Star Struck

An Encyclopedia of Celebrity Culture

Sam G. Riley, Editor

GREENWOOD PRESS
An Imprint of ABC-CLIO, LLC

A B C 〜 C L I O

Santa Barbara, California • Denver, Colorado • Oxford, England

Library of Congress Cataloging-in-Publication Data
Star struck : an encyclopedia of celebrity culture / Sam G. Riley, editor.
    p. cm.
   Includes bibliographical references and index.
   ISBN 978-0-313-35812-8 (hard copy : alk. paper) — ISBN 978-0-313-35813-5
(ebook)
    1. United States—Civilization—1970—Encyclopedias. 2. United States—Social
life and customs—1971—Encyclopedias. 3. Popular culture—United States—Encyclopedias.
4. Celebrities—United States—Encyclopedias. 5. Celebrities in mass media—Encyclopedias.
6. Mass media—Social aspects—United States—Encyclopedias. 7. Fame—Social
aspects—United States—Encyclopedias. I. Riley, Sam G.
   E169.12.S73   2010
   302.230862′1—dc22   2009030649

ISBN: 978-0-313-35812-8
EISBN: 978-0-313-35813-5

14 13 12 11 10   1 2 3 4 5

This book is also available on the World Wide Web as an eBook.
Visit www.abc-clio.com for details.

Greenwood Press
An Imprint of ABC-CLIO, LLC

ABC-CLIO, LLC
130 Cremona Drive, P.O. Box 1911
Santa Barbara, California 93116–1911

This book is printed on acid-free paper ∞

Manufactured in the United States of America

For Janie, Mary, Brady, and Carter—
celebrities one and all

Contents

List of Entries

Preface

The aim of this book is to present a reasonable, balanced look at as many aspects of American celebrity culture as possible. The editor's intention is to keep the book as free as possible of academic jargon. Entries about individual celebrities do not appear inasmuch as celebrities are so numerous; to have done otherwise would have made the book more biographical. This reference work focuses on more than eighty aspects of American-style celebrity; however, within these alphabetically arranged entries, many individual celebrities are named and discussed. The entries herein are of three assigned lengths: 2,500 words, 1,500 words, and 500 words—give or take a bit.

This encyclopedia of American celebrity focuses on the period from 1950 through the early 21st century but allows for appropriate historical background. Joining the editor, who is a journalism professor, in writing these entries are other scholars, most of whom are professors of journalism or communication, as well as a few writers who are not university faculty or who are from other disciplines. Randle Carpenter, for example, is a practicing lawyer in New York City and comments on celebrity lawyers. Amy Widmayer worked for Condé Nast in early 21st-century New York City and is ideally suited for writing about supermodels and fashion designers. Robert Sugarman's academic area is popular-culture studies; he was uniquely positioned to write the entry on circus celebrity and its changed nature. Ken Muir, who writes on athletic celebrity, is a sociology professor.

The book, which contains 40 illustrations, offers a timeline, which should be especially useful for readers who, unlike the editor, are too young to have lived through the period of the book's emphasis. Entries that are cross-referenced are indicated by boldfaced terms within the entry text and also are listed following "See also" at the end of entries, as warranted. At the end of each entry, brief citations are listed under the heading For Further Reading. A fairly extensive bibliography, mainly of recent work on celebrity, appears at the end of the book, followed by a general index and, in turn, biographical information about the editor and contributors.

Acknowledgments

Thanks to Virginia Tech's Department of Communication for administrative support for this book and to a number of my colleagues, here and elsewhere, for joining me in writing entries. Special thanks go to Janie and Mary Chadwick for their expertise on children's television and to Steven Berry for his suggestions regarding the entry on hip-hop and rap. Thanks, too, to Larry and Patti Cowley for their enthusiastic contributions to the entry titled Temporary Celebrity.

Introduction

A celebrity is a famous person who receives heavy media attention, who is popular due to personal qualities that go beyond actual accomplishments, and whose identity is suitable for some degree of merchandising. In today's America, most, although not all, celebrities come from some part of the vast entertainment industry, which includes sports.

Of all that has been written and said about celebrity, the two most oft-repeated remarks came from a historian and an artist. In his insightful 1961 book *The Image: A Guide to Pseudo-Events in America*, historian Daniel Boorstin contended that a celebrity is someone who is famous for being famous—a human pseudo-event. To educated readers, most of whom are not among the famous, this dismissive view of celebrity as something essentially hollow is an appealing notion. On closer examination, however, it does not stand up to reason. To be sure, some celebrities fit Boorstin's description quite well; two recent examples are Anna Nicole Smith and Paris Hilton. But most celebrities have gained their renown by actual, substantial accomplishment. Tiger Woods, for instance, is a major celebrity, and he got that way through hard work that made him the world's best golfer. Somewhere in between is such an individual as Vanna White. Few Americans would fail to recognize her name, even though her considerable renown came by way of looking decorative while turning cards on a quiz show—not the loftiest of accomplishments. Yet signs at the city limits of Myrtle Beach, South Carolina, proudly proclaim to visitors that this ocean-side community is the hometown of Vanna White. Although Boorstin's "famous for being famous" remark was more glib than insightful, it must be admitted that when people hear someone famous is in their vicinity, they will want to see the celebrity, even if they have no idea why or how that person gained such celebrity.

Whenever celebrity is discussed, three terms are bandied about that are used more or less interchangeably: fame, celebrity, and stardom. Of the three, fame has the broadest meaning. Fame comes to any public figure, but celebrity to only some.

Fame brings with it admirers as well as detractors. Celebrity brings fans, and occasional stalkers. Fame's admiration generally implies quiet respect, while celebrity's fandom or stardom brings about a specious feeling of intimacy that the hardcore fan feels for the celebrity. Fame suggests something earned by solid accomplishment, whereas celebrity and its movie cousin, stardom, imply not only accomplishment, but also good looks, glitz, glamour, media hounding, and consequent heavy exposure and excited adulation. Celebrity is marked by intense interest in an individual's personal life as opposed to his or her professional accomplishments—a desire to know what the celebrity is "really like." Finally, celebrity has come to imply the "branding" of individuals so that, like a product, stars can be used to make money not just for themselves, but also for other people and companies.

The definitive account of old-style fame is Leo Braudy's 1986 book *The Frenzy of Renown: Fame and Its History.* In it, Braudy points out the rulers of antiquity, figures from the Bible and from other holy books, saints through the centuries, successful explorers, military conquerors or heroes, and members of the nobility or aristocracy—all of whom were famous and functioned as the celebrities of their time. Some gained celebrity by their goodness, but far more of them achieved it by harsh, even murderous treatment of their fellow humans. Some were born to greatness, others came up the hard way despite the odds. As recently as the early to mid-1800s, the principal celebrities tended to be government and military leaders, major inventors, a few luminaries from the serious arts, people of great wealth (either earned or inherited), and other individuals from the more dignified, sober walks of life.

But that was before the coming of mass media, mass availability of illustration, and mass entertainment. After those three forces had taken hold, only a few of the aforementioned celebrity types still made the leap from fame to celebrity. The public now had such attractive alternatives at their disposal in the persons of powerful athletes, glamorous movie stars, and singers whose crooning was sent out to all of America by radio or phonograph—in short, entertainment figures. Few politicians could compete for comparable public adulation. Most office seekers have simply looked like well-to-do white men in dark suits talking a lot without saying much. Furthermore, their continuous partisan bickering, pomposity, and influence peddling have rendered them less than admirable or trustworthy. Every four years, of course, politicians put on a show of portraying themselves as "just plain good old boys" or "men and women of the people," but most such attempts are transparent and look phony; and after the hoopla of an election has passed, both winner and loser retreat to their mansions or $1,000-a-night hotel suites to make deals and hobnob with the captains of industry.

Should it really be surprising that the luminaries of stage, screen, radio, television, and athletics are turned to as a more attractive alternative? Not only are they more physically attractive than most politicians and other "serious people," but also, to rise from obscurity, they have had to deliver. To become celebrities, most have had to do more than talk big and make dubious promises. And while being born wealthy is a huge help to anyone hoping to rise high politically, circumstances of birth have had little to do with entertainment-world accomplishment and celebrity. Perhaps without having to actually think about this distinction, many Americans have felt it. Entertainment-world success was and is democratic—open to all comers—a big plus in appealing to egalitarian-minded Americans.

More must be said about the distinction between the hero and the celebrity. A difference is that the hero seldom seeks out publicity, whereas the celebrity must do so—at least until a lofty level of celebrity has been achieved. Untold numbers of individuals who fought in World War II and were genuine heroes were so conflicted to have survived when so many died that they have refused to talk, even to family members, about what they saw and did during the fighting. Many real heroes, then, remain unrecognized, but a person is not a celebrity until recognition has occurred. Also, the hero usually does something for the benefit of others, while the celebrity is more likely characterized by self-seeking motivations and actions. Another difference is that heroism depends on a person's internal values or traits (honesty, caring, and loyalty), whereas celebrity has more to do with one's exterior. Not all celebrities are beautiful or handsome, of course, but most certainly fit that description. Even among athletes, who must depend mainly on true physical accomplishment, the best looking often become the biggest celebrities. Having unusually good looks always has been important in the movie business, and television has followed suit, even in selecting on-camera talent for news shows. More recently, and more surprisingly, an examination of individuals chosen to be magazine editors and newspaper columnists reveals a predisposition to hire the attractive. Due to media convergence, companies want writers and editors who also will look good as talk show guests or as "talking heads."

Coupled with looks in today's celebrity culture is the matter of youth. One would be hard-pressed to believe that in today's Hollywood, an actor such as Humphrey Bogart could become a major star. He was simply not pretty enough, and when he began acting, he was too old to appeal to the kind of people who today buy most of the movie theater tickets. The youthful present-day theatergoer would much prefer a leading man no older than twenty-five or thirty at the outside, who had lifted his share of weights. In what has come to be referred to as today's "youth culture," the celebrity must be suitably young or else do whatever it takes to appear as young as possible. Diet and exercise can help only so much, but Botox and cosmetic surgery have come to the rescue, not just for celebrities, but for ordinary Americans, who want to look young, too. The early years of the new century appear to be a time for taking corrective action, not for "aging gracefully." Among the young, the desire to look as much as possible like their favored celebrities is a powerful force. Among boys, the temptation to "buff up" or to excel at sports with the help of anabolic steroids is considerable; anorexia and bulimia among young girls constitute a serious health problem despite the massive, if ironic, media attention these disorders have received. Yet is it any wonder that these problems persist when movie after movie, show after show, magazine cover after cover, display, with drumbeat regularity, the current ideal "look" for men and for women? And among the very young, we observe the dreadful spectacle of child beauty pageants, in which parents, wanting to start their little girls on the road to celebrity, tart them up to look like miniature prostitutes and shove them out onto the runway. Similarly, how many fathers are consumed with the desire for their sons to excel at sports, whether the boys are physically equipped for it or not?

It is difficult to imagine life before the dissemination of such "ideal" images was technologically possible, but in the great scheme of things, it was not all that long ago that photography was invented, or that improved printing technologies made possible the distribution of photographic images to an enormous audience. It was not so long ago that the phonograph allowed people to spend less time personally playing musical instruments or singing to one another and instead become fans of other people who could sing or play better. Not so long ago, sports began to change from mere games to big business, while radio came along and allowed huge audiences to simultaneously hear music or enjoy other forms of entertainment. Consider how relatively recent an innovation is the motion picture, and try to imagine how exciting its novelty must have been for people in the movies' formative years. Today's students even must rely on their imagination to picture life without television, but some of their older professors can remember it well. When today's students age a while and have children of their own, these offspring in turn will have to imagine life before the Internet and the changes this newer medium has wrought.

Without pictures, still or moving, celebrity culture could not have burgeoned, but the two biggest factors in its growth unquestionably have been movies and television. The movie star is and has been, like his or her image on the theater screen, larger than life. The movie star rather quickly replaced the wealthy, aristocratic, and fashionable with a new kind of celebrity hero and heroine. For many Americans, the major movie star became the very pinnacle of celebrity, someone to be looked up to just as when we sit back in our theater seat and literally look up at the large, elevated screen. Boys and adult males wanted to be like the suave leading men, the urban tough guys, or the Western heroes who could shoot the gun out of the outlaw's hand, then ride off into the sunset, ready for the next adventure. Girls and women wanted to look as seductively glamorous as the goddesses of the big screen. Then, in the 1950s, for most Americans, came television, with its dramas, Westerns, variety shows, and sitcoms. Again, most fans secretly wanted to be like those people on the screen, but there was a difference. The new television celebrities did not evoke quite the same level of awe as did the big-screen movie stars, but instead they were people with whom we were more likely to form imaginary bonds of "friendship" or "intimacy." The friendship and intimacy were specious, of course, but they seemed real enough if not thought about in a rational manner; and we were glad to feel, not think. This was true when television was a new medium, and it is probably even more true today. Rock-and-roll pioneer Jerry Lee Lewis sang in the 1950s about a "whole lot of shakin' going on," but at a deeper level, there was a whole lot of feelin' going on. Thinking simply wasn't, and isn't, as easy or as much fun as feeling, and our preference for feeling various emotions is perfectly catered to by movies, television, and, intermingled with both those media, popular music in its many forms. If anything, music is likely the most personal medium of them all. And as if these offerings were not enough, sports developed as another highly organized, profitable kind of public entertainment that also could be celebrated on the movie screen and brought to us regularly by television, radio, and the print media. Soon after the end of World War II, Americans became the best-entertained people on the face of the earth, and surely we still fit this description.

These media are the source of most celebrity, although the Internet has made its own contribution, especially in allowing vast numbers of Americans to seize a tiny corner of celebrity for themselves, even though this kind of renown is usually fleeting. The lure of "being somebody" in the sense of being even a small-caliber celebrity is strong. Americans see celebrity nearly everywhere. It is hard to get people to contribute to a charity unless that charity is fronted by a big-name celebrity. Those Americans who still read for pleasure, and this group keeps getting smaller, reflexively buy even the potboilers dashed off by well-promoted celebrity writers. People place their hope for eternal salvation in celebrity television evangelists, and to lure young church-goers, many churches have resorted to the use of drum sets and electric guitars. Some universities put their academic programs on starvation diets while spending princely sums on bringing in celebrity lecturers. The biggest celebrity on most campuses, of course, is the football coach, whose compensation is usually many times that of the university president. The celebrity culture, the youth culture, the entertainment culture, and U.S. popular culture in general have largely blended together in present-day America. The effects of this blending have left more questions than provided answers, despite the earnest efforts of many people to explain it all.

Some critics chide Americans for having become absolutely sappy over celebrity; others point out that our enormous interest in the comings and goings of celebrities is simply the modern version of the way earlier people gossiped about pretty much the same things: sexual entanglements, murders, accidents, natural disasters, noble or unusual births, oddities, and the like. It is true, if somewhat disconcerting, that most of the same things that fill today's tabloids also filled the broadsides published and sold before even newspapers appeared. And it is probably true that our preoccupation with celebrity and our entertainment-steeped popular culture render us to some extent less rational, more prone to seeing the world through the filter of Hollywood movies, and to see politics and even war through the template of ball games. At the same time, this veneer of entertaining unreality is in part what makes people from all over the world want to come to America.

An unfortunate effect of our celebrity, entertainment, youth, and popular culture is that, as a people, we demonstrate interests that appear to have become more narrow. Boys are expected to be mainly interested in sports, girls in their own sports or shopping. To meet their obligations as fans, both genders are expected to be keenly interested in popular music, movies, some television—especially reality shows, which often seem mainly designed to show nice-looking young people wearing skimpy outfits—and the interactive joys of the Internet. Virtually all media content, including what now passes for news, has been forced into the mold of entertainment. A popular bumper sticker reads, "If it's not fun, why do it?" As cheery a thought as this might be, one is glad that, when one's appendix needs to come out, that sticker is not on the bumper of our local surgeon. And when students hit the job market, it is remarkable how little appears in the job ads under the heading "Fun." A second regrettable aspect of our present pop culture is the extent to which everything depends on constant selling. Few celebrity talk show guests are not conducting their interviews to promote or sell something. Even the U.S. federal government, which in earlier times nagged us to save some of what we earned, now urges us to spend, spend, spend to keep the wheels of commerce turning. Meanwhile, all values begin to look like financial values.

Whichever position on celebrity one takes, many questions remain. Does our celebrity-laden entertainment culture place undue emphasis on sex? Romantic love? Material success? Does what we see our favorite celebrities do, own, or wear on screen create unrealistic expectations of the part of young admirers, who expect their own lives to turn out in similar fashion? Or, are the examples provided by these celebrities inspirational and motivating? Do television and movies overemphasize violence? Do the media and the celebrities they showcase, in fact, provide a template for imitative violence, or does viewing such content provide a harmless release for people's violent feelings? Does too much attention to celebrity and entertainment in its many appealing forms make us dream too much and do too little, or are they merely a welcome diversion from the mundane? Because entertainment is America's biggest export, and because many U.S. celebrities are known around the world, does what we are selling amount to devious cultural imperialism, or should we Americans relax and be happy we have such attractive goods to sell to the world?

Long ago, President Calvin Coolidge remarked that "The business of America is business." Today, with jobs disappearing by the thousands, empty storefronts, shuttered factories, and failing or endangered banks, one wonders whether his remark remains valid. Or, should we "fess up" and admit that, in today's America, "The business of America is entertainment"?

Timeline

1776   Benjamin Franklin, who is sent to France as U.S. commissioner, becomes the new nation's first international celebrity.

1829   Andy Jackson, hero of the Battle of New Orleans, takes office as America's first Populist celebrity president.

1830s   The Industrial Revolution reaches the United States.

1833   The first "penny paper," the *New York Sun*, is sold on the streets of New York.

1837   Samuel Morse introduces his telegraph.

1842   The rotary press speeds printing.

1844   Mathew Brady opens his portrait studio in New York City and begins to photograph famous Americans.

1845   The lurid *National Police Gazette* is launched by George Wilkes.

1850   Jenny Lind, "The Swedish Nightingale," is brought to America at great expense by showman P. T. Barnum.

1863   Samuel Clemens steps into the persona of Mark Twain and becomes one of America's first major celebrities.

        The wedding of General and Mrs. Tom Thumb (Charles Stratton and Lavinia Warren) takes place.

1871   P. T. Barnum opens his first circus.

1873   The lavishly illustrated *Daily Graphic: An Illustrated Evening Newspaper* appears in New York.

1877   Thomas Edison invents the phonograph and also records the human voice.

1880   Halftone technology improves print illustrations.

1882   British literary celebrity Oscar Wilde tours the United States.

1883   Buffalo Bill Cody's Wild West Show premieres and tours America.

1889   The first cylinder and disc recordings are sold.

Edison perfects his kinetograph motion picture camera and his kinetoscope projection device.

George Eastman introduces celluloid film.

1890   Samuel Warren and Lewis Brandeis publish a law review article that leads to the creation of privacy law.

1894   Edison opens the first kinetoscope parlors for viewing bits of film.

1896   Guglielmo Marconi patents wireless telegraphy.

Edison introduces the Vitascope projector; nickelodeon theaters begin opening.

1899   Magician Harry Houdini concentrates on escape acts and gains international celebrity.

1903   *The Great Train Robbery*, the first U.S. movie to tell a story using film editing, appears.

1905   Neon signs are introduced, allowing celebrities to literally "see their name in lights."

1906   The Victrola, the first popular player of disc records, is introduced.

1910   The earliest movie magazines appear.

1911   *Photoplay* and *Motion Picture Story* magazines are launched.

1915   The earliest U.S. epic movie, *The Birth of a Nation*, premieres.

1916   Westinghouse engineer Frank Conrad becomes the first "disc jockey" by broadcasting recorded music on radio out of his garage.

1919   The tabloid *New York Daily News* launches the era of "jazz journalism."

1920   The first commercial radio stations go on air.

1921   Rudolph Valentino's title role in *The Sheik* makes him Hollywood's leading male sex symbol.

Celebrity comedian Fatty Arbuckle is charged with rape and murder, showing the way to tabloid-style coverage of sensational crime.

1923   *Time*, the first successful U.S. news weekly, is founded by Henry Luce.

1924   Early Asian American actress Anna May Wong appears with Douglas Fairbanks in the silent film *The Thief of Baghdad*.

The tabloid *New York Graphic* is published by flamboyant self-promoter Bernarr Macfadden.

1925   Greta Garbo of Sweden comes to Hollywood and becomes one of silent film's first sex symbols.

The standard speed for phonograph records becomes 78 rpm (revolutions per minute).

1927   *The Jazz Singer*, the first U.S. "talkie," appears.

Charles Lindbergh becomes a heroic celebrity after his solo flight across the Atlantic Ocean.

Following the release of the movie *It*, Clara Bow becomes a national celebrity as "The It Girl."

Child star Mickey Rooney appears in his first of many movies, *Orchids and Ermine*.

1929   The Oscars (Academy Awards) originate to honor film achievement.

1930   John Wayne appears in the first of his Western movies, *The Big Trail*.

1932   The movie *A Farewell to Arms* appears and helps Ernest Hemingway become a celebrity author.

African American singer, actor, lawyer, and activist Paul Robeson appears on Broadway in *Show Boat*.

1933   President Franklin D. Roosevelt furthers his New Deal policies, and his personal celebrity, via a series of radio speeches couched as "fireside chats."

1935   Howard Hughes, wealthy industrialist and movie producer, increases his celebrity by setting the speed record for powered flight.

The *Fibber McGee and Molly* radio show appears, introducing a variety of stereotypical yet comic characters.

1936   FM radio is introduced by Edwin Armstrong, providing better sound quality for music.

African American athlete Jesse Owens debunks Hitler's "master race" claims in the Berlin Olympics.

1937   Actress Zsa Zsa Gabor marries for the first of nine times.

1938   African American boxer Joe Louis beats German champ Max Schmeling, becoming world heavyweight champion.

1939   Television is introduced to the public at the New York World's Fair.

In an early endorsement deal, baseball's homerun king Babe Ruth plugs Red Rock Cola.

One of America's favorite epic movies, *Gone With the Wind*, premieres.

The National Baseball Hall of Fame and Museum opens.

1940   Disc jockey Martin Block, for whom the term "disc jockey" was coined, goes national with his *Make Believe Ballroom* radio show.

1941   The George Foster Peabody Awards originate to honor broadcast accomplishment.

1944   The Hollywood Foreign Press Association's Golden Globes originate, honoring work in film and television.

1946   Danish pianist and comedian Victor Borge first performs his classic "phonetic punctuation" comedy routine.

Commercial television is introduced.

1947   Jackie Robinson breaks the color barrier in major league baseball.

"Buffalo" Bob Smith's successful children's television show *Howdy Doody* begins its long run on NBC.

The Tony Awards honoring Broadway theater originate.

1948   Television drama shows begin to appear.

The magazine *TV Guide* is launched.

1949   Hollywood studios begin to produce programming for television.

The Emmy Awards program is instituted for television.

Italian operatic bass Ezio Pinza appears in *South Pacific* on Broadway.

Child actors David and Ricky Nelson join the cast of their parents' radio show, *The Adventures of Ozzie and Harriet.*

Baseball player Eddie Waitkus is shot and badly injured by a female stalker.

1950   Stan Freberg's hit record "John and Marsha" spoofs "cheesy" soap operas.

Jon Arthur opens his children's show *No School Today* on American Broadcasting Company (ABC) television.

1951   The hugely popular sitcom *I Love Lucy* appears on television.

The 45 rpm record becomes popular in the United States.

1952   Gene Kelly performs what may well remain the best movie dance number ever in *Singin' in the Rain.*

Generoso Pope introduces *The National Enquirer*, soon to be imitated by other tabloid magazines.

Karl Lagerfeld begins his career in couture and ready-to-wear design.

1953   Bill Haley records the first rock and roll music.

Andy Griffith achieves instant celebrity with his comedy record "What It Was, Was Football."

1954   The transistor radio hits the market.

Elvis Presley cuts his first record, "That's All Right," for Sun Records.

Marlon Brando makes the t-shirt popular in the movie *On the Waterfront.*

Celebrity "Red baiter" Sen. Joseph McCarthy's star dims in the Army-McCarthy hearings.

Fashion designer Coco Chanel makes her comeback after a fifteen-year hiatus.

1955   Harland Sanders, founder of Kentucky Fried Chicken, begins franchising his restaurants and appearing in his own ads and commercials.

Gunsmoke, television's longest-running Western, premieres.

The movie *Rebel Without a Cause* makes James Dean a major celebrity.

Three children's television shows appear: Bob Keeshan's *Captain Kangaroo, Pinky Lee,* and *Soupy Sales.*

1956   Comedy duo Dean Martin and Jerry Lewis split and pursue solo careers.

Brigitte Bardot of France brings European-style sex appeal to America in the movie *And God Created Woman*.

The Obie Awards originate and honor off- and off-off Broadway theater.

1957 Comedy team Bud Abbott and Lou Costello end their partnership.

Jamaica's Harry Belafonte records "Banana Boat Song" and popularizes calypso music.

Pioneering Asian American actor Sessue Hayakawa appears in *The Bridge on the River Kwai*.

1958 The 33 1/3 rpm stereo long-playing record is introduced.

Economist Kenneth Galbraith publishes *The Affluent Society*, addressing America's consumer society.

The telephoto lens for thirty-five-millimeter cameras becomes popular.

The Grammy Awards originate, honoring musical achievement.

1959 The air-crash deaths of rock and roll's Buddy Holly, Ritchie Valens, and the Big Bopper (J. P. Richardson) cause February 3 to be remembered as "the day the music died."

The term "paparazzi" first appears in the Federico Fellini film *La Dolce Vita*.

1960 The presidential debates between Richard Nixon and John F. Kennedy are televised and change the way political campaigns are run.

Child actor Ron Howard assumes the role of Opie on *The Andy Griffith Show*.

1961 Historian Daniel Boorstin publishes *The Image: A Guide to Pseudo-Events in America*, which addresses, among other things, celebrity.

1962 Scottish actor Sean Connery is the first movie actor to play James Bond.

The Tonight Show with Johnny Carson premieres.

Blonde sex symbol Marilyn Monroe dies from a possible drug overdose.

1963 President John F. Kennedy is assassinated.

African American actor Sidney Poitier stars in three fine films and ushers in a more accepting era for black actors.

The television series *That Was the Week That Was* appears in the United States and lampoons very nearly everything.

Bob Dylan records his song "Blowin' in the Wind."

The American Music Awards originate and compete with the Grammys.

1964 The U.S. Supreme Court, in *New York Times v. Sullivan*, makes it difficult for celebrities or other public-figure plaintiffs to win libel or privacy suits.

Controversial stand-up comic Lenny Bruce is convicted of obscenity.

1965 African American actor Bill Cosby appears in the television action series *I Spy*.

1966   Movie actor Ronald Reagan is elected governor of California.

All television networks begin broadcasting prime-time content in color.

1967   Thurgood Marshall becomes the first African American justice on the U.S. Supreme Court.

The Country Music Awards originate.

1968   Civil rights leader Martin Luther King, Jr., and U.S. attorney general Robert Kennedy are assassinated.

The comic television variety series *Rowan & Martin's Laugh-In* appears.

Artist Andy Warhol says that, in the future, we all will have our fifteen minutes of fame; he is shot and wounded by a hanger-on.

Fred Rogers brings *Mr. Rogers's Neighborhood* to children's television.

1969   Television shows its stuff by televising images from the Moon.

Ukulele-strumming singer Tiny Tim (Herbert Khaury) has his brightest fifteen minutes of fame when he marries "Miss Vickie" on the Johnny Carson Show.

Dave Thomas founds Wendy's and soon begins to appear in an eventual 800 television commercials for his company.

The British Broadcasting Company's (BBC's) comedy sketch show *Monty Python's Flying Circus* comes to U.S. television.

1970   Singer Janis Joplin dies of a drug overdose.

1971   Singer Jim Morrison of "The Doors" dies mysteriously at age twenty-seven.

1972   The first of the *Godfather* Mafia movies appears.

Actor David Carradine is "the face that launched a thousand kicks" with his role in the television series *Kung Fu.*

Paparazzi photographer Ron Galella loses to Jacqueline Kennedy Onassis in her invasion-of-privacy suit.

Celebrity physician and author Benjamin Spock runs for the U.S. presidency.

1973   Child actor Andy Lambros tapes the "Oscar Mayer wiener" commercial jingle.

An American Family, perhaps the first reality television show, airs on Public Broadcasting Service (PBS).

1974   Television evangelists Jim and Tammy Faye Bakker achieve dubious celebrity via their *PTL Club* television show.

People magazine appears.

1975   Comic sketch and variety show *Saturday Night Live* premieres.

Actor Jack Nicholson plays the prototypical anti-hero role in the film *One Flew Over the Cuckoo's Nest.*

1976   HBO (Home Box Office) is launched.

1977   The first *Star Wars* movie premieres, spawning both sequels and prequels.

1980   Ronald Reagan is elected president of the United States.

Both ESPN (Entertainment and Sports Programming Network) and CNN (Cable News Network) begin broadcasting.

1981   Celebrity-oriented magazine *US Weekly* is launched.

The first VJs (video jockeys) appear with the founding of MTV (Music Television).

1982   Gannett begins publishing *USA Today*, considerably affecting U.S. newspapers.

Lenny Skutnik becomes a temporary celebrity by rescuing a woman from the icy Potomac River.

1983   The CD (compact disc) is introduced to the U.S. market.

The Rock and Roll Hall of Fame and Museum opens in Cleveland, Ohio.

1984   *The Cosby Show* airs.

The movie *The Karate Kid* gives martial arts instruction a huge boost.

Tiny, feisty Clara Peller achieves celebrity in a Wendy's commercial, rasping, "Where's the beef?"

1986   The *Oprah Winfrey Show* appears on television in Chicago, then nationally.

Movie star Clint Eastwood is elected mayor of Carmel, California.

1989   Sitcom actress Rebecca Schaeffer is shot to death by a stalker.

1990   The Billboard Music Awards originate.

1991   The *Jerry Springer Show* appears, testing the lower limits of taste.

Anthony Hopkins plays one of film's most fearsome villains as cannibalistic serial killer Hannibal Lecter in *Silence of the Lambs*.

1992   Presidential candidate Bill Clinton appeals to young and minority voters by playing saxophone on *The Arsenio Hall Show*.

1993   Tennis star Monica Seles is stabbed and badly injured by a deranged man.

The World Wide Web goes public, thanks to Tim Berners-Lee.

1994   Football great O. J. Simpson is tried and acquitted for a double homicide.

Nirvana lead vocalist Kurt Cobain commits suicide.

1995   The Internet goes from government to public.

1996   Golfer Tiger Wood begins his phenomenal professional career.

1997   Britain's Princess Diana dies in an automobile accident in Paris.

British author J. K. Rowling becomes a huge success with the publication of her first *Harry Potter* book.

Matt Drudge's *The Drudge Report* evolves from an e-mail newsletter into a popular Web site.

1998   President Bill Clinton's sexual relationship with White House intern Monica Lewinsky results in impeachment charges the following year.

Margaret Ray, longtime stalker of late-night host Dave Letterman, commits suicide.

Richard Branson, English billionaire founder of the Virgin brand, tries to fly around the world in a hot-air balloon.

1999   The American Film Institute names Katharine Hepburn as the greatest Hollywood actress.

Turkish schoolteacher Mahir Cagri's Borat-like Web site draws millions of visitors, making him an international celebrity of sorts.

Wrestler Jesse Ventura is elected governor of Minnesota.

2002   Recognizing the importance of the Internet and its worldwide reach, the International Fan Club Organization replaces the National Association of Fan Clubs.

American Idol is launched on U.S. television.

2003   Bodybuilder and action star Arnold Schwarzenegger is elected governor of California.

Basketball star Kobe Bryant is charged with sexual assault. Charges were later dropped.

Magician and animal trainer Roy Horn of Siegfried and Roy is seriously injured by a white tiger during a performance.

Omnipresent celebrity Martha Stewart is sentenced to a brief prison stay.

The Star goes from tabloid to glossy magazine.

The first Emmy for reality television goes to *The Amazing Race*.

2005   Gonzo journalist Hunter S. Thompson commits suicide.

2006   California adopts a statute designed to rein in the paparazzi.

In the movie *Borat!* actor Sacha Baron Cohen successfully exposes unfortunate aspects of American culture.

Al Gore, former U.S. vice president, becomes a celebrity with the screening of his documentary film *An Inconvenient Truth*, addressing global warming.

2007   Famous for being famous blonde Anna Nicole Smith dies at age thirty-nine, setting off a media frenzy.

Entertainer Michael Jackson is found not guilty of child molestation charges.

Golfer Tiger Woods becomes America's highest-earning athlete ever.

2008   Barack Obama becomes the biggest presidential celebrity since John F. Kennedy.

2009   Singer and dancer Michael Jackson, known as the "King of Pop," dies at the age of fifty.

A

AFRICAN AMERICAN

That Barack Obama was the Democratic Party's successful presidential candidate in the 2008 race is dramatically symbolic of the progress made in the last half century by a racial minority long held down by discrimination. As this progress gradually occurred, black celebrities served as role models for African Americans and other minorities and as eye-openers for white America. Jack Johnson became the preeminent boxer of the early 1900s. Track and field great Jesse Owens rubbed Adolf Hitler's nose in the Nazi myth of the "master race" at the 1936 Olympics. Joe Louis was universally admired as America's heavyweight champion boxer in the mid-1900s. In music, Paul Robeson's rich bass voice and acting talent made him a celebrity in the 1930s, and operatic contralto Marian Anderson gained similar fame. Three decades later, the Rev. Martin Luther King, Jr.'s civil rights activism made him not only a celebrity, but arguably the most admired American of his century. In sport, music, film, writing, **comedy**, television, social activism, and political life, black America has produced many celebrities.

Musicians

Before the movie industry allowed African American actors to fill roles that were not subservient or comic, black entertainers made their mark in music. Their earliest success was achieved in **jazz**, a predominantly black musical form. One such jazz icon was New Orleans trumpeter and singer Louis Armstrong, whose Dixieland style appealed to most Americans. Performing on radio and on tour were the bands of jazz greats Edward "Duke" Ellington and William "Count" Basie. Black jazz greats have been many: saxophonist John Coltrane, pianist Thelonious Monk, and trumpeters John "Dizzy" Gillespie and Miles Davis. Well liked for his smooth jazz-pop blend was crooner Nathaniel "Nat King" Cole. Versatile Sammy Davis, Jr., sang, danced, acted, played several instruments, and did comedy. Davis's celebrity was enhanced by his membership in the otherwise all-white "Rat Pack" group of good-time pals led by singer Frank Sinatra. Introducing a new musical style to America in the 1950s and becoming a major celebrity was Jamaican singer Harry Belafonte, whose bongo drum-punctuated calypso music swept the nation.

The real musical sea change of the 1950s, however, was **rock** and roll, an electrifying musical form performed by both black and white musicians. Its deepest roots were in the historically black rural southern blues, in which the singer tells of life's hard times, usually accompanied by an acoustic guitar and perhaps a harmonica. Newer urban blues performers sang of their troubles in northern cities. A second contributor to rock and roll was gospel music, with its emotional clapping and swaying; and a third was the more upbeat boogie-woogie sound of big-band jazz. Rock and roll was a reaction to the saccharine, lily-white pop music that had dominated radio and the recording industry. For most teens, it represented rebellion, sexual promise, more attention to their peers, and a new awareness of still-segregated black America. In the early 1950s, the major studios refused to sign most black recording artists, whose work instead appeared on independent labels, and radio stations refused airtime to the new black rock performers.

A rock and roll pioneer was Chuck Berry, whose 1955 hit "Maybellene" excited teens. Little Richard (Richard Penniman) screamed and pounded his way through "Tutti-Fruitti" in 1955. Bouncy Antoine "Fats" Domino recorded "Blueberry Hill" in 1956, and thrilling teens with his oddly shaped electric guitar and gargantuan speakers

was Bo Diddley (Elias McDaniel). In the 1960s, Chubby Checker (Ernest Evans) gained instant celebrity with the song and dance craze "The Twist." These early black singers were joined by white performers such as Elvis Presley, Jerry Lee Lewis, and Buddy Holly.

A smoother sound was produced by black doo-wop groups such as the Platters, Coasters, Drifters, and Dell-Vikings. Black rock and roll took a temporary back seat in the early to mid-1960s to British groups such as The Beatles, The Rolling Stones, and The Who. Then in the late 1960s, two varieties of black music emerged: soul and Motown. Also, electric guitar soloists came into vogue, the best of whom was Jimi Hendrix. From the South came soul, from the North, the Motown sound. Raw, emotional soul music was performed by Ray Charles, James Brown ("The Godfather of Soul"), and laid-back Sam Cooke. Called the "Queen of Soul" was Aretha Franklin. Motown, both a sound and a record label, was a creation of Detroit's Berry Gordy, Jr. Singer Smokey Robinson was a Motown mainstay, as were such groups as Martha and the Vandellas, Diana Ross and the Supremes, The Temptations, and Gladys Knight and the Pips. Marvin Gaye recorded there, as did Steveland Morris, at age thirteen, whose stage name was Little Stevie Wonder. The ultimate Motown success story is that of Michael Jackson, the "King of Pop." A similar recording star is Prince (born Prince Rogers Nelson).

Black women who became early singing celebrities include Josephine Baker, Lena Horne, Ella Fitzgerald, Sarah Vaughan, and Pearl Bailey. Greatest of them all was Billie Holiday,

"Lady Day." Holiday's sad personal story was told in the 1972 film *Lady Sings the Blues*, starring Diana Ross. Known for her sultry voice and slinky portrayal of Catwoman in the 1960s *Batman* television series was Eartha Kitt. Likewise, singer Della Reese (Delloreese Early) appeared on the show *Touched by an Angel*, and Diahann Carroll had her self-named show, the *Diahann Carroll Show*. Whereas rock and roll was dominated by male singers, soul music was not. Tina Turner's down-and-dirty blend of rock and soul made her a major celebrity, as did Dionne Warwick's softer style. More recent singers of soul, pop, and jazz include Natalie Cole, daughter of Nat King Cole; Whitney Houston; and Janet Jackson. Even more recent are Mariah Carey; Brandy (Norwood); Aaliyah (Haughton), who died in a 2001 plane crash; Beyonce (Knowles); Fantasia (Barrino); and Rihanna (Robyn Rihanna Fenty).

The end of the 1960s brought in a period of hard rock, followed in the mid-1970s by punk rock, both of which were dominated by whites. In the 1980s, a new, more iconoclastic street culture appeared in the nation's urban neighborhoods: **hip-hop**, which manifested itself in sprayed graffiti, break dancing, baggy pants worn low, tattoos, and hypermacho disrespect for women. The music of the hip-hop culture is rap, in which the words are spoken rather than sung over a driving, distinctive beat. Some of rap's pioneers include **disc jockeys** such as Afrika Bambaataa and DJ Kool Herc (Clive Campbell). Early rappers included Grandmaster Flash (Joseph Saddler) of the Bronx and The Furious Five; Harlem's Kurtis Blow (Curtis Walker); and on the West Coast, gangsta rappers Dr. Dre (Andre

Young), Ice Cube (O'Shea Jackson), Ice T (Tracy Marrow, known to older Americans for his role on *Law & Order: Special Victims Unit*); Snoop Dogg (Cordozar Broadus); and Tupac Shakur, who was shot and killed in 1996.

Feuds and shootouts became common among rappers. Ja Rule (Jeffrey Atkins) and Fat Joe (Joseph Cartagena) have both feuded with 50 Cent (Curtis Jackson), and Jay-Z with Nas (Nasir Jones). Many a rapper has spent time behind bars and has survived multiple shootings. One who did not survive was The Notorious B.I.G. (Christopher Wallace), shot to death in 1997 in response to Tupac's killing. Most older Americans are oblivious to the astronomical earnings of successful rappers, such as LL Cool J (James Smith), Nelly (Cornell Haynes), Ludacris (Christopher Bridges), Master P (Percy Miller), Lil Wayne (Dwayne Carter), and Sister Soljah (Lisa Williams).

Actors

In Hollywood, the breakthrough to real celebrity for black actors was made by Sidney Poitier, born in the Bahamas. A series of fine films in the 1960s starting with *Lilies of the Field* (1963), which earned Poitier an Oscar for best actor, established him as a major star. The movie industry is now quite hospitable to black actors, and many talented performers have followed Poitier's lead. James Earl Jones, known for his Jovian voice, had to overcome stuttering before becoming an actor. Louis Gossett, Jr., briefly played professional basketball before working in movies and television; Morgan Freeman has become one of the most admired of all

Hollywood actors; husky Carl Weathers's biggest role was as Apollo Creed in the *Rocky* films; and Billy Dee Williams played Lando Calrissian in *Star Wars*. Three of the biggest black male stars since Poitier are Denzel Washington; Jamie Foxx, who played Ray Charles in *Ray* (2004); and Will Smith, who in 2008 was one of the most highly paid of all movie actors. Other black actor-celebrities include Danny Glover, Samuel L. Jackson, Laurence Fishburne, Blair Underwood, and Cuba Gooding, Jr. The actor-dancer who played "Chicken George" in *Roots* is Ben Vareen, and other black dancers are the late Gregory Hines and tap superstar Savion Glover. America's most famous African American film producer-director is Shelton "Spike" Lee. Among America's best black actresses have been Dorothy Dandridge, Cicely Tyson, Leslie Uggams, Nell Carter, Whoopie Goldberg (Caryn Johnson), Vanessa Williams, Halle Berry (the first black woman to receive an Oscar for best actress in 2001 for *Monster's Ball*), and Queen Latifah (Dana Owens).

Known mainly for their television work are Robert Guillaume (*Soap; Benson*), James Avery (*Fresh Prince of Bel-Air*), Mr. T (Laurence Tureaud, of *The A-Team*), and Isaiah Washington (*Grey's Anatomy*). The queen of **talk show hosts** is Oprah, whose *Oprah Winfrey Show* and many other endeavors have made her a billionaire and the nation's wealthiest African American. Willowy **supermodel** Tyra Banks has hosted *The Tyra Banks Show*, and other black talk show hosts have included Montel Williams, Bryant Gumbel, Arsenio Hall, and Star Jones. In television news, the earliest black network anchor, in 1971, was Max Robinson of American Broadcasting Company (ABC). Charlayne Hunter-Gault pioneered as a national correspondent for Public Broadcasting Service (PBS); and other standouts have included CNN anchor Bernard Shaw, Ed Bradley of *60 Minutes*, PBS pundit Gwen Ifill, and NBC anchor Lester Holt.

The premier black comedian-actor is Bill Cosby, who began on television in the action series *I Spy*, then had his own sitcom, *The Bill Cosby Show*. Veteran performer Red Foxx (John Sanford) starred on *Sanford and Son*; Clerow "Flip" Wilson had his *Flip Wilson Show*, where he played the smart-mouthed Geraldine and the glib Rev. Leroy of The Church of What's Happenin' Now; the late Richard Pryor was noted for his edgy humor about race; and Dick Gregory is remembered more for his activism than for his comedy. Having emerged from *Def Comedy Jam* on Home Box Office (HBO) is the late Bernie Mac (Bernard McCullough). Other outstanding stand-up comics include Sinbad (David Atkins), megastar Eddie Murphy, BET's (Black Entertainment Television's) Cedric the Entertainer (Cedric Kyles), political-social satirist Chris Rock, and sketch comedy star Dave Chappelle.

Athletes

Sports have provided great riches for those young men and women who have risen to the top of their game. Of the major revenue sports, baseball led the way in racial integration, but the percentage of players who are black is far greater in professional basketball and football, where at least two-thirds of all players are black. In professional baseball, the figure is not much more than 10 percent, which is roughly the same in professional soccer. Professional ice hockey and the "country club sports," golf and tennis, have few black players, although golf has been dominated through the early 21st century by the world's finest golfer, Tiger Woods, part black and well on his way to becoming the first billionaire **athlete**. Women's tennis has two African American celebrities: sisters Venus and Serena Williams. Earlier black tennis stars were Althea Gibson and Zina Garrison; and standouts among black male tennis celebrities have been Arthur Ashe, Mali Vai Washington, and James Blake.

One of the first sports to allow black competitors is boxing. Since Joe Louis, the greatest fighter of them all has been Muhammad Ali (Cassius Clay), who won the heavyweight title three times. Other fine heavyweights include Floyd Patterson, Sonny Liston, George Foreman, Mike Tyson, and Evander Holyfield, who had part of an ear bitten off in a bout with Tyson. In the lighter-weight categories were Sugar Ray Robinson (Walker Smith), Rubin "Hurricane" Carter, "Marvelous" Marvin Hagler, and Sugar Ray Leonard (Ray Charles Leonard). Another boxing-world celebrity is promoter Don King.

The legendary tall men of professional basketball, many of them black, date from 7′1″ Wilton "Wilt the Stilt" Chamberlain, who set records for rebounding and scoring, both on the court and with his female admirers. Next came 7′2″ Kareem Abdul-Jabbar (Louis Alcindor). A mere 6′9″ is Earvin "Magic" Johnson, who contracted HIV and is now an advocate for safe sex.

Tattooed and bling-laden, Dennis Rodman gained his celebrity from a combination of rebounding and attitude; Patrick Ewing was a fine center; "Sir" Charles Barkley was a fierce power forward; and tall (7′1), brawny (325-pound) Shaquille O'Neal has been a true superstar, and one who carried on a famous feud with teammate Kobe Bryant, shooting guard. At age eighteen, LeBron James, a 6′8″ forward, went straight from high school to the pros.

In football, a small sample of celebrity-quality players includes running back Walter Payton, intimidating tackle Charles "Mean Joe" Greene, running back O. J. Simpson, and quarterback Donovan McNabb.

In baseball, the first black major league player, in 1947, was second baseman Jackie Robinson, who portrayed himself in the 1950 movie *The Jackie Robinson Story*. In his honor, all major league teams retired Robinson's number, 42. Other early standouts were first baseman Willie Stargell, catcher Roy Campanella, and pitcher Don Newcombe. Great black batters include Willie Mays, Hank Aaron, Reggie Jackson, Dave Winfield, and home-run record-holder Barry Bonds, whose legacy is clouded by charges of steroid use.

Olympic celebrity is often short-lived, but a woman Olympian whose fame has endured was sprinter Wilma Rudolph, winner of three gold medals in the 1960 games. What Jesse Owens did to Hitler, Rudolph did to the Soviets. Around 1960, however, most black track athletes were still being turned away from collegiate competition. Finally, students at New York University and a few other northern universities protested this form of discrimination, and soon sport, a great equalizer, became a way for young black athletes to prove their worth.

Writers

African American celebrities from the more somber fields of endeavor include a number of prominent **authors**. Some, like Zora Neale Hurston and Langston Hughes, were part of the Harlem Renaissance movement. Alex Haley's fame rests mainly on his book *Roots: The Saga of an American Family* (1976). James Baldwin, Toni Morrison (the first African American to earn the Nobel Prize for Literature for *Beloved* in 1993), and Alice Walker are known for their novels; Ishmael Reed is known for skewering American conservatives. Maya Angelou (Marguerite Johnson) is loved for her memoir writing and her verse, and two other prominent contemporary black poets are Rita Dove and Nikki Giovanni.

Activists

The civil rights movement created its own celebrities, both before and after Martin Luther King. Known all over the country was Elijah Muhammad (Elijah Poole), who led the Nation of Islam and the Black Muslims. Rosa Parks was a demure woman whose brave act of civil disobedience led to the Montgomery, Alabama, bus boycott and launched the protests led by the Reverend King. A fiery proponent of black rights until his 1965 murder was Malcolm X (Malcolm Little), and mainstays of the Black Panther Party were Stokley Carmichael and H. Rap Brown. Three contemporary activists are Al Sharpton; National Association for the Advancement of Colored People Chair Julian Bond; and Jesse Jackson, whose recent peccadilloes have lessened his standing.

Politicians

Other leaders of note who have gained celebrity include Thurgood Marshall, the first black U.S. Supreme Court justice, and Clarence Thomas, who took his seat on that court in 1991 amid considerable controversy. Debonair Adam Clayton Powell, Jr., of Harlem was elected to the U.S. House of Representatives in 1945; Shirley Chisholm of New York became the first black congresswoman in 1969; Edward Brooke of Massachusetts was the first black to be elected to the U.S. Senate, in 1966; and Carol Moseley Braun of Illinois became a senator in 1993. A memorable congresswoman from Texas was Barbara Jordan, and another famous but unrelated Jordan was Vernon Jordan, Jr., who was president of the Urban League and an advisor to President Bill Clinton. Military hero General Colin Powell served as secretary of state under President George W. Bush as did his replacement, in 1992, Condoleezza Rice. *See also*: **Criminals**; **Disputes and Feuds**; **Divas**; **Dream Girls**; **Drugs and Alcohol**; **Endorsements**; **Fads**; **Family Celebrity**; **Fan Clubs and Sites**; **Former Sports Stars as Media Celebrities**; **Hobbies and Sports**; **Lawyers**; **Martial Arts**; **Military Celebrity**; **News Media Figures**; **Nicknames**; **One-Name Celebrity**; **Pseudonyms**; **Setbacks and Obstacles**; **Sex and Scandal**; **Sidekicks**; **Suicides**; **Supermodels**; **Temporary Celebrity**; **Tough Guys**.

Sam G. Riley

For Further Reading

Cripps, Thomas. *Making Movies Black.* New York: Oxford University Press, 1993.

Friedlander, Paul, with Peter Miller. *Rock and Roll: A Social History.* Boulder, CO: Westview Press, 2006.

Lapchick, Richard. *Mashing Barriers: Race and Sport in the New Millennium.* New York: Madison Books, 2001.

Miller, Patrick B., and David Kenneth Wiggins, eds. *Sport and the Color Line.* New York, London: Routledge, 2004.

Watkins, S. Craig. *Hip Hop Matters.* Boston: Beacon Press, 2005.

Wiggins, David Kenneth. *Out of the Shadows: A Biographical History of African American Athletes.* Fayetteville: University of Arkansas Press, 2006.

www.africanamericans.com.

www.blackflix.com/celeb.

ANTI-HERO, THE

The anti-hero is a protagonist who behaves ignobly. Anti-heroes lack honesty, courage, and grace. They bumble through life confused. Like Willy Loman in Henry Miller's *Death of a Salesman*, they radiate doubts and ambivalence regarding cultural expectations. They reject the status quo.

Rebels with a Guitar?

Rock and roll abounds with examples. Warren Zevon turned terminal cancer into a publicity gimmick and posthumously won two Grammy awards. His songs "Detox Mansion," "Mr. Bad Example," and "My Dirty Life and Times" reflect his anti-hero reputation for gun-toting rages, substance abuse, womanizing, and irreverent wit. Zevon influenced several generations of singers. Today, fans hear his music on the **Internet**. Zevon attained celebrity with *Excitable Boy*, which featured "Werewolves of London." Although that album went gold in sales, Zevon never again enjoyed great commercial success. While battling lung cancer, he recorded *Wind,* which won a Grammy in 2003, soon after Zevon had died.

In 1967, Jim Morrison, lead singer of The Doors, released the hit, "Light My Fire." His poetic lyrics about death, **sex**, **drugs**, and rebellion against authority frightened parents. Nevertheless, realizing that fans ignored his insights, Morrison unraveled in disappointment and died mysteriously at the age of twenty-seven.

Elvis Presley shook up conservatives with his gyrating hips and played anti-heroes in *Jail House Rock* and numerous other movies. Like Presley, Janis Joplin became a cultural icon of the outsider who gained wisdom from tribulations. Although the twenty-seven-year-old singer died from a heroin overdose in 1970, Joplin's songs, like "Me and Billy Magee" or "Mercedes" remain popular.

Scranton, Pennsylvania, *Times Tribune* critic Chris Kelly designated Johnny Cash, "the Man in Black," as the original anti-hero of pop culture. Cash said he wore symbolic black for the poor, the hungry, and the imprisoned. Cash's marriage to June Carter, daughter of **country** music legend "Mother Maybelle" Carter, helped him conquer addiction and depression. Cash

Jack Nicholson appears at his diabolical best in Witches of Eastwick, *1987. Courtesy of Photofest.*

sang about outcasts whom society denied the chance to pursue the American Dream, and he was among the first to appreciate Bob Dylan's music.

Cash profoundly influenced Dylan, a young folk musician of the early 1960s who sang "Blowing in the Wind" and other message songs. Always a renegade, Dylan segued into rock and roll with an electric guitar and his trademark harmonica. As America's roaming troubadour, he spent the 1990s and early 2000s on the road, often singing the folk songs he wrote at the beginning of his career.

Dylan's most message-oriented song, "Times They Are a Changing," has appealed to several generations of human rights and peace protesters. Blending controversial views with hardcore punk anthems, Andy Martin and Dave Fanning organized a punk rock band "Anti-heroes" in the 1980s.

A decade later, *New York Times* critic Neil Strauss called the band Slipknot (Matt McDonough, drummer, and Pete Murray, vocals) "antiheroes made of steel."

Projecting a steely persona helped Barbara Stanwyck (*Double Indemnity*, 1944) and Bette Davis (*Dangerous*, 1935) eschew vapid "leading lady" roles. In the 1950s, James Dean (*Rebel Without a Cause*, 1955), Marlon Brando (*On the Waterfront*, 1954), and Marilyn Monroe with Clark Gable (*The Misfits*, 1961) explored the depths of human emotions via anti-hero roles.

Heroes Earn Respect but Celebrities Purchase Fame

In *Hidden History* (1987), Daniel J. Boorstin and coauthor Ruth Frankel Boorstin concluded that while heroes often remain anonymous, celebrities exist only through name recognition. Heroes risk their lives to save others, explore new territory, question the status quo in defense of human rights. Selfishness, vanity, and obsession with fame frequently motivate celebrities. H. L. Mencken observed that many readers cannot fathom genius or true heroism, and so writers dilute great individuals with the traits of ordinary folks to enable less gifted souls to relate to them.

Heroes from mythology and history did not seek renown. The Boorstins explained that one of the first major celebrities, Charles Lindbergh, had joined the ranks of heroes on May 21, 1927, by completing the transatlantic flight from Long Island to Paris. Before Lindbergh left, he signed an agreement with the *New York Times*, hired a clipping service, and set a $50 limit to avoid paying the tab for the rest of his life. Overnight, he became famous. Boorstin concludes that the brave aviator abandoned his calling to pursue celebrity and dropped into obscurity after accepting an award from Hitler.

In the 1950s, Communist hunter Sen. Joseph McCarthy from Wisconsin also enjoyed brief celebrity. Like Lindbergh, McCarthy's prejudices eventually backfired on him. In *The Hero in History*, Sidney Hook concludes that the continuum between hero and anti-hero shifts with time and national climate. Therefore, at first, followers called McCarthy a populist godsend, but later many denounced him. Jules Archer makes a similar point in *The Unpopular Ones*, a collection of essays about influential nonconformists, such as birth control pioneer Margaret Sanger, who did not become a celebrity but changed the world.

A Flash in the Pan?

When Louise Fletcher played Nurse Ratched opposite Jack Nicholson in *One Flew Over the Cuckoo's Nest* in 1975, few remembered her television appearances eleven years earlier. Overnight, both she and Nicholson were famous. Film critics called him the conquering anti-hero of roles that Spencer Tracy and Humphrey Bogart had played in the 1940s. After Fletcher won the Oscar, the press courted her. However, her film career plummeted into semi-eclipse as she appeared in a few television roles such as Kai Winn, the cold schemer fans loved to hate in *Star Trek Nine*, some science-fiction movies like 1987's *Flowers in the Attic*, and in 2007 as Mrs. Martha Wilson in *Dennis the Menace Christmas*. In marked contrast, Jack Nicholson's name remains well known, tabloids still track him, and juicy roles continue to showcase his talent. Starring in some forty-one movies, Nicholson has often played anti-heroes.

Geraldine Page's nickname was the First Lady of American Theater. She dedicated her life to her craft, won an Oscar in 1987 for *The Trip to Bountiful*, was nominated several times for a Broadway Tony and appeared first in radio and later in television dramas. She did not become a celebrity because she focused on perfecting her skill, creating repertory theaters to train young actors, and performing where audiences were not accustomed to seeing Broadway shows. She dedicated her life to making a difference instead of to making headlines. Appropriately, Page won the 1987 Wise Owl Award from the U.S. Retirement Research Foundation.

While Page was certainly no flash in the pan, Tiny Tim (Herbert Khaury) became a household name suddenly when he wed seventeen-year-old "Miss Vicki" (Victoria Budinger) on the Johnny Carson Show on December 17, 1969, garnering the largest rating for a late-night talk show to date. He had sung "Tiptoe through the Tulips with Me" while strumming a ukulele on *Rowan & Martin's Laugh In* and other television programs. Almost as abruptly as he had captured the public imagination with his long, brown straggly hair and strange mannerisms, Tiny Tim dropped off the pop-culture radar screen. He continued to perform at charity fundraisers, at a Halloween "spook-tacular" outside Boston, on television commercials, and in Las Vegas; and he cut several albums that became cult favorites. A fatal heart attack interrupted his last performance of "Tiptoe through the Tulips with Me" on November 30, 1996, in Minneapolis.

Anti-Heroes Push Down Facades

Marilyn Monroe and Joseph Cotton both qualify as anti-heroes in *Niagara*, the 1953 suspense film about a pretty young wife who plots with her lover to kill the much older, envious husband. Cotton strangles his unfaithful wife. The grim story raises questions about May-September marriages and the corrosive effects of jealousy. Monroe today lives on in fan clubs, on Web sites, and as an icon of Hollywood glamour. However, Monroe was a talented, versatile actor who played villains as readily as daffy blondes.

Cinematic anti-heroes force audiences to recognize and confront social problems. For example, Sally Field's *Norma Rae* (1979), drinks, smokes, and goes out a bit yet supports her children. Risking everything to unionize a textile mill, she exposes the poverty inherent in company towns. In *The Last King of Scotland* (2006), Forest Whitaker's portrayal of Idi Amin traces the breakdown of an idealist into a paranoid, murderous traitor. Occasionally, even repulsive psychopaths such as Anthony Hopkins in the 1999 thriller *Silence of the Lambs* and Javier Bardem in *No Country for Old Men* (2007) do something good. In *There Will Be Blood* (2007), however, Daniel Day-Lewis plays a mogul whose obsession with power completely erodes his sense of decency.

Playing anti-heroes has added to the luster of many celebrities, including the following: Vivian Leigh (*Gone With the Wind*, 1939), Broderick Crawford (*All the King's Men*, 1959), Elizabeth Taylor (*Who's Afraid of Virginia Woolf?* 1966), Steve McQueen (*Bullitt*, 1968), Gene Hackman (*The French Connection*, 1971), Charles Bronson (*Death Wish*, 1974), Faye Dunaway (*Network*, 1976), Michael Douglas (*Wall Street*, 1987), Joe Pesci (*Good Fellas*, 1990), Catharine Zeta-Jones (*Chicago*, 2003), Jennifer Hudson (*Dreamgirls*, 2006), Laura Linney (*The Savages*, 2007), and George Clooney, Tom Wilkinson, and Tilda Swinton (*Michael Clayton*, 2007). *See also*: **Awards and Ceremonies; Dream Girls; Politics; Temporary Celebrity; Tough Guys.**

Paulette D. Kilmer

For Further Reading

Boorstin, Daniel J., and Ruth Frankel Boorstin. *Hidden History: Exploring Our Secret Past*. New York: Harper & Row, 1987, 284–296.

Deardorff, Donald L., II. *Hero and Anti-Hero in the American Football Novel: Changing Conceptions of Masculinity from Nineteenth Century to the Twenty-First Century*. Lewiston, NY: Mellen, 2006.

Hook, Sidney. *The Hero in History: A Study in Limitation and Possibility*. Boston: Beacon Press, 1955.

Wector, Dixon. *The Hero in America: A Chronicle of Hero-Worship in America*. Ann Arbor: University of Michigan Press, 1966.

Wloszczyna, Susan. "Anti-Heroes Aren't New for Oscars," *USA Today*, February 21, 2008, www.usatoday.com/life/movies/movieawards/oscars/2008-02-20-anti-heroes-side_N.htm.

Wrestler Andre the Giant enters the ring. Courtesy of Photofest.

ARRESTS OF CELEBRITIES

An anonymous pre-Revolutionary Russian proverb advised: "Be righteous before God; be wealthy before a judge." Today, we might make that "wealthy and famous" considering the frequent leniency shown by our courts to celebrity miscreants. Some judges, of course, have been as firm with celebrities as with anyone else, but often America appears to have a dual standard of justice: one for the rich and famous, another for the rest of society. Perhaps this tendency toward leniency helps account for the ding-dong regularity of celebrity arrests. Once upon a more genteel time, it was rare to see celebrities hauled into court on **criminal** charges. Now, although celebrities rarely commit **murder**, rape, armed robbery or burglary, arrests of our entertainers on **drug** charges and driving under the influence of alcohol are remarkably common. Our media have adopted a sort of nudge-nudge, wink-wink attitude about celebrity substance abuse, and besides, if legal trouble comes calling, high-powered lawyers and offers of large financial settlements often make the trouble go away. Fans who imitate their loose-living celebrity idols, and who land in court, usually find it much more difficult to hire top legal counsel or to spend the trouble away.

Murder

Among the few celebrities to have been charged with murder was Sid Vicious (born Simon Ritchie), bass player for the English punk rock group The Sex Pistols. The drug-addled rocker was charged with the 1978 stabbing death of his girlfriend. Soon after her death, he attempted **suicide** and shortly thereafter died of a heroin overdose. As to publicity generated, the Sid Vicious case paled in comparison to the media circus that attended the murder arrest and trial of former football star O. J. Simpson, charged in 1994 with murdering his wife and a male friend. In a racially charged trial, Simpson was found not guilty despite compelling evidence to the contrary. In 2007, he was arrested and charged with the armed robbery of sports memorabilia in a Las Vegas hotel. Simpson's bail was revoked when he attempted to contact a defendant in violation of court orders. He was convicted in 2008.

Sex Crimes

Moviemaker Roman Polanski worked out a plea bargain in 1978 regarding having had sex with a thirteen-year-old girl, and then fled to France. Should he return to the United States, he theoretically would face prison time. Boxer Mike Tyson was convicted of rape in 1992 and spent three years in prison. Charged with sexual assault in 2003 was NBA (National Basketball Association) player Kobe Bryant. His accuser dropped the criminal charges, and a settlement was reached in the civil suit she had filed against him. Generating huge publicity worldwide were the various arrests on child molestation charges of entertainer Michael Jackson. He was able to reach an out-of-court settlement of the charges brought against him in 1993, but in 2003 was charged with seven counts of the same offense. In his trial, held in 2005, Jackson was acquitted on all counts, after which he moved to Bahrain in the Persian Gulf.

Assault

Andre the Giant (born Andre Roussimoff), all 540 pounds of him, was charged with assaulting a cameraman in 1989. Tattoo-covered NBA star Dennis Rodman was arrested in 1999 for allegedly assaulting his wife and fellow celebrity, Carmine Electra, who eventually dropped charges. Also arrested for spousal assault, in 2002, was wrestler "Stone Cold" Steve Austin, as was the "godfather of Soul," singer James Brown, in 2004. R&B (rhythm and blues) singer Lou Rawls was arrested in 2003 for assault and battery on his girlfriend, boxer Joe Frazier was arrested in 2004 for assaulting a woman who was the mother of one of his children, and rap performer Vanilla Ice (born Robert Van Winkle) was arrested in 2008 for assaulting his wife. The charges against Van Winkle were eventually dropped. Rapper Jay-Z (born Shawn Carter) was arrested in 1999 and charged with stabbing a record executive, rap artist Eminem (born Marshall Mathers III) was arrested in 2000 for assaulting a man he saw kissing his estranged wife, and actor Ryan O'Neal was arrested in 2007 for the assault of his adult son. Arrested in 1989 and sentenced to three days in jail was longtime Hollywood celebrity Zsa Zsa Gabor, who slapped a Beverly Hills police officer who had pulled her over. No stranger to arrest, Adam "Pacman" Jones of the NFL (National Football League) was arrested in 2007 and charged with biting a bouncer and threatening to kill another man in a nightclub. Kid Rock (born Robert James Ritchie) was arrested in 1991, 1997, 2005, and 2007, the last two times on charges of assault and battery. Busta Rhymes (born Trevor Smith) was arrested in 2008 for assaulting a fan and a driver, and Boy George (born George O'Dowd) was charged in 2007 with assault and false imprisonment for allegedly keeping a Norwegian man a prisoner in the musician's home. A handful of women celebrities have also been hauled into court on assault charges, including Mindy McCready (2007), Foxy Brown (born Inga Marchand, 2007), and model Naomi Campbell (2000 and 2007).

Larceny

Many CNN (Cable News Network) viewers might be surprised that **talk show host** Larry King was arrested in 1971 on grand larceny charges, which he beat thanks to the statute of limitations. In 1975, most of the world was caught up in the arrest of media heiress Patricia Hearst, who had been kidnapped in 1974 by an urban revolutionary group called the Symbionese Liberation Army (SLA). Miss Hearst was found guilty of having participated in an SLA bank robbery in San Francisco, but her seven-year sentence was commuted by President Jimmy Carter. Later, she was granted a full pardon by President Bill Clinton. In 1983, soul singer James Brown was arrested for assaulting a police officer and served three years. A seven-year sentence was handed down to boxer Hector "Macho" Camacho in 2007 for burglary of a computer store, and in 2008, basketball player Isaiah Rider was arrested on charges of grand theft auto.

Drugs

Celebrities' number-one crime of choice has been drug offenses. Pioneers in this regard were drummer Gene Krupa, in 1943, and actor Robert Mitchum, in 1948, both for possession of marijuana. Arrested for the same offense have been such other celebrities as Tex-Mex singer Freddy Fender (1960), Beetle George Harrison (1961),

singer David Bowie (1976), and Beetle Paul McCartney (1980). More recent marijuana arrests have included tennis star Jennifer Capriati (1994), country singer Willie Nelson (1995), dancer Savion Glover (1996), Bob Denver and Dawn Wells of *Gilligan's Island* (1998 and 2008, respectively), basketball greats Allen Iverson (1997) and Kareem Abdul-Jabbar (1998), singer Amy Winehouse (2007), and actor Kevin Gage (2008). In addition, baseball star Orlando Cepeda was arrested in 1976 and charged with smuggling marijuana.

Arrested for possession of various hard drugs were musician Jimi Hendrix (1969); actor Stacy Keach (1984), who actually served nine months; rap artist 50 Cent (born Curtis Jackson, in 1994); actor Robert Downey, Jr. (1996); "celebutantes" Nicole Ritchie (2003, 2006) and Lindsay Lohan (2007); boxer Mike Tyson (2006, 2007); actor Tom Sizemore (2004); singer Bobby Brown (2007); rapper Lil Wayne (2008, born Dwayne Carter); and actor Gary Dourdan of *CSI* (2008). Conservative and outspokenly antidrug pundit Rush Limbaugh was taken into custody in 2006 for attempting to "doctor shop" to get multiple painkiller prescriptions, but got off with a fine.

Drunken Driving and Public Drunkenness

The second-most-frequent cause of celebrity arrests has been driving under the influence (DUI). This offense, plus reckless driving, nipped actor Steve McQueen in 1972. Among the many other celebrities charged with DUI or reckless driving have been actors Nick Nolte (2002) and Robert Conrad (2003); country singers Wynonna Judd (2003) and Glen Campbell (2003);

actors Rip Torn (2006) and Mel Gibson (2007); Lindsay Lohan (2002), Paris Hilton (2006), and Nichole Ritchie (2006); actors Kiefer Sutherland (2007), Mickey Rourke (2007), Rebecca De Morney (2007), and Gary Collins (2008); guitarist Richie Samboro of Bon Jovi (2008); and Hollywood madam Heidi Fleiss (2008). Rocker Ozzy Osbourne was arrested in 1984 for public drunkenness, as was up-and-coming young actor Shia La Beouf in 2007.

Shoplifting

A hard-to-understand crime for wealthy celebrities is shoplifting. Actress Winona Ryder's 2001 arrest for taking clothes from a Saks Fifth Avenue store excited considerable public curiosity, and in 2008, actress Bai Ling of *Lost* was charged with taking magazines and batteries from an airport shop.

Other Charges

A high-profile celebrity morals charge involved comic actor Pee Wee Herman (born Paul Reubens), arrested in 1991 for lewd conduct in the form of masturbation in a movie theater. He was arrested again in 2002 on child pornography charges. Also generating great public comment was the 1995 arrest of actor Hugh Grant, caught making use of the services of a prostitute. Arrested in 2007 and given a twenty-three-month prison sentence for operating a dog-fighting ring was Atlanta Falcons quarterback Michael Vick, and receiving a three-year sentence in 2008 for failing to file income taxes was actor Wesley Snipes.

Some years ago, a criminal arrest would have greatly embarrassed most celebrities, but a May 2008 *Time* magazine item revealed that Senegalese-American hip-hop singer Akon (born Aliuane Thiam) had actually inflated the extent of his rap sheet to bolster his "street credibility." *See also*: **African American**; **Athletes**; **Hip-Hop and Rap**; **News Media Figures**; **Rock and Pop**.

Sam G. Riley

For Further Reading

Benedict, Jeff. *Public Heroes, Private Felons: Athletes and Crimes Against Women*. Boston: Northeastern University Press, 1997.

Newton, Michael, and John L. French. *Celebrities and Crime*. New York: Chelsea House, 2008.

Olsen, Marilyn. *Arrested! Celebrities Caught in the Act*. New York: Hatherleigh Press, 2002.

www.hollyscoop.com/celebrity-arrests.

www.totalcriminaldefense.com/celebrity-arrests.

ARTISTS

The term "celebrity artists" encompasses two meanings: (1) professional artists who have gained celebrity and (2) celebrities who are amateur artists in addition to doing whatever gained them their fame. As to the full-time, professional artists of recent times, when it comes to gaining widespread celebrity, many have been called but few chosen, as the old saying has it. We live in a time of popular, not fine art, which limits the number of painters and sculptors whose names become household words in America.

Professional Artists

One whom virtually all literate Americans likely would have heard of was the Spanish artist Pablo Picasso, who was born in 1881 and died in 1973. Many an onlooker has scratched his or her head over this artist's cubist paintings, pictures of prostitutes and gloomy abstracts. Georgia O'Keeffe (born in 1887) is remembered primarily for her work as a New Mexico painter of vivid desert landscapes, clouds and flowers; she died in 1986. The creator of the mobile, Alexander Calder, produced hanging, kinetic artworks out of metal rods and pieces of sheet metal. He also did standing metal sculptures, painted, and designed tapestries and carpets. He was born in 1898 and died in 1976. Born in the same year as Calder was English sculptor Henry Moore, who became well known in America for his abstract, rounded, reclining bronze or marble figures. Many of his works were done in large scale, intended for public spaces rather than private collections, and they made Moore a very wealthy artist.

A real artist with a camera was Ansel Adams, born in 1902, whose photographs beautifully depicted the Sierra Nevada mountain range, capturing the grandeur of Yosemite, Mount Rainier, Glacier National Park, and various stands of Sequoia trees. Adams died in 1984. Abstract expressionist Willem de Kooning, born in 1904 in the Netherlands, came to the United States in the mid-1920s and painted mainly women and landscapes. He died in 1997. One of the most colorful and eccentric of artists was Spain's Salvador Dali, also born in 1904. Dressed in a long cape, carrying a cane, wearing a waxed and

Eccentric artist Andy Warhol looks every bit the part in his oversized eyeglasses and wild mop hairstyle. Courtesy of Photofest.

upturned mustache, speaking of himself in third person, and affecting a bug-eyed stare, Dali was prolific in a variety of media: painting, drawing, sculpture, photography, film, and fashion. He is perhaps best remembered for his soft, melting clocks and watches, which hung limply over tree limbs or drooped languidly over the sharp edges of buildings. Dali died in 1989.

The master of splatter, sometimes called "Jack the Dripper," was Jackson Pollock, born in 1912. Working with his canvas placed flat on the studio floor, this abstract expressionist would apply paint by pouring, dripping, and splattering it. Pollock died in a car wreck in 1956. Another abstract expressionist of similar age to Pollock was Robert Motherwell, whose stark use of black came to public attention in part due to the many speeches he gave around the country before his 1991 death. Enjoying far wider public acclaim, although not so lavishly praised by professional art critics, is Andrew Wyeth, born in 1917 to illustrator N. C. Wyeth and father to Jamie Wyeth. Known for his realistic depictions of the lovely countryside of Chadds Ford, Pennsylvania, and for his many studies of his favorite models, Christina, Siri, and Helga, the celebrated Wyeth divided his time between Chadds Ford and Cushing, Maine. Wyeth died in 2009.

In an America dominated by popular, not high culture, Roy Lichtenstein, with his comic-book or comic-strip style, achieved success among the avant-garde. His paintings linked art and America's commercial mass media; he died in 1997. Even more of an art-world celebrity was Andy Warhol (born Andrew Warhola), who painted the everyday objects of the U.S. consumer culture and also did many portraits of his fellow celebrities. With his mop of white hair and deadpan facial expression, Warhol was the most eccentric artist since Salvador Dali, an image furthered by the odd cast of characters who peopled his New York City studio, which he called The Factory. He was shot in 1968 by one of these hangers-on, Valerie Solanas, but recovered. Two decades later, in 1987, Warhol died of a heart attack following surgery. A more recent artist with a sizeable studio of assistants is Jeff Koons, who likes to transform ordinary objects into shiny metal pieces of pop art.

A different kind of abstract expressionist was Robert Rauschenberg, who picked up "found objects" on the streets of New York and literally put them into his paintings. He died in 2008. Perhaps the most unusual of all these artists are the husband and wife team of Christo and Jeanne-Claude, who share the same 1935 birthday. Their work often involves wrapping bridges or buildings or altering the look of landscapes by stretching long expanses of cloth-like fences. He was born in Bulgaria, she in Morocco, and the couple came to the United States in the 1960s. Of all this period's artists who have gained celebrity in America, the most accessible to a large public was Norman Rockwell, painter and illustrator, who did many portraits of notables but is mainly celebrated for the covers and other illustrations he did for two magazines: *Saturday Evening Post* and *Look*. Professional art critics tend to look down their patrician noses at Rockwell's work, yet it had great warmth and recorded America as it once was. He died in 1978.

Celebrity Artists

One kind of "celebrity artist" is the entertainer who likes to paint or sculpt. Such individuals are many, although some of these famous weekend artists produce work that not only tends to the abstract, but also could be said to be more like pistachio than Picasso. One of the most talented and most serious of these amateur artists is singer Tony Bennett, who signs his work with his birth name, Anthony Benedetto, and who says that he paints every day. He prefers watercolor, does portraits of fellow celebrities and still-life pictures but is probably at his very best with landscapes. Another celebrity watercolorist with talent is Gene Wilder. Actor Tony Curtis is a competent artist, though not especially original, and quite good at both painting and sculpture was actor Anthony Quinn. Other celebrities with above-average talent are Richard

Chamberlin; Jane Seymour; Vigo Mortensen, whose abstract pictures show a real grasp of color; Ronny Wood of The Rolling Stones, who has depicted his fellow musicians; Martin Mull, whose work is inventive in its combining of color with black and white; Elke Sommer, whose work has an old-world style; and Anthony Hopkins, whose choices of subject matter tend toward the weird but who makes great use of color. Jazz great Miles Davis had talent for painting, as did longtime actor Buddy Ebsen. Budding **tough guy** actor Michael Madsen, who, like Vigo Mortensen, also writes poetry, shows talent, and Peter Falk is quite good at pencil drawing. Two more performers who could sketch well were singer Janis Joplin and comic impressionist Rich Little; and both former Jefferson Airplane/Starship **rock** singer Grace Slick and rock guitarist Jimi Hendrix have done some good artwork. Sylvester Stallone's abstract efforts are not bad at all; Johnny Depp is fair; singer Joni Mitchell's work rates one thumb up; and the paintings of Grateful Dead singer and guitarist Jerry Garcia show that he had formal art training.

In the not-quite-so-gifted group might be placed three former Beetles: Ringo Starr, Paul McCartney, and the late John Lennon; Dennis Hopper; The Millennium's bassist John Entwhisle; former singer with The Monkees Mickey Dolenz; heavy-metal musician Marilyn Manson; actor Pierce Brosnan; song and dance man Tommy Tune; U2 singer and activist Bono; versatile musician Moby; folk singer Joan Baez; actress Tina Louise; comedian Phyllis Diller; boxing great Muhammad Ali; and combative entertainer Rosie O'Donnell. Then again, art is in the eye of the beholder, and the creating of art, whether good or bad, is not only pleasant work, but therapeutic. Besides, in an America so taken with celebrity, artsy performers do not really have to be all that good to sell lithographs, seriographs, or other reproductions of their work—sometimes for impressive sums. *See also*: **Athletes**; **Talk Show Hosts**.

Sam G. Riley

For Further Reading

Cherbo, Joni Maya, and Margaret Jane Syszomirski. *The Public Life of the Arts in America.* New Brunswick, NJ: Rutgers University Press, 2000.

Joachimides, Christos M., et al. *American Art in the 20th Century: Painting and Sculpture, 1913–1993.* New York: Te Neues Pub. Co., 1993.

www.limelightagency.com.

www.poplifeart.com.

www.rockstargallery.net/celebrityartists.

ASIAN AMERICAN

The road to U.S. celebrity was long a difficult one for Asian and Asian American entertainers. The man and woman who broke ground in Hollywood for performers of their ethnicity were Sessue Hayakawa and Anna May Wong, each of whom had a career that spanned silent pictures and "talkies." Hayakawa appeared in roughly eighty films, founded his own production company and considered his best role to have been as Colonel Saito in *The Bridge on the River Kwai* (1957); he died in 1973. The beautiful Anna Wong played with Douglas Fairbanks in *The*

Thief of Baghdad in 1924, with Marlene Dietrich in *Shaghai Express* (1932), and with Lana Turner in *Portrait in Black* (1960). She was to have appeared in *Flower Drum Song* but died of a heart attack at fifty-six. She is often referred to as the first Asian international film star and as America's earliest Chinese American star.

Keye Luke, another Chinese American actor, was "Number-One Son" in some of the *Charlie Chan* mystery films, acting with Warner Oland, who had the title role. Oland was actually Swedish but had vaguely Asian features. The fact that he was the first Charlie Chan owes much not only to his acting abilities but also to the ethnic discrimination of the time. Luke appeared in the *Dr. Kildare* movies and as Kato in the *Green Hornet* series. In 1972, he played the title role of Charlie Chan on television and is perhaps best known of all for his role as Master Po on the *Kung Fu* television show. Racial discrimination also worked in an odd way for African American actress Juanita Hall, whose appearance was sufficiently Asian that she appeared as Bloody Mary in *South Pacific* and as Auntie Liang in *Flower Drum Song*.

Korean American actor Philip Ahn acted with Gregory Peck in *The Keys to the Kingdom* (1944) and was in *Love Is a Many-Splendored Thing* (1955); *Around the World in Eighty Days* (1956); *Paradise, Hawaiian Style* (1966) with Elvis Presley; and *Thoroughly Modern Millie* (1967). Ahn died in 1978. Two Japanese actors who

Bruce Lee (left) takes on Kareem Abdul-Jabbar in the movie Game of Death, *1978. Courtesy of Photofest.*

became well known in America for their work in the movies of Akira Kurosawa were Toshiro Mifune and Takashi Shimura. In *The Seven Samurai* (1954), Shimura played the matchless swordsman and Mifune the wild, emotional novice warrior. Shimura died in 1982 and, after having appeared in roughly 170 films, Mifune died in 1997.

Following Anna Wong, the next Asian woman to gain U.S. stardom was France Nuyen, who was of French-Chinese background. She played the lovely Liat in *South Pacific* (1958), took the title role in the Broadway version of *The World of Susie Wong*, and appeared in Amy Tan's story set to film, *Joy Luck Club* (1993). The third Asian woman to become a major Hollywood star was Hong Kong–born Nancy Kwan, who starred opposite William Holden in the film version of *The World of Susie Wong* (1960) and the following year in *Flower Drum Song*. Her later movies never matched her first two in quality, but Kwan often appeared on television shows such as *Hawaii Five-O* and *Kung Fu*. In *Flower Drum Song* with Kwan and in the Broadway version was Japanese American actor James Shigeta, who also appeared in Japanese movies and on such American television shows as *Perry Mason* and *Little House on the Prairie*.

Three celebrity character actors of Asian lineage have been Burt Kwouk, Harold Sakata, and Pat Morita. Kwouk appeared as Cato, Inspector Clouseau's diabolical valet and ill-fated sparring partner, in six of the *Pink Panther* movies, beginning in 1975 with *The Return of the Pink Panther* and ending in 1993 with *Son of the Pink Panther*.

The name Cato was taken from the *Green Hornet* radio show, in which that character was originally Japanese, but after the attack on Pearl Harbor, suddenly became Filipino. Sakata, originally a Japanese American wrestler and also an Olympic silver medalist in weightlifting, appeared in *Goldfinger* (1964) as that arch-villain's bodyguard, Oddjob, who cut down his victims by flinging his steel-brimmed bowler hat at them. A good guy–**tough guy** role, Mr. Miyagi, the elderly but effective karate master in *The Karate Kid,* was played by veteran actor Pat Morita, who prior to that had held the television sitcom role of Arnold on *Happy Days*. Morita had spent part of his youth in a World War II–era Japanese internment camp in Arizona; he died in 2005.

Omitted in this entry are the Asian **martial arts** actors and actresses, who are covered in an entry of their own. An exception is the versatile Malaysian actress Michelle Yeoh, best known for her action roles such as the one she played in *Crouching Tiger, Hidden Dragon* (2000). Yeoh, whose early hopes of becoming a ballerina were dashed by an injury to her spine, drew considerable attention with her graceful performance in the 2005 film *Memoirs of a Geisha* and in the 2007 independent film *Far North*. Also in *Memoirs of a Geisha* was Japanese actor Ken Watanabe, who made his early reputation in Japanese movies performing samurai roles. Among his better U.S. movie roles were a samurai overlord in *The Last Samurai* (2003) and a Japanese general in Clint Eastwood's *Letters from Iwo Jima* (2006). Yet another actor appearing in *Memoirs of a Geisha* is Koji Yakusho, who earlier had done a fine job of acting, and dancing, in the Japanese movie *Shall We Dance?* (1997), in which he starred opposite the supremely graceful Japanese **dancer** and actress Tamiyo Kusakari. The fact that many U.S. movie goers are reluctant to go to subtitled movies starring people whose names are hard to pronounce or remember led to a less-than-stellar U.S. remake of that film in 2004 starring Richard Gere and Jennifer Lopez. The best-known Asian movie directors today are Ang Lee from Taiwan and Indian American M. Night Shymalan. Lee's credits include *The Wedding Banquet* (1993), *Sense and Sensibility* (1995), *Crouching Tiger, Hidden Dragon* (2000), and *Brokeback Mountain* (2005). Shymalan's movies usually deal in the supernatural; he has directed two films starring Bruce Willis, *The Sixth Sense* (1999) and *Signs* (2002) and one with Mel Gibson, *Unbreakable* (2000).

Known mainly for her work on the soap *General Hospital* and on other television shows is Tia Carrere, whose ancestry is a mix of Chinese, Filipino, and Spanish. A well-known stereotype of Asian Americans is that they are unusually intelligent. Young Japanese actor Masi Oka, who plays the delightful character Hiro on the television series *Heroes*, certainly fits that stereotype, inasmuch as his intelligence quotient is reportedly around 180. Lisa Ling, of Chinese descent, is one of the cohosts of the daytime television chat show *The View*. As such, she might just be a bigger celebrity in 2008 than her fellow Chinese American Connie Chung, who has been a television journalist since the 1970s. Part journalist, part daytime entertainer is the respected Ann Curry, anchor of *Today* since 1997

and host of *Dateline* since 2005. Curry's mother is Japanese, her father American. An unusual entertainer is Shoji Tabuchi, who sings, plays fiddle, and does stand-up comedy at the highly profitable Shoji Tabuchi Theater in Branson, Missouri. Although trained as a violinist, this Japan-born entertainer certainly knows where the big money is in America.

Fine Arts

Among the few Asian American celebrities in the fine arts, the best known is cellist Yo-Yo Ma, who trained at Julliard, is considered the world's finest cellist, and who has extended his talents to the popular arts by his work on movie scores. Like Ma, who also began performing as a prodigy, is violinist Chee-Yun, who began performing in the United States at age thirteen. Among conductors, few of whom ever become true celebrities in America, the best known Asian is Japanese: Seiji Ozawa, who for many years was music director of the Boston Symphony Orchestra. Among **authors**, Amy Tan, who published *Joy Luck Club* in 1989, is probably the biggest Asian American celebrity; and among **fashion designers**, New York–based Vera Wang is likely the best known.

Athletes

Surely the biggest celebrity **athlete** with Asian ancestry is golf sensation Tiger Woods, who is usually indentified as African American, but is also one-fourth Thai and one-fourth Chinese, plus one-eighth Native American and one-fourth Dutch. He is, in short, multiracial; and he is also the highest-earning athlete of all professional athletes, on track to become the first billionaire in sports. Three women professional golfers who also have achieved U.S. celebrity status are Korean American Grace Park; Aree Song, whose father is Korean and mother Thai; and Michelle Wie, also Korean American. An Asian American tennis celebrity, now retired, is Michael Chang, who won the French Open in 1989 and whose even-tempered sportsmanship made him a crowd favorite.

The sport that has attracted the greatest number of players of Asian background into the professional ranks is baseball. Chan Ho Park, pitcher, was the first Korean player in the U.S. major league when he joined the Los Angeles Dodgers in 1994. In 1995, that same team hired Japanese pitcher Hideo Nomo. Both men went on to pitch—for enormous salaries—on other major league teams. Another Japanese standout is outfielder and excellent batter Ichiro Suzuki, who came to the United States in 2001 to play for the Seattle Mariners. Fewer Asians and Asian Americans have played professional football, although an early standout was quarterback Roman Gabriel, whose parents were Filipino. Unusually large for that position, Gabriel was in 1962 the first person of Asian ancestry to be an NFL (National Football League) starting quarterback. Another NFL notable is the Dallas Cowboys' Dat Nguyen, who in 1999 was the first Vietnamese American in the league. Nguyen now coaches for that team. In men's professional basketball, two Asians stand out: Wang Zhizhi and Yao Ming, both Chinese. Wang, 7'1", joined the Dallas Mavericks in 2001, played for two other U.S. teams and then returned to China to rejoin that

country's national team. Yao, even taller at 7'6", was in 2008 the tallest of all the professional players. He signed with the Houston Rockets in 1997, remains a potent force in the sport and has had many highly paid product-endorsement deals. Another Chinese basketball player, who stood 6'8", is a woman: Zheng Haixia, who signed with the Los Angeles Sparks in 1997 and a year later returned to China to coach.

In professional figure skating, two Asian names predominate: Michelle Kwan and Kristi Yamaguchi. Both women have won Olympic medals for the United States plus many other skating honors. Kwan is the daughter of Chinese immigrants to America; Yamaguchi is Japanese American. Also performing on skates is Richard Park, professional ice hockey player, who was born in the Republic of Korea. His older countryman, Sammy Lee, won two Olympic gold medals for platform diving, in 1948 and 1952. *See also*: **Classical Music**; **Dancers**; **Dream Girls**; **News Media Figures**; **Rock and Pop**.

Sam G. Riley

For Further Reading

Anon. *Guide to Asian Artists and Performers*. New York: Asia Society, 1990.

http://asians.net/Fashion.

http://goldsea.com/Personalities.

ATHLETES

It was a sunny afternoon in St. Louis, Missouri, as the St. Louis Browns hosted the Detroit Tigers in a double-header at Sportsman's Park. The Tigers had won the first game of the twin-bill and Bill Veeck—the Browns' owner, a self-promoting showman—had promised his many sponsors a special show. Veeck did not disappoint.

Between the two games, Veeck had an on-field show featuring several midgets leaping out of a ceremonial "birthday cake." The show was a bust. People murmured that Veeck had lost his showman's touch. But Veeck had grander plans in mind.

In the bottom of the first inning, after the Tigers had not put a runner on base and the Browns prepared for its half of the inning, a new player emerged from the Browns' dugout and approached the plate. Standing just over three and one-half feet tall and wearing uniform number 1/8 on his

Browns jersey, twenty-six-year-old Eddie Gaedel calmly stepped into the batter's box as the crowd roared its approval. Veeck smiled, knowing he had solidified his claim to baseball immortality.

Home-plate umpire Ed Hurley immediately called timeout as the Tigers' manager protested the appearance of the tiny Gaedel in the Browns' lineup. Veeck also had readied himself for any challenge. Presented with the official lineup for the second game, along with Gaedel's recently signed contract, there was little the veteran umpire Hurley could do. Hurley finally motioned to the Tigers' pitcher to proceed with the game.

Gaedel, who had been instructed to crouch as low as possible, took his

Heavyweight champion Muhammad Ali delivers a crushing right to Ken Norton in their 1973 bout. Courtesy of Photofest.

Tiger Woods shows his concentration after an iron shot. Courtesy of Photofest.

place and, under strict orders not to swing, he took his stance. Presented with a strike zone of just less than two inches, Tiger pitcher Bob Cain, struggling to control his own laughter, walked Gaedel, who trotted to first base doffing his cap to the crowd. He was immediately replaced by a pinch runner and never again played in a major league baseball game.

Gaedel's celebrity was short-lived, however; he never cashed in on his celebrity and was killed a few years later in an armed robbery in Chicago.

Mass Media and the Rise of Sports Celebrity

The purpose of this entry is to examine the rise of sport celebrity and the role of the mass media in fueling that rise. A typology of forms of sport celebrity is presented to better understand the ephemeral and enduring nature of sport celebrity.

The first rule of celebrity is that one can achieve celebrity simply by being known, not by renown. It would be, of course, impossible to identify the first sport celebrity, but consider the early Greek sporting events—the birth place of most modern sports. Around the fifth century B.C.E., the Greeks introduced a particularly brutal form of combined boxing and wrestling: the *pankration*. Rules regulating strikes or body blows to the "soft parts" of one's opponent were put into place after a certain combatant struck a blow to an opponent's midsection, twisted his fist inward, and then removed his hapless victim's intestines. Rules also were changed, in part, because of another wrestler of the same era who gained fame (or infamy) for his ability to break his opponents' fingers to ensure submission. These two athletes, and others, gained notoriety among their countrymen, but little was more widely known about these athletes. It took the enterprising Roman Empire to give a boost to the legitimacy of sports heroes.

Once the Greeks were conquered, Rome began altering the sporting events the Greek citizens had come to enjoy as a means for Rome to "advertise" its dominance over Greece. The cult of sport celebrity may well have been born as the Romans altered the early Greek competitions and introduced the games of the Coliseum where gladiators faced off against other gladiators, slaves against slaves, gladiators against Christians and, finally, lions and tigers against gladiators and Christians. The gathering throngs were plied with wine and bread, and the dramatic mass spectacle of sport was born.

Obviously, during these early games, people in the rest of Europe—or the rest of the world—had little if any conception of the exploits of the Greek wrestlers or of the Roman gladiators. These athletes' renown was geographically restricted. So, when and where did sport celebrity begin to gain larger, more widespread audience?

The answer lies in the rise of the mass media in general and the electronic media in particular. Consider the story of Jack Johnson. White heavyweights of the early 1900s refused to fight Johnson, the undefeated black champion. As he moved through the ranks toward a possible world championship bout, Johnson had to prove himself with little, if any, media support. Radio broadcasts of his fights would often "inexplicably" lose their signal when Johnson was winning a fight over a white boxer. African American supporters in his home state of Texas would spill into the streets to celebrate Johnson's victories, when news was available, yet local authorities often would cancel broadcasts of Johnson's fights in anticipation of potential "race riots." Johnson held the title for four years before media publicity and a racist legal system chased him into exile in Cuba. His crime was emblematic of the times: Johnson had married a white woman.

Johnson's case fits well into the model of the power elite's use of the "under class" as tools of capitalist amusement. Sports throughout the early part of the 20th century in the United States remained a display of the power elites' control over the masses. Prize fight champions (excluding African Americans) were showcased as a demonstration of the elites' power over the common people. This notion of control over a commodity was hardly unique as the war lords in ancient Japan held sumo matches between competing villages pitting their finest wrestlers against the next village's finest. Winners were said to have the blessing of the gods and also represented the prospect of a better harvest for the village the wrestler represented.

But again, there is the issue of the spread of celebrity. Outside of the rural prefects of Japan, who knew, or cared, about the exploits of the sumo?

The ability of the media to frame interest in a social event or to create individual superstars should come as no surprise. Media researchers and social theorists have long argued that the media help contribute to ideological hegemony. In addition, advertising of a news event, the story's placement, and the amount of play the story ultimately will receive are deliberately thought out. The rise of Michael Jordan to superstar status was a direct result, in addition to his ability to play basketball, of Nike's calculated advertising strategy wherein Jordan would be the only professional athlete to shill Nike products. Once Jordan's global stardom was ensured, Nike began "collecting" other professional athletes, especially African American standouts, to sell shoes and athletic clothing. The Jordan name is iconic in that the mere mention of his name became a tagline in advertising. Gatorade sports drink's initial advertising campaign of the early 1990s asked, "Do you want to be like Mike?" This was later reduced to simply "Be like Mike."

How did this commoditization of athletes begin? It took a media controlled by elites working in conjunction with wealthy team owners, to bring sporting contests to the masses and get people excited about not just the result of the sporting event, but also the actors (players) in the drama. Thorsten Veblen, in his *Theory of the Leisure Class* (1912), noted that most sporting events were initially produced for the entertainment value they supplied to wealthy elites. Working-class individuals, it was argued in the early 20th century, should not spend their time engaging in these sporting activities, as it would take away from work that supplied the leisure class with its riches.

The stroke of genius that transformed leisure-time sporting events into professional-class sporting events appears to have coincided with the rise of the print media in the late 1920s. Most major cities in the early half of the 1900s had competing newspapers. Sports sections of those early newspapers rarely carried more than a summary of a previous day's baseball or football game. Competition between daily newspapers began to turn away from crime and political reporting as wealthy sports team owners began buying interests in newspapers. Newspapers held a strangle hold on the marketing of reporting of sporting events for nearly four decades. The print media began to lose readers with the onset of the electronic media in the late 1940s and early 1950s. Radio broadcasts of sporting events had been around during the print media's rise to power on the sporting scene, but the wealthy elites who controlled the media and sports teams could not earn much money from the broadcast of, say, a baseball game only in New York City, or St. Louis, or Chicago. Interest had to be generated on a global scale, players

had to be compensated on a grander scale, and scandals had to be invented and then exposed for athletes to become a commodity to be brokered to the masses. Superstars were needed to complete this capitalistic coup d'état. Enter George Herman Ruth, "The Babe," who popularized American baseball in a way that set the standard for nearly all American athlete-celebrities.

Women's contribution to sport, with a few notable exceptions, has been woefully underreported in the mainstream media and limited until fairly recently in the work of academic writers. Women played basketball in roughly the same numbers as men at all levels after its initial introduction by James Naismith in 1891. It was only after basketball went professional with touring teams in the 1920s that women became unwelcome in the sport. Women's athletics continued to struggle in the shadow of men's athletics despite the ongoing interest in women's sports since the introduction of Title IX in 1972.

Typologies of Sport Celebrity

Like the inevitable arguments that arise over the list of, say, the greatest baseball players of all time, arguments can be made over the selection of the criteria for inclusion in any of the three categories of sport celebrity outlined below. A concerted effort also is made for inclusion of women sports celebrities with the understanding that mainstream American sports such as football, baseball, and basketball will necessarily exclude many great women athletes.

The reader's own interest in a particular sporting event or fascination with a certain team or player will, of course, color the selection and placement of athletes into the typographic scheme shown below, a scheme not designed to inspire arguments, but to identify criteria necessary for an athlete to become a sports celebrity. The earlier examples of certain sports celebrities give rise to the opinion that celebrity can be categorized easily. From the fleeting celebrity of Eddie Gaedel to the enduring supercelebrity of stars such as Babe Ruth and Michael Jordan, sports celebrity can be categorized as follows:

Category One: One-Shot Wonders

Fleeting, one-shot wonder sports celebrities would include individuals such as Eddie Gaedel or another Eddie: Eddie "The Eagle" Edwards, who gained short-lived fame as a ski jumper during the 1988 Winter Olympics. Olympic officials were embarrassed at the attention Edwards garnered despite his woeful performance. Another Eagle in this category would be Vince Papale who, in the 1980s, became the oldest noncollege football player to play professional football. Papale was thirty years old when he tried out for and made the roster of the Philadelphia Eagles American football team. His career lasted just two years.

Category Two: Sport-Specific Athletes

Sports celebrities who only the most die-hard, sport-specific fans would recognize fall into this category, which contains the greatest number of athletes simply by recognition of the sheer number of athletic events that exist worldwide. From soccer and rugby to cricket and American football (collegiate and professional) fans of these sports would readily be able to identify their favorite athletes through either the athlete's fame or infamy. Athletes in this category would include Margaret Court and Billie Jean King (tennis); Sir Donald Bradman and William Grace (cricket); George Best, and Gheorghe Hagi (soccer); Bill Russell, Wilt Chamberlin, Kareem Abdul Jabbar, and Dr. J (basketball); Steve Yzerman, Maurice Richard, and Bobby Orr (hockey); and Dick Butkus, Bob Lilly, and Bart Starr (football).

Category Three: Superstars

Sports celebrity *superstars* are athletes that fans and non-fans alike would recognize. This category is reserved for individuals who have achieved such fame that it sufficient to merely mention either the athlete's first or last name, such as Pele, Ronaldo, or Maradano (soccer); Jordan, Magic, "Pistol Pete," and Bird (basketball); Nicklaus, Tiger, and Hogan (golf); Sorenstam, Lopez, and Zaharias (golf); Evert, Navratalova, and Graf (tennis); Earnhardt, Petty, and Pearson (NASCAR); The Babe, Cobb, and Mays (baseball); Unitas, Favre, and Brown (professional football); Zinzan, Pienaar, and Lomu (rugby union); and Gretzky, Lemieux, and Howe (hockey). Finally, it could be argued that a separate category could be added for the one individual known worldwide simple as "The Greatest" . . . Muhammad Ali. *See also*: **African American; Endorsements; Halls of Fame; Newspapers' Role; One-Name Celebrity; Pseudonyms; Temporary Celebrity.**

Ken Muir

For Further Reading

Gans, Herbert. *Deciding What's News: A Study of CBS Evening News, NBC Nightly News, Newsweek, and Time.* New York: Vintage Press, 1978.

Gramsci, Antonio. *The Prison Notebooks,* Vol. 1. New York: Columbia University Press, 1991.

Miller, Patrick B., and David K. Wiggens. *Sport and the Color Line: Black Athletes and Race Relations in Twentieth-Century America.* New York: Routledge, 2004.

Muir, Kenneth B. "Corporate Change and Neutral Newspaper Editorials." *Mass Communications Review* 23 (1993): 77–87.

Veblen, Thorstein. *Theory of Leisure Class.* New York: Modern Library, 1934.

Ernest Hemingway strikes a self-satisfied pose, having dispatched a leopard. Courtesy of Photofest.

AUTHORS

Today's American is more likely a viewer than a reader. While the nation's rate of complete illiteracy is only 1 percent, an estimated 40 million adult Americans are functional illiterates. Some studies claim that somewhere around 30 to 40 percent of Americans never read another book after their formal schooling ends, and only 30 percent report having been in a bookstore during the previous year. Such individuals, although not illiterate, are more nearly alliterate in that they can read but do not choose to do so, at least not for pleasure. Due to these sobering facts, authors, as celebrities, are hardly in the same league as movie stars or sports heroes, yet some authors manage to be both read and read about. As in other fields of endeavor, celebrity is more likely achieved if the individual is photogenic, or even better, "mediagenic"—glib and willing to be interviewed, as well as physically attractive. Exceptions include J. D. Salinger and Thomas Pynchon, two writers who have fiercely clung to privacy, a practice so unusual in publicity-hungry America that their celebrity has been enhanced due to novelty.

Among U.S. authors, the great pioneer of self-promotion was Samuel Clemens, who in the late 1800s stepped into and lived in the white-suited persona of Mark Twain. The suit, if not the **pseudonym**, has been revived in more recent years by New Journalist turned novelist and essayist Tom Wolfe. Twain lacked the 21st century's abundance of communications media with which to promote himself, but he boosted his celebrity by making stage appearances, thereby reaching non-readers. Today, Wolfe dons a white or pastel suit and delivers well-paid talks on university campuses, accomplishing the same end as Twain's. Also, he makes television **talk show** appearances, the venue where hype reigns supreme.

Book publishing has changed greatly since Twain's day, when it was a cottage industry in which many small firms competed. Since then, bigness has taken over. In the early 21st century, a handful of major publishing houses churn out the lion's share of books published. **Corporate** publishers tend to be cautious and often are reluctant to take a chance on an unproven or unknown writer. But celebrity sells, and books by, or ostensibly by, celebrities are easy to publish. These books are usually ghost written, although some celebrity authors are honest enough to include the ghost writer's name on the cover.

Celebrity writers known to be good sellers can publish "pot-boilers," books of limited originality, but with the familiar name on the dust jacket. A trick of the trade is the well-publicized awarding of a princely advance on royalties before publication, which convinces readers that the book must be worth buying. Corporate publishers also have television and film interests, which ensures that their books will make it onto screens, where the big money awaits. The author is hyped and marketed as though he or she were a branded product. This system is good for profits but promotes confusion as to what constitutes a "good book." Generally, if it sells well, a book is deemed "good." Still, one corner of the book market has welcomed quality work from formerly marginalized groups, including women and minority writers, and authors from developing countries.

Movie stars and television personalities like having their names on books; authorship lends them gravitas or prestige. Some celebrities are the actual authors of these books, others contribute ideas to their ghost writer, and still others are probably in the position of the corporate executive who reads a theretofore unseen speech handed to him or her by the public relations department. In all likelihood, comic actor Steve Martin did all or most of the writing for his several humorous books. The same would appear true of Woody Allen, Carl Reiner, William Shatner, Rupert Everett, Leonard Nimoy, Ethan Hawke, Alan Dershowitz, and Carrie Fisher. Since they are not known for writing, one wonders about novels attributed to Pamela Anderson, Joan Collins, Victoria Beckham, Goldie Hawn, Lucille Ball, and Ed McMahon. Among celebrities whose books show a coauthor on the cover are Kirk Douglas, John McEnroe, Martina Navratilova, Hugh Laurie, Ed Koch, Jerry Seinfeld, Spike Lee, Jane Seymour, and Bette Midler. An especially hot market for celebrity authors, who usually make use of a coauthor, is children's books. Katie Couric, Tiki and Ronde Barber, Elizabeth Taylor, Will Smith, John Lithgow, Mario Cuomo, LeAnn Rimes, John Travolta, Jamie Lee Curtis, Billy Crystal, Bill Cosby, Jay Leno, Maria Shriver, Henry Winkler, Dolly Parton, Jimmy Buffet, Julie Andrews, and Madonna have published in this genre.

Probably the genre in which it is most difficult for a writer to gain celebrity is verse. The only poetry to capture the imagination of contemporary American youth appears to be rap. Few serious poets are celebrities, although James Dickey, Rita Dove, Toni Morrison, and Maya Angelou are exceptions.

Americans who read for pleasure have made novelists the authors most likely to achieve celebrity. In the mid-1900s, the two outstanding celebrity novelists were macho Ernest Hemingway and voice of the South, William Faulkner. Some novelists have written one book so well received that their celebrity came quickly: J. D. Salinger (*The Catcher in the Rye*), Jack Kerouac (*On the Road*), Philip Roth (*Portnoy's Complaint*), Alice Walker (*The Color Purple*), Leon Uris (*Exodus*), Erich Segal (*Love Story*), Amy Tan (*The Joy Luck Club*), James Clavell (*Shogun*), Robert Waller (*The Bridges of Madison County*), and Terry McMillan (*Waiting to Exhale*). Adaption of such novels to the screen greatly enhances the celebrity of the author.

Other authors' celebrity comes from an accumulation of their work: Tom Wolfe, Pat Conroy, Kathy Acker, Terry McMillan, Gore Vidal, Normal Mailer, Kurt Vonnegut, Anne Tyler, Dean Koontz, Larry McMurtry, and Salman Rushdie, whose fourth novel, *The Satanic Verses*, also brought him death threats from militant Islam. Flamboyant Truman Capote declared himself the greatest of all short-story writers and also produced novellas and nonfiction. Appreciated for use of humor or satire are John Irving, Tom Robbins, Margaret Atwood, and Barbara Kingsolver.

Hugely popular with leisure readers are the books of mystery and crime writers such as British authors Dorothy Sayers, whose enduring sleuth was Lord Peter Wimsey, Agatha Christie (Hercule Poirot, Miss Marple), Ngaio Marsh (Detective Roderick Alleyn), and Ian Fleming (James Bond). John Le Carre was born David Cornwell; his specialty is the espionage novel. Other writers who deal in espionage are Tom Clancy, Ken Follett, and Robert Ludlum. A more recent English mystery writer is Ruth Rendell, creator of Chief Inspector Wexford. American mystery authors of celebrity include "Ellery Queen" (actually Frederic Dannay and Manfred Lee), Mickey Spillane, creator of private eye Mike Hammer, Dashiell Hammett (Sam Spade), Raymond Chandler (Philip Marlowe), and Erle Stanley Gardner (Perry Mason). More recent mystery authors to gain celebrity include Patricia Cornwell (Dr. Kay Scarpetta), Sue Grafton (Kinsey Millhone), Elmore Leonard, Walter Mosley, James Patterson (Alex Cross), Mary Higgins Clark, and Sharon McCrumb (Elizabeth MacPherson). Enjoying great celebrity are lawyer-mystery writers Scott Turow and John Grisham, and the crown prince of the comic murder mystery is Miami newspaper columnist Carl Hiaasen. Hottest seller of all has been Dan Brown, author of *The Da Vinci Code*, an unusual mystery story that excited great controversy.

Fantasy tales of enormous scope suitable for big-budget movies or movie series have been the province of the British. A great rags-to-riches story is that of fantasy writer J. K. Rowling, now a billionaire thanks to her *Harry Potter* series of novels and their movie adaptations. Others were Englishman J. R. R. Tolkien (*Lord of the Rings*) and Irish writer C. S. Lewis (*Chronicles of Narnia*). A celebrity for his prolific outpouring of dark, macabre books is

Maine's Stephen King. Another writer of the macabre is John Saul—successful with suspense and horror stories—and Anne Rice of New Orleans is celebrated for her vampire novels and other tales of the supernatural. In the field of science fiction, the most prolific author was Isaac Asimov, a Russian American. Other standouts include Michael Crichton, Arthur C. Clarke, and Ray Bradbury.

More than half of all U.S. paperback sales come from another genre: the romance novel, for which most readers are women. This popular genre is, at the same time, the most reviled among literary critics. The literary quality of these books is not high. Little originality should be expected in these stories of girl meets boy, girl and boy fall in love, with obstacles eventually overcome to allow a happy or at least promising ending; and the cover art for these books sets the standard for "cheesy." Romance novels come in a number of varieties. Some are torrid, others are mild or inspirational. Most have contemporary settings, but perhaps one-fifth are historically set. Some are modestly suspenseful, and others are humorous. Some involve science fiction and a newer variety is the multiethnic romance. The largest publisher of these books is Toronto-based Harlequin Enterprises, a worldwide seller. Queen of the genre is Danielle Steel, author of more than 50 romance novels and reportedly the bestselling fiction writer in contemporary America. Linnea Sinclair writes science-fiction romances, Philippa Gregory and former beauty queen Lisa Kleypas write historical romance tales, and celebrity-in-the-making Crystal Hubbard specializes in the multiethnic romance novel. Other

names in the romance novel field are Kathleen Woodiwiss, Nora Roberts, Jayne Ann Krentz, and Jude Deveraux. *See also*: **Comedy**; **Lawyers**; **Movies' Role**; **Privacy and Right of Publicity**; **Pseudonyms**.

Sam G. Riley

For Further Reading

Glass, Loren Daniel. *Authors Inc.: Literary Celebrity in the Modern United States, 1880–1980*. New York: New York University Press, 2004.

Moran, Joe. *Star Authors: Literary Celebrity in America*. London; Sterling, VA: Pluto Press, 2000.

http://gossip.celebritycowboy.com/40-celebrity-auhors.

www.abebooks.co.uk/docs/Children/cele brityChildrenAuthors.

www.hycyber.com/MYST/a_list.

www.springfieldlibrary.org/reading/celebrity.

AWARDS AND CEREMONIES

Awards are presented to recognize and to reward excellence. Some offer trophies or medals as a visual sign of excellence, while others proffer monetary reward. Usually, the award's prestige has the greatest impact, providing the recipient a life-long identity as a winner. Some awards recognize individuals and others honor group efforts; some acknowledge the product and others the process. Awards might reflect specific genres or celebrate accomplishment across a medium. Among the entertainment awards dedicated to television, cinema, music, and theater that establish or validate celebrity are the following:

Television Awards

The Emmy Awards (instituted in 1949) recognize excellence in television and are administered by three sister organizations focusing on different television programming divisions: the Academy of Television Arts and Sciences (prime time), the National Academy of Television Arts and Sciences (daytime, sports, news, and documentary), and the International Academy of Television Arts and Sciences (international). Academy members cast ballots in their field of expertise. The Emmy statue, a winged woman holding an atom, represents art (the winged muse) and science (the atom). The Alfred I. duPont–Columbia University Award (1968) is an American award honoring excellence in broadcast journalism administered by the Columbia University Graduate School of Journalism; it is considered the broadcast equivalent of the Pulitzer Prize.

Cinema Awards

Dedicated to excellence in filmmaking achievement, the Academy of Motion Picture Arts and Sciences's most famous award is The Oscars, or the Academy Awards (1929). Officially named the Academy Award of Merit, the statuette known as "Oscar" is a knight standing on a reel of film, hands gripping a sword, 13.5 inches tall and weighing 8.5 pounds. Voting is limited to those with Academy membership, established by invitation only, consisting of more than 6,000 motion picture professionals divided into fifteen branches representing different disciplines in motion pictures. Critics' awards include those presented by the Broadcast Film Critics Association Awards (the Critics Choice Awards, 1995) and the National Board of Review of Motion Pictures (1908). The Independent Spirit Awards (1984) recognize the year's best achievements in independent film. MTV Movie Awards (1992) are based on fans' votes, awarding the "Golden Popcorn" in categories ranging from Best Villain to Best New Filmmaker. The Golden Raspberry Awards (the Razzies, 1981) recognize the worst acting, screenwriting, songwriting, directing, and films each year. Razzies, voted upon by the Golden Raspberry Award Foundation (GRAF), whose membership is open to the public, give a plastic raspberry, spray-painted gold and mounted on a plastic base. Razzie nominations are announced the day before the Motion Picture Academy announces Oscar nominations, and Razzies are awarded one day before the Academy Award ceremony.

Music Awards

The Grammy Awards (1958, originally the Gramophone Awards, still the honor's symbol), presented by the National Academy of Recording Arts and Sciences of the United States, pay tribute to artistic achievement, technical proficiency, and overall excellence in the recording industry without regard to album sales or chart position. The American Music Awards, created by Dick Clark (1973) to compete with the Grammys, are awarded by popularity via a poll of music buyers. The Country Music Association Awards (CMA,

1967) are given by the first trade organization formed to promote a musical genre. Based in Nashville and founded in 1967, twelve categories of annual awards are voted on by business members of the Country Music Association. Contrasting the CMA is the Academy of Country Music Award (ACM, 1964), which represents the Country and Western Music Academy in Los Angeles to promote country music in the western states. The *Billboard* Music Awards (1990) honor winners based on popularity established by *Billboard* magazine's year-end music charts, created from Nielsen data for sales, downloads, and airplay. The MTV Video Music Awards (1984) celebrate the top music videos of the year. Winners receive a statue of an astronaut on the moon, one of MTV's earliest representations. The Gospel Music Association (GMA, 1969) Dove Awards recognize outstanding achievements in Christian music, including musical styles such as **rock and pop**, and **hip-hop and rap**, country, gospel, and praise and worship. Perhaps less known but carrying greater prestige is the Pulitzer Prize for Music (1943), presented for a distinguished musical composition by an American that has had its first performance or recording in the United States during the year. Years of criticism that the award went only to music following the European classical tradition led to a rules change in 2004, extending the honor to a full range of American musical excellence, from **jazz** to opera, musical theater to classical symphony, choral music to movie scores.

Theater Awards

The Antoinette Perry Awards for Excellence in Theatre (the Tony Awards, 1947) celebrate achievement in live American theater and generally are regarded as the theater's equivalent to the Oscars, the Grammys, and the Emmys. Now presented annually by the founding American Theatre Wing and the Broadway League, the Tonys honor twenty-seven categories of Broadway productions and performances and also confer noncompetitive Special Tony Awards and Regional Theatre Tony Awards. The disk-shaped medallion includes the masks of comedy and tragedy on one side and the profile of Antoinette Perry (an actress, director, producer, and the wartime leader of the American Theatre Wing) on the other. Similar to the Tony Awards for Broadway productions, The Obie Awards (Off-Broadway Theater Awards, 1956) are presented by *The Village Voice* newspaper to off- and off-off Broadway productions in New York City. The Helen Hayes Awards (1983) are presented annually by the Washington Theatre Awards Society to resident and nonresident productions in the Washington, D.C., area, honoring excellence and recognizing professional theater. The New York Drama Critics Circle Award (1935) is awarded yearly to the best new play of the season, with additional awards for musicals and foreign or American plays as well as citations for special achievement. The second-oldest U.S. theater award after the Pulitzer Prize for drama, it represents twenty-two drama critics based in the New York City metropolitan area from daily newspapers, magazines, and wire services, excluding the *New York Times*, whose editorial position prohibits critics from participation in awards. The Drama Desk Awards (1955) are presented by theater critics, writers, and editors, celebrating creative stage productions off Broadway, off-off Broadway, and legitimate not-for-profit theaters wherever they are located. Finally, the Pulitzer Prize for Drama (1918) pays tribute to an American playwright whose drama preferably is original in its source and deals with American life.

Awards Crossing Media Platforms

A number of other awards are given by groups that recognize several entertainment media. The Hollywood Foreign Press Association's Golden Globes (HFPA, 1944) reward American film and television's roles in disseminating information about American culture and traditions through foreign news media. Its statue is a golden globe circled by a strip of motion picture film mounted on a pedestal. A unique tradition of the non-profit HFPA is its annual selection of Miss or Mr. Golden Globe, the child of a well-known performer who assists in the Golden Globe ceremony. The Screen Actors Guild Awards (1995) honor performers for acting in film and television and are affiliated with the American Federation of Labor–Congress of Industrial Organizations (AFL-CIO). A craft labor union founded 1936 as the Screen Directors Guild, the Directors Guild of America offers the Directors Guild of America Awards (1960), recognizing directorial excellence in film and television. The George Foster Peabody Awards are the oldest annual awards for distinguished achievement and meritorious service by individuals, networks, stations, and other organizations. Administered by the Henry W. Grady College of Journalism and Mass Communication at the University of Georgia, they began with

radio in 1941, added television in 1948, CD-ROM and multimedia in the late 1990s, and the World Wide Web in 2002. The Kennedy Center Honors (1978) recognize America's artistic legacy in dance, theater, music, and variety, as well as American artists and those of other nations who have achieved prominence here. Rewarding a lifetime of work, The Kennedy Center Honors have been compared with a knighthood in Britain or the French Legion of Honor. The National Association for the Advancement of Colored People (NAACP) Image Awards (1969) celebrate outstanding achievements and performances of people of color in the fields of motion picture, television, music, and literature. The Teen Choice Awards (1999) honor the year's biggest achievements in music, movies, sports, and television, as voted on by teens ages thirteen to nineteen; winners are awarded a large surfboard. Similarly, the Nickelodeon Kids Choice Awards (1986) reward the year's biggest television, movie, and music acts with an orange blimp trophy, as voted on by people (mostly children) who watch the Nickelodeon cable channel. The TV Land Awards commemorate American television shows now off the air. Begun in 2003, it spoofs other entertainment award ceremonies, with input from voters on TV Land's Web site who select their favorite individual actors and television series. The Saturn Awards (1972) are presented annually by the Academy of Science Fiction, Fantasy and Horror Films to honor top works in these genres in film, television, and home video. Clio Awards (1959) reward creative excellence in advertising and design for American and international television, print, radio, Internet, outdoor, integrated campaign, innovative media, content and contact, and student work. *See also*: **African American**; **Child Celebrity**; **Country and Western**.

Beth M. Waggenspack

For Further Reading

American Theatre Wing. *The Tony Award: A Complete Listing of Winners and Nominees with a History of the American Theatre Wing*. Portsmouth, NH: Heinemann, 2001.

Franks, Don. *Entertainment Awards: A Music, Cinema, Theatre and Broadcasting Guide, 1928 through 2003*. Jefferson, NC: McFarland, 2004.

Hyatt, Wesley. *Emmy Award Winning Nighttime Television Shows, 1948–2004*. Jefferson, NC: McFarland, 2006.

Piazza, Jim, and Gail Kinn. *The Academy Awards: The Complete Unofficial History Revised and Updated*. New York: Black Dog and Leventhal Publishers, 2004.

B

BLOGGERS

Blogs (the term is a contraction of the words "Web log") have become a ubiquitous feature of the World Wide Web's landscape. Blogs are frequently updated Web sites offering news, commentary, images, video, or other content. Blog authors, colloquially called "bloggers," often upload their blogs' content to the Web using automatic publishing systems that allow blogs to be created and updated without advanced Web programming or design skills.

Technorati, a search engine site devoted to blogs, included more than 100 million blogs in its tracking list by 2008, although it is unclear exactly how many blogs exist in the universe of blogs (the "blogosphere"). Many blogs maintain only a small audience, functioning as personal blogs akin to online diaries or are topical blogs addressing a niche audience. Others have millions of readers. Some popular blogs owe their notoriety to the preexisting fame of their authors, such as *The Huffington Post*, which was cofounded by author and columnist Arianna Huffington and has featured contributions from notables ranging from long-standing U.S. Sen. Ted Kennedy to *Seinfeld* cocreator Larry David. Other famous blogs, such as the technology-oriented *Boing Boing* or the *Gawker* news and gossip site, are group efforts that draw the individual members of their staff comparatively little attention.

In some cases, though, blogs have provided a path to fame or minor celebrity for creators otherwise lacking in notoriety. The eponymous blog penned by Perez Hilton, a *nom de plume* used by Mario Armando Lavandeira, Jr., has been visited by millions. Lavandeira's blogging fame has also led to numerous television appearances, including a starring role in a **reality television** program on the VH1 (Video Hits 1) network.

Matt Drudge's *The Drudge Report*, which started as an e-mail newsletter and evolved in 1997 into an ascetically designed, blog-like Web site featuring hyperlinks to stories on various news sites and occasional original news briefs, attained worldwide prominence when it was the first news source to report then-President Bill Clinton's

35

affair with White House intern Monica Lewinsky. Drudge has since hosted a television program on the FOX News network and a nationally syndicated radio program.

Drudge has also published a book, as have other bloggers who have received blog-related book deals ("blooks" to some). They include Jessica Cutler, who was fired from her job as a U.S. congressional staff assistant for her *Washingtonienne* blog's salacious accounts of sexual affairs with Washington notables. Cutler subsequently published a novel and appeared in *Playboy* magazine. Ellen Simonetti's *Queen of Sky: Diary of a Dysfunctional Flight Attendant* led to her firing from Delta Airlines, but also led to bylines in news media and a book. Salam al-Janabi, an Iraqi blogger using the pseudonym Salam Pax, started his *Where Is Raed?* blog to keep in touch with friend Raed Jarrar while Jarrar attended graduate school in Jordan. Prior to, during, and after the 2003 U.S. invasion of Iraq, Janabi's accounts from Baghdad garnered widespread attention and were later published as a book. Typically, however, a blogger's fame fails to translate to print; as of July 2008, the only "blook" to appear on the *New York Times*'s bestseller list is *I Hope They Serve Beer in Hell*, a collection of purportedly autobiographical stories from blogger Tucker Max focusing on prodigious alcohol consumption, graphic sexual portrayals, misogyny, and belligerence. *See also*: **News Media Figures**; **Temporary Celebrity**.

James D. Ivory

For Further Reading

Banks, Michael A. *Blogging Heroes: Interviews with 30 of the World's Top Bloggers*. Indianapolis, IN: Wiley Publishing, 2007.

Perlmutter, David D. *Blogwars: The New Political Battleground*. New York: Oxford University Press, 2008.

Technorati. http://technorati.com.

C

CHILD CELEBRITY

Ever since America's entertainment media began to develop, child performers have risen to the level of celebrity. One of the most precocious and successful of Hollywood's child actors was Mickey Rooney, born Joe Yule, Jr., in 1920 into a show-business family. As his success grew, he adopted the stage name Mickey Rooney, made his first movies with Judy Garland in 1937, and did a series of Andy Hardy movies. Rooney was a child star whose success continued throughout a long life. A contemporary child actor of Rooney's was Jackie Cooper, who began his career in the *Our Gang* comedies in 1929 and, like Rooney, had continued success in the movies. Other *Our Gang* stars who became celebrities were the cowlick-haired Carl Switzer (Alfalfa) and cute Darla Hood, who played under her own name, Darla.

Rooney's female equivalent was Shirley Temple, "discovered" at age four. The bright-eyed, talented moppet appeared in many movies, singing, dancing, and melting hearts. A somewhat older child star who became a huge success with the 1939 movie *The Wizard of Oz* was Judy Garland, a small child with a big voice. Another song-and-dance child star was Donald O'Connor; and a rare **one-name celebrity** was Sabu, a child from India who played in *The Elephant Boy* (1937). Playing "Boy" in the 1930s and 1940s opposite the greatest of Tarzans, Johnny Weismuller, was Johnny Sheffield. Child model turned actress Terry Moore (born Helen Koford) was in her first movie at age eleven; her celebrity grew later in life due to her marriage to reclusive tycoon Howard Hughes, dating Henry Kissinger, and, in 1984, posing nude for *Playboy* magazine. Margaret O'Brien became a child celebrity in 1944 after acting with Orson Welles in *Jane Eyre* (1944), and beautiful Elizabeth Taylor began acting in 1942 at age ten, later working her way into starlet status, then into more mature roles. Of comparable beauty was Natalie Wood (born Natalia Zakharenko), who began acting at four and made a big hit in 1947 as a little girl in the Christmas movie *Miracle on 34th Street*. *Song of the South* (1946)

Cute as a button, Miley Cyrus smiles for the cameras at the Teen Choice awards. Courtesy of Photofest.

and *Treasure Island* (1950) provided celebrity to child actor Bobby Driscoll, and Jane Powell (born Suzanne Bruce) enjoyed success in children's roles, although her career peaked with her ingénue performance in the musical film *Seven Brides for Seven Brothers* (1954). Similarly, Dean Stockwell started acting at age seven, was a hit in *Anchors Aweigh* (1945), but had only limited success as an adult actor. Sal Mineo was sixteen when he played James Dean's sidekick Plato in *Rebel Without a Cause* (1955).

Remembered for his shrieks in the Western movie *Shane* (1953) was Brandon de Wilde, eleven at that time; he died tragically in an automobile accident at age thirty. Tuesday Weld began modeling at age three and progressed into television and movie work. Like Weld, Sandra Dee (born Alexandra Zuck) began as a child model, entered

film work at age fourteen, and became America's poster girl for innocence and cuteness. Patty Duke broke into movies at seven and Broadway at twelve, later starring in *The Patty Duke Show*. Haley Mills, a Disney favorite, came from a family of actors and began her film career at thirteen. Hollywood-great Ron Howard's first work on stage and television was at age two; his earliest movie role came at age five. In 1960, the five-year-old Howard's celebrity was sealed when he became Opie on *The Andy Griffith Show*; in 1974, as a teenager, Howard began his next iconic role, Richie Cunningham, on the sitcom *Happy Days*. Kurt Russell began acting at age ten and has enjoyed a long adult career with Disney. A looming change in Hollywood's use of child stars was foreshadowed in 1962 in the film *Lolita*, the story of a dirty old man seduced by an underage nymphet, played by fourteen-year-old Sue Lyon. By this time, the entertainment industry had begun to address children more as if they were adults (and adults as if they were children), and some child actors would be called on thereafter to take on roles that would be less innocent and more seductive or suggestive.

Mark Lester was a winning lad who played the title role in *Oliver* in 1968, and Linda Blair, unforgettable in *The Exorcist* (1973), began her movie career at age eleven. Jodie Foster launched her movie career at age three, worked in Disney television, and in 1973, was Becky Thatcher in *Tom Sawyer*. Tatum O'Neal, born to show-business parents, was in her first movie at nine and appeared in *Paper Moon* (1973) with her father, Ryan O'Neal. Mackenzie Phillips began acting at fourteen and a year later appeared in

American Graffiti (1973). Brooke Shields first worked as a child model and broke into movies in 1977 at age twelve. Classically beautiful early in life, she became a star by 1978 in *Pretty Baby* and appeared partially nude in *The Blue Lagoon* (1980). Little Ricky Schroder was in *The Champ* (1979) at nine, and Aileen Quinn, eleven, got the title role in *Annie* (1982). Matt Dillon began acting at fifteen, and in 1980 was in *Little Darling.* The late River Phoenix, who died of a cocaine and heroin overdose, was sixteen when he appeared in *Stand by Me.* His contemporary Christian Slater also was in his first film at sixteen, but had appeared on Broadway at age eleven. One of the most memorable of all performances by a child actor was that of Peter Billingsley, who played Ralphie in *A Christmas Story* (1983); Billingsley had begun making commercials when he was two and had appeared in more than 100 before landing the role of Ralphie.

Phenomenally successful twins Mary-Kate and Ashley Olsen had their first television roles in 1987 at nine months old on *Full House* (1987–1995) and at twelve, were on a second show, *Two of a Kind* (1998–1999). They have appeared in movies since 1992 and are now among Hollywood's wealthiest celebrities. At sixteen, Winona Ryder made her film debut in *Heathers* (1989) and appeared in *Beetlejuice* (1988) at eighteen. Kirsten Dunst debuted in 1989 at age seven in Woody Allen's *Oedipus Wrecks*; Christina Ricci was in the movie *The Addams Family* (1991) when she was eleven; at age nine, Anna Paquin delivered an Oscar-winning performance as Flora in *The Piano* (1993); and Scarlett Johansson, who started acting at ten, was fourteen when

she appeared in *The Horse Whisperer* (1998). At twelve, Daniel Radcliffe assumed his title role in the hugely popular *Harry Potter* movie series. Emma Watson was eleven when she appeared in the first *Harry Potter* movie (2001) as Hermione, and, in that same movie, Rupert Grint, then thirteen, played the role of Ron Weasley. Another child actor was Dakota Fanning, who had done commercials since age five, was ten while in *War of the Worlds* (2004), and was twelve in *Charlotte's Web* (2006).

Television

Television has produced a long succession of child celebrities. Two of the earliest such performers had already gained celebrity in radio, before moving smoothly into the new medium. David and Ricky Nelson were twelve and eight, respectively, in 1949 when they joined the cast of their parents' radio show *The Adventures of Ozzie and Harriet* (1944–1949). This popular show appeared on television from 1952 to 1966, after which Ricky's successful career as a pop singer was cut short by a 1985 plane crash. The show that made David and Ricky famous reflected the suburban ideal of the 1950s. Another early child star of television was Keith Thibodeaux, who in 1951 at age six got the part of Lucille Ball's son on the sitcom *I Love Lucy* (1951–1960). Another such child celebrity of the 1950s was Tommy Rettig, who played Jeff on the *Lassie* series from 1954 to 1957; Rettig took this job at age thirteen, the same age at which perky Annette Funicello joined the cast of the *Mickey Mouse Club* (1955–1959) and became the most popular of all the

"Mousekateers." In 1957, nine-year-old Jerry Mathers, already a show-business veteran, took the title role in *Leave It to Beaver* (1957–1963).

Popular in the 1960s was nineteen-year-old Burt Ward (born Bert Gervais, Jr.), the envy of all boys as Robin the Boy Wonder on the *Batman* series (1966–1968). At age ten in 1963, Barry Livingston made a hit as Ernie on the sitcom *My Three Sons* (1960–1972). Red-haired, wisecracking, and precocious, Danny (born Dante) Bonaduce appeared on the sitcom *The Partridge Family* (1970–1974) at age ten in 1970. A hugely popular child star of 1970s television was Melissa Gilbert, age ten in 1974 when she began playing Laura on *Little House on the Prairie* (1974–1984). Valerie Bertinelli began as Barbara at age fifteen in 1975 on *One Day at a Time* (1975–1984), and Gary Coleman was ten in 1978 when cast as Arnold on *Diff'rent Strokes* (1978–1985). Scott Baio, fresh from a role in the 1976 musical *Bugsy Malone*, was sixteen when in 1977 he became Chachi, younger cousin of "The Fonz," on *Happy Days* (1974–1984). A cute child actor of the 1980s was Emmanuel Lewis, who took the title role in *Webster* (1983–1987) at age twelve in 1983; another was Keisha Knight Pulliam, who appeared on *Sesame Street* (1969–) when she was three and in 1984 at age five, became Rudy on *The Cosby Show* (1984–1992). An older child celebrity who appeared on that show was Malcolm-Jamal Warner, cast as Theo at age fourteen. Fred Savage was eleven in 1988 when he starred as Kevin in *The Wonder Years* (1988–1993).

A child actor of the seductive sort was Christina Applegate, who at fifteen became the dim, oversexed Kelly on the tasteless but hilarious *Married with Children* (1987–1997). Cute, innocent, and yet "adultized" was Neil Patrick Harris, who at sixteen took the title role in *Doogie Howser, M.D.* (1989–1993). Tabloid princess Lindsay Lohan was in a soap opera at ten and in the 1998 film *The Parent Trap* at eleven. Dangerously cute Raven-Symone Pearman was four when she became Olivia on *The Cosby Show*; she remained cute but became saucier in her later show *That's So Raven* (2003–2007). Jaleel White, twelve, played Steve Urkel on *Family Matters* (1989–1998); Jeremy Suarez was eleven when he joined *The Bernie Mac Show* (2001–2006); and Justin Berfield was fourteen when he began playing one of the brothers in *Malcolm in the Middle* (2000–2006). Shia La Beouf was also fourteen when in 2000 he took the title role of Louis Stevens on the Disney Channel's *Even Stevens* (2000–2003). His popularity grew in 2007 with his work in the film *Transformers*. In the role of the cheerleader, Claire, on *Heroes* (2006–) is Hayden Panettiere, seventeen when cast in 2006, and now a glamorous teen star.

Disney

Many of the child-actor successes of the early 2000s work for Disney. Most of these teenage celebrities both act and sing. Mitchel Musso is a pop rock and **hip-hop** singer who has played Oliver on the *Hanna Montana* (2006–) series. Appearing as Lilly on that show is Emily Osment, who also sings; and playing Alex on the Disney Channel's *Wizards of Waverly Place* (2007–) is Selena Gomez, who, with her fellow sixteen-year-old Demi Lovato, sings on

Barney and Friends (1992–). Lovato also was a cast member of the Disney Channel movie *Camp Rock* (2008), as was fifteen-year-old Alyson Stoner. Stoner also appeared on another Disney show, *The Suite Life of Zack and Cody* (2005–2008), which featured teenage identical twins Dylan and Cole Sprouse, regarded as "hot" young stars by America's huge youth audience. Other teen heartthrobs from *Hanna Montana* and also the 2008 movie *Camp Rock* are the three pop-rock singers who perform as The Jonas Brothers: Nick, Joe, and Kevin, who in *Camp Rock* were 16, 19, and 21. Without doubt the biggest child star of the early 2000s has been Miley Cyrus (born Destiny Hope Cyrus), daughter of **country** singer Billy Ray Cyrus. This perky, energetic performer "became" Hanna Montana at age twelve and soon was one of the best-paid entertainers of the decade. In 2008, she was involved in controversy over photos of her taken for the magazine *Vanity Fair* by photographer Annie Leibovitz; some observers deem the shots too suggestive for a fifteen-year-old. Making a big hit in 2008 is *Kit Kittredge*, a non-Disney movie produced by Julia Roberts. Starring in the title role is twelve-year-old Abigail Breslin, whose earlier smash success was in *Little Miss Sunshine* (2006).

Music

Musical celebrity has had its share of child stars, a phenomenon that began a long time ago in **classical music** with prodigies such as Wolfgang Amadeus Mozart, Frederic Chopin, Niccolo Paganini, Franz List, and Felix Mendelsohn, and continued with more recent notables such as Fritz Kreisler, Gian Carlo Menotti, Jascha Heifetz, Yehudi Mehnuhin, and Yo-Yo Ma. But classical music is not what excites the youth culture and produces most of America's present-day celebrities. Nor is **jazz and blues** or folk music. Most of today's musical celebrities, young or old, perform **rock and pop**, hip-hop, or country and Western.

Perhaps the first big child celebrity in popular music in the 1950s was Ricky Nelson, who had around fifty top 100 hits from 1957 to his tragic demise in 1985. The four sisters who sang as The Lennon Sisters ranged in ages from nine to sixteen when they debuted on *The Lawrence Welk Show* (1955–1982) in 1955, and Chicano rock singer Richie Valens was seventeen when he recorded *Donna* in 1958. Valens died in the 1959 plane crash that also killed singers Buddy Holly and Jiles Richardson (the Big Bopper).

A rockabilly singer who began performing when she was six, a little girl with a huge voice, was Brenda Lee (born Brenda Tarpley). Her big break came at age eleven with the help of veteran country star Red Foley, and in 1960, she recorded *I'm Sorry* and *Sweet Nothin's*. Fabian (born Fabiano Forte) began attempting to sing at fourteen as "The Fabulous Fabian." He was put on stage mainly for his looks, although his singing ability gradually improved. The Jackson Five signed with Motown Records in the 1960s, but later split up. The late Michael Jackson, clearly the group's great talent—even at age five when the group began performing— became the undisputed "king of pop" in the 1980s. The five Beach Boys were ages fifteen through nineteen in 1961 when they began recording, and the great English group The Beatles ranged in age from seventeen to twenty in 1960 when they appeared. Stevie Wonder (born Steveland Judkins) began performing at twelve and had his first hit at thirteen. During his early years in the business, he was billed as "Little Stevie Wonder."

Donny Osmond was four when he first appeared on *The Andy Williams Show* (1959–1971); and he went on to become a squeaky-clean teen heartthrob. His siblings appeared as The Osmond Brothers, later as The Osmonds, to accommodate sister Marie; and from 1976 to 1981, Donny and Marie had their own variety television show. Rhythm and blues–pop singer Brandy (born Brandy Norwood) cut her first album at age fifteen; the dapper Usher's successful career was launched at age thirteen on the program *Star Search* (1985–1995, 2002–); and country–pop performer LeAnn Rimes made her first single, *Blue*, at thirteen. Other country music prodigies include Ricky Skaggs, who began performing at age six in the 1960s, and Alison Krauss, fiddler and singer, who in the early 1980s, began her recording career at age fourteen. Another *Star Search* launch was Britney Spears, on the show in 1992 at age eleven, who spent two years on the *Mickey Mouse Club* (1995–1996), and then went up and down in popularity from there.

Glamorous Jessica Simpson, singer and actress, got her first recording contract at eighteen; and Pink (born Alecia Moore) began her career at fourteen, making her debut single at nineteen. Alicia Keys was four when she joined *The Cosby Show* cast, and she made her first rhythm-and-blues single at sixteen. Rapper Lil' Romeo (born Percy Romeo Miller) was only twelve when he scored a huge hit in 2001 with his single *My Baby*. Born in Barbados, Rihanna (born Robyn Rihanna Fenty) made her debut album at seventeen.

Commercials

A modest number of children have attained at least **temporary celebrity** by acting in television commercials. Cute and blonde, identical twins Jayne and Joan Boyd became the original Doublemint Chewing Gum twins in 1959. Other sets of twins followed, and most did noncommercial television thereafter. "Bankrollably" cute child talents have included Andy Lambros, the four-year-old "Oscar Meyer boy," who sang his famous jingle in 1973; and equally cute Hallie Kate Eisenberg, "the Pepsi girl" in the late 1990s and early 2000s.

Youth Culture

Whether as tykes or teens, child actors have been an important part of America's celebrity culture, which in recent times has often appeared to be almost synonymous with the youth culture. At very early ages, some of these talented youth have been able to make enormous amounts of money. Some of them have had parents who handled their child stars' finances responsibly, others have not. Many are the child celebrities who feel that they were more or less robbed of their childhoods by the adult-like demands of rehearsals, multiple takes, and the like or who resent their "stage-door parents" having pushed them to make the money while they could. Some child performers have transitioned smoothly into adult success in their field; examples include Ron Howard, Jodie Foster, and Stevie Wonder. Many others have not, have been numbered among the forgotten people of show business, and have turned to more mundane methods of earning a living. Some of these discarded figures have retained enough of the earnings from their unusual childhoods to be financially fixed for life, yet others ended their youthful careers broke. The entertainment industry's insatiable demands for physical perfection have led many child celebrities, as they age, toward eating disorders. The nudge-nudge, wink-wink treatment accorded to adult entertainers who use recreational drugs has caused many a child star to follow suit, sometimes with deadly consequences. In sum, the lot of the child star is no doubt exciting, but it has its downside. Most children grow up directed by their parents and teachers. So, too, are child celebrities, but they also must answer to directors, producers, voice coaches, recording executives, network executives, commercial sponsors, publicists, and the ever-hungry media. These children are celebrated, but they are to one degree or another exploited as well. *See also*: **Comedy**; **Dream Girls**; **Drugs and Alcohol**; **Early Deaths**; **Family Celebrity**; **Movies' Role**; **Television's Role**.

Sam G. Riley

For Further Reading

Aylesworth, Thomas G. *Hollywood Kids: Child Stars of the Silver Screen from 1903 to the Present.* New York: Dutton, 1987.

Kenneson, Claude. *Musical Prodigies: Perilous Journeys, Remarkable Lives.* Portland, OR: Amadeus Press, 1998.

Ryan, Joal. *Former Child Stars: The Story of America's Least Wanted.* Toronto: ECW Press, 2000.

www.younghollywoodhof.com.

CHILDREN'S SHOW HOSTS

Since the mid-1900s, some of the most significant celebrities to the very young have been the colorful individuals who have hosted radio and television programs aimed at preadolescents. Americans who grew up in the era before television are likely to remember with fondness the American Broadcasting Company (ABC) radio program *No School Today* (1950–1958), which originated in Cincinnati in 1947 as *Big John and Sparkie*. The host of these shows was Jon Arthur (born Jon Goerss), a bespectacled, whimsical-looking man who did voices, including the squeaky voice of the elf-like puppet Sparkie, who wanted to be a real boy. This show opened with the catchy theme song "Teddy Bear's Picnic" and was remarkable in that it competed well against television during the newer medium's first decade of popularity.

Also originating in 1947 was the pioneering children's television show *Howdy Doody*, launched several years before most American homes had a television set. This popular show ran until 1960. Like radio's Sparkie, Howdy Doody was a puppet—in this case an eleven-string marionette. Hosting the NBC show was jovial Bob Smith, who adopted the stage name Buffalo Bob. He wore buckskins, and the red-headed

Howdy was dressed in cowboy boots, a Western-style shirt and jeans, and a bandana. Smith did the voice of Howdy Doody and interacted with other puppet characters, including Howdy's little-remembered sister, Heidi Doody, and the wonderfully named character Princess Summerfall Winterspring. Buffalo Bob's human sidekick was Clarabell the Clown, who, à la Harpo Marx, honked horns in place of speaking. The original Clarabell was Bob Keeshan, who departed the show in 1952 and became Captain Kangaroo on CBS. A 1954 heart attack slowed Smith's work, and a variety of guest hosts appeared in his place. The voice of Howdy was then done by Allen Swift, "the Man of a Thousand Voices."

Using a ventriloquist's dummy was Paul Winchell (born Pinkus Wilchinski), a New York ventriloquist and inventor. In the early 1940s, Winchell had appeared briefly on radio with his dummy, Jerry Mahoney. His Saturday morning television series, *The Paul Winchell and Jerry Mahoney Show*, ran on NBC from 1950 to 1954. His later show, *Winchell-Mahoney Time*, appeared from 1965 to 1968.

Another popular children's television show was *Smilin' Ed's Gang* (1950–1955), which appeared at one time or another on each of the three major networks. Jolly, avuncular James Edwin McConnell was Smilin' Ed, who from 1929 to 1953 had hosted radio's *Buster Brown Show* for children. Smilin' Ed's most memorable character on those shows was a tuxedo-clad frog puppet, Froggy the Gremlin. When Smilin' Ed uttered the stock line, "Plunk your magic twanger, Froggy," the listener would hear a loud "boing," which, for reasons not easy to explain, was

absurdly funny. Upon McConnell's death in 1954, his role was assumed by portly, yodel-voiced Andy Divine, and the show, retitled *Andy's Gang*, played until 1958.

One of the zaniest of children's programs was NBC's *The Pinky Lee Show* (1955–1956), hosted by slapstick comic Pinky Lee (born Pincus Leff). The frenetic Lee appeared in baggy pants and a suit and hat of ferocious gaudiness. A second 1955 launch, on ABC, was *The Soupy Sales Show*, which ran until 1967, then reappeared in 1979 for a second run with Viacom. Former disc jockey Sales (born Milton Supman) had immigrated with his parents to America from Hungary. His signature on-air prank was the pie-in-the-face act—with the target being his own as well as others, including that of Frank Sinatra. The third and longest-lasting launch, in 1955, was *Captain Kangaroo*, which ran until 1984. In the host role as the Captain was rotund Bob Keeshan, who played Clarabell the Clown on *Howdy Doody*. An older man by the time he became the Captain, Keeshan dressed in a suit with exaggerated piping, wore his hair in bangs and sported a bushy mustache. He ran this semieducational show with the help of Mr. Green Jeans (actor Hugh Brannum), a handyman in green overalls. The versatile show featured puppets, animals, and a talking clock. In the show's later years, comedian Bill Cosby was a semiregular.

The lone woman to host a popular children's show was puppeteer-ventriloquist Shari Lewis (born Sonia Hurwitz). Lewis was introduced to a national audience in 1956 on *Captain Kangaroo*, then in 1960 landed her own program, *The Shari Lewis Show*, which ran until 1963. Her most memorable puppet was Lamb Chop, and other popular puppet characters included Charlie Horse and Hush Puppy. After 1963, Lewis continued to make occasional television appearances and also published about three dozen children's books.

Breaking the customary mold of the jolly, chubby show host was Presbyterian minister Fred McFeely Rogers, a slight, hypergentle man whose *Mister Rogers's Neighborhood* lasted from 1968 to 2001. Mister Rogers opened each show by entering his imaginary Neighborhood of Make Believe singing his own composition, "Won't You Be My Neighbor" and assuring his young viewers that he liked them just the way they were. His cast was a mix of puppets, such as King Friday XIII, Henriette Pussycat, and the semineurotic Lady Elaine Fairchild, and human characters, including Mr. McFeely (the "speedy delivery" man, played by David Newell), Chef Brockett (Don Brockett), and the lovely Lady Aberlin (Betty Aberlin). The "neighborhood" was actually a model train layout.

Children in the 1980s likely watched *Pee-wee's Playhouse*, hosted by Pee-wee Herman (born Paul Rubenfelds). This CBS series ran from 1986 to 1991. Herman, whose character was that of an eternal child and whose outfit resembled Pinky Lee's, was small, zany and somewhat effeminate. Like *Mister Rogers's Neighborhood*, Herman's show offered a mix of puppets and human guests, such as Oprah Winfrey and singer Little Richard. Herman's show ended after his July 1991 **arrest** for exposing himself in an adult movie theater.

A big success of the 1990s and early 2000s was Nickelodeon's *Blue's Clues*, a semi-interactive educational show running from 1996 to 2006. Its host for the first seven seasons was a thoughtful-looking young man, Steve Burns, who left the show in 2002 to pursue a music career. His replacement for the remainder of the show's run was twenty-four-year-old Donovan Patton, whose "host name" was Joe. *Blue's Clues* involved the host's and viewers' attempts to solve a puzzle with the help of clues left by a dog named Blue. The show was extremely popular, not only in the United States, but also in approximately sixty other countries.

Not all children's shows have hosts. One such show is the phenomenally popular *Sesame Street*, which features the many puppets created by producer Jim Henson. This show has reached the children of around 120 nations since its 1969 inception. Also lacking a host were *The Electric Company* (1971–1977) and *The Muppet Show* (1976–1981). In place of a regular, continuing host, *The Muppet Show* used a guest star to host each episode. Still other children's shows, such as *The Wiggles*, have human talent but no host; and others, such as the *Teletubbies*, show only cartoon characters. *See also*: **Comedy**; **Television's Role**.

Sam G. Riley

For Further Reading

Hollis, Tim. *Hi There, Boys and Girls! America's Local Children's TV Programs*. Jackson: University Press of Mississippi, 2001.

Jordan, Amy B., and Kathleen Hall Jamieson. *Children and Television*.

Thousand Oaks, CA: Sage Publications, 1998.

www.old-time.com/kidshows/index.

www.tvacres.com/child.

CIRCUS CELEBRITIES

As American circus changed in the second half of the 20th century, so did American circus celebrity. The Golden Age of American circus that began in the 1870s when circuses first traveled on trains was ending. In the Golden Age, circus celebrities were center-ring stars who shone amid massive shows—the largest had three rings and four stages and were presented in giant tents and arenas to audiences as large as 15,000. The celebrities' names—Lillian Leitzel, May Wirth, The Riding Hannefords, and Clyde Beatty—were well known because their acts had been featured in colorful lithographs that advertised the circuses in store windows and on barn sides before the shows came to town.

By the 1950s, thanks to the loss of cheap labor, changing modes of advertising, the development of alternate forms of entertainment such as film and television, and the growth of suburbs that ate up land that had provided circus lots, circuses downsized and the largest, like Ringling Brothers and Barnum & Bailey, moved indoors.

During the 1950s, the last Golden Age circus celebrities were still performing. The Wallendas on the high wire continued as one of the most exciting acts in the business. The act, which featured human pyramids crossing the high wire with no safety net, had first appeared in this country in 1928. Eventually, the Wallendas presented a seven-person pyramid. Four men made up the lower level. The first and second men wore yokes on their shoulders supporting a bar that ran between them. The two men behind them did the same. On the second level, two men stood on the bars. They were similarly yoked, and the bar between them supported a woman who carried a chair. All carried heavy balancing poles. Each of the four men on the bottom took simultaneous steps when commanded by Karl Wallenda, the leader of the troupe who stood at the back, until they reached the center of the wire. The woman then placed the chair on the bar on which she had been standing and climbed onto it. When she stood up straight on the chair's seat, the ringmaster announced, "No Princess was ever carried with greater care," and the troupe completed its trip across the wire. In 1962, some of the Wallendas fell while performing in Detroit. Two died and a third was paralyzed, but Karl Wallenda, with a cracked pelvis, performed the following night and continued to perform smaller versions of the act until his death from a fall in 1978. The Wallendas had always been circus celebrities, but after the publicity that attended their fall, their fame grew still greater, and several of the next generations of Wallendas continued to perform versions of the act.

Wild animal trainer Clyde Beatty, who had begun performing in the 1920s, appeared in tents and arenas until his death in 1956. Lou Jacobs, the clown celebrity who was featured in advertising and performances for Ringling Brothers and Barnum & Bailey, joined the show in 1922 and continued with it until his retirement in 1987.

A post–Golden Age era circus star who achieved similar celebrity status was the German acrobat, and horse, elephant, and tiger trainer, Gunther Gebel-Williams, who joined the Ringling show in 1969. With the postwar development of performing arenas that could accommodate a two-year tour of the Big Show, a second Ringling unit was created around elements first leased, and then bought, from the German Circus Williams. This made it possible for a different Ringling unit to play the arenas each year. Gebel-Williams arrived with the Williams Circus. His ability to control three rings of elephants with voice commands, his prodigious energy, and his charm, which reached the farthest seats in the arena, enabled him to remain supreme in the Ringling Red Unit from 1969 until his retirement in 1990.

The difference in performance style between Beatty and Gebel-Williams suggests the change that took place in circuses and in public perceptions of circus. Beatty and Gebel-Williams were both exceptional, theatrical performers, but in totally different ways. Beatty's lion and tiger act was a "fighting" act. Wearing a hunter's hat and brandishing a pistol with blanks, he dominated fierce adversaries. A feature of his act was the moment when he appeared to stare down a snarling tiger and force it into submission. Gebel-Williams, unarmed, presented his tigers as partners in a dynamic demonstration of human and animal skill. As increasing opposition to the use of wild animals in circuses grew, led by organizations like PETA (People for the Ethical Treatment of Animals), Gebel-Williams's act reflected the new respect for animals.

In addition to Williams, some performers achieved a celebrity that, through advertising and television, extended beyond the world of circus. The Italian musical clown David Larible was featured in a number of Ringling Blue Unit shows and the short lived one-ring Ringling boutique show *Kaleidoscape*, but he did not achieve the level of celebrity that Gebel-Williams had. The acrobatic clown Bello Nock, who moved from the Big Apple one-ring circus to Ringling, did achieve the kind of status Gebel-Williams had in the Ringling Red Unit. One event, a pre-performance show for small children, was called *Bellobration*. An American-born member of the Swiss acrobatic Nock family, Bello mastered the sway pole, the high wire, and all kinds of acrobatics. His high-spirited energy easily filled the largest arena. His makeup was unique. The most prominent feature was his red-blonde hair swept up in an outrageous pompadour.

Another clown who achieved celebrity status beyond the world of circus was Barry Lubin, whose feisty Grandma became a virtual trademark of the Big Apple Circus; Grandma regularly appeared in the Macy's Thanksgiving parade and other events. Lubin, who chose not to play all dates with the circus, created clone Grandmas who often stood in for him, which raises interesting questions about how transferable celebrity is and whether an individual performer's work in a live medium can be franchised in this way. Lubin, as Grandma, made many guest appearances with other circuses.

There were also celebrities within the world of circus even if they were not well known beyond the ring. Sylvia Zerbini worked in various American circuses doing solo trapeze and presenting a liberty horse act. When she joined the Ringling shows, she combined the two acts. After touring with Ringling's *Kaleidoscape*, Gold Unit, and Blue Unit, she continued to perform with other shows.

Flying acts create a special excitement, and a number of flyers achieved celebrity in the circus world. Tito Gaona did his first triple somersault in 1964 and by 1990 had done this feat about 13,000 times. He also did a "double double" (a double somersault with a double twist) in his family's act. Miguel Vasquez achieved a quadruple somersault in 1982 but was unable to do it on a regular basis.

In the 1960s, the Flying Cavarettas were teenage flyers. The brother was the catcher and his four sisters took turns as flyers. Terry Cavaretta made it to the *Guinness Book of Records* as the woman who had achieved the most triple somersaults. After settling in at Circus Circus in Las Vegas, the act continued to perform for twenty-five years.

The King Charles troupe, a unicycling version of the Harlem Globetrotters, was a comic sensation on Ringling and other shows for more than a generation. Led by Feld Management, which owned the Ringling franchise, circuses became racially integrated. The days when all celebrity circus performers were white and only workers and sideshow performers were African American ended.

Smaller circuses, in tents or in arenas, could seldom afford celebrity performers. However, after *perestroika,* the arrival in America of circus artists trained in the subsidized circus systems of Eastern Europe raised the general level of skill in American circuses. The spectacular aerial act the Cranes, which depicted the spirits of dead Soviet soldiers transformed into cranes, was developed after years of nurturing in the Soviet system. It first played in the United States with touring Russian circuses and then took up residence in Reno, Nevada.

In the last quarter of the 20th century, a new interest in circus skills training for recreational and professional purposes led to the creation of circus schools based on the Eastern European model, most notably the National Circus School in Montreal. Such schools, along with the new youth circuses, meant that young people could prepare for circus careers without having been brought up in circus families.

Cirque du Soleil, which was founded in 1984 and by the end of the 1990s had become the largest circus organization in the world with a huge training center in Montreal and many touring and permanent shows, maintained a house style that was virtually anti-celebrity. Although unique acts were featured, most of the performers were kept anonymous, often hidden behind elaborate costumes and makeup. The surreal Cirque du Soleil style was widely emulated.

While circus in its traditional form was downsized and as circus skills training was professionalized, circus became part of a performance continuum that included ballet, vaudeville, puppetry, theater, and gymnastics. Thus, traditional circus skills appeared in other media than the circus. Not only was the nature of circus redefined, the Cirque du Soleil influence fostered spectacle at the expense of individual celebrity, a rarity in today's entertainment culture. *See also*: **Television's Role**.

Robert Sugarman

For Further Reading

Albrecht, Ernest. *The New American Circus.* Gainesville: University Press of Florida, 1995.

Albrecht, Ernest. *The Contemporary Circus: Art of the Spectacular.* Lanham, MD: Scarecrow Press, 2006.

Gebel-Williams, Gunther, and Toni Reinhold. *Untamed: The Autobiography of the Circus's Greatest Animal Trainer.* New York: William Morrow, 1991.

Opera's great tenor Luciano Pavarotti performs in "Idomeneo" at the Met in 1983. Courtesy of Photofest.

CLASSICAL MUSIC

In an America solidly dominated by popular, not high culture, relatively few singers, musicians, or conductors who devote their lives to serious music go beyond fame and pass into the profitable realm of celebrity. To gain U.S. celebrity, a musician must not only be exceptional at his or her work, but also must provide the added incentive of personal interest that the public demands. One can achieve this by being unusually good looking, dabbling in some form or forms of popular music on the side, having a well-publicized dispute with a rival musician, or living an unusual or flamboyant lifestyle.

Only a few opera performers out of many have become genuine celebrities in America. Born in the United States to Greek parents, soprano Maria Callas not only sang like an angel, but went from fame to celebrity thanks first to her long love affair with Greek shipping tycoon Aristotle Onassis and secondarily to published reports of a feud with rival singer Renata Tebaldi, an Italian soprano who often performed at New York's Metropolitan Opera (the Met). Director of that important institution in the early years of the new century was American coloratura soprano Beverly Sills (born Belle Silverman in Brooklyn, New York). Sills made many efforts to take the high-culture stiffness out of opera via her many television appearances, including hosting a **talk show** of her own; and who could resist the charm of an accomplished opera star with the nickname "Bubbles"? Other American opera stars to reach celebrity status included three African American singers: Marian Anderson, the first black singer to perform at the Met; throaty Leontyne Price, who is known for her role in *Aida*; and Marilyn Horne, who also recorded popular music and appeared on various television shows. One of today's most popular sopranos is Renee Fleming, who also has recorded with soft-rock singer Michael Bolton, has appeared on Garrison Keillor's radio show *A Prairie*

Home Companion, and whose voice is on the soundtrack of the 2003 *Lord of the Rings* movie. Three additional recent or contemporary operatic superstars have been Swede Birgit Nilsson, Italian American Anna Moffo, and Australian Joan Sutherland.

Among operatic bass singers, the biggest celebrity since 1950 was Italian Ezio Pinza, who not only spent more than two decades at the Met, but also gained wide celebrity with his rendition of "Some Enchanted Evening" in the 1949 stage musical *South Pacific*. The debonair Pinza was especially popular with female fans. The most controversial operatic bass was the remarkably talented and versatile African American singer, actor, lawyer, and activist Paul Robeson, who left America to live in England and was an admirer of Russia's Joseph Stalin. Robeson, who toured the world performing the title role in *Othello*, a role he first played in 1930, is also remembered for his earlier performance in *Show Boat*, in which he first appeared in 1929. Two more celebrity bassos were Jerome Hines (born Jerome Heinz), who put in just over forty seasons at the Met and who stood 6'6", and Robert Merrill (born Morris Miller). Merrill sang on popular radio and worked the Borscht Belt during his younger years before gaining widespread public recognition by singing the national anthem on each opening day at Yankee Stadium, starting in 1969.

Most popular of all male opera stars have been the tenors. The great celebrity of the 1950s was Mario Lanza, whose parents were Italian and who played the earlier operatic sensation Enrico Caruso in the film *The Great Caruso* (1951). In more recent years, three heavily promoted superstars, known collectively as "The Three Tenors," have been the late Italian sensation Luciano Pavarotti and two Spaniards: Placido Domingo and Jose Carreras. The three men performed several concerts together and also recorded together, beginning in 1990 and concluding in 2003. They were active in raising money for charitable causes, including research on leukemia, from which Carreras himself has recovered after lengthy treatment.

Among the classical pianists who achieved celebrity since 1950 have been Polish American Arthur Rubinstein and Russian American Vladimir Horowitz, both of whom made numerous recordings, which helped further their celebrity. Better known to a wide U.S. audience was German American Andre Previn. Although he was director or conductor of three major symphony orchestras, Previn also played **jazz** piano and composed or adapted the scores for a number of movies, including *Gigi* (1958), *Porgy and Bess* (1959), *Irma la Douce* (1963), *My Fair Lady* (1964), and *Paint Your Wagon* (1969). Thunderously popular in his youth was Harvey "Van" Cliburn, who at twenty-three in 1958 won the International Tchaikovsky Piano Competition in Moscow. Following this win, he became the only classical musician ever to be given a ticker-tape parade in Manhattan.

Like the pianists, virtuoso violinists' celebrity is usually restricted to a modest segment of the U.S. populace. Those who appreciate serious music, however, have included among their own celebrities romanticist Fritz Kreisler, who no longer gave concerts during the 1950s but who still made recordings then, and the remarkably versatile Jascha Heifetz. Two more violinists, whose deaths came near the turn of the new century, were both Russian-born: Yehudi Menuhin and Isaac Stern. Equally talented but more inclined to extend the reach of his talents through popular music is Israeli American Itzhak Perlman, who has played the scores for the movies *Schindler's List* (1993) and *Memoirs of a Geisha* (2005) and who occasionally plays jazz violin. Somewhat less well known are Joshua Bell and Korean prodigy Chee-Yun, who performed at age thirteen with the New York Philharmonic.

Very likely the biggest classical music celebrity in 2008 is Chinese American cellist Yo-Yo Ma, who also was a prodigy. While enjoying the reputation as the world's greatest living cellist, Ma has not only played music as varied and unexpected as bluegrass and tango, but also has performed musical scores for such films as *Seven Years in Tibet* (1997), *Crouching Tiger, Hidden Dragon* (2000), and *Memoirs of a Geisha* (2005) and has performed with singer Sting and pianist Condoleezza Rice, former U.S. secretary of state (2005–2009). The very opposite of the stereotypically temperamental artist, Ma has shared his talents with children via appearances on *Sesame Street* and *Mr. Rogers's Neighborhood*. The other two great cellists of the late 1900s, both now deceased, were Spaniard Pablo Casals and Russian Mstislav Rostropovich. An important figure in having the guitar recognized as a serious instrument was Spain's Andres Segovia, who died in 1986 but performed well into his eighties. The best-known classical guitarists in the early 21st century are Californian Christopher Parkening and Australian-Englishman John Williams, who has provided the theme music for

The Deer Hunter (1979) and has played with fusion group *Sky*.

Only a handful of conductors have become limited-audience celebrities in the United States. Italian Arturo Toscanini, German Otto Klemperer, Pole Leopold Stokowski, and Hungarian American Eugene Ormandy have been among the select few. Leonard Bernstein was the first U.S.-born conductor to gain international celebrity. Bernstein had his widest audience in 1957 when he composed the score for the Broadway musical and later movie *West Side Story*. Earlier, he had written the score for the movie *On the Waterfront* (1954). Three additional conductors to achieve some measure of celebrity have been Italian Riccado Muti, French American Lorin Maazel, and U.S. conductor of Russian ancestry Leonard Slatkin. *See also*: **African American**; **Asian American**; **Child Celebrity**; **Movies' Role**; **Television's Role**.

Sam G. Riley

For Further Reading

Ehn, Hope. *On-Line Resources for Classical and Academic Musicians: A Guide through the Wilds of the Internet*. Newton Centre, MA: H. Ehn, 1994.

Pincus, Andrew L. *Musicians with a Mission: Keeping the Classical Tradition Alive*. Boston: Northeastern University Press, 2002.

Yoshihara, Mari. *Musicians from a Different Shore: Asians and Asian Americans in Classical Music*. Philadelphia: Temple University Press, 2007.

COMEDY

Americans adore comedy: that which makes people laugh. The public's need for comedy to smooth the rough edges of life has propelled a remarkable number of performers into celebrity. Unlike singers, **dancers**, romantic actors, or **athletes**, comic celebrities can scale the heights without being handsome, beautiful, or physically powerful. They merely have to be funny—something not just anyone can manage. Some comedy is slapstick, or dependent on pratfalls or physical movement. Some is vocal, or cerebral, or dark, or satirical, or romantic, or farcical. Some is gentle, some harsh and controversial. Some comic celebrities do solo stand-up routines, while others act in sketches, interacting with other actors. All, however, exploit the comic possibilities of incongruity, exaggeration, surprise, tension, and ambivalence.

Stand-Up Comics

The early 1950s were the final days of old-time, pretelevision radio, where vocal comedy had been king. In radio, one of the greats was ex-vaudevillian Fred Allen, whose *Allen's Alley* featured stereotypical yet hilarious characters. When the show closed in 1948, Allen performed other radio comedy into the early 1950s, continuing his running "feud" with fellow comedy pioneer Jack Benny. Concurrent with *Allen's Alley* was the show *Fibber McGee and Molly*, which lasted until 1959. Jim and Marian Jordan played the title roles, interacting with such characters as blowhard Throckmorton

Comic actor Robin Williams sings for the troops at Aviano Air Base in Italy, backed by Kid Rock on guitar. Courtesy of the Department of Defense.

P. Gildersleeve (Harold Peary), Mayor LaTrivia (Gale Gordon, who parodied New York's Mayor Fiorello LaGuardia), and Wallace Wimple (Bill Thompson, also the voice in "Droopy the Dog" cartoons), a little man terrorized by Sweetieface, his "big ol' wife." A fine Jewish radio comedy show that in 1950 migrated to television was *The Goldbergs*, starring Gertrude Berg. Also moving successfully from radio to television was *The Jack Benny Show*, in which the self-deprecating Benny portrayed himself as a vain (always age thirty-nine) miser with a "money bin" in his mansion, where he was attended by the gravel-voiced Rochester (Eddie Anderson).

Other radio-to-television moves were made by ventriloquist Edgar Bergen, whose *Edgar Bergen/Charlie McCarthy Show* pitted him against two dummies: smart-mouthed Charlie and simpleton Mortimer Snerd; Red Skelton, whose NBC show featured his own characters, the most unusual of all being Heathcilffe the seagull; and Bob Hope, a megacelebrity comic of radio, nearly 300 television specials, and roughly sixty movies. Hope, master of the corny one-liner, was much honored for his many shows for U.S. troops stationed abroad. Like many of the other comics mentioned in this entry, Hope appeared in movies, as well.

Americans of the 1950s also enjoyed comedy on record albums. One of the best such comics was Danish immigrant pianist Victor Borge, who combined music and humor. His one-man show *Comedy in Music* lasted for roughly 850 performances in New York during the 1950s, and his "phonetic punctuation" routine remains a classic. Some refer to Stan Freberg as the last

of the radio comics, but he also is remembered for his comic albums and singles. His 1950 hit "John and Marsha" spoofed soap operas, with Freberg doing both voices, repeating "John" and "Marsha" in increasingly breathless tones. Freberg went on to parody Johnnie Ray, Harry Belafonte, and Elvis Presley; and his send-up of Laurence Welk's saccharine music and bubble machine was a tremendous hit. Virtually every college boy of the 1950s was also familiar with Oscar Brand and his album *Bawdy Songs and Back Room Ballads*. Less vulgar but just as funny was the album work of portly Allan Sherman, who gained instant celebrity in 1962 with *My Son, the Folk Singer*, a collection of Jewish-themed parodies. One of his best songs, "Hello Muddah, Hello Fadduh" appeared on a later album. One of the most intellectual musical comics of that era was math instructor Tom Lehrer, who used his wit and his piano to satirize political and social issues. His song "Fight Fiercely, Harvard" was one of the best comic put-downs ever. Finally, another "piano comedian," Mark Russell, became a celebrity in the early 1960s for his work in the lounge of Washington, D.C.'s Shoreham Hotel, where he skewered politicians. This "sit-down comic" also did television specials featuring political satire.

Other comics achieved celebrity with nonmusical albums. Andy Griffith was an instant success with his 1953 album *What It Was, Was Football*, on which the game is viewed for the first time by a clueless rube. Southern "redneck humor" was also the stock in trade of a later comic, Jerry Clower, who began recording in 1970. A talented parodist whose career suddenly disappeared was Vaughn Meader, whose album impersonating John F. Kennedy's upper-crust New England accent was removed from store shelves after the president's assassination. Other impressionists known more for their television appearances have included Rich Little, who appeared in the 1960s doing Richard Nixon, Johnny Carson, and many other figures, and his contemporary David Frye, who impersonated Nixon, Lyndon Johnson, Ed Sullivan, Cary Grant, and William F. Buckley, Jr.

Like boxers, stand-up comics must stand in the spotlight alone and either sink or swim, whether in comedy clubs, on television, or elsewhere. Henny Youngman's long stand-up career lasted from the 1930s to the 1990s and relied heavily on poking fun at his wife. Portly "Borscht Belt" comic Buddy Hackett made many television and movie appearances. The "king and queen of mean" were acid-tongued, quick-witted Don Rickles and mock-venomous Joan Rivers, both regulars on Johnny Carson's *Tonight Show*, as were their contemporaries Shecky Green, Alan King, Myron Cohen, and the most manic comedian of the 1950s, Jonathan Winters, often remembered for his sweet and sour little-old-lady character, Maudie Frickert.

Stand-up comics of the 1960s include deadpan, cerebral Bob Newhart; urban "little man" Woody Allen; the Bill Gates of self-deprecation, Rodney Dangerfield; political satirist Jackie Mason; and Foster Brooks, whose comic persona was a loveable, sentence-mangling drunk. The 1970s produced versatile Robert Klein, the perpetually confused-looking Gary Shandling, and the edgier humor of

such performers as political comic David Brenner, Hispanic comedian Freddie Prinze, and pull-no-punches black comic Richard Pryor. African American stand-up comics who followed in the 1980s were Whoopie Goldberg, who borrowed the first part of her stage name from the whoopee cushion; Sinbad (born David Adkins), advocate of clean humor; stand-up and sketch comic Dave Chappelle; and Jamie Foxx, whose perhaps greatest contribution to show business came later in his superb movie portrayal of singer Ray Charles. Three other 1980s stand-up performers were women: Roseanne Barr, often portraying the hard-pressed housewife; pretty comic Brett Butler; and Ellen DeGeneres, who broke new ground as the first openly lesbian comic on the circuit. Other male comics of that era include Bobcat Goldthwait; Drew Carey; prop comedy performer Carrot Top (born Scott Thompson); cherubic John Pinette; smasher of watermelons and other objects Gallagher; and wordplay comic Mitch Hedberg, who died at thirty-seven of **drug** toxicity.

Coming online in the 1990s or thereafter have been brilliant, deadpan Steven Wright; **rock** and roll parodist Weird Al Yankovic; redneck humorist Jeff Foxworthy; Korean American Margaret Cho; Russian-born Yakov Smirnoff (born Yakov Pokhis); laid-back Dane Cook; Rita Rudner; and black comics Cedric The Entertainer (Cedric Kyles), the late Bernie Mac (Bernard McCullough), and fast-talking Chris Tucker.

Stand-up comics who pushed the limits of taste or were especially outrageous began to appear in the 1940s with controversialist Lenny Bruce

(Leonard Schneider), remembered for his 1964 obscenity conviction; he was posthumously pardoned in 2003. Redd Foxx (born John Sanford) began his comic career doing remarkably gross album humor but went on to do gentler humor on television in *Sanford and Son*. Andy Kaufman played Latvian taxi driver Latka on the sitcom *Taxi*, did perhaps the finest Elvis impression ever, but made audiences gasp with his intergender wrestling and his realistic mock feud with pro wrestler Jerry Lawler. Sam Kinison was known for his intense, crazed rants, and Andrew Dice Clay (Andrew Silverstein) possibly reached the apex of the offensive and profane in comic routines.

Comedy Shows

Some of the most memorable comedy of this period was performed on comic variety shows. Earliest was *That Was the Week That Was*, which originally aired in 1962 on the British Broadcasting Company (BBC), then in the United States in the following year. Its lampooning of the establishment was hosted by David Frost and featured stand-up, music, and sketch numbers by Woody Allen, Alan Alda, Steve Allen, Tom Lehrer, and many others. *Rowan & Martin's Laugh-In* ran from 1968 to 1973. Hosts included Dan Rowan, straight man, and Dick Martin, "doofus"; but the real comic stars were cast members Ruth Buzzi playing Gladys Ormphby, horny and hideous spinster; her nemesis Tyrone F. Horgeigh, played by Arte Johnson, who also appeared as Wolfgang the Nazi soldier; tiny, mild Henry Gibson (born James Bateman) as a poet; Lily Tomlin as Ernestine, rude telephone operator; and

Flip Wilson dressed as the streetwise Geraldine. The show supplied the nation with odd catchphrases, such as "Here come da judge," "Verrry enterrestink," and "The devil made me do it."

Another comic ensemble appearing at the end of the 1960s was BBC's *Monty Python's Flying Circus*, with its surreal animation and hilarious sketches starring John Cleese, Eric Idle, Terry Gilliam, Terry Jones, and Michael Palin. Their skits, such as "Nudge Nudge, Wink Wink," "The Dead Parrot," "The Job Interview," and "The Lumberjack Song" remain fresh in the memories of their viewers, both in Britain and America. In 1975 came the long-lived *Saturday Night Live* (SNL), which has continued into the 21st century. Some of its early sketches featured Chevy Chase as a network anchorman ("Good evening. I'm Chevy Chase—and you're not."); Bill Murray as a painfully bad lounge singer; Dan Aykroyd in one great role after another; John Belushi in the "Chee' burger" sketch and, paired with Aykroyd, as "The Blues Brothers"; Gilda Radner as the manic Roseanne Roseannadanna and Baba Wawa, a takeoff on newswoman Barbara Walters. Later came Eddie Murphy in "Mr. Robinson's Neighborhood," a spoof of Fred Rogers; Billy Crystal as Fernando, a takeoff on Hollywood shallowness; Dana Carvey as Church Lady; Martin Short as supernerd Ed Grimley; Joe Piscopo as Frank Sinatra; guest star Steve Martin, teaming with Aykroyd as "Two Wild and Crazy Guys"; Don Novello as the strangely hip Father Guido Sarducci; and John Lovitz as "The Pathological Liar" and "Master Thesbian." Still later SNL standouts have included Chris Farley, Adam Sandler, Victoria

Jackson, Dennis Miller, Chris Rock, and Sarah Silverman.

More recent comedy shows have been *Politically Incorrect*, starring Bill Maher; *The Daily Show* with Jon Stewart; and a *Daily Show* spin-off, Stephen Colbert's *Colbert Report* (pronounced Col-bare Ray-por). Also irreverent have been the late-night talk shows, among which the greatest was *The Tonight Show with Johnny Carson*, which ran from 1962 until Carson's retirement in 1992. Carson's own portrayals of "mentalist" Carnac the Magnificent and Floyd R. Turbo, plaid hunting jacket and goofy cap-clad right-winger, appeared alongside guests that included many stand-up comics. Replacing Carson until May 2009 was Jay Leno. A late-night competitor for a brief time starting in 1962 was *The Steve Allen Show*, and in 1982 appeared the so-called late-late show that has appealed greatly to young viewers: *The Late Show with David Letterman*. A competitor is *Late Night with Conan O'Brien*, which began in 1993 and concluded in 2009 when O'Brien took over *The Tonight Show*. Comic Joan Rivers, formerly a guest host for Johnny Carson, briefly hosted her own such program, *The Joan Rivers Show*, but in 1987 it was replaced by the first late-night program with an African American host, *The Arsenio Hall Show*, which ran until 1994.

American television sitcoms and their stars are legion. A pioneer was Lucille Ball in *I Love Lucy*, which premiered in 1951. The next year came Jackie ("And awa-a-a-ay we go") Gleason in *The Honeymooners* and later *The Jackie Gleason Show*. Dick Van Dyke had his first televised comedy show in the early 1960s, and in 1967 appeared *The Carol Burnett Show*, with Burnett, Harvey Korman, and Tim Conway. *The Mary Tyler Moore Show* opened in 1970 and *M*A*S*H* in 1972. A funny show with a serious social message was *All in the Family*, launched in 1971. Using verbal irony, Carroll O'Connor played the lead role as a racial bigot. Gabe Kaplan starred in *Welcome Back Kotter* starting in 1975, and Robin Williams in *Mork and Mindy* in 1978. Other top sitcoms among the many have been *Cheers* (1982), *The Cosby Show* (1984), *Seinfeld* (1989), *Frasier* (1993), and *Boston Legal* (2004).

Double Acts

A staple of comic performance since the days of vaudeville has been the comic duo, or double act, in which one partner is the "straight man," tossing setup lines to the funny partner. In movies, radio, and television, George Burns played straight man to his "ditsy" wife, Gracie Allen. Bud Abbott played opposite the bumbling Lou Costello, a popular duo in the 1940s and 1950s, as were smooth, handsome singer Dean Martin and manic, gawping Jerry Lewis. Short-lived but wonderful was the comedy duo of Sid Caesar and Imogene Coca on *Your Show of Shows* during the very early days of television. Celebrities in the 1950s were Bob and Ray (Bob Elliott and Ray Goulding), a radio duo who moved to television. The 1960s *Smothers Brothers* show featured straight-man Dick and perpetually confused Tommy Smothers, and the growth of America's drug culture was reflected in the 1970s and 1980s in the comedy of Cheech and Chong. Perhaps the best comic duo in the early 2000s has been on television's *Boston Legal*. There, William Shatner and James Spader play two mega-zany lawyers, although it is hard to say which is the straight man.

Good comedic movies are plentiful, but the American Film Institute has rated the funniest ever as *Some Like It Hot* (1959), with Marilyn Monroe, Jack Lemon, and Tony Curtis. The Institute rated Dustin Hoffman's *Tootsie* (1982), Peter Sellers's *Dr. Strangelove* (1964), and Woody Allen and Diane Keaton's *Annie Hall* (1977) as numbers two, three, and four. Other comic movies rated in the top twenty were *Blazing Saddles* (1974, No. 6), *M*A*S*H* (1970, No. 7), *The Graduate* (1967, No. 9), *Airplane!* (1980, No. 10), *The Producers* (1968, No. 11), *Young Frankenstein* (1974, No. 13), *The Odd Couple* (1968, No. 17), and *The Apartment* (1960, No. 20). Underrated at number twenty-six was Peter Sellers's satiric masterpiece, *Being There* (1979); and a glaring omission from the Institute's top 100 list was *Trading Places* (1983), starring Dan Aykroyd and Eddie Murphy. *See also*: **African American**; **Children's Show Hosts**; **Criticisms of Celebrity Culture**; **Fads**; **Movies' Role**; **News Media Figures**; **Talk Show Hosts**; **Television's Role**.

Sam G. Riley

For Further Reading

Berger, Phil. *The Last Laugh: The World of Stand-up Comics*. New York: Cooper Square Press, 2000.

Breitbart, Andrew, and Mark Ebner. "The Death of Comedy." In *Hollywood Interrupted*, 257–276. New York: John Wiley & Sons, 2004.

Epstein, Lawrence J. *Mixed Nuts: America's Love Affair with Comedy Teams*. New York: PublicAffairs, 2004.

Garner, Joe. *Made You Laugh: the Funniest Moments in Radio, Television, Stand-up and Movie Comedy*. Kansas City, KS: Andrews McMeel, 2004.

Krutnik, Frank. *Hollywood Comedians, the Film Reader*. London: Routledge, 2003.

Nachman, Gerald. *Seriously Funny: the Rebel Comedians of the 1950s and 1960s*. New York: Pantheon Books, 2003.

Zoglin, Richard. *Comedy at the Edge: How Stand-up in the 1970s Changed America*. New York: Bloomsbury, 2008.

www.infoplease.com/ipea.

CORPORATE CELEBRITY

President Calvin Coolidge famously remarked that "The business of America is business," yet relatively few corporate titans have ascended to celebrity. Furthermore, many who have managed to do so have become celebrities at least in part out of notoriety. Some of our nation's earliest celebrity business people to gain heavy publicity and excite widespread public interest are remembered today as the "robber barons," men who became incredibly rich by way of sharp practices and cornered markets. Among the most successful were John Jacob Astor (furs, real estate), Cornelius Vanderbilt (railroads, shipping), Leland Stanford (railroads), Jay Gould (railroads), Henry Flagler (railroads, real estate development), J. P. Morgan (finance), Andrew

Microsoft founder Bill Gates joshes with Secretary of Defense Robert Gates and Marine General Peter Pace. Courtesy of the Department of Defense.

Mellon (banking), John D. Rockefeller (oil), and James Duke (tobacco, electric power). Of these men, the first to die was Astor, in 1848, and the last, Mellon, in 1937. Other early business celebrities included gold- and silver-mining titan George Hearst and his flamboyant son, publisher William Randolph Hearst; Henry Ford (automobiles); and P. T. Barnum of circus fame.

As U.S. media became ever more important, Americans took great interest in individuals such as animator and film producer Walt Disney; dapper, aristocratic magazine publisher Henry Luce, who with Briton Hadden, started *Time*, *Life*, *Fortune*, and *Sports Illustrated*; the rags to riches head of the National Broadcasting Company (NBC) and Radio Corporation of America (RCA), David Sarnoff; and William S.

Paley, who built CBS, the Columbia Broadcasting System. The last of these individuals to die was Paley, in 1990.

To gain celebrity, a corporate figure requires more than just financial success. In a culture in which the biggest celebrities tend to be movie stars and **athletes**, the corporate celebrity usually needs special dash or glamour. Such a figure was the enormously wealthy playboy industrialist, pilot, engineer, and film producer Howard Hughes, whose fortune was enormous for his time. Hughes had personal magnetism to spare and was known for romancing actresses Terry Moore and Jane Russell before falling prey to mental illness that turned him into an eccentric and recluse for some years prior to his death in 1976. In possession of another large fortune was J. Paul Getty, founder of Getty Oil and also of special interest to the public because of his collections of art and antiquities. Portions of his collection are available for public view at Los Angeles's beautiful Getty Museum, the most lavishly funded museum (free to the public) in the world thanks to Getty, who, like Hughes, died in 1976.

More lovable was Harland Sanders, founder of the Kentucky Fried Chicken (KFC) chain. Known as Colonel Sanders because he had been made an honorary Kentucky colonel, he dressed the part in string tie and white suit. In front of his franchise restaurants stood a larger-than-life plastic statue of Sanders, arms open in a vaguely religious gesture, beckoning customers. His image was still tied to the company after he sold it in 1964, although in 1971 he sued the new owner, Heublein Inc., alleging misuse of his image. Sanders died in 1980 and was to business the kind of success story that Elvis was to music. Another American who made a remarkable fortune but never lost his common touch was Sam Walton, founder of Wal-Mart and Sam's Club, a man whose personal fortune in the early 1990s was said to be more than $58 billion. America has always liked titans who choose to live like regular guys, as did Walton until his death in 1992. Another fast-food celebrity was KFC alumnus and founder of Wendy's Old Fashioned Hamburgers, Dave Thomas. It is often a mistake for business owners to be their own television front man, but Thomas, exuding good-natured folksiness, made a great success of it. He is said to have appeared in more commercials than any other individual—more than 800—before his 2002 death.

Among the now-deceased celebrities of the corporate world were a number of women. One was Estee Lauder, born Josephine Esther Mentzer, cofounder with her husband of a successful cosmetics business. The fashionable Estee outlived her husband by many years and died in 2004. A similar success story was that of Mary Kay Ash, who founded Mary Kay Cosmetics, which employed other women as direct marketers of the company's line. The most successful of these women were rewarded with a pink Cadillac. Ash died in 2001, much admired. Far less admired but well known was billionaire New York hotelier and commercial real estate magnate Leona Helmsley. Her celebrity was magnified in 1989 when she was convicted of tax evasion and began serving nearly two years in prison. Her enormous celebrity was largely due to her dismissive "let-them-eat-cake" attitude toward what she once called America's "little people." She died in 2007. Two individuals from other nations who were extremely well known in the United States were French **fashion designer** and perfume marketer Gabrielle "Coco" Chanel and Greek shipping and airline tycoon Aristotle Onassis. Chanel's elegant sense of style appealed greatly to American women in the mid decades of the 1900s, and she was especially admired for popularizing what generations of women have called "the little black dress." Her death came in 1971. Onassis was fairly well known in America due to his long affair with opera great Maria Callas, but his celebrity grew exponentially in 1968 when he married John F. Kennedy's widow, Jacqueline Kennedy, the greatest celebrity of her time. Onassis died in 1975.

Of contemporary, living corporate celebrities, many are connected with the communications media or computer technology. One of the most singular of media tycoons is Cable News Network founder Ted Turner, who made brilliant business decisions while sometimes giving the impression that he was slightly daft. Gap-toothed yet striking in appearance, the Atlanta-based Turner became even more of a celebrity in 1991 when he married controversial actress Jane Fonda, and again when the two divorced a decade later. As of 2009, he boasted the nation's largest buffalo herd and sold buffalo meat products in his chain of Montana Grill restaurants. Less glamorous than Turner (funny how a few billion dollars can make a man seem more so) is Australian-born News Corporation mogul Rupert Murdoch, whose worldwide media holdings make him impossible to ignore. Known most widely for his "You're fired" role on television reality show *The Apprentice* is "The Donald," Donald Trump. His self-promotion, showy lifestyle, and hotel and entertainment holdings, plus his marriages to beautiful women, have made him one of America's most recognized business figures. Less widely known, at least until his outspoken campaigning for Hillary Clinton and against Barak Obama, is America's first black billionaire, Robert L. Johnson, founder of Black Entertainment Television and owner of the Charlotte Bobcats basketball team. Also no stranger to controversy is television host and magazine publisher Martha Stewart, who has controlling interest in the company Martha Stewart Living Omnimedia. She was, in addition, the style spokesperson for Kmart discount stores. Stewart suffered from media overexposure, causing some people to take

delight in her conviction in 2004 and subsequent brief imprisonment for lying about her handling of ImClone stock. Her reputation survived the prison stay, and she continues to appear seemingly everywhere offering home-making advice. Even better known than Stewart and minus the prison record is television host, movie actress, magazine publisher, and billionaire philanthropist Oprah Winfrey. Winfrey has been open about her own life, which has not always been easy, and she very likely is the most popular woman in America. Finally, billionaire film-makers Steven Spielberg and George Lucas are among these contemporary celebrities. *Jaws*, *E.T.* and *Jurassic Park* firmly established Spielberg; and the *Star Wars* and *Indiana Jones* films did the same for Lucas.

Computer celebrity's reigning monarch is Bill Gates, the shy, slightly nerdy-looking Microsoft founder. In 2008, he was thought to be the world's third-richest person, with a net worth of around $58 billion. Gates stepped down in 2000 and now devotes much of his time to philanthropy. Behind Gates in wealth are Oracle Corporation founder and chief executive Larry Ellison, known for his affinity for automobile and yacht racing, and the less flamboyant Michael Dell, founding chief executive of Dell, Inc., which at first sold its computers directly to the public rather than through stores. Two other computer billionaire celebrities are Jeff Bezos, founder and chair of Amazon.com, and founding chief executive of Apple Inc. and founder of Pixar Animation Studios Steve Jobs, widely publicized as America's lowest-paid chief executive, with an annual salary of $1. Jobs, bearded and casually clad in jeans and a pullover, likes to serve as company spokesman and does it effectively. Finally, Ross Perot, founder of Electronic Data Systems, a data-processing firm, became a celebrity when he twice ran unsuccessfully for the White House, in 1992 and 1996. The colorful Texan was outspoken in his criticism of the **globalization** trend that, as he predicted, outsourced American jobs to Mexico and beyond, a trend Perot called the "giant sucking sound." He now controls another company, Perot Systems.

Rounding out the current crop of corporate celebrities are individuals whose wealth comes from other sectors of the economy. Richest of them all is Warren Buffett, the "Sage (or Oracle) of Omaha." His estimated $62 billion fortune came from stock trading as chief executive of Berkshire Hathaway. Like Steve Jobs, Buffett takes only a token salary and lives in a modest house. In 2006, he announced plans to give to charity most of his massive fortune, much of it through the auspices of the Bill and Melinda Gates Foundation. Former Chrysler Corporation Chief Executive Officer Lee Iacocca, now a philanthropist, gained celebrity status with his television appearances for Chrysler and, before that, for Ford Motor Company, his books, his political support for George H. W. Bush, and his more recent criticism of inept national politicians and overpaid corporate executives. Two more corporate celebrities are fugitive billionaire commodities trader Marc Rich, who lives in splendor in Switzerland thanks to having been pardoned in 2001 by outgoing President Bill Clinton from a tax evasion conviction, and dashing Englishman Richard Branson, now Sir Richard Branson,

known to the U.S. public for his Virgin brand, which has been applied to Virgin Atlantic Airways, Virgin Records, and many other businesses. *See also*: **Criminals**; **Dream Girls**; **International Celebrity**; **Magazines' Role**; **Movies' Role**; **Politics**; **Television's Role**.

Sam G. Riley

For Further Reading

Dingle, Derek T. *Black Enterprise Titans of the B.E.100s: Black CEOs Who Redefined and Conquered American Business*. New York: J. Wiley, 1999.

Josephson, Matthew. *The Robber Barons: The Great American Capitalists, 1861–1901*. New York: Harcourt, Brace, 1934.

http://entrepreneurs.about.com.

COUNTRY AND WESTERN

Country and Western music as a distinctive style emerged from hillbilly and folk traditions in the American South in the 1930s. Musicians gained fans by appearing on radio barn dance shows appealing mainly to rural Southern and Midwestern audiences. Most influential were the western Virginia Carter Family, who specialized in Appalachian tunes, and Jimmy Rogers, the Alabama "singing brakeman," who blended blues, cowboy, black, and work songs, streamlining folk music for an industrial era and making it a viable commercial property. In the late 1940s Hank Williams modernized country music and was, until his untimely death in 1953 from self-destructive use of drugs and alcohol, a huge influence on generations of country singers with great songs such as "Your Cheatin' Heart," "Hey Good Looking," and "Jambalaya." Williams often celebrated the "honky tonk" culture of bars and fast living. Patsy Cline, "the Queen of Country Singers," also achieved enduring fame with songs such as "Crazy" and "Sweet Dreams." She died in a plane crash in 1963 at the height of her career.

By the 1950s the mainstream country music of Williams and Cline became part of a broader concept, country and Western, that included several other rural-based traditions with sizeable audiences. The Western swing of Bob Wills and his Texas Playboys integrated country and **jazz**. Hugely popular Western films boosted the cowboy songs of Gene Autry, Roy Rogers, and the Sons of the Pioneers. Kentucky-born Bill Monroe and his Blue Grass Boys and the Stanley Brothers from Virginia mixed black and Appalachian folk music to create bluegrass. Johnny Cash and Carl Perkins developed a large youth following by blending **rock** and country to create rockabilly. Cash, known as "The Man in Black," maintained his popularity and iconic status until his death in 2003. The Grand Ole' Opry radio broadcasts from Nashville developed a mass national audience and increased the celebrity value of top acts like Williams, Cline, Kitty Wells, and Roy Acuff.

The emergence of rock and roll in the 1950s prompted the country music industry to incorporate more pop production, creating the smooth Nashville sound that attracted more urban working-class fans and was the most commercially oriented and successful style from the late 1950s through the 1980s. Keyboards, strings, and electric guitars often replaced fiddles and steel guitars. This music was designed to cross over into pop and did so quite often. Eddie Arnold sold 60 million records with his smooth voice. "Gentleman" Jim Reeves also found a pop music audience with his sentimental songs, his popularity enduring after his death in an airplane crash in 1964. Fans enjoyed following the stormy personal lives of stars like George Jones and Barbara Mandrell. But top country acts rarely reached the superstar status of such rockers as Elvis Presley and The Beatles even as their audience grew in the Midwest and West.

By the 1960s, many country and Western songs, appealing particularly to people of modest income, were drenched in consumerism, patriotism, and acceptance of one's often difficult lot in life, and represented more conservative family values than did rock music. One female star, Tammy Wynette, advised disenchanted women to "Stand by Your Man." Only once in a while would a rebellious country musician like Johnny Paycheck suggest that people "take this job and shove it." Furthermore, country music was sometimes employed in support of U.S. foreign policy objectives such as the Vietnam War. Merle Haggard had a major hit with "Okie from Muskogee" in 1969, a song saturated with patriotic platitudes, criticism of war protesters and **drugs**, and exaltation of mainstream, small-town values. Later, after the terrorist attacks of 9/11, country musicians entered the debate over the Iraq War. Toby Keith supported U.S.

military action with his "Courtesy of the Red, White, and Blue," while Haggard, a maverick who sympathized with average American workers, questioned the war and its human cost.

Some of the music reflected social changes. Singers like Kitty Wells, Loretta Lynn, Dolly Parton, and, later, Mary Chapin Carpenter articulated the sentiments of many working-class women, providing a certain feminist sensibility by "talking back" to men: "It Wasn't God Who Made Honky Tonk Angels" (Wells), "Don't Come Home A'Drinking With Lovin' on Your Mind" (Lynn), "9 to 5" (Parton), and "He Thinks He'll Keep Her" (Carpenter). Lynn, one of the most celebrated singers, was raised poor in a Kentucky coal-mining camp and married at fourteen; her music reflects her gritty mountain heritage. For example, in 1975, she released two controversial songs: "One's on the Way" and "The Pill." The first expressed the reality for many working-class women who got married and pregnant too early and were trapped in the tedium and drudgery of their lives; the second endorsed the birth control pill.

Through the 1970s and 1980s, with increasing number of fans in the West, Midwest, and even parts of the Northeast, country music diversified. Some country musicians absorbed folk and singer-songwriter influences, often with an acoustic sound and an emphasis on lyrics. One pioneer of this strand was Emmylou Harris, who began as a folksinger but then integrated folk, rock, and bluegrass into country. Many of these singer-songwriters have been folkish storytellers, often from Texas, with intensely loyal followings, like Steve Earle, Guy Clark, Lyle Lovett, Tom Russell, and Townes Van Zandt.

Like Williams, Van Zandt died too young from reckless substance use.

An even more radical challenge to Nashville came from the "Outlaws," mostly based in Austin, Texas; Austin became a rival to Nashville with a grittier, more eclectic music scene, often showcased on the popular Public Broadcasting Service (PBS) series "Austin City Limits." The "Outlaws" rebelled against the Nashville formula, production techniques, and clean-cut image, favoring an edgier sound influenced by folk, blues, Western swing, rock, and honky-tonk traditions. Willie Nelson and Waylon Jennings, longhaired, bearded, and jeans-wearing, were the leaders, demanding creative control and mostly using acoustic instruments. They and their comrades, including Johnny Cash and Kris Kristofferson, idolized Hank Williams and Bob Wills as well as cowboys (as symbols of restless freedom) and avoided the celebrity culture of Nashville. Nelson still has a devoted following. Later the folk, rockabilly, Western swing, cowboy, and bluegrass-tinged music of Harris, the Texans, Haggard, and others with a rougher sound became known as "alternative country" or "Americana" music, a category separate from and more inclusive than Nashville country but with a much smaller fan base.

In the early 21st century, some of the most inventive country music comes from the women in Nashville and Austin, including singer-songwriters like Kathy Mattea, Suzie Bogguss, Nanci Griffith, Pam Tillis, Mary Chapin Carpenter, Iris DeMent, Roseann Cash, and Gillian Welch, all of whom write their own material. Most are college educated and were influenced by folk music. Some of their music provides a challenge to male chauvinism or uncaring politicians. The bluegrass-influenced Dixie Chicks became immensely popular by playing on sex appeal while offering music with attitude. This attitude got them in trouble when lead singer Natalie Maines's public criticism of her fellow Texan, President George W. Bush, for launching the Iraq War prompted many country fans to abandon the Chicks and radio stations to ban their songs, but also increased their appeal to urban and college audiences.

Only in the 1990s would country music attract a large urban and suburban middle-class audience around the nation, aided by the development of Country Music Television and hundreds of radio stations with a country format. This development has come with the transformation of the Nashville Sound into New Country, a slick, polished, pop-influenced style without much grit that purists, such as the fans of Haggard and Nelson, criticize as a betrayal of country music traditions. Young, attractive superstars use showmanship, video images, and their celebrity lifestyles to leave behind the rural Southern hayseed image of earlier country music. This is the style of Reba McEntire, who later became a television star, Shania Twain, and Faith Hill, as well as male singers, often wearing cowboy hats, including George Strait, Randy Travis, Vince Gill, Travis Tritt, Trace Adkins, Kenny Chesney, and Garth Brooks. Brooks became the major male country superstar, the top selling solo artist in U.S. history, and attracted huge concert audiences by adapting his stage show to replicate the dynamics of a stadium rock show. New Country favorites Twain and Hill exude sex appeal.

These musicians have brought country into the pop music mainstream, with a presence on adult contemporary radio stations. Meanwhile, various traditionalists with a less pop-oriented sound, such as Alan Jackson and Dwight Yoakum, also have found a following. Jackson's songs contain humor ("She's Got the Rhythm and I've Got the Blues") and often address the small-town roots of country music, as in "Little Man." Like rock and pop music, the country music industry has fragmented into several styles—pop-flavored New Country, the traditionalists, Americana, bluegrass—each with their own fan base and set of celebrities. *See also*: **Jazz and Blues**; **Rock and Pop**; **Television's Role**.

Craig A. Lockard

For Further Reading

Escott, Colin. *Lost Highway: The True Story of Country Music*. Washington, DC: Smithsonian Press, 2003.

Malone, Bill C. *Country Music, U.S.A.* 2nd rev. ed. Austin: University of Texas Press, 2002.

Oermann, Robert K. *America's Music: The Roots of Country*. Atlanta, GA: Turner Publishing, 1996.

Willman, Chris. *Rednecks and Bluenecks: The Politics of Country Music*. New York: The New Press, 2005.

CRIMINALS

Like it or not, celebrity has its dark side, wherein certain criminals become celebrities, either temporary or more nearly permanent, depending on the nature and scope of their misdeeds. The person who holds up a convenience store or who breaks into houses by dark of night is not likely to attract much public interest, nor is the embezzler or the extortionist or the clever rascal who robs people via computer fraud. The criminals who ascend to the status of "dark-side celebrities" tend to be key figures in organized crime, serial killers, or other kinds of mass murderers, or religious leaders who use their special position for criminal purposes and when caught are revealed as moral hypocrites.

Gangsters and Mafia

Of all the many kinds of criminals busily plying their trades, those who have most interested moviemakers, and through them, the rest of American society, are the gangsters who have risen

Convicted murderer Charles Manson appears in handcuffs. Courtesy of Photofest.

to the top of organized crime. Surely the greatest celebrity of this sort was Alphonse "Scarface Al" Capone, who died in 1947 following a spectacular career in bootlegging, smuggling, and influence-buying as head of what became known as "The Chicago Outfit." His colorful nickname and smiling public face, the immense scope of his criminal dealings, and his frequent shootouts with rival underworld figures rendered him perfect copy for media consumers. Another Prohibition-era gangster, deceased in the 1950s, was George "Machine Gun" Kelly. The capture of Kelly by the Federal Bureau of Investigation did much to enhance the reputation—the institutional celebrity—of that government agency and its "G-Men."

Most colorful and most exploited by Hollywood of all organized criminals have been the Italian American organized crime figures collectively known as the Mafia, the Cosa Nostra, or simply, the mob. By the later years of the 1900s, U.S. law enforcement had managed to reduce the influence of these mob "families," even though these organizations are far from having been completely eradicated. Other mob celebrities who died in the second half of the 20th century include Charles "Lucky" Luciano, who specialized in heroin and morphine distribution, operating out of New York; Frank Costello, who took over the Luciano family and became the "boss of bosses" in the United States; Peter "Horseface" Licavoli, a Detroit "Don," or family head, who controlled mob operations in the Midwest; Vito "Don Vito" Genovese and his "pupil," Carlo "Don Carlo" Gambino, who went on to found his own powerful mob family; Sam

"Momo" Giancana, a Chicago mob boss; Carmine "Lilo" Galante of New York's Bonanno crime family; Tony "Big Tuna" Accardo, in Chicago; Simone "Sam the Plummer" DeCavalcante in New Jersey; Joseph "Joey" Gallo, a New York mobster who built cooperative bridges with African American criminals; and Anthony "Tony the Ant" Spilotro, a Chicago enforcer remembered for his Las Vegas casino operations. All these men were dead by the end of the 1900s, having provided America's mainly peaceful media consumers a spectacular, bloody trail of irresistible mayhem so very different from their everyday lives.

Two Mafia deaths of 2002 were John Gotti and Giuseppe "Joe Bonanas" Bonanno, both of New York. The handsome Gotti, who courted publicity and who was a natty dresser, was known as "The Dapper Don" and, for his longstanding ability to "beat the rap," as "The Teflon Don." Gotti's luck eventually ran out, and he died in prison. Bonanno, unusual among Mafiosi in that he disliked his nickname, headed his own crime family. Also unusual was Vincent "The Chin" Gigante, who died in 2005. His huge frame matched his last name, and the ex-boxer, who was for some time head of New York's Genovese family, did his best to stay out of prison by wandering the streets of Greenwich Village dressed in slippers and bathrobe, muttering and gesturing wildly in order to line up the insanity defense. In 2003, Gigante admitted that his apparently crazed wanderings were a ruse, and he died in prison. Other Mafia figures who attracted heavy publicity and are still living as of 2008 include Carmine "The Snake" Persico, a head of the Colombo family; Salvatore "Sammy the Bull" Gravano, who broke mob tradition and turned informant in the early 1990s; and Jimmy "The Weasel" Fratianno, a Los Angeles and Cleveland crime boss who also became an informant in the 1990s.

These men, and others like them, have provided the raw material for Hollywood's treatment of the Mafia. Although the mob is on hard times compared with its glory days, it lives on in popular culture through many movies and television series. Some observers have compared the pop-culture mystique of the Mafia to that of the Old West. Both genres involved the use of guns to settle things, and both featured strongmen who did not need others to protect them and were not hamstrung by society's conventions. Also, both genres showed individuals who often were pictured as the societal underdog, the lone man who by raw power has to "fight the system." As America changed from predominantly rural to urban, mobster movies gradually took over from the earlier, frontier-based Westerns. Two pioneering gangster movies were *Little Caesar* (1931), starring a scowling Edward G. Robinson, and *Scarface* (1932), in which Paul Muni's title role was based on Al Capone. Since that time, many gangster movies have been made, but standouts that helped preserve the Mafia mystique include *Key Largo* (1948), *The Black Hand* (1950), *Al Capone* (1959), and *The Brotherhood* (1968). Films such as these, plus television shows like *The Untouchables* (1959–1963) paved the way for the success of the best Mafia movie of them all, *The Godfather* (1972) and its two sequels, which told the story of the fictitious Sicilian American family the

Corleones. More recently, the popular HBO (Home Box Office) series *The Sopranos*, which premiered in 1999, has kept the mob mystique on the public mind. Recent Mafia movies have included *Goodfellas* (1990), *The Funeral* (1996), *Analyze This* (1999), and its sequel, *Analyze That* (2002). In an increasingly polarized America, it is easy for ordinary people to feel forgotten or ignored and to fantasize about being, or making use of, a powerful godfather who will make his followers' enemies his own. Popular as they are, Mafia-based movies and television shows have not been without their critics. Various Italian American interest groups, such as the Order of the Sons of Italy, have complained that these films and shows cause other Americans to see all Italians as inherently criminal and untrustworthy. Still, Italian Americans not only attend, but also act in, these shows and films, and Italy itself remains a favorite destination of the American tourist.

Serial and Spree Killers

Even more gruesome than organized crime and its popularity with fans is the public attention lavished on mass murderers. Leading the pack in number of victims, in America, at least, are Timothy McVeigh and his accomplice Terry Nichols, responsible for the deaths of 168 people in the 1995 bombing of the Federal Building in Oklahoma City. In second place is Gary Ridgeway, the so-called Green River Killer of Washington State, thought to have killed forty-eight. Sadly, the number of serial or spree killers has grown in recent decades, but among those who became dark-side celebrities have been handsome Ted Bundy, serial killer of thirty-five young women; Chicago's John Wayne Gacy, who enjoyed entertaining children while dressed as a circus clown but killed thirty-three boys and young men; spree killer Seung-Hui Cho, who shot and killed thirty-two victims at Virginia Tech on April 16, 2007; cannibalistic Jeffrey Dahmer, killer of seventeen men and boys; Robert Hansen, who kidnapped, raped, and murdered fifteen prostitutes; and Charles Whitman, the "Texas Tower Shooter," spree killer of fourteen in 1966 in addition to killing his own wife and mother. Individuals who killed fewer victims but who received unusually heavy media attention include Chicago's Richard Speck, killer of eight student nurses; hippie commune leader Charles Manson, found guilty of the highly publicized Tate-LaBianca murders in 1969; and antihomosexual, antiabortion survivalist bomber Eric Rudolph, who killed three but injured around 150. Sadly, some dim but well-meaning people regarded Rudolph as a folk hero, at least until he was captured in 2003.

Not a killer, but a criminal who, although more than likely dead since 1971, continues to intrigue people today, is Dan "D. B." Cooper, who hijacked a Boeing 727, was paid a ransom of $200,000, and jumped with his loot from the plane over a remote and rugged region of Washington State. Two serial killers captured in 2002 were John Allen Muhammad and his young accomplice Lee Boyd Malvo, the Beltway Snipers, who shot and killed ten random victims that year. Gaining his primary celebrity forty-one years after the three murders for which he was partly responsible was

Edgar Ray Killen. Killen had been a Baptist minister and Ku Klux Klan organizer in Mississippi until the 1964 deaths of three civil rights activists for which he was convicted of manslaughter in 2005.

Religious Leaders

Many religious leaders have embarrassing moral lapses, but some have also broken the law and have been held accountable for their crimes. One such individual is Jim Bakker, who with his then-wife Tammy Faye Bakker, became well known on the Rev. Pat Robertson's television program *The 700 Club*. The couple then founded their own organization, The PTL Club, which stood for "Praise the Lord," although critics said it should be "Pass the Loot." The Bakkers built a Christian theme park, Heritage USA, in Fort Mill, South Carolina, and via their own satellite system, solicited contributions from viewers while, without apparent shame, spending lavish sums on themselves. They were investigated for making bogus offers, thanks in part to investigative reporting done by *The Charlotte Observer*, and in 1987, Bakker was charged with making payments to a young woman named Jessica Hahn to keep her from suing him for rape, bringing about his resignation. He was found guilty of mail fraud, wire fraud, and conspiracy and sentenced to forty-five years in prison, but he was granted parole after having served five years. He now has a new television show produced in Branson, Missouri.

Sun Myung Moon, founder of the Unification Church, was found guilty in 1982 for filing false income tax forms, a fine how-do-you-do for someone who claims to be the Second Coming of Christ. The Korean-born Moon moved to the Untied States—the land of opportunity—in 1971 and became an outspoken supporter of Republican presidential candidates, especially Richard Nixon and Ronald Reagan. Among his many business properties is the *Washington Times* newspaper, published in the nation's capital.

A polygamist Mormon fundamentalist who ordered his followers to kill a number of people in the 1970s was Ervil LeBaron, who died in prison in 1981. In 1979, the wife of L. Ron Hubbard, Scientology's founder, was found guilty of wiretapping and theft of documents from offices of the Internal Revenue Service. Thereafter, Mary Sue Hubbard was stricken from the rolls of that church. In 2005, Matthew Hale, head of the World Church of the Creator (also called the Creativity Movement) got forty years for attempting to arrange the murder of a federal judge. This church is a white-supremacist organization that advocates a white America purged of Jews and dark-skinned people. Executed in 2006 for ordering the killing of an entire family was Jeffrey Lundgren, who called himself a prophet of the Reorganized Church of Jesus Christ of Latter Day Saints; and imprisoned in 2007 for arranging illegal marriages between older men and very young girls was Warren Jeffs, leader of a polygamist Mormon sect called the Fundamentalist Church of Jesus Christ of Latter Day Saints. Jeffs was sentenced to ten years.

The crimes of ministers discussed above cannot hold an altar candle to the scandal that came to light in 2002 involving child abuse perpetrated by

Roman Catholic pedophile priests. The individual priest whose case brought this widespread problem into the public spotlight was Father John Geoghan of the Boston Diocese, who had been switched from parish to parish for years amid continued charges that he had sexually abused children. Eventually, Geoghan was ousted from the priesthood, tried, and imprisoned. The Church eventually settled with eighty-six of his victims for a reported $10 million. In 2002, Geoghan was strangled to death by another inmate. The Church's problems mushroomed, and more than 4,300 U.S. priests were charged with similar offenses. Their crimes have cost the Catholic Church more than $570 million in settlements, and roughly 800 U.S. priests have been removed from their ministries. The Church has apologized at the highest levels, and the U.S. Conference of Catholic Bishops created the National Review Board for the Protection of Children and Young People in an attempt to regain credibility and trust. It appears, however, that further sex-abuse charges, including those brought by abused adults, lie ahead. Sex crimes by clergy are not by any means unique to the Roman Catholic Church, yet in this religion, the problem has been most severe and dramatic, making Father Geoghan and his cardinal, Boston's Bernard Law, dark-side celebrities of considerable wattage. *See also*: **Movies' Role**; **Pseudonyms**.

Sam G. Riley

For Further Reading

Claitor, Diana. *Outlaws, Mobsters and Murderers: The Villains—The Deeds*. New York: Mallard Press, 1991.

Corrina, Joseph. *Mobsters: A Who's Who of America's Most Notorious Criminals*. North Dighton, MA: World Publications Group, 2003.

DeStefano, George. *An Offer We Can't Refuse: The Mafia in the Mind of America*. New York: Faber and Faber, 2006.

Olla, Roberto. *Godfathers: Lives and Crimes of the Mafia Mobsters*. Richmond, UK: Alma, 2007.

Paoli, Letizia. *Mafia Brotherhoods: Organized Crime, Italian Style*. Oxford and New York: Oxford University Press, 2003.

Willis, Clint. *Wise Guys: Stories of Mobsters from Jersey to Vegas*. New York: Thunder's Mouth Press, 2003.

www.newgrounds.com/bbs/topic/83723.

www.onewal.com/maf-nick.

www.priestsofdarkness.com/stats.

CRITICISMS OF CELEBRITY CULTURE

In the latter half of the 20th century, Americans began to realize that they were creating a celebrity culture, and that it was not altogether good. Parents, popular pundits, and scholars criticized the cult of celebrity and the media that brimmed with it.

One scholar declared that America's preoccupation with celebrities in the 1950s amounted to mass gossip. By the 1960s, the tabloid press had found its calling in covering the famous, with at least one historian lamenting that culture was manufacturing celebrities instead of seeking heroes. In the 1970s, celebrity coverage became an industry of its own, and the celebrity became the symbol of entertainment media as well as a target on which to lay blame for society's shortfalls.

In the 1980s, critics wondered whether the distraction of widespread entertainment would mean the demise of the culture itself. Entertainment of the 1990s was criticized by new media in addition to conventional media. By 2000, the federal government was castigating entertainment media, despite the fact that some politicians themselves had become celebrities.

In the summer of 2008, celebrity criticism reached a crescendo with Sen. John McCain, Republican presidential candidate, spearheading his attack against rival Sen. Barack Obama with scathing accusations that the Democratic senator was a celebrity. In the run-up to national convention performances, McCain counted on this accusation to carry the negative connotations of mass celebrity and to provide him with a platform for questioning the Democrat's leadership ability. McCain's accusation set off volleys of criticism and countercriticism, both of the presidential hopefuls and of celebrity itself.

The Political Is Personal

Celebrities were once widely known as movie stars, since their images on the big screen gave the actors a larger-than-life presence. The film industry built a star system, which it relied on to market movies. Television adopted the role of star-maker that the movie industry had held during the early 20th century. Alongside the growth of television

rose a fiercely image-oriented popular culture.

Those who appeared on television became celebrities, even if they were not entertainers but journalists or politicians. By the 1960s, audiences were tending to judge people's moral character by their mediated image. Richard M. Nixon attributed the loss of his first presidential bid to the fact that he did not look good on television. Politicians' activities off camera were dutifully recorded on the record by society columnists at newspapers, particularly in Washington D.C., where politicians are a mainstay of social life. But journalism was changing. Articles about politicians and socialites that ignored their flaws and *faux pas* were increasingly recognized as unpaid promotion pieces and not up to the reportorial standards of modern journalism. By the end of the 1960s, the free ride for politicians was coming to an end.

A society columnist at the *Washington Post* who wrote about politicians acquired a reputation for reporting what they said and did, even if it was the type of behavior that had been traditionally omitted from publication, such as getting stumbling drunk, yelling at the hired help, or making statements that were contrary to the politician's public platform. The social and the political are often inseparable sources of power in the nation's capital, and criticism in social situations can easily translate to loss of political clout.

Those journalists who bucked traditional promotional coverage sometimes found themselves being wooed away from critically covering celebrities to become celebrities themselves. In the 1970s, the announcement that someone was moving from working in print media to performing on television conferred instant celebrity status. But taking a job in front of the camera meant a certain loss of control over their own images; they would ever after be portrayed in the conventional media as others saw them, and in the tabloid press, as it wished to cast them. A move to the visual media created a celebrated public figure that was at the same time vulnerable to intensely personal attacks.

First impressions can be lasting impressions, particularly if they play on stereotypes, which have the power to frame subsequent coverage and perceptions. For example, depiction as a sex symbol diminishes a woman's credibility in areas of expertise, substituting the popularity of celebrity as her worth. In much the same way that a first impression frames a celebrity's public reception, a celebrity's final image can frame historical memory, such as that of Elvis Presley (the King of Rock 'n' Roll), whose final image haunts the popular psyche and encourages attempts to banish it through iterations and imitations of the youthful Elvis. With the high penetration of 21st-century technology and the democratization of celebrity ideology, impressions are becoming as fleeting as stardom itself.

Tabloids, Trades, and Commodities

The **tabloid** press that emerged in post–World War II America developed a reliance on celebrity coverage and became synonymous with a lower standard of journalism. At the heart of tabloid success is an extreme personalization of celebrities, which creates a false intimacy with the audience. Voyeuristic detail of the stars' lives that appeared in the tabloid press encouraged public criticism of their personal lives. Such controversy fueled circulation as well as box office sales. From the big screen to the smaller screen of television, and in amusements such as sports, stars became commodities on which billion-dollar industries were built.

Through a reliance on celebrity gossip for news, publications using the tabloid format, such as the *National Enquirer,* became equated with unethical information-gathering practices and sensational content. Privacy was invaded, quotes were created, and photographs were manipulated. While most celebrities were said to ignore tabloid gossip, some stars, such as comedienne Carol Burnett, brought successful libel lawsuits against tabloids for printing false information. Those working in the mainstream press heaped criticism on the tabloids to create a journalistic distance, contrasting their own efforts against the lowbrow press to define conventional publications as the nation's legitimate journalism. Yet, for the tabloids, professional censure and unreliable content did not translate to a decline in circulation. Their popularity skyrocketed, with circulation peaking in the 1980s, as the decline in readership of the legitimate press was beginning its slide in earnest.

As technology was reshaping celebrity culture in the 1990s, and *People* magazine and *Entertainment Tonight* were mainstays of popular consumption, advertisers were criticizing the business-to-business publications of the entertainment industry for being behind the times. When long-standing trade publications such as *Variety* began to address the industry in the context of its technological restructuring, advertisers again criticized the trade magazines, not for lack of coverage but perhaps lack of understanding, stating that they were perpetuating negative coverage of technology and the changes it was bringing to the entertainment industry.

Youth at Risk

With the emergence of each new medium, concern over its potential to corrupt children has driven criticism of celebrity culture. In the 1950s, a psychiatrist wrote a bestselling book on the dangers of comic books and their superheroes, saying that their vulgarity and violence could influence young readers and override parental authority. Television took control of content further out of parents' hands by bringing its own visual storytelling into the family living room, and color television could draw children into its reality even more effectively. Criticisms of media's danger to children resurfaced with the advent of the **Internet** and easy access to unfiltered global communications through unsupervised computer terminals.

High profiles carry high expectations, but with celebrities, the American work ethic has been shown shortcutting the American Dream. Larger-than-life celebrities with images cast as role models are rewarded for behaving badly. Many people have questioned the legitimacy of elevating stars as cultural success stories, even when they display illegal or what many Americans consider immoral behavior. The presumption of noble character as the complement to physical prowess has time and again been misplaced. Regardless of behavior, professional

athletes are often allowed to engage in high-profile competition, while parents wrestle with buying their children designer athletic wear emblazoned with monikers of the fallen heroes.

Celebrity status has meant ubiquitous presence and youth appeal for hosts of entertainment figures. Parents deride stars who appeal to the young when these celebrities do not model appropriate behavior, which includes the way they dress. Criticism is leveled at the **fashion** industry, which makes available clothing that imitates stars' attire, particularly when it produces school outfits for young girls that more resemble the traditional wear of prostitutes or female impersonators. With this backing of sports, entertainment, fashion, and the promotional complex, in commercial culture, celebrities often command far more power than their critics.

Comparisons with other occupations have often cast cultural priorities into question. Celebrities draw criticism because of their salaries, which are much higher than common laborers, professional service providers, and even many executives. Commonly cited in these debates is the example that teachers are required to take on increased responsibility with fewer resources and no financial gain, while stars abdicate social responsibility and sign multi-million-dollar contracts.

Many people have expressed concern that celebrities and the industries they represent are subverting the core values of American culture. At the turn of the century, the federal government was leveling criticism at the entertainment industry. It cited the media's violent content and their practices of marketing entertainment and advertising products to children as reasons for increased regulation and federal oversight. Fears of children's unfettered access to the Internet have fueled similar criticisms of media content and business practices in recent years.

Danger to Democracy

Critics have lamented the fall from hero to media personality in an exponentially expanding cultural iconography. Unlike archetypal heroes whose stories ennobled a population, celebrities are manufactured by society to reflect a fictionalized self more cosmetically attuned than grandly idealized. Widespread is the industry practice of creating celebrities to represent complex issues in simplified terms to secure audience identification and consumer loyalty. The phenomenon of celebrity creation has helped to craft the perception that the complexities of 21st-century culture can seemingly be understood through the visual language of celebrity images.

Stars are created in much the same manner that manufactured public relations events are now considered news. And news, particularly journalism embedded in the entertainment medium of television, is itself entertainment. In a profit-driven society, news has become just another product. When news content is not about the personal lives of celebrities or delivered by edgy celebrities, it does not rise to the top in the new marketplace of images, which has replaced the marketplace of ideas. But the business of maintaining a democracy relies on an informed and active population, not on its entertainment value.

Tabloids, and their competitive carryover, the tabloidization of the conventional media, have been blamed for dumbing down culture. Critics have decried for decades Americans' preoccupation with entertainment. The citizenry no longer cares about, or cares to participate in, the business of culture, unless it is the entertainment business. A shift in the 21st century has been to a democratizing of celebrities. Television shows that create stars through amateur competitions have attained enormous popularity, as have so-called **reality television** series, which employ common people instead of the big-name actors and expose them to mass audiences. Critiqued as a propagation of mediocrity, such shows and their newly minted stars are produced in a media context driven by competition with the Internet.

The Internet has enabled more mass audience and content producers and generated more gossip than could have been imagined by the 1950s critics of the tabloid press. Yet, in the early 21st century, the conventional press is under corporate control, and so it does not possess the unencumbered voice to criticize the mediocrity driving the marketplace. As the bottom line becomes the top priority, conventional media are losing the resources to countermand an increased emphasis on entertainment and the predominance of the uninformed individual as cultural spokesperson.

In the early 21st century, the star-making machinery is being transferred to another screen, that of the Internet, which is driving a digital democratization of celebrity status as well as intensification in criticism. Celebrities jockey for star positioning in a multimedia environment, with Internet start-ups seeking old-school stars and traditional media hunting brand new Web celebrities for the survival of their dwindling profit margin. Internet users create Web logs about celebrities and blog to gossip about and criticize their favorite stars' latest indiscretions. Individuals use social networking to propagate, and to despair over, the latest celebrity rumors. Numerous Web sites have been created for the purpose of mocking stars and casting aspersions on celebrity culture.

A dim host of self-nominated stars is shifting the Internet from an information highway to an entertainment strip. Individuals revel in the lack of intermediaries as they put themselves and their creations onto the Web for global consumption and a glimmer of stardom. Critics condemn the onslaught of unfiltered information and the instantaneous conferral of celebrity status in a communications environment in which scatological humor draws accolades.

Critics fret that this cluttered cosmos is the democratic ideal gone terribly wrong. Therefore, placing a political rival in the context of celebrities and socialites is positioning him or her in an array of flickering stars that serve as guideposts to a future as elusive as their own stardom. While such accusations provide grudging acknowledgment of the rival's star status, they also carry the threat that that very celebrity could be the downfall of democracy. *See also*: **Arrests of Celebrities; Magazines' Role; Movies' Role; News Media Figures; Politics; Television's Role**.

Therese L. Lueck

For Further Reading

Boorstin, Daniel J. *The Image: A Guide to Pseudo-Events in America*. 5th ed., rep. New York: Atheneum, 1975.

Lowenthal, Leo. "The Triumph of Mass Idols." In *Literature, Popular Culture, and Society*, 109–140. Englewood Cliffs, NJ: Prentice-Hall, Inc., 1961.

Macdonald, Myra. "Rethinking Personalization in Current Affairs Journalism." In *Tabloid Tales: Global Debates over Media Standards*, edited by Colin Sparks and John Tulloch, 251–266. New York: Rowman & Littlefield, 2000.

Neimark, Jull. "The Culture of Celebrity." *Psychology Today* May/June (1995): 54–57, 84.

Postman, Neil. *Amusing Ourselves to Death: Public Discourse in the Age of Show Business*. New York: Viking, 1985.

Rathesar, Romesh, and Joel Stein. "Everyone's a Star.Com." *Time* (March 27, 2000): 70–76.

Schickel, Richard. *Intimate Strangers: The Culture of Celebrity in America*. 2nd ed., rep. Chicago: Ivan R. Dee, 2000.

www.tmz.com.

CULINARY

The modern celebrity chef came of age in the television era in which mass audiences salivated over the culinary creations of James Beard, Julia Child, and, later, Emeril Lagasse and Rachel Ray. Yet the celebrity chef predated television by more than 100 years. In 1829, uppercrust Parisians flocked to taste Antonin Careme's revolutionary recipes in the first "age of gastronomy," when great chefs were celebrities, at least in France. Variations of Careme's dishes—for example, his *Potage a la Regance* and *Perche a la Hollandaise*—are still served around the world.

In the 21st century, the most well-known chefs are television stars. For example, Lagasse, known by his first name Emeril, has been called the "cooking Elvis." By age forty-four, the personable chef had amassed a cooking empire of restaurants, cookbooks, television shows, and branded products worth many millions.

James Beard, called the "father of American cooking," experimented with his own television show, *I Love to Cook*, in 1946 and 1947 before founding the influential James Beard Cooking School in the mid-1950s. But it was Julia Child who became the first American celebrity television chef. At age fifty in 1963, she debuted her show *The French Chef* on public television and pulled American viewers into a world of new, exciting foods.

Others followed Child's lead, including British-born Graham Kerr, who became the "Galloping Gourmet" in the 1960s, and Martha Stewart, whose media empire was built on the simmering stock of her 1980s televised cooking lessons. The Food Network debuted in 1993, feeding its audience's appetite for new, interesting cuisine. Viewers could become vicarious gourmets without any knowledge of food or cooking.

But is the modern celebrity chef indicative of a true gastronomic revolution? Critics argue that televised cooking shows simply offer consumption-based fantasy and make cooking appear simpler than it is in reality. Others argue that celebrity chefs have

Celebrity chef Emeril Lagasse autographs cookbooks, October 2006. Courtesy of U.S. Army.

brought new people into the kitchen, introducing them to the joys of cooking.

Other celebrity chefs include Cajun cuisine specialists Justin Wilson and Paul Prudhomme; Jeff Smith, television's "Frugal Gourmet"; Savannah's Paula Dean; and California's Giada De Laurentiis. Television has turned cooking into a ball game–like competition on the show Iron Chef America, featuring Bobby Flay, Catherine "Cat" Cora, and others.

Celebrities among America's "foodies" are such chefs as Patrick O'Connell of the Inn at Little Washington in Washington, Virginia, and Thomas Keller of The French Laundry restaurant in Yountville, California. Famed chef-owners of restaurant chains include Michael Mina and Wolfgang Puck. *See also*: **Corporate Celebrity**; **Television's Role**.

Janice Hume

For Further Reading

Adema, Pauline. "Vicarious Consumption: Food, Television and the Ambiguity of Modernity." *Journal of American and Comparative Cultures* 23, no. 3 (Fall 2000).

de Ravel, Anne. *Cooking on the Road with Celebrity Chefs*. Ventura, CA: Woodall, 2006.

Ketchum, Cheri. "The Essence of Cooking Shows: How the Food Network Constructs Consumer Fantasies." *Journal of Communication Inquiry* 29, no. 3 (July 2005): 217–134.

Lurie, Karen. *TV Chefs*. Los Angeles, CA: Renaissance Books, 1999.

Rossant, Juliette. *Super Chef: The Making of the Great Modern Restaurant Empires*. New York: Free Press, 2004.

CULT FILMS AND FIGURES

A cult film attracts a devoted group of followers or obsessive fans, often despite being a financial or critical flop on initial release. There is no "cult film genre"; these movies range in taste and style as well as form and content. Cult films can become the source of a thriving, elaborate subculture, and they develop cult followings because of their production values, strange narratives, memorable and quotable dialogue, eccentric or quirky characters, or shocking subject matter.

There films include cult Westerns (*Johnny Guitar*, 1954); cult musicals (*The Sound of Music*, 1965; *The Rocky Horror Picture Show*, 1975); cult drug movies (*Reefer Madness*, 1936; *Easy Rider*, 1969); cult teen movies (*American Graffiti*, 1973; *Animal House*, 1978; *Ferris Bueller's Day Off*, 1986; *Dazed and Confused*, 1993); cult blaxploitation films (*Sweet Sweetback's Baadasssss Song*, 1971; *Shaft*, 1971; *Foxy Brown*, 1974); Japanese horror cult movies (*Godzilla*, 1954); sword and sandal cult films (*Hercules*, 1959); and others considered cult because they are simply strange or evoke a unique mood or atmosphere (*Harold and Maude*, 1971; *Pee-wee's Big Adventure*, 1985; *The Big Lebowski*, 1998). Some cult films blur genres or explode their rules (*Alien*, 1979; *Blazing Saddles*, 1974). Probably the most popular

Tim Curry appears in his iconic role in The Rocky Horror Picture Show, *1975. Courtesy of Photofest.*

genres that become cult films are horror, science-fiction, and fantasy films because of their out-of-reality premises.

Cult film figures usually are admired by a devoted group of fans, and they, too, defy clear-cut classifications. Actor Christopher Walken is famous, but as a cult film figure, Walken is better known for his quirky mannerisms. Lon Chaney, Sr. was known as "The Man of a Thousand Faces." Vincent Price, who could be counted on for his eloquent voice and droll attitude, made cult films ranging from low-budget Roger Corman adaptations of Poe's tales, horror films like *House of Wax* (1953) or *The Fly* (1958), and *Dr. Goldfoot and the Bikini Machine* (1965). Other actors have attained cult status for their characters: Lon Chaney, Junior, (*The Wolf Man,* 1941), Bela Lugosi (*Dracula,* 1931), Boris Karloff (*Frankenstein,* 1931, *The Mummy,* 1932); and, more recently, Harris Glenn Milstead, better

known by his drag persona Divine (*Pink Flamingos,* 1972; *Polyester,* 1981; *Hairspray,* 1988); Pam Grier (*Foxy Brown,* 1974); Brad Dourif (voice of Chucky in *Child's Play,* 1988); and Ron Perlman (*Hellboy,* 2004; *Quest for Fire,* 1981).

Directors also attain cult film figure status. Quentin Tarantino created nonlinear storylines and idealized violence in films such as *Reservoir Dogs* (1992), *Pulp Fiction* (1994), and *Kill Bill* (Vol. 1, 2003, Vol. 2, 2004). Ed Wood won a posthumous Golden Turkey Award as the worst director ever for such cult films as *Glen or Glenda?* (1953) and *Plan 9 from Outer Space* (1959), often referred to as the worst movie ever. Roger Corman developed low-budget exploitation cult films such as *Little Shop of Horrors* (1960) and *The Wild Angels* (1966). Russ Meyer is revered for campy sexploitation movies like *Faster, Pussycat! Kill! Kill!* (1966). Tom Laughlin commented on social and political issues while developing his near-mythic, enigmatic hero in *The Born Losers* (1967) and *Billy Jack* (1971). David Lynch's *Blue Velvet* (1986) was both film noir and surrealistic. John Waters developed the Dreamlanders, an acting group responsible for **kitsch** and eccentric cult films like *Pink Flamingos* (1972), *Polyester* (1981), and *Hairspray* (1988). George Romero's *Night of the Living Dead* (1968) inaugurated a zombie-apocalypse craze. The Coen Brothers—Joel (director) and Ethan (producer)—offer quirky, offbeat cult films such as *Raising Arizona* (1987), *Fargo* (1996), and *The Big Lebowski* (1998). Sam Raimi offered the cartoon-like, splatter-filled *Evil Dead* (1983). Frank Darabont's allegorical, life-affirming prison story *The*

Shawshank Redemption (1994) gained cult status on video release. Some cult films and their directors achieve special recognition. For example, David Lynch's avant-garde *Eraserhead* (1977), selected as culturally, historically, or aesthetically significant by the U.S. Library of Congress, is preserved in the National Film Registry. The same is true for Alfred Hitchcock's suspense-horror film *Psycho* (1960), with its legendary scenes that received four Academy Award nominations.

And then there are the cult film characters themselves, those who transcend their initial stories and live on as costumes, toys, novels, comic books, video games, action figures, collectibles, poster idols, and pop-culture references.

These characters include the monsters from Universal Studios: Frankenstein, Dracula, the Werewolf, the Mummy, the Invisible Man, the Creature from the Black Lagoon, and the Phantom of the Opera. After film series of their own, *Alien* (1979) and *Predator* (1987) demonstrated crossover power of two large franchises in 2004's *Alien vs. Predator*. A litany of nightmarish, undead serial killers, many inspired by Hitchcock's *Psycho*, are exemplified by Freddy Krueger (the wisecracking burned-alive character from *A Nightmare on Elm Street* series, 1984–2003); Chucky (a murderer whose soul gets stuck in a doll, featured in four films beginning with *Child's Play*, 1988); Jason Voorhees (the hockey-mask slasher of eleven *Friday the 13th* films, 1980–2003; in the last one, a crossover film clashed Jason with Freddy); Michael Myers (psychotic killer star of nine *Halloween* slasher films, 1978–2007); Hannibal Lecter, M.D.

(cannibalistic serial killer and star of five films, made most famous by Anthony Hopkin's Academy Award–winning performance in *Silence of the Lambs*, 1991); the Jigsaw Killer (a dying man who kidnaps victims and places them in brutal tests, *Saw* series, four films 2004–2007); Leatherface (main character with a human-skin mask, blood-soaked butcher's apron, and chainsaw featured in nine *Texas Chainsaw Massacre* slasher films, 1974–2006); *Puppet Master* (puppet maker brings puppets to evil life, ten films, 1989–2004); and Pinhead (*Hellraiser*, seven films, 1987–2005).

A group of cult film figures resulted from exploitation of nature's unknowns or the dangers from space. King Kong (1933) became a cultural icon. Ray Harryhausen's creations, including the fictional Rhedosaurus, awakened from the Arctic Circle by an atomic bomb test in *The Beast From 20,000 Fathoms* (1953), began the "creature features" that reflected nuclear fear. The Japanese monsters often fought each other, beginning with the mutated prehistoric lizard Godzilla (originally *Gojira*, 1954) that established the kaiju film (translated as "strange beast"). This was followed by other strange environmentally mutated or newly discovered monsters such as Rodan (a pseudo-pteranodon, 1956); Gamera (a flying pseudo-turtle, 1965); Mothra (a giant butterfly-moth, 1961); Ghidorah (Godzilla's greatest foe, a three-headed, two-tailed, winged golden dragon space monster, 1964); and Hedorah, the Smog Monster (1971). Ridley Scott's *Alien* (1979) antagonist was a highly aggressive extraterrestrial creature who stalks and kills a spaceship crew. The giant great white shark of Steven Spielberg's *Jaws* (1975) created panic at the seashores, while *Tremors* (1990) offered Graboids, subterranean worm creatures that terrorize a small town.

All cult figures are not monsters, though. James Cameron's *Terminator* (1984) featured a cyborg assassin sent back from the future by intelligent machines to kill a future hero; however, in a sequel, a reprogrammed Terminator returned to protect the same human. The comedy *Beetlejuice* (1988) introduced a bio-exorcist hired by a dead couple who want to remove the new owners of their house. *Harold and Maude* (1971) featured a morbid younger man and an energetic, impulsive senior citizen. Beach movies were popular in the 1960s, representing surfing, **rock** and roll, and beach bunnies; cult figures included *Gidget* (1959) and Annette Funicelo and Frankie Avalon (who teamed up with Funicelo in several films, including *Beach Blanket Bingo*, 1965). The Superheroes (Superman, Batman, the Toxic Avenger, the Crow, Spiderman, and the XMen) possess superhuman abilities and demonstrate them in action-packed films. Biker movies, usually in which the biker is an outlaw or rebel, are represented by *The Wild One* (1953) and the drug-dealing, counterculture cyclists in *Easy Rider* (1969). Frank the Bunny with *Donnie Darko* (2001) predicts the world's end. Frank Capra's *It's a Wonderful Life* (1946) features suicidal George Bailey, who, on Christmas Eve, is shown the value of his life. Perhaps the best-known cult film figure, though, is the Dr. Frank-N-Furter the sweet Transsexual Transylvania transvestite in *The Rocky Horror Picture Show* (1975), a bizarre musical parody that still packs theatres with participating audiences in midnight showings.

Cult films were given wider exposure by the American cult television comedy series *Mystery Science Theater 3000* (MST3K, 1988–1999). The series featured a man and his robot sidekicks trapped in space by an evil scientist, forced to watch a selection of terrible movies. They kept sane by offering a running, wisecracking commentary on the film. During its 198 episodes and one feature film, MST3K attained a loyal fan base, a 1993 Peabody Award, and several Emmy nominations. Another source of information about cult movies is the May 23, 2003, issue of *Entertainment Weekly*, which published a list of the Top 50 Cult Movies.

The Cult Film Archive is located at Brunel University in London, England (http://www.brunel.ac.uk/about/acad/sa/artresearch/smrc/cultfilm/). In addition to a large library of cult films, books, slides, stills, posters, and soundtracks, the Archive's collection also contains 600 hours of exclusive interview footage of leading cult film figures from around the world.

Cult movie figures, along with their movies, break the rules of good and bad taste, just as they challenge genre conventions. For a film, its director, or cast to achieve cult status, viewers must see it as out of the ordinary in a difficult-to-describe fashion. An aura holds fascination for those who are drawn to these films. These viewers become so fiercely devoted that they want to spread the word. *See also*: **Comedy**; **Movies' Role**; **Television's Role**.

Beth M. Waggenspack

For Further Reading

Havis, Allen. *Cult Films: Taboo and Transgression*. Lanham, MD: University Press of America, 2008.

Mathijs, Ernest, and Jamie Sexton. *Cult Cinema: An Introduction,* Boston: Blackwell, 2009.

Mathijs, Ernest, and Jamie Sexton. *The Cult Film Reader*. New York: Open University Press, 2007.

Paul, Louis, and Tom Weaver. *Tales from the Cult Film Trenches: Interviews with 36 Actors from Horror, Science Fiction and Exploitation Cinema*. Jefferson, NC: McFarland, 2007.

D

DANCERS

While still appreciated in some quarters, dance is not at the apex of its popularity in the first decade of the 2000s. Few dancers of any kind currently enjoy the level of celebrity of, say, **hiphop and rap** artists, **rock and pop** performers, **country and Western** singers, actors and actresses, or **athletes**.

This is especially true where ballet or the serious arts of any kind are concerned. Seldom do top ballet stars command the enormous following necessary to top-level celebrity. One such dancer who beat the odds and scaled the celebrity heights was Rudolf Nureyev, who was born in Siberia, became a star in Russia with the Kirov Ballet, and defected to the West in 1961. He performed both ballet and modern dance in the United States, was in a number of movies, and was well connected socially, yet became a wealthy recluse before dying of AIDS in 1993. The only male ballet dancer to achieve celebrity similar to Nureyev's has been another Russian from the Kirov: Mikhail Baryshnikov, who

defected in 1974. Like Nureyev, he also danced in films. Unlike Nureyev, who spent much of his time in Austria, Italy, and France, Baryshnikov has worked mainly in New York.

The prima ballerinas who have gained the most acclaim with U.S. audiences have been English dancer Margot Fonteyn, a favorite Nureyev partner; Patricia McBride, who danced with Baryshnikov; and U.S. dancer Suzanne Farrell, associated with Washington, D.C.'s Kennedy Center since her 1983 retirement from performing.

Show-business dancers, whose work is naturally more accessible to larger audiences, have also been on the decline so far as full-scale celebrity is concerned. The great post-1950 dancers of the movies, stage, or clubs were preceded by great talents who were even better known in their day. Two such African American performers were Bill "Bojangles" Robinson, who danced mainly for black audiences during his long career, and Josephine Baker, a U.S.-born dancer and singer who in 1937 became a citizen of France but who danced in America as recently as

Athletic dancer Gene Kelly shows off his gravity-defying abilities in this 1950 publicity shot. Courtesy of Photofest.

the early 1970s. Another was Irish-American Jimmy Cagney, who played **tough guy** movie roles and also danced with furious energy in the 1942 movie *Yankee Doodle Dandy*.

A great star from the late 1920s through the 1970s was Fred Astaire (born Frederick Austerlitz). Skinny by present-day standards for leading men, Astaire starred in many musicals and other films and was a fashion icon as well as a consummate dancer. A song and dance man of Broadway, Las Vegas, and Hollywood was Sammy Davis, Jr., often remembered as a member of singer Dean Martin's hard-drinking "Rat Pack" in the 1960s. Heavily influenced by Davis was the more recent tap dancer and singer Gregory Hines, who died a decade after his award-winning role in the 1993 film *Jelly's Last Jam*. Influenced in turn by Hines is tap sensation Savion Glover,

who starred in *Bring in da Noise, Bring in da Funk* in 1996.

Many U.S. fans of Hollywood musicals might well name as their favorite dancer *Singin' in the Rain* (1952) star Gene Kelly. This muscular yet graceful dancer worked on Broadway in the 1930s and became a hit in Hollywood in the 1940s, though his greatest roles came in the early 1950s. Also dancing in *Singin' in the Rain* was Donald O'Connor, and an electrifying dancer in the musical films *Seven Brides for Seven Brothers* (1954) and *West Side Story* (1961) was Russ Tamblyn. More recent dancing celebrities include long-legged (6'6") Tommy Tune, mainly famed for his work on Broadway; heart-throb actor-dancer Patrick Swayze of *Dirty Dancing* (1987) fame; and John Travolta, whose big dance roles were in *Saturday Night Fever* (1977) and *Grease* (1978).

Among many women who danced in Hollywood films, some of the very best were Eleanor Powell, a star of the 1930s and 1940s; Astaire partner Ginger Rogers (born Virginia McMath); Ann Miller (born Johnnie Collier); and another Astaire partner, Cyd Charisse (born Tula Finklea).

The biggest recent hit in the world of dance has been the worldwide interest generated by the reality television show *Dancing with the Stars*, which originated in Britain and spread to Australia and then thirty-two more nations, including the United States. The U.S. version first aired on American Broadcasting Company (ABC) in 2005 and remains hugely popular. In these shows, celebrities of varying "wattage" pair with professional dancers and compete in foxtrot, tango, waltz, and various other ballroom dances. *See also*:

African American; **Divas**; **Movies'
Role**; **Reality Television's Role**.

Sam G. Riley

For Further Reading

Delamater, Jerome. *Dance in the Hollywood Musical*. Ann Arbor, MI: UMI
Research Press, 1981.

Miller, Norma, and Evette Jensen.
*Swingin' at the Savoy: A Memoir of
a Jazz Dancer*. Philadelphia, PA:
Temple University Press, 1996.

Montague, Sarah. *The Ballerina: Fa-
mous Dancers and Rising Stars of
Our Time*. New York: Universe
Books, 1980.

DISC JOCKEYS

An unusual type of celebrity is the disc
jockey, or DJ, a person who plays pre-
recorded music for radio, club, dance,
or other audiences. The newer television equivalent of the DJ is the VJ, or
video jockey. Countless thousands of
individuals have worked as DJs in U.S.
communities, and although most of
these people have in no way achieved a
level of celebrity akin to that of a
movie star or top **athlete**, they nevertheless have been heard (but often
unseen) celebrities to legions of teenagers. Even so, when finally seen in
person by listeners, much of the magic
was lost, in that many DJs' appearance
in no way matched their big voice.

The earliest radio broadcast of a
phonograph record apparently occurred
in 1906, when Canadian radio pioneer
Reginald Fessenden broadcast a recorded selection from Handel. First to
act as a DJ was Westinghouse engineer

Frank Conrad, who in 1916 played
records in his Pennsylvania garage and
began taking song requests from listeners. The first true celebrity DJ was Martin Block, who in 1935 played records
on radio during breaks in the Lindbergh
kidnapping trial. Borrowing from a
West Coast DJ, Block began broadcasting *Make Believe Ballroom* later that
same year and in 1940 took the show
national. The term "disc jockey" was
coined to describe Block by columnist-
commentator Walter Winchell.

Known as "Moondog," Alan Freed
was a New York City celebrity DJ in
the early years of **rock** and roll, a term
he is said to have originated. Another
highly popular New York rock and roll
DJ of the 1950s was Murray "The K"
Kaufman. Less known yet beloved by
teenagers far and wide were fast-talking, patter-spouting DJs on Nashville's
powerful WLAC: Gene Nobles and his

*Legendary disc jockey Wolfman Jack howls
into his microphone. Courtesy of Photofest.*

Tarzan-call emitting engineer, "the ape man"; John R. Richbourg; and Bill "Hoss" Allen. In the 1960s appeared celebrity DJ "Wolfman Jack," born Robert Smith, who worked out of New York and Los Angeles, then transitioned to television and movies. An earlier move from radio to television was made by Dick Clark, whose television dance show *American Bandstand* ran from 1952 to 1989. A top DJ of the 1970s was Los Angeles's Casey Kasem, with his *American Top 40 Countdown.*

DJ celebrity is associated mainly with three U.S. cities. In New York, examples were Bruce "Cousin Brucie" Morrow, and African American DJ and sportscaster Hal Jackson; in Los Angeles, examples include Robert W. Morgan, Gary Owens, and Rick Dees of *Rick Dees Weekly Top 40* fame. In Chicago, DJ luminaries include oldies DJ Dick Bartley and witty Larry Lujack, plus African Americans Herb "The Cool Gent" Kent, Yvonne Daniels, and Tom Joyner.

VJs appeared in 1981 with the founding of cable network MTV (Music Television); introducing music videos were Nina Blackwood, Martha Quinn, Mark Goodman, J. J. Jackson, and Alan Hunter. *See also*: **African American**; **Hip-Hop and Rap**; **Talk Show Hosts**; **Television's Role**.

Sam G. Riley

For Further Reading

Cox, Jim. *Music Radio*. Jefferson, NC: McFarland, 2005.

Reighley, Kurt B. *Looking for the Perfect Beat*. New York: Pocket Books, 2000.

Souvignier, Todd. *The World of DJs and the Turntable Culture.* Milwaukee, WI: Hal Leonard Corp, 2003.

DISPUTES AND FEUDS

With celebrity comes inflated ego; with inflated ego comes competitive ill feelings—exactly what National Broadcasting Company (NBC) boss David Sarnoff was talking about many years ago when he remarked that competition might bring out the best in products, but it often brings out the worst in people. At least some "feuds" between celebrities come about as a means of generating publicity or increasing viewership. Such was, in fact, the case with one of the entertainment world's most famous "feuds," between early comics Fred Allen and Jack Benny, who were good friends but saw their supposed feud as a popular running gag and kept it going for at least ten years. It began when Allen teased Benny about his violin playing. Benny countered with a crack about Allen's "Clown Hall Tonight" show, a takeoff on its actual name, *Town Hall Tonight*. The two men "guested" on each other's shows; their rule was that the guest would be given the funniest line that figured into the "feud."

Most of the early show-business feuds were real, however, and usually involved professional jealousy. Major Hollywood star Betty Davis offended fellow actress Joan Crawford in the mid-1940s, saying she could not act. The two women continued to despise each other, even when working together on the successful film *Whatever Happened to Baby Jane* (1962). The

American Film Institute later picked Davis as the second-greatest film star of them all, Crawford tenth greatest. Less public but still full of rancor was the strained personal relationship between comedian Lou Costello and his straight man, Bud Abbott. The two men were a team from 1931 to 1957 and, sadly, each ended his career in bankruptcy. That feud's direct descendant was the sudden breakup in 1956 of a later **comedy** duo, Dean Martin and Jerry Lewis, who thereafter had little to do with one another. It appears that Martin felt his talents were stifled by Lewis's highly popular mugging and clowning. Each performer had reasonable success as a solo act, Lewis continuing to gangle and gape, and Martin singing, acting, and joining Frank Sinatra's "Rat Pack."

Among the stars and the beautiful people, disputes are common. Jerry Hall and her **supermodel** predecessor Janice Dickinson feuded over the affections of rocker Mick Jagger, Heidi Klum and Ellie MacPherson squabbled over rights to the identifying slogan "The Body," Joan Collins and Linda Evans clashed repeatedly while working on *Dynasty,* and late-night host Johnny Carson refused ever again to speak to comic Joan Rivers when she abandoned her guest hosting on *The Tonight Show* and launched her own competing program on a rival network at the same hour. New *Tonight Show* hard feelings arose in 1992 when NBC picked Jay Leno as Carson's successor rather than David Letterman. A year later, aging comedian Milton Berle, who had often dressed in drag on his shows, was angered by drag queen–recording artist RuPaul (born RuPaul Andre Charles) at the 1993 MTV

(Music Television) Video Awards when RuPaul intimated that Berle was wearing adult diapers.

In 1984, Paul McCartney and Yoko Ono were upset when Michael Jackson outbid them (at $47 million) for The Beatles catalogue. At the outset of the U.S. invasion of Iraq, Natalie Maines of the Dixie Chicks was verbally attacked and called treasonous by country singer Toby Keith. Janet Jackson and Madonna traded insults, and singer Dolly Parton saw no humor in Howard Stern's gross garbling of one of her audio books. Two very different celebrities feuded and went to court over a crude, tasteless spoof in a 1983 *Hustler* magazine about the Rev. Jerry Falwell's first time having sex. The reverend sued for libel, invasion of privacy, and intentional infliction of emotional distress, but after all appeals, won nothing. Billionaires Donald Trump and Mark Cuban exchanged insults over competition between Trump's *The Apprentice* and Cuban's short-lived rival show *The Benefactor.*

Sports celebrities, too, have their feuds, both real and promotional. Muhammad Ali and Joe Frazier boosted interest in their fights by trading verbal jabs and calling each other names. Motivation was questionable when Mike Tyson told the media he would rip out Lennox Lewis's heart and eat his children and later got into a scuffle before their bout, which Lewis won. Lakers teammates Shaquille O'Neal and Kobe Bryant were on the outs after O'Neal criticized Bryant about needing to be more of a team player, and Bryant fired back that Shaq should not show up each season out of shape and overweight; the two later made up. The pressures of Olympic skating came to light in 1994 when Nancy Kerrigan had a knee injured in an attack by rival skater Tonya Harding's ex-husband. Harding eventually admitted complicity.

Among recent show-business feuds, the Barbara Walters–Star Reynolds dispute looms large. The two women had been longtime cohosts of *The View*. Reynolds was fired and reportedly advised to make up some reason for her departure. Instead, she surprised executive editor Walters by announcing her firing on air. Reynolds was replaced by abrasive Rosie O'Donnell, who earlier had chided Reynolds for being less than truthful about having gastric bypass surgery to lose weight. In this kind of feud, no one comes out looking good. At least they did not come to blows, as did Christina Aguilera and Kelly Osbourne, who reportedly tussled at a nightclub after trading insults, as did Paris Hilton and Shanna Moakler at another club. Scraps between male celebrities have included *Survivor* contestant Johnny Fairplay who jumped on Danny Bonaduce, then wished he had not, and *Laugh Factory* comic Andy Dick, who was beaten up by fellow comic Jon Lovitz for joking about the Phil Hartman murder case.

Minor tiffs among celebrities are a dime a dozen, but things really get rough in the seamy world of **hip-hop and rap** music. Some hip-hop feuds, of course, are at least in part done to get the desired kind of publicity. Such seems to have been the case with Jay-Z (born Shawn Carter), America's wealthiest rapper, and his competitor Nas (born Nasir Jones). Some of these disputes remain confined to words, as when Eminem (born Marshall Mathers) called Moby (born Richard Hall) a

"little girl" at an awards show and threatened him with violence. Shots were exchanged among the supporters of rappers 50 Cent (born Curtis Jackson) and The Game (born Jayceon Taylor). The same was true in a dispute between rappers Foxy Brown (born Inga Marchand) and Lil' Kim (born Kimberly Jones). Most deadly of all was the feud between Tupac (born Tupak Shakur) and The Notorious B.I.G. (born Christopher Wallace). The latter was shot to death in 1996, the former in 1997; both murders are unsolved. *See also*: **African American**; **Athletes**; **Comedy**; **Movies' Role**; **Publicity**; **Reality Television's Role**; **Supermodels**; **Talk Show Hosts**; **Television's Role**.

Sam G. Riley

For Further Reading

Hadleigh, Boze. *Celebrity Feuds!: The Cattiest Rows, Spats, and Tiffs Ever Recorded*. Dallas, TX: Taylor, 2000.

Land, Myrick. *The Fine Art of Literary Mayhem; A Lively Account of Famous Writers and Their Feuds*. New York: Holt, Rinehart and Winston, 1963.

www.celebrityfeuds.com.

www.hollywoodlife.net/index.php/ category/celebrity-feuds.

www.hollyscoop.com/celebrity-feuds.

www.tmz.com/2006/07/15/celebrity- family-feuds.

DIVAS

The term "diva" is elastic in meaning; however, in popular culture, usage refers to a woman of considerable celebrity derived from significant accomplishment combined with glamorous appearance and a larger-than-life personality that commands attention both professionally and personally. The diva has "attitude" and a demanding manner that contribute to her imposing persona. The term appears to have been used first to describe performers in the field of opera in the same way that "prima donna" has been used to refer to standout ballerinas. Later, the term began being used to refer to certain popular singers and movie actresses. On rare occasions, it is applied to prominent businesswomen such as Martha Stewart (The Domestic Diva), is used as a descriptor for drag queens and for women especially admired by gay men, and is even used to describe glamorous and successful female wrestlers.

Opera stars who have been called divas include such greats as Maria Callas of Greece, who was sometimes dubbed "La Divina"; Birgit Nilsson of

Domestic diva Martha Stewart combines cakes and flowers. Courtesy of Photofest.

Sweden; Joan Sutherland, Australian coloratura; Italian-born lyrical soprano Renata Tebaldi; Americans Beverly Sills, Eileen Farrell, and mezzo-soprano Marilyn Horne; and Leontyne Price, the first African American operatic diva, renowned especially for her performances of *Aida*.

From its operatic origins, the term "diva" was first used to describe prima donnas of popular music, but certainly not all of them. To be a pop diva, a singer would have to be a top star whose work was in great demand, and most such performers had the reputation of having a demanding ego. Contemporary examples include Barbara Streisand, Cher (born Cherilyn Sarkisian), Liza Minnelli, Bette Midler (The Divine Miss M); and perhaps the biggest diva of them all, Madonna (born Madonna Louise Ciccone and often called "The Queen of Pop"), whose earnings as an entertainer have been astronomical. Bridging the gap between the operatic and the popular is Sarah Brightman, known mainly for her success in musical theater. Some African American women singers, too, are referred to as divas. Showing the way was Billie Holiday (Lady Day), whose exceptional talent and work for Columbia Records gave her a formidable reputation. More recent examples have included Tina Turner (born Anna Mae Bullock), who went on to a fine solo career after breaking up with her musician husband Ike Turner; versatile Aretha Franklin (The Queen of Soul); glamorous and equally versatile Diana Ross; and Whitney Houston (The Voice), known for her blending of pop and gospel.

To a lesser degree, the word "diva" has been applied to quite a number of accomplished actresses, especially those who are strong women known to be independent, demanding, or "high maintenance." Early examples are Berlin's Marlene Dietrich; exotic Swede Greta Garbo; husky-voiced, Alabama-born Tallulah Bankhead; formidable Joan Crawford; top star Katharine Hepburn; intense Bette Davis; beautiful but bipolar Vivien Leigh; and megastar Elizabeth Taylor.

Reportedly known as divas among the gay community are such celebrities as loud, brash, pushy, yet self-effacing comedian Joan Rivers (born Joan Molinsky), one of Hollywood's poster girls for plastic surgery; Joy Behar (born Josephina Occhiuto), a stand-up comic who was on the television show *The View* and who worked as a Jenny Craig spokesperson; outspoken improv comedian Kathy Griffin; and pop singer Taborah (born Taborah Adams). A different sort of diva well known to the gay community was Dame Edna Everage, a character played, in drag, by Australian comic Barry Humphries. This brassy character, with lilac hair and outlandish eyeglasses, delighted not only gays, but no less a dignitary than Queen Elizabeth of England, who in 2007 honored Humphries by making him a Commander of the Order of the British Empire. Another actor known for his drag persona was Harris Milstead, better known as his character Divine. In America, one of the best-known cross-dressing roles in movie history was Tim Curry's character Dr. Frank-N-Furter in the cult movie *The Rocky Horror Picture Show* (1975).

A final category of women routinely called divas are such female wrestlers as Chyna (Joan Laurer), Sable (Rena Mero), Victoria (Lisa Marie Varon), Molly Holly (Noreen Greenwald), Ivory (Lisa Moretti), and Kelly Kelly (Barbara Jean Blank), all of whom ply their popular, profitable trade for World Wrestling Entertainment.

In addition, San Francisco has its Hotel Diva, Key West its dance club called Divas, and Washington, D.C., has a women's football team called the D.C. Divas. Additionally, a line of talking Barbie Dolls is marketed as "Barbie Chat Divas," and in 1979, the ever-inventive entertainer-director Frank Zappa named his youngest daughter Diva Thin Muffin Pigeen Zappa. One could say the term has caught on. *See also*: **African American**; **Athletes**; **Classical Music**; **Comedy**; **Cult Films and Figures**; **Dream Girls**; **LGBT Celebrity**; **Martial Arts**; **Movies' Role**; **Rock and Pop**.

Sam G. Riley

For Further Reading

Burns, Lori, and Melisse Lafrance. *Disruptive Divas: Feminism, Identity and Popular Music*. New York: Routledge, 2002.

Inness, Sherrie A. *Disco Divas: Women and Popular Culture in the 1970s*. Philadelphia: University of Pennsylvania Press, 2003.

Kord, Susanne, and Elisabeth Krimmer. *Hollywood Divas, Indie Queens, and TV Heroines*. Lanham, MD: Rowman & Littlefield, 2005.

Nathan, David. *The Soulful Divas*. New York: Billboard Books, 1999.

Parrish, James Robert. *Hollywood Divas: The Good, the Bad, and the Fabulous*. New York and London: McGraw-Hill, 2002.

www.divasthesite.com.

DIVORCES

The history of celebrity divorce is filled with eye-popping superlatives. Holding the apparent record for the magnitude of a celebrity divorce settlement is the reported $168 million that basketball great Michael Jordon's ex-wife Juanita received in 2006. Many Hollywood stars have been married and divorced multiple times, but at or near the top is Hungarian beauty Zsa Zsa Gabor, married nine times since 1937. Her sister Magda married six times, one of which was to Zsa Zsa's ex-husband, actor George Sanders; and sister Ava, known mainly for her role on the television sitcom *Green Acres*, married five times. On the heels of Zsa Zsa in terms of number of marriages and divorces is actress Elizabeth Taylor, whose eight marriages and seven divorces involved a hotel heir, three actors (she married and divorced Richard Burton twice), a singer, a U.S. senator, and a construction worker.

An oft-divorced socialite was Barbara Hutton, heiress to the Woolworth dime store fortune, who favored European princes, counts, and barons and who divorced seven times. She also divorced actor Cary Grant and Dominican playboy racecar driver and polo player Porfirio Rubirosa, whose sexual prowess was the stuff of legend. Rubirosa had already been divorced, very profitably, by another American socialite, Doris Duke, heiress to dual fortunes in tobacco and electric utilities. That most debonair of all Hollywood leading men, Cary Grant, had five wives and four divorces. Two of those marriages were to actresses Betsy Drake and Dyan Cannon, and his final marriage was to a public relations woman who

was nearly a half-century younger than Grant. Marrying ever-younger women has also held appeal for self-promoting business celebrity Donald Trump. His first wife, Ivana Zelnickova of Czechoslovakia, reportedly came away with at least $40 million in their 1992 divorce.

Among entertainment greats whose divorces attracted much public comment was singer Frank Sinatra; two of his four marriages were to actresses Ava Gardner and Mia Farrow. The beautiful Ava had three marriages to fellow entertainers: actor Mickey Rooney, band-leader Artie Shaw, and Sinatra. All three marriages ended in divorce.

Exciting great interest were the marital problems of actress Jane Fonda, who wed and in 1973 divorced French moviemaker Roger Vadim, said to have received a $2 million settlement from her; divorced political activist Tom Hayden in 1990; and divorced Ted Turner in 2001. Turner had been divorced twice before marrying Fonda.

A classic love-triangle divorce scenario resulted in the 1980 divorce of actress Farrah Fawcett-Majors from *Six Million Dollar Man* star Lee Majors, who was blindsided by a one-time friend, actor Ryan O'Neal. Mary Tyler Moore, who during most of the 1970s gave American television viewers a preview of life as lived by the urban single girl on *The Mary Tyler Moore Show*, split with broadcast executive Grant Tinker in 1979. Their polite, amicable, yet highly publicized divorce was granted in 1982. English sex goddess Joan Collins, whose U.S. celebrity benefited from her role on the soap opera *Dynasty*, alleged physical violence when she sued handsome young Swede Peter Holm for divorce in 1986. Holm's efforts to attach half her income ended in 1988 with a modest settlement.

In 1979, America's attention turned to the marital woes of baseball great Pete Rose, at that time the nation's highest-paid ballplayer. Rose had been hit with a paternity suit in 1978 but only intensified his womanizing. His expensive divorce was finalized in 1980, but his betting habits caused him even greater grief by the end of that decade. Also divorced in 1980 was 1976 Olympic decathlon winner Bruce Jenner, who reached a settlement with the woman who had supported him during his extensive training. Soon thereafter, he married again, this time to former *Hee-Haw* cutie and final girlfriend of Elvis Presley, Linda Thompson. In 1987, that marriage also ended with an amicable settlement. Another high-profile sports hero, handsome and talented Redskins quarterback Joe Theismann, divorced his first wife in 1984 for actress Cathy Lee Crosby, a relationship that ended following Theismann's career-ending injury. Yet another sports-world divorce that got heavy press was that of boxer Mike Tyson, who was always a man of extremes. He had compiled a record of more than three dozen arrests while growing up, became the youngest ever heavyweight champ in 1986, and by 1988 was reportedly the highest paid of all athletes. His marriage to beautiful and brilliant actress Robin Givens seemed a stark contrast from the start and ended in an acrimonious 1989 divorce that included the added spectacle of Givens suing Tyson for libel.

Celebrity divorces continue to be a major entertainment medium of their own. A disproportionate amount of Americans' attention has been directed at the domestic and other woes of pop icon Britney Spears, who has made hundreds of millions of dollars from her entertaining and endorsements. One of her marriages, to longtime friend Jason Alexander, lasted all of fifty-five hours and ended in annulment; but getting far more public attention was her 2007 divorce from her former backup dancer Kevin Federline. The divorces that prompted the most jokes were the three divorces of late-night host Johnny Carson. The settlement in his 1972 parting with wife Joanne involved a $500,000 lump sum plus $100,000-a-year alimony, and his 1985 divorce from model Joanna resulted in a $20 million settlement. An enormous divorce settlement in 1995 involved singer Neil Diamond, whose wife received a reported $150 million following their thirty-two-year marriage.

Although most celebrity divorce settlements involve the husband giving up assets to the wife, the 1997 divorce of actress Kirstie Alley resulted in a reported $6 million settlement going to actor Parker Stevenson. Entertainer Janet Jackson gave up more than $10 million to Rene Elizondo in their 2003 settlement, and Jennifer Lopez settled in 2001 with Chris Judd for roughly $15 million. In 2006, Victoria Principal's divorce settlement with plastic surgeon Harry Glassman was reported to have cost her $25 million plus one of the couple's homes, and tennis star Chris Evert lost $7 million and a vacation house to her Olympic skier husband, Andy Mill. Another high-profile divorce settlement occurred in 2008 when former Beatle Paul McCartney paid Heather Mills more than $48 million. As a result of such divorces, and in keeping with a general societal trend, many younger celebrities are slower to marry, and when they do, are more likely to sign a prenuptial agreement.

Other celebrity divorces that drew great public interest were those of Liza Minnelli, whose one-year marriage to David Gest ended amid charges and countercharges in 2003; Donald Trump's divorces from wives Ivana in 1988 and Marla Maples in 1999; and the 2008 split of model Christie Brinkley from her architect-husband Peter Cook, who reportedly was having an affair with an eighteen-year-old girl. *See also*: **Athletes**; **Corporate Celebrity**; **Dream Girls**; **Movies' Role**; **Rock and Pop**; **Supermodels**.

Sam G. Riley

For Further Reading

Albert, James A. *Pay Dirt: Divorces of the Rich and Famous*. New York: Berkley Books, 1991.

www.forbes.com/2007/04/11/celebrity-women-alimony-biz.

DREAM GIRLS

The dream girl, glamour girl, **sex** symbol, femme fatale—could there be any other human type more emblematic of Hollywood, a place where producers make sure that the women look like Venus and the men like Mars? These beautiful women chosen to be merchandized as the stuff of dreams are what most women reportedly want to look like and what most men arguably just want. They come in many varieties: sultry, shy, voluptuous, delicate, hard, kitten-soft, imperious, tall, short, foreign, and domestic. But all are beautiful according to the standards of their time. Of them all, the single dream girl who appears to have best captured the world's imagination was Marilyn Monroe—that is, if the ability to generate money long after one's demise is any indication. When it comes to making money for one's estate or for others, Monroe is the female counterpart to Elvis Presley.

Just who was the first Hollywood dream girl is open to debate, but two women who might be considered for this honor (both now deceased) are sultry, Swedish-born Greta Garbo, remembered for such silent films as *Flesh and the Devil* (1926) and *Grand Hotel* (1932), and lovely girl-next-door Clara Bow, known as "The It Girl" after her film *It* in 1927, the same year she starred with Gary Cooper in *Wings*. The "It" referred to in her nickname was, of course, sex appeal, which she had in abundance.

In the 1930s, talking pictures welcomed a new crop of lovelies to the screen. In 1930, Jean Harlow (born Harlean Harlow Carpenter) established a Hollywood archetype, the platinum blonde, in the Howard Hughes film *Hell's Angels*. Harlow's acting ability was minimal but her "vampish" beauty great. Because she died of kidney failure at age twenty-six, she did not have time to develop as an actress, although she was in quite of number of less-than-stellar films. Some dream girls were imports, such as naughty, worldly, German-born Marlene Dietrich, who made a big hit in 1930 in *The Blue Angel*. Dietrich, who died in 1992, performed into the 1970s. Red-haired

Actress Marilyn Monroe flashes her brightest smile in Gentlemen Prefer Blondes, *1953. Courtesy of Photofest.*

Maureen O'Sullivan, the first Irish lass to become a movie star, appeared in six Tarzan movies beginning in 1934 with *Tarzan and His Mate*, in which the scanty costumes worn by O'Sullivan as Jane and Romanian-American Johnny Weissmuller as Tarzan, plus their jungle lifestyle, were considered scandalous. The female lead character, Scarlett O'Hara, in the epic movie *Gone With the Wind* (1939), was played by English actress Vivien Leigh, whose dream girl image went from hard and calculating to soft, if insipid, and back again. Fay Wray did a fine job of depicting the fair damsel in need of rescue in *King Kong* (1933); also in that year, Katharine Hepburn appeared in *Morning Glory*. Hepburn's personal image was unusual: beautiful yet strong, classy, smart, and independent. She

went on to a long, stellar career and, in 1999, was declared the greatest of all female stars by the American Film Institute.

The early 1940s saw performances by three very different dream girls. Swedish-born Ingrid Bergman showed deft acting talent in her love-conflicted role in *Casablanca* (1942), one of the best movies ever made. Full-figure girl Jane Russell burst onto the movie scene in *The Outlaw* (1943), and in that same year, African American actress Lena Horne appeared in *Stormy Weather*. Gene Tierney played the delicate, haunting title character in *Laura* (1944), the same year in which Betty Grable and her celebrated legs starred in *Pin Up Girl* and became just that, the number-one pinup for the troops in World War II. In 1946, Lauren Bacall was in *The Big Sleep*, Veronica Lake starred in *The Blue Dahlia,* and Lana Turner featured in *The Postman Always Rings Twice*. Rita Hayworth joined Grable as a favorite pinup after *The Lady from Shanghai* (1948); another import, Austrian Hedy Lamarr, was in *Samson and Delilah* (1949). Classically beautiful Ava Gardner also began making movies in this decade, but her better roles came later in such films as *The Snows of Kilimanjaro* (1952) and *The Night of the Iguana* (1964).

Two stars in 1950s musical films were French actress Leslie Caron (*An American in Paris,* 1951) and leggy dancer Cyd Charisse (*Singin' in the Rain,* 1952). Blonde bombshell Marilyn Monroe dazzled in *How to Marry a Millionaire* (1953) and also showed that she had comic talent. Mamie Van Doren joined the ranks of Hollywood's blonde dream girls in *Forbidden* (1953), as did statuesque Jayne Mansfield (born Vera Jayne Palmer) in *The Girl Can't Help It* (1956), and sexy Italian import Gina Lollobrigida appeared in *Beat the Devil* in that same year. Grace Kelly, a well-bred but smoldering blonde, appeared in *Rear Window* in 1954, the same year that African American star Dorothy Dandridge appeared in *Carmen Jones*. Kim Novak triggered many fantasies in *Picnic* (1955), and Elizabeth Taylor showed near-perfect good looks coupled with real acting ability in *Cat on a Hot Tin Roof* (1958). For sheer sex appeal, however, the gold standard in the 1950s was French starlet Brigitte Bardot, for whom the term "sex kitten" was coined. When her movie *And God Created Woman* appeared in 1956, religious groups picketed in front of some U.S. theaters that showed it—and were nearly trampled underfoot by hordes of teenage boys who watched the movie several times.

The 1960s gave audiences interesting new talent. Janet Leigh made a lovely victim in *Psycho* (1960), and Italian Sophia Loren looked amazingly constructed in *El Cid* (1961). In 1961, Natalie Wood was sweetly girlish in *West Side Story* but was very much grown up in *Gypsy* (1962). Few American men or boys were not secretly in love with slender, delicate Audrey Hepburn after seeing *Breakfast at Tiffany's* (1961). Sue Lyon played a nymphet in *Lolita* (1962), Swiss bombshell Ursula Andress was megadecorative in *Dr. No* (1962), and Julie Christie was delectable in *Doctor Zhivago* (1965). Three more dream girls of this decade were voluptuous Raquel Welch (born Jo Raquel Tejada), who appeared in *One Million Years B.C.* in 1966; starlet Sharon Tate (*Valley of the Dolls,* 1967), one of the murder victims of the Charlie Manson gang in 1969; and Jacqueline Bissett from England (*Bullitt,* 1968).

Blessed with an eye-popping mane of blonde hair was Farrah Fawcett (*Myra Breckinridge,* 1970), and an appropriately carnal-looking Ann Margaret appeared in *Carnal Knowledge* in 1971. Diane Keaton became an urban yuppie sex symbol in *Annie Hall* (1977), and Bo Derek in *10* (1979) lived up to the movie's title—in appearance, at least.

New faces and figures of the 1980s included blonde Goldie Hawn (*Private Benjamin,* 1980); ravishing German actress Nastassia Kinski, born Nastassja Nakszynski (*Cat People*, 1982); coolly beautiful French star Catherine Denevue (*The Hunger,* 1983); and blonde environmentalist Daryl Hannah (*Splash*, 1984). Twinkly-nosed and blonde, Kim Basinger appeared in *Nine and a Half Weeks* in 1986; willowy Michelle Pfeiffer was in *The Fabulous Baker Boys* in 1986; and Julia Roberts played in *Steel Magnolias* in 1989 and continues to be one of Hollywood's most popular dream girls.

The 1990s brought a lively new crop of screen sirens: Demi Moore (*Ghost*, 1990), very nearly perfect-looking Sharon Stone (*Basic Instinct*, 1992), elfin Kirsten Dunst (*Interview with the Vampire*, 1994), flirty-eyed Alicia Silverstone (*Clueless*, 1995) and the unusual-looking yet magnetically attractive Renee Zellweger (*Jerry Maguire*, 1996). Jennifer Lopez, now the most successful of Hispanic stars, was a hit in *Selena* (1997) and Cameron Diaz an even bigger hit in *There's Something About Mary* (1998). South African American Charlize Theron was in *Mighty Joe Young* in 1998; and probably the decade's biggest new stars were willowy Nicole Kidman, who appeared in *Eyes Wide Shut* in 1999, and pouty-lipped Angelina Jolie (*Girl Interrupted*, 1999).

The turn of the new century brought with it an outpouring of new beauties. Regal Penelope Cruz from Spain (born Penelope Cruz Sanchez) was in *All the Pretty Horses* (2000), demure and intelligent-looking Israeli American Natalie Portman (born Natalie Hershlag) was in *Cold Mountain* (2002), African American lovely Halle Berry was in *Monster's Ball* (2002), Danish American Scarlett Johansson was in *Lost in Translation* (2003), and in 2005, slender Keira Knightley appeared in *Pride and Prejudice* and Jessica Alba featured in *Sin City*. In 2006 appeared Ann Hathaway (*The Devil Wears Prada*), Jessica Biel (*The Illusionist*), and singer-turned-actress Beyonce Knowles (*The Pink Panther*; *Dream Girls*). Two eye-catching newcomers emerged in 2007: Brazilian Alice Braga (*I Am Legend*) and Canadian cutie Ellen Page (*Juno*).

The details of what is deemed most desirable change a bit from time to time, but a good thing about dream girls is that unlike oil, a limitless supply of this commodity is available, allowing movie producers to film, paparazzi to chase, magazines to objectify, **talk show hosts** to interview, women to evaluate, and men to salivate. *See also*: **African American**; **Dancers**; **Hispanic/Latino**; **International Celebrity**; **Movies' Role**; **Rock and Pop**.

Sam G. Riley

For Further Reading

Lisanti, Tom. *Glamour Girls of Sixties Hollywood*. Jefferson, NC: McFarland & Co., 2008.

Pascall, Jeremy. *Hollywood and the Great Stars: The Stars, the Sex Symbols, the Legend, the Movies, and How It All Began*. New York: Crescent Books, 1975.

Pitts, Leonard. *The Glamour Girls of Hollywood*. Cresskill, NJ: Sharon Publications, 1984.

DRUGS AND ALCOHOL

Overindulgence in and addiction to drugs and alcohol are hardly limited to the culture of celebrities: anyone might succumb to the problem. Some individuals are more dominated and defined by their dependency than others, but the status that comes with celebrity notoriety seems to amplify the connection of real human beings with the abuse of substances.

When we think of celebrity culture and its seemingly inherent link with drugs and alcohol, we often consider the stars we know who fell victim to their addictions. This list is long and inevitably will grow, but there is much more to the connection between fame and drugs and alcohol than the bits of trivia and the tragic outcomes that we may glean from the popular media.

Some argue that substance abuse by celebrity-artists is one of the crucial elements of their artistry, intensity, uniqueness—a sort of deal with the devil that is made to tap into otherwise-hidden creative energy. Would Jean Michele Basquiat (famous and influential graffiti and neo-expressionist 1980s artist) *be* Basquiat if he were not using heroin? Would Jimi Hendrix have had his Experience without the influences of drugs and alcohol? Would comedian Mitch Hedburg have been as hilarious as he was or even have been able to get on stage without the chemicals he consumed? Would Bob Dylan have written "Mr. Tambourine Man" without psychedelic influence? Are drugs necessary for the attainment of true self-actualization and boundless creative expression and energy? It is true that the Beat writer William S. Burroughs would most likely never have been inspired to write the novels *Junkie* or *Naked Lunch* without the influences of heroin and morphine? But does that mean that such experience is necessarily part of making great art? The question of whether or not drugs offer the celebrity-artist a mainline to creative

intensity is up for debate and definitely worthy of some consideration.

Some celebrities are famous specifically because of their public support of various drugs. Dr. Timothy Leary was by far one of the most famous and outspoken advocates for psychedelic drug use, specifically for LSD (lysergic acid diethylamide—created, studied, and promoted by Swiss chemist Albert Hoffman), which Leary believed provided powerful spiritual and psychological benefits. He published numerous books on this topic and has been an influential icon of American counterculture for decades. World-renowned **author**, physician, and nutritionist Dr. Andrew Weil is a self-proclaimed mycophile (psychedelic mushroom user), who believes strongly that their consumption can stimulate imagination and intuition. Other celebs who are famous for extolling the virtues of psychedelics or marijuana include Abby Hoffman (1960s activist), Ram Daas (Harvard professor and spiritual leader), Hunter S. Thompson (journalist and author), Allen Ginsberg (poet), Jim Morrison (musician), Lou Reed (musician), Jean-Paul Sartre (philosopher), Aldus Huxley (writer), Bob Marley (musician), Michel Foucault (French philosopher), Ken Kesey (Beat writer), Muddy Waters (blues musician), John Lennon (musician, activist), and Willie Nelson (musician, activist). Many American comedians have made it part of their routine to speak openly about their drug and alcohol use as self-defamation, critique, or pure humor. Consider the stand-up routines of Robin Williams, Richard Pryor, Lenny Bruce, Mitch Hedberg, George Carlin, Bill Hicks, Joan Rivers, Steve Martin, and Sam Kinison. Dean Martin and Jackie

Gleason's famous **comedy** routines often involved getting smashed while on stage and then exaggerating their drunkenness.

The term bohemian (deriving from Bohemia, a region in the Czech Republic) was first used colloquially in France and then in the English language beginning in the 19th century to describe artists, actors, writers, and musicians who lived a marginalized, unconventional, antiestablishment lifestyle. Bohemianism involved indulgence in drugs and alcohol, casual sexual practices, volunteer poverty, and a tendency toward a nomadic (or Gypsy) lifestyle—living in different cities around the globe so as to not be bound to any single state or system. The Italian painter and sculptor Amedeo Modigliani was a bohemian in every sense of the word and met an early end at age thirty-five due to alcohol, narcotics, and poverty. Many famous people can in fact be described as living bohemian lifestyles, especially in 1960s America. Included in this list are Bob Dylan, Talitha Getty, Allen Ginsberg, Jack Kerouac, and other Beat poets, writers, and artists. In the 21st century, the term bohemian is used superficially to describe a "look" or fashion that resembles that past lifestyle, or to romantically describe a celebrity or artist who appears to have some characteristics of the classic bohemian, as does Tom Waits.

The self-destruction that results from alcohol or drug dependency is far from being romantic, celebrity or no. The pain, depression, and wasting that goes with chemical dependency is often extreme—for the abusers, as well as for their friends, family, and fans. To say that a celebrity is more likely to be faced with substance-abuse problems would be accurate. A study conducted by A. M. Ludwig in 1995 showed that famous people are twice as likely as the general population to have alcohol-related problems. This increased propensity toward substance abuse can stem from a number of different factors; however, few experts agree on the causes of addiction or even its definition. Basically, individual characteristics, including personality and psychological state; environmental factors; and drug and alcohol properties, and the effects they have on the chemical composition of the brain, are all interconnected in addiction.

For celebrities, a tendency toward addiction can be made even more complicated by a variety of influences. These influences include the feeling of having to live up to the exaggerated expectations of others (through the media), constant public scrutiny and **paparazzi** presence, demanding work and tour schedules, having to be "extroverted" for public appearances, intensity of creative work, being seen and treated as a commercial product (dehumanized or trivialized by the media), influences of large sums of money and the presence of hangers-on (peer pressure, the entourage), easy access to all substances, extreme focus on the self, and fear of failure. Add any of these to the other complex factors that can spur addiction and it is easier to see how famous people might be at a much greater risk of entering the downward spiral of drug and alcohol addiction.

Many legendary celebrities have fallen victim to their addiction(s). Cocaine, heroin, or cocaine and morphine (speedball) addiction claimed Chet

Baker, John Belushi, Len Bias, Chris Farley, Andy Gibb, Billie Holiday, Janice Joplin, Bradley Nowell, River Phoenix, Dee Dee Ramone, Layne Staley, Sid Vicious, and Hank Williams. A long list of celebrities have died from alcohol poisoning or complications from alcohol abuse, including John Bonham, Montgomery Clift, W. C. Fields, F. Scott Fitzgerald, William Holden, Jack Kerouac, Veronica Lake, Mickey Mantle, Keith Moon, Jim Morrison, Jack Nance, Oliver Reed, Dylan Thomas, and Spencer Tracy. Pharmaceutical overdose has taken the lives of many an icon: Truman Capote, Dorothy Dandridge, Nick Drake, Judy Garland, Howard Hughes, Heath Ledger, Bruce Lee, Marilyn Monroe, and Elvis Presley.

Although substance abuse did not kill Ray Charles, Johnny Cash, or Charlie Parker, it certainly took a dramatic toll on their careers and personal lives. A number of celebrities have survived their addictions and have made it part of their life's work to tell their complex stories and through them perhaps influence others who are battling addiction. Drew Barrymore, who gained celebrity status at age eight with the movie *E.T.*, has been instrumental in inspiring those facing drug and alcohol problems in public appearances and through her autobiography, *Little Girl Lost* (1990). Many rockers have also written of their fame and brushes with self-destruction: Anthony Kiedis in *Scar Tissue* (2004), Slash and Anthony Bozza in *Slash* (2007), Nikki Sixx in *The Heroin Diaries: A Year in the Life of a Shattered Rock Star* (2005), Eric Clapton in *Clapton: The Autobiography* (2007), and Marianne Faithfull in *Faithfull: An Autobiography* (1994).

But there are also celebrities who continue to navigate the spiral of addiction while under the magnifying glass of the media—some because they want to be, others simply because their stories sell. We may know about Nick Nolte's multiple **arrests** for driving under the influence, Robert Downey, Jr.'s infamous exploits while under the influence, and Diana Ross's or Rush Limbaugh's battles with addiction because we saw it on the news. We tend to target our celebrities to be our fonts for entertainment via **reality television**. Our fascination with celebrities, drugs, and alcohol is seen all over the media in shows like *Celebrity Rehab with Dr. Drew* that trivialize and exploit addiction, VH1's (Video Hits 1) *True Hollywood Story* (romanticized tragedy), on E!, MTV (Music Television), all varieties of **talk shows**, and in **magazines** and **tabloids**. The Betty Ford Center, a clinic for narcotic and chemical dependency rehabilitation located in Rancho Mirage, California, is a household name because of media reports on the scores of celebrities who have checked in in the hope of rescuing their lives and salvaging their careers.

By nature, humans are curious animals who are fascinated by the morbid, such as gladiator battles, public executions, or slowing down to look at a car wreck. We have a strong tendency toward cultural voyeurism, the desire to secretly and safely observe the personal and intimate lives of others, and this is especially relevant in the ways we consume celebrity vices. The more scandalous a story, the better the sales. As a consumer culture, we create the need for stories about celebrities. One cannot blame the media for the exploitation of celebrity drug and alcohol issues because, in the end, we are the problem. It is all part of the human condition—like it or not. *See also*: **Country and Western; Disputes and Feuds; Early Deaths; Hispanic/Latino; International Celebrity; Jazz and Blues; Movies' Role; News Media Figures; Rock and Pop.**

Nancy Jurek

For Further Reading

Fisher, Carrie. *Postcards from the Edge*. New York: Pocket Books, 1990.

Long, John. *Drugs and the 'Beats': The Role of Drugs in the Lives and Writings of Kerouac, Burroughs and Ginsberg*. Virtualbookworm.com, 2005.

O'Day, Anita. *High Times Hard Times*. New York: G. P. Putnam's Sons, 1981.

Thompson, Hunter S. *Fear and Loathing in Las Vegas: A Savage Journey to the Heart of the American Dream*. New York: Vintage, 1989.

Wolfe, Thomas. *The Electric Kool-Aid Acid Test*. New York: Farrar, Straus & Giroux, 1968.

E

EARLY DEATHS

Not to be confused with unexpected deaths, this category of early deaths considers celebrities who died before age fifty. Each decade experienced its own set of shocking early deaths. However, the 1960s and 1990s arguably contain the most morose such headlines.

In 1955, twenty-four-year-old *Rebel Without a Cause* screen heartthrob James Dean was killed in a car accident on the California coast. Four years later, twenty-two-year-old up-and-coming rocker Buddy Holly perished in an airplane crash following a concert in Green Bay, Wisconsin.

The most legendary early deaths of the 1960s began with the thirty-six-year-old sex bomb Marilyn Monroe's apparent overdose in her Los Angeles apartment, which was ruled "probably suicide" by coroners, but has kept conspiracy theorists busy ever since. President John F. Kennedy was assassinated at age forty-six in 1963, and in 1968, his younger brother Robert F. Kennedy, age forty-three, was also the victim of an assassin's bullet; at that time, Robert Kennedy was representing the state of New York in the U.S. Senate. Also in 1963, Patsy Cline, a thirty-year-old country musician at the top of her career, was killed in an airplane crash leaving Kansas City. In 1967, voluptuous pinup gossip queen Jayne Mansfield died at age thirty-four, when her convertible slid underneath the back of a tractor-trailer. The next year, shockwaves rippled through the country when preeminent civil rights leader Martin Luther King, Jr., age thirty-nine, was assassinated in Memphis. A year later came the grisly news of twenty-six-year-old actress Sharon Tate's murder; she was eight and a half months pregnant when she was murdered by Charles Manson cult members.

The 1970s, while somewhat less dramatic on the celebrity death front, witnessed the drug overdoses of two very different icons: rocker Janis Joplin, who died in 1970 in Los Angeles at age twenty-seven, and Warhol muse Edie Sedgewick, who died at twenty-eight in Santa Barbara, California.

Actor James Dean looks cooler than cool during the filming of Giant, *1956. Courtesy of Photofest.*

The 1990s was another unfortunate decade for fame's younger set. Actor River Phoenix, often compared to James Dean, was twenty-three when he collapsed and died from a drug overdose in Los Angeles in 1993. The next year, grunge icon Kurt Cobain, twenty-seven, committed suicide by shooting himself in the head in his Seattle home. The next two years saw gang murders—the gunshot killings of twenty-five-year-old rapper-actor Tupac Shakur in 1996 and twenty-four-year-old rapper The Notorious B.I.G. in 1997. Two other such deaths were those of British and American royalty: Princess Diana, who was thirty-six when she died in a car accident in Paris in 1997, and John F. Kennedy, Jr., who died in 1999 at age thirty-eight when the airplane he was piloting went down in the Atlantic Ocean, killing him, his wife Carolyn Bessette, and her sister Lauren.

The most prominent early deaths in the first decade of the 21st century both

included drug overdoses. Tabloid queen Anna Nicole Smith was thirty-nine when she was found unresponsive in her Bahaman hotel room in 2007, and Heath Ledger was twenty-eight in 2008 when he was found dead in his Manhattan apartment. *See also*: **Criminals**; **Cult Films and Figures**; **Drugs and Alcohol**; **Hip-Hop and Rap**; **Politics**; **Rock and Pop**; **Tabloids' Role**.

Elizabeth Hendrickson

For Further Reading

Donnelley, Paul. *Fade to Black: A Book of Movie Obituaries*. London: Omnibus Press, 2005.

Largo, Michael. *The Portable Obituary: How the Famous, Rich, and Powerful Really Died*. New York: Harper Paperbacks, 2007.

Parish, James Robert. *The Hollywood Book of Death: The Bizarre, Often Sordid, Passings of More than 125 American Movie and TV Idols*. New York: Contemporary Books of McGraw Hill, 2001.

ENDORSEMENTS

Since 1939, when Atlanta's Red Rock Cola paid the great slugger Babe Ruth to endorse their soft drink, many a celebrity has made megabucks from fronting for or endorsing commercial products and services. The companies that have paid them have bet that the celebrity-crazed public, and especially the young, will so want to dress like, eat and drink like, cut their hair like, and perhaps even drive like their beloved celebrity idols that entertainment-world endorsements will at the very least increase consumer awareness of individual brands. It is possible that a brand will create a positive impression thanks to a celebrity endorser and that the endorsement will encourage consumers to see the product as desirable or trustworthy, thereby imparting a largely subconscious "tidal pull" in the direction of the product being endorsed. Older Americans might recall many of the early endorsement deals on television, such as Robert Young for Sanka instant coffee, Joe DiMaggio for Mr. Coffee, John Cameron Swayze for Timex watches, Roy Orbison for Coca-Cola, Edie Adams for Muriel cigars, Florence Henderson for Polident, Jimmy Stewart for Campbell soups, Bing Crosby for Minute Maid orange juice, Anita Bryant for Florida orange juice, Ricardo Montalban for Chrysler, and Andy Griffith for Kraft cheese products.

Among endorsers of the products we drink, Burt Bacharach and Angie Dickinson fronted for Martini & Rossi wine, Wayne Gretsky and Ed McMahon for Budweiser beer, Charles Barkley for Coors beer, Lindsay Wagner for Diet Rite cola and Nescafe, Pat Boone for Maxell House coffee, and Andre Agassi for Mountain Dew. Among drink manufacturers, Pepsi appears to have placed the most faith in celebrity endorsements, including Michael J. Fox, Cuba Gooding, Jr., Michael Jackson, Don Johnson, Madonna, Shaquille O'Neal, Sammy Sossa, and Britney Spears. McDonald's has favored sports figures such as Charles Barkley, Michael Jordon, and Yao Ming, but at other times it has used comedic actors Jason Alexander and Kelsey Grammer. Jason Alexander has also fronted for Kentucky Fried Chicken, Sherman Hemsley for Denny's restaurants, Queen Latifah and Ringo Starr for Pizza Hut, and Shaquille O'Neal for Burger King and Taco Bell.

America's foremost golfer, Tiger Woods, has endorsed Wheaties, Buick, Titlist golf balls, Nike shoes, and the American Express card; boxer George Foreman has fronted for Frito-Lay snacks and for his own grills; Elvis Presley, who usually shied away from endorsement deals, did ads for Southern Maid doughnuts; Jay Leno for Doritos; and model Fabio flexed and posed for I Can't Believe It's Not Butter. Endorsers for women's beauty products and services have included Sybil Shepherd and Jessica Alba for L'Oreal hair coloring, Jane Seymour for rival hair-coloring product Loving Care, Julia Louis-Dreyfus for Clairol Nice 'N' Easy hair products, Catherine Deneuve and Nicole Kidman for Chanel perfumes, and Brandy for Cover Girl makeup.

In recent years, corporations have, for the most part, tried to select celebrity endorsers who are a sensible match with their products. To do otherwise would be expensive due to the enormous fees that many of these endorsers command. Buick has received bad press for making a questionable match with Tiger Woods, inasmuch as Buick is seen as an older person's car. On the other hand, the use of snuggly Joey Heatherton made sense for advertising Serta mattresses, Sarah Ferguson (The Duchess of York) worked convincingly for Weight Watchers, beefy Robert Mitchum was right for promoting beef products, and who better than Brooke Shields for making Calvin Klein jeans look good. Many times, then, companies probably get more than their money's worth from expensive endorsement deals with celebrities, but at other times, advertisers have done well by using an unknown in their commercials—and then watching that person *become* a celebrity. Such was the case with Andy Lambros, the cute-as-a-button child who sang the much-loved Oscar Meyer jingle or feisty little old lady Clara Peller who rasped, "Where's the beef?" in Wendy's commercials. Although many business owners and chief executives are well advised to remain off camera, Wendy's founder Dave Thomas, Frank Perdue for Perdue Chicken, Harland Sanders for his fried chicken chain, and Orville Redenbacher for his popcorn line all became household-name celebrities by touting their own products.

Another caveat for companies that contract with a celebrity endorser is that unforeseen things can happen to sour the deal and endanger the company image. Madonna was dropped by Pepsi in 1989 following the release of one of her graphic videos. When basketball's Magic Johnson revealed in 1991 that he was HIV-positive, his endorsements were not continued. Martha Stewart's arrangements with Kmart were severed when she was convicted of lying about a stock sale and imprisoned in 2004. In that same year, Slim-Fast dropped Whoopie Goldberg because of her remarks critical of George W. Bush. McDonald's and Nutella distanced themselves from basketball star Kobe Bryant in 2003 when he was accused of rape, although Nike continued to use his endorsement. In 2005, Reebok dropped rapper 50 Cent due to his "gangsta" image and Hardee's took heat from its suggestive commercials featuring slinky Paris Hilton. A combination of misbehaviors on

the part of quarterback Michael Vick cost him a number of profitable endorsement deals. Vick lost AirTran after making a vulgar gesture at angry fans after a disappointing game. He lost Reebok and other deals after he pled guilty to the dog-fighting charges that sent him to prison in 2007. Still other endorsement deals have been ditched by companies when company officials decided that the high-cost celebrity commercials they were running were actually better publicity for the celebrities involved than for the company and its products. Examples involved Pepsi and both troubled entertainer Britney Spears and Beyonce Knowles, plus Chrysler and its endorser Celine Dion. A 2006 National Consumer Council–sponsored study concluded that celebrity-endorsement commercials were declining slightly in number, and another study sponsored by the Luxury Institute showed that luxury products and services tend to receive little benefit from celebrity endorsements.

Even so, in 2003, Madonna was signed for Gap, Justin Timberlake for McDonald's, Anna Kournikova for the Multiway Sports Bra, and Fran Drescher for Old Navy. In 2004, Beyonce was contracted by L'Oreal, David Beckham by Gillette razors, and Howie Long for Chevy trucks. Madonna began endorsing Versace in 2005, and in that year, Gwyneth Paltrow began fronting for Estee Lauder, Donovan McNabb and his mother were featured for Campbell's Chunky Soup, and Teri Hatcher began pushing Clairol Nice 'N' Easy hair coloring.

Another aspect of this topic is political endorsement by celebrities. It is difficult to know the actual effect at the polls of highly paid celebrities who attempt to influence the voting of their fans, yet celebrity endorsement of candidates remains active. Celebrity endorsement of presidential candidates is nothing new, of course. As far back as the days of the silent pictures, stars have taken political sides. In 1920, Warren Harding had the support of Al Jolson, Mary Pickford, Douglas Fairbanks, and other early Hollywood luminaries for what turned out to be a remarkably lackluster administration. Some entertainers, such as W. C. Fields, did not so much endorse a candidate of choice as oppose the one he liked least—in his case, Franklin D. Roosevelt. Hollywood was big for the glamorous candidate John F. Kennedy, led by Frank Sinatra and his pals, but Wilt Chamberlain was a Nixon supporter. **Country and Western** stars mostly favored Jimmy Carter: Loretta Lynn, Willie Nelson, Johnny Cash, and Charlie Daniels, for example. Also in Carter's corner were Muhammad Ali, Elizabeth Montgomery, Neil Simon, Dionne Warwick, and numerous other notables, while Ronald Reagan had the support of James Cagney, Robert Stack, Dean Martin, Frank Sinatra, Pat Boone, Wayne Newton, and more.

As the 2008 presidential election campaign began, John McCain was endorsed by Sylvester Stallone and pitcher Curt Schilling; Mitt Romney by Donnie and Marie Osmond; Chris Dodd by Paul Simon; John Edwards by Kevin Bacon, Harry Belafonte, and Lance Armstrong; Dennis Kucinich by Tim Robbins, Kevin Bacon, Willie Nelson, and Larry Flynt; Rudy Giuliani by Bo Derek, Jeff Gordon, Robert Duvall, and Adam Sandler; Mike Huckabee by Chuck Norris and Ric Flair; Hillary Clinton by the unlikely combination of Martha Stewart and rapper 50 Cent; and Barack Obama by Oprah Winfrey, Scarlett Johansson, and George Clooney. During the long and arduous Democratic primary race, Hillary picked up the support of Quincy Jones, BET billionaire Robert Johnson, Jerry Springer, Sean Penn, Carly Simon, Janet Jackson, Madonna, Barbara Streisand, and Jon Bon Jovi. Obama received the endorsements of Stevie Wonder, Usher, Zach Braff, Will Smith, Halle Berry, Jessica Biel, and Herbie Hancock. *See also*: **African American**; **Athletes**; **Child Celebrity**; **Corporate Celebrity**; **Dream Girls**; **Movies' Role**; **Politics**; **Rock and Pop**; **Setbacks and Obstacles**; **Sex and Scandal**; **Television's Role**.

Sam G. Riley

For Further Reading

Celebrity Sell: Star Endorsements in the Classic Age of Advertising. London: Prion, 2001.

Luscri, Carmela, and Judith Foster-Langford. *Food and Advertising: Celebrity Endorsements.* Adelaide, Australia: The Association, 1986.

www.thecelebritycafe.com/features/13298.

www.mentalfloss.com/blogs/archives/10386.

www.radaronline.com/exclusives/2008/02/battle-of-the-celebrity-endorsements.

www.tvacres.com/advertising_endorsements.

F

FADS

When celebrities say, wear, or do something that catches on with the media and their consumers, Americans often engage in imitation, which really must be the sincerest form of flattery. We partake of celebrity-originated fads to form psychological bonds with our favorite celebrities; establish kinship with our like-minded fellows; appear "cool" or in the know; and, perhaps, avoid having to think enough to be original. Most celebrity-related fads fall into two categories: fad expressions and fad purchases.

Fad Expressions

Sometimes a celebrity will say something catchy in just the right way, with just the right timing, accent, or inflection. Recognizing the utility of what they or their writers have created, celebrities will continue using these signature expressions. Bolstered by repetition, these expressions will be accepted into the culture and eventually will be repeated, as by a tape recorder, by countless members of the far-flung media audience. Some such expressions will enjoy popularity but will fade from use fairly quickly; others will become engrained in our mediated culture for a remarkably long span of years or even decades. Anyone sufficiently old as to have been a listener in the days of pre-1950s radio who hears the words, "Now, cut that out" will instantly identify that sentence with comedian Jack Benny and also will recall the way those words were said. Similarly, those who witnessed the early years of television, will hear "How sweet it is!" or "Mmmmmm boy, you're fat" and automatically will link these expressions to the rotund Jackie Gleason and *The Jackie Gleason Show*. Like the popular music of our youth, expressions such as these continue to bring us pleasure for a long time.

Some celebrity catchphrases catch on not so much due to the cleverness of the content but to the way the words are spoken. Anyone can repeat the words, "You look marvelous, absolutely marvelous," but only an accomplished mimic could adequately imitate the way these words sounded on *Saturday Night Live* when uttered by Billy Crystal in a faux-Hispanic accent, sounding more or less like, "Eee-yew rook mah-v'lous." Similarly, viewers loved it when Steve Martin, who played on that same show alongside Dan Aykroyd as the Czechoslovakian Festrunk brothers, wound up and let fly the manic line, "Because we are . . . two wild and crazy guys." Few can accurately mimic Martin, but many attempt it just the same. This curious fact is perhaps a part of the magic of show business. Fans recall and repeat "You rang?" although few have the vocal ability to match the way the hulking Lurch (actor Ted Cassidy) said it on *The Addams Family*. Nor can the average fan tell someone to "Kiss my grits" quite the way Flo (actress Polly Holliday) did on the sitcom *Alice*, or the Germanic way Sergeant Schultz (actor John Banner) of *Hogan's Heroes* intoned, "I know noth-ink!" Nor can we match the leer in the voice of actor Telly Savalas as Kojak when he slyly asked, "Who loves you, baby?" or comic actor Don Adams's clipped, nasal way of starting a thought with, "Would you believe . . ." on *Get Smart*, or the crazed enthusiasm of Jimmy Walker's all-purpose exclamation, "Dyn-o-mite!" on *Good Times*, or Bill Cosby's "Hey, hey, hey" as Fat Albert.

Many a Trekkie has "blessed" his or her pals with Mr. Spock's *Star Trek* line, "Live long and prosper," and even more have borrowed the *Star Wars* catchphrase, "May the force be with you." Many others have chided someone with the sitcom *Maude*'s star Bea Arthur's dismissive assurance that, "God'll get you for that." Viewers in untold numbers have aped Stephen Colbert of *The Colbert Report* and his telling usage of the word "truthiness" to mock political "spin" that displaces fact in modern life. The dismissive and oft-repeated "I don't *think* so" was used frequently by Jerry Seinfeld, Macauly Culkin in the movie *Home Alone,* and David Schwimmer of the sitcom *Friends.* Another *Seinfeld* character, Elaine (Julia Louis-Dreyfus), is largely responsible for the sudden popularity of "Yadda, yadda, yadda" in place of "Blah, blah, blah."

The cast of the sitcom *Cybill* popularized the happy "cha-ching" way of exclaiming "Yessss!" as well as "Get a life" and the cutesy "Valley Girl" usages "As if . . ." and "Hell-ooooo?" The successful movie and television portrayal of all things California as our nation's *summum bonum*, in fact, has had almost magical power over the way America's teenagers and emerging adults speak, especially when conversing among themselves. In this faddish argot, young America speaks what might be called "the like patois," sprinkling Los Angeles–accented "likes" throughout whatever they say, as in, "'Like, ya know, like,' he went," "Like, as if, . . ." and "I went, like, 'Get over it, dude.'"

A remarkable outpouring of fad words and phrases originated in two very popular television comedy shows, *Rowan & Martin's Laugh-In* (1968–1973) and *Saturday Night Live* (1975–current). *Laugh-In* catchphrases still in use, although many of their users might not realize the origin, include the remarks of the floozy character played by Jo Ann Worley: "Sock it to me" and "Blow in my ear and I'll follow you anywhere"; Dick Martin's "Look that up in your Funk & Wagnalls" and

"You bet your bippy"; or, when Martin botched his lines and messed up a joke, Dan Rowan's rejoinder, "Sure, that's easy for you to say." Comedian Flip Wilson, cross-dressed as the naughty character Geraldine, gave the nation "The devil made me do it" and "What you see is what you get" and, in addition, recycled the old vaudeville line, "Here come da judge." Peeking at something from behind a potted plant and dressed as a Nazi soldier, *Laugh-In*'s Arte Johnson, holding a cigarette European style, would deliver a thickly accented "Verrrrry Eenterest-ink."

A worthy successor to *Laugh-In* in the production of widely repeated fad expressions was *Saturday Night Live* (SNL). Who could ever forget or resist repeating Garrett Morris's line as he parodied retired baseball player Chico Escuela: "Base-a-bol been berry, berry good to me" or Gilda Radner's sweetly anticlimactic "Never mind . . ." at the end of one of her rants as the perpetually confused middle-aged character Emily Litella? As the self-righteous Church Lady, Dana Carvey created the classic put-down line, "Now, isn't that special," which he would follow by breaking into his "little superior dance." Carvey and Kevin Nealon, dressed in padded outfits and flexing furiously, poked fun at Arnold Schwarzenegger through their characters Hans and Franz, Germanic bodybuilders, invariably using the stock line, "Ve are here to pump . . . you up." In his Sprokets sketches, Mike Myers, clad in black as German minimalist Dieter, often suggestively offered to let people "Touch my monkey," and in another of his characters, Jewish housewife Linda Richman, Myers would sigh, "Oy, I am sooo verklempt."

Martin Short, playing SNL's super-nerd Ed Grimsley, skipped and gangled about, muttering, "I must say, I must say." As The Pathological Liar, chubby Jon Lovitz would conclude his all-too-obvious lies with a sly, purposely unconvincing, "Yeah, that's the ticket," and with Tom Hanks as The Girl Watchers, would signal the sidewalk approach of a beautiful girl with "Hell-oooo . . . Hell-oooo," and after she snubbed him, "Gooood bye . . . Too rich for my blood." Several more catchphrases entered the pop-culture lexicon through two unlikely SNL characters, Wayne and Garth (Mike Myers and Dana Carvey) as a pair of silly, music-sated teens who punctuated their inane thoughts with "Excellent!" and "Party on!" This duo also popularized an odd "reverse usage" in which they would make a statement, then pause and append "Not!" to reveal their real meaning. In like manner, they would often end a segment with "No way," then after a pause, "Way!" These strange usages were recycled everywhere, including uses by highly placed political figures who wanted to sound "cool."

While most celebrity-uttered catchphrases emerge from the movies and even more from entertainment television, some originate in television commercials and become so ingrained in popular culture that the people who uttered them become at least minor celebrities. When restaurant chain Wendy's wanted to accentuate the size of the beef patty in its hamburger relative to its competition, the company was fortunate to find feisty little old lady Clara Peller, who inspected her burger, scowled, and rasped at the clerk in the drive-in window, "Where's the beef?" Since then, this line has been applied to lack of substance in situations without number. Many Americans with expanding waistlines have often borrowed from a long-ago Alka Seltzer commercial the line, "I can't believe I ate the whole thing," and frequently adapted to fit new uses is a line from a Vicks Formula 44 commercial in which a lab-coat wearing young actor says with smarmy confidence, "I'm not a doctor, but I play one on TV." Another example is "I've fallen and I can't get up," etched into America's vocabulary by a 1990s LifeCall medical alarm commercial.

Fad Purchases

In our celebrity-oriented society, Americans are quick to buy products that link them with their favorite celebrities. Of all these objects, perhaps the most common is the t-shirt bearing a celebrity likeness or name. It is ironic that the wearing of the t-shirts in general was a fad that began in the 1950s with one of the biggest movie stars of that time, Marlon Brando. Until the release of the movie *The Wild Ones*, the t-shirt was customarily worn as an undergarment, but upon seeing the muscular, brooding Brando flex his way through that movie in a white t-shirt with the already short sleeves rolled up even higher to accentuate the manly flexing, teens and older boys, wanting to look like Brando, began wearing t-shirts without another shirt on the outside, sleeves rolled high, usually revealing less than Brando-like biceps. Since that time, the t-shirt has become a bedrock item of the U.S. economy, and many of these garments honor favorite rockers, rappers, Hollywood stars, television

personalities, and sports stars. Right behind the t-shirt as celebrity fad merchandise are the celebrity sweatshirt and posters featuring celebrities in all their commercialized glory.

While celebrity-connected fad purchases make up only part of all fad items, the overall economic impact is still huge, and celebrities' power over how Americans want to appear is significant. Looking back to the 1950s, the Frisbee, hula hoop, and boomerang did not stem from celebrity beginnings, yet little boys of that decade either had or wanted a coonskin cap so as to identify with frontiersman Davy Crockett, ably played by Fess Parker. Also iconic in the 1950s was the wearing of rock and roll's Elvis Presley and Jerry Lee Lewis–style long sideburns and ducktail haircuts. Elvis's fad contribution in the 1960s, shared with Sonny and Cher and many other musical entertainers, was the wearing of bellbottom slacks and jeans. The turtleneck owed much of its popularity in that decade to movie stars Steve McQueen, Paul Newman, and others. John Lennon of The Beatles helped popularize dark-rimmed glasses; Nancy Sinatra and her one and only hit song "These Boots Are Made for Walking" did the same for go-go boots; and the greatest celebrity of that era, Jackie Kennedy, made the bouffant hairdo widely if not well imitated.

Hollywood's most sweeping addition to movie-merchandise tie-ins in the 1970s was *Star Wars* and its sequels, accompanied by the sale of a mighty armada of action figures, spacecraft, and the like. Rakish Burt Reynolds, in his movies such as *Smokey and the Bandit* (1977), stimulated the sale of "muscle cars," and sex symbol and actress Farrah Fawcett's magnificent mane of blond hair was the joy of many a hair salon owner due to women's desire to imitate her.

During the 1980s, entertainer Madonna popularized the wearing of underwear on the outside as well as fingerless lace gloves, and *Miami Vice* television star Don Johnson stimulated the sale of brighter-colored men's clothing. In the 1990s, women's "big hair" and other styles gave way to what came to be called "The Rachel," so named for Jennifer Aniston's sitcom character of that name on *Friends*. Another fad of the decade was to buy items from the J. Peterman mail-order catalog, whose character was portrayed by actor John O'Hurley, Elaine's boss on *Seinfeld*. As more movie stars and singers, even some women, began to sport tattoos, so went the nation's youth—good news for tattoo parlors. After the turn of the new century, the great bike racer Lance Armstrong, who overcame cancer and kept winning races, started a successful fundraising fad to bolster support for cancer research: the yellow LiveStrong wristband. Various flat-tummied starlets and models made low-riding jeans a big seller, and the MTV (Music Television) show *Pimp My Ride* was good for certain businesses but did little to improve young America's taste in automobiles.

Another commercial tie with celebrity is in the matter of celebrity-endorsed diets. Some such diets make money for the celebrity whose name is attached to them, while others are merely tried by certain celebrities and after subsequent publicity, are tried by their fans. Celebrities tied in one way or another to certain diets include actresses Jennifer Aniston, Renee Zellweger, Kate Winslet, Gwyneth Paltrow,

and Uma Thurman as well as Victoria Beckham, Christina Aguilera, and Mariah Carey. *See also*: **Athletes**; **Comedy**; **Corporate Celebrity**; **Dream Girls**; **Endorsements**; **Movies' Role**; **Rock and Pop**; **Television's Role**.

Sam G. Riley

For Further Reading

Best, Joel. *Flavor of the Month: Why Smart People Fall for Fads*. Berkeley: University of California Press, 2006.

Hoffmann, Frank W., and William G. Bailey. *Arts and Entertainment Fads*. New York: Haworth Press, 1990.

Panati, Charles. *Panati's Parade of Fads, Follies, and Manias: The Origins of Our Most Cherished Obsessions*. New York: HarperPerennial, 1991.

Savan, Leslie. "Yadda, Yadda, Yadda." *Time* (December 16, 1996): 88; Savan, Leslie. *Slam Dunks and No-Brainers: Language in Your Life, the Media, Business, Politics, and, Like, Whatever*. New York: Knopf, 2005.

Skolnik, Peter L., Laura Torbet, and Nikki Smith. *Fads: America's Crazes, Fevers and Fancies from the 1890s to the 1970s*. New York: Crowell, 1978.

www.crazyfads.com.

http://theskinnywebsite.com.

FAMILY CELEBRITY

In entertainment, some family groups, such as the Marx brothers, have performed together as a unit. Other celebrity families, the Fonda family for example, are known for doing the same type of work although they perform separately. In **politics**, the Kennedy family has been a major family dynasty of considerable celebrity, as have the Rockefellers in the financial sphere.

An early example of those who have performed as a family unit was the so-called royal family of vaudeville, who were billed as "The Seven Little Foys." The group toured the nation from 1914 until the end of the 1920s singing and doing impersonations, and was the subject of a 1955 Bob Hope musical movie titled *The Seven Little Foys*. Performing in early films, usually separately, were the Barrymore family siblings: Lionel, Ethel, and John. Their nephew was actor John Drew Barrymore, father of daughter Drew Barrymore of *E.T.* (1981) and *The Wedding Singer* (1998) fame. Of considerable renown were Douglas Fairbanks, who specialized in swashbuckling roles in silent movies, and his son, Douglas Jr., who appeared in movies from 1916 until his last film, *Ghost Story*, in 1981. A more recent family of remarkable actors, the Redgraves, hail from England. Michael Redgrave (*The Importance of Being Earnest*, 1952; the filmed adaptation of *1984*, which was released in 1956) had two daughters, Vanessa (*Isadora*, 1966; *Girl Interrupted*, 1999) and Lynn (*Georgy Girl*, 1966). The Redgrave daughters also have achieved success on Broadway and television.

Among many successful Hollywood acting families, the name Fonda looms large. Henry Fonda was a major star of his time, appearing in such classic films as *Mister Roberts* (1955), *12 Angry Men* (1957) and *On Golden Pond*

(1981). A celebrity partly due to her family, partly to her beauty, and partly for her controversial stand protesting the Vietnam War, Henry's daughter Jane became famous with her roles in *Cat Ballou* (1965) and space-spoof *Barbarella* (1968). Her flagging celebrity received a boost in 1991 when she married and, a decade later, divorced media tycoon Ted Turner. Her younger brother, Peter, the family nonconformist, is most remembered as an actor for his role as "Captain America" in *Easy Rider* (1968). His daughter, Bridget Fonda, was a child actor in *Easy Rider* and went on to appear in *Godfather, Part III* (1990) and to star in *Single White Female* (1992). Other Hollywood families of actors include sisters Zsa Zsa and Eva Gabor, celebrated mainly for their heavy accents and sophisticated good looks; Kirk Douglas and his equally accomplished son Michael; Jon Voight and pouty-lipped daughter Angelina Jolie; Lloyd Bridges and his actor sons Beau and Jeff, plus Beau's son Jordan; and Martin Sheen (born Ramon Estevez) and his children who have followed in his film footsteps: Charlie, Emilio, Ramon Jr., and Renia. In addition, composer Carmine Coppola fathered celebrity director Francis Ford Coppola and actress Talia Shire. Francis's daughter Sofia now directs, as well.

Among singing families, the 2007–2008 toast of the town on television and on tour are Miley Cyrus (Hannah Montana, darling of the teens and tweens) and her father, Billy Ray Cyrus, formerly known for his one big country hit song, "Achy Breaky Heart." Earlier **country and Western** singing greats were Hank Williams, Hank Jr., Hank III, and Hank Jr.'s daughter Holly; others are the Judds: mother Naomi, who sings with daughter Wynonna, and is also mother to actress Ashley Judd. A little bit country and a little bit **rock** and roll are the Osmonds, Donny and sister Marie, backed up by siblings Alan, Wayne, Merrill, Jay, and Jimmy. Performing from the 1960s until 1990, the Motown group The Jackson Five included siblings Michael, who became a major solo star, plus Jackie, Tito, Jermaine, Marlon, and Randy. The group was known for a variety of styles, including rhythm and blues, soul, pop, and disco. Songs such as "I'll Be There" and "Never Can Say Goodbye" appealed greatly to young white audiences. Other Jackson family performances included sisters Janet, LaToya, and Maureen ("Rebbie").

Greatest of all comedic family entertainers were the Marx brothers: Groucho (Julius), Gummo (Milton), Zeppo (Herbert), Chico (Leonard), and Harpo (Adolph). Starting in the early 1900s in vaudeville, the brothers went on to work in clubs, casinos, film, and television. Their antics took the meaning of the word "zany" to a new level. Groucho became the best known of the group and performed solo into the 1950s. With the advent of television, a new form of comedy was established: the sitcom, or situation comedy. The first family-group sitcom was *The Adventures of Ozzie and Harriet*, starring the Nelson family: mom, dad, and sons David and Ricky. The wholesome show, a reflection of American family life in the 1950s, ran from 1952 until 1966. Ricky Nelson went on to become a popular solo singer following his 1972 hit "Garden Party"; he died in a plane crash in 1985. A striking contrast to Ozzie and Harriet is a more recent television show, *The Osbournes* (2002), featuring outrageous former heavy-metal rock star Ozzy Osbourne, wife Sharon, daughter Kelly, and son Jack. This semifunctional, foul-mouthed family appealed to a large audience in a time when the rule of thumb seems to be the stranger, the better.

In sports are plentiful examples of like father, like son (or daughter); however, in no sport is family a bigger factor that in automobile racing. Family dynasties such as the Earnhardt family are venerated to extreme: for example, when someone noticed a goat with what appeared to be Dale Earnhardt's racecar number in its hide, fans flocked to see it like pilgrims to Lourdes. Father Ralph, son Dale (who died in a 1998 crash), and grandson Dale Jr. are much beloved by NASCAR followers. Another such family began with driver Lee Petty and continued with his remarkably successful son Richard, his grandson Kyle, and great-grandson Adam, who died in a 2000 race. Al Unser, brother Bobby, Al Jr., and Al III are a competing family dynasty. Still another includes Bobby Allison, brother Donny, and Bobby's sons Clifford and Davey, both of whom perished in crashes. Born to race in NASCAR is Chrissy Wallace, daughter of Mike Wallace and niece of Rusty and Kenny Wallace. Italian-born naturalized U.S. citizen Mario Andretti is one of the greats of racing, and keeping it in the family are his sons Jeff and Michael, plus grandson Marco and nephew John.

In loftier circles, Americans have their own "royal families" of politics, the most recent example being U.S. presidents George Herbert Walker Bush and son George W. Bush, plus George

W.'s younger brother and Florida governor Jeb Bush. Before the Bush family was the Kennedy clan, descended from the wealthy Joseph and Rose Kennedy. Probably the most popular U.S. president of modern times was John F. Kennedy, assassinated in 1963; he and wife Jacqueline were **international celebrities**. Also hugely popular, especially among the young, was Robert Kennedy, who served as U.S. attorney general before his assassination in 1968. The last remaining Kennedy brother, Edward (Ted), was a U.S. senator from Massachusetts from 1962 to 2009. Of families whose celebrity derives principally from their wealth, the greatest has been the Rockefellers. John D. Rockefeller made his fortune in oil and eventually turned over most of his business affairs to son John D. Jr., who produced John D. III, director of the Rockefeller Foundation; Nelson, former U.S. vice president and New York governor; David, president of Chase Manhattan Bank; and Laurance, a conservationist who was important in the resort business and in conservation circles. *See also*: **African American**; **Athletes**; **Child Celebrity**; **Comedy**; **Corporate Celebrity**; **Movies' Role**.

Sam G. Riley

For Further Reading

Landes, David S. *Dynasties: Fortunes and Misfortunes of the World's Great Family Businesses*. New York: Viking, 2006.

Schroeder, Alan. *Celebrity-in-Chief: How Show Business Took Over the White House*. Boulder, CO: Westview Press, 2004.

Wright, Ed. *Celebrity Family Trees: The World's Most Celebrated and Scandalous Dynasties*. New York: Barnes & Noble, 2006.

www.findarticles.com/p/articles/mi.

FAMOUS FOR BEING FAMOUS

The gradations within contemporary fame increasingly run the gamut from people distinguished for their extraordinary talents to those recognized simply for their recognizability. Daniel J. Boorstin seemed to foreshadow this cultural inclination in his 1961 book, *The Image: A Guide to Pseudo Events in America*, when he wrote that Shakespeare once divided the famous into three classes: those born great, those who achieved greatness, and those who had greatness thrust upon them. Boorstin added that it never occurred to

Paris Hilton is the very embodiment of the "California girl" in The Hottie and the Nottie, *2008. Courtesy of Photofest.*

Shakespeare to add a fourth category: those who hired public relations agents or press secretaries to make themselves appear great.

Each decade seems to feature its own cast of famous-for-being-famous characters. Zsa Zsa Gabor cultivated her recognition through public appearances and nine high-profile marriages between the 1930s to the present. Heiress and socialite Edie Sedgwick blasted into cultural consciousness as Andy Warhol's muse during the 1960s, before her untimely death in 1971 at age twenty-eight. The 1970s ushered in dissimilar but nevertheless electric celebrities, such as personality Brett Somers, popular for her risqué behavior on the hit television show *Match Game,* and heiress Patty Hearst, kidnapped, allegedly brainwashed, and arrested in 1975 with members of the Symbionese Liberation Army (SLA). In contrast, the 1980s were speckled with pseudo-celebrities ranging from supermodels such as Elle MacPherson and Cindy Crawford, to Mr. T, the mohawked and bejeweled star of television's *A-Team*. But it was the 1990s that introduced America to the most extensive era of those famous-for-being-famous celebrities. The decade was chockablock with photogenic folks caught in unconventional and sometimes unfortunate situations. Anna Nicole Smith, a now-deceased stripper-turned-model-turned-billionaire-widow, illustrates the former. Kato Kaelin, a witness during the O. J. Simpson trial, represents the latter. Coverage of their tribulations involved all mainstream media outlets, from celebrity tabloids to the nightly news. That shift no doubt influenced our culture's celebrity consumption patterns and, from the 1990s to the present, introduced reality television stars into the mix, creating celebrities such as Paris Hilton, Nicole Ritchie, and the cast of *The Hills* (2006–) and *The Bachelor* (2002–).

But what makes these last two decades truly significant within the cultural sphere is their relationship to technology. While certainly every generation boasts its share of infamous characters, advancements in media dissemination have quickened the production and consumption of these personalities. Web sites can promptly post **paparazzi** photos of the starlet du jour, thus feeding the fame frenzy surrounding the celebrity by beckoning print publications to follow suit in their own coverage. As media platforms gauge audience response to the different celebrity gradations, the lines distinguishing merit from mere "knowingness" begin to blur, and these audiences are left with a democratic, though potentially homogeneous, roster of familiar faces. *See also*: **African American**; **Criminals**; **Dream Girls**; **Supermodels**; **Tough Guys**.

Elizabeth Hendrickson

For Further Reading

Halpern, Jake. *Fame Junkies: The Hidden Truths behind America's Favorite Addiction*. New York: Houghton Mifflin Company, 2007.

Gamson, Joshua. *Claims to Fame: Celebrity in Contemporary America*. Berkeley: University of California Press, 1994.

Orth, Maureen. *The Importance of Being Famous: Behind the Scenes of the Celebrity Industrial Complex*. New York: Henry Holt and Company, LLC, 2004.

FAN CLUBS AND SITES

Since the early years of moviemaking fan clubs have allowed admirers of stars to enjoy a sense of kinship not only with the star, but also with fellow fans. Singers and other musicians also have had their own fan clubs, as have star **athletes** and television personalities. Not just individual celebrities, but bands, some television shows, and some movies also have fan clubs of their own. Most of these fan clubs are small—no larger than a few hundred members, if that. Some fan clubs still operate the old-fashioned way; their contact with members is through the mail and through the publication of paper fan newsletters. The coming of the **Internet**, however, has brought about considerable change; and in the 21st century, many fan clubs exist only online. Other fan clubs operate both ways. The online fansite approach provides great flexibility, offering not only biographical and career information about a celebrity, but also a less limited array of pictures and listings, discussion boards, links to fanzines or related sites, and video and audio add-ons. Another distinction is that some fan clubs are "official," or sanctioned by the celebrities they serve, whereas others are independent. Certainly one change brought about by the growing number of online fansites has been an intensification of merchandise tie-ins. Some observers regard Americans' current celebrity worship as sad and regrettable, while others point out that the parasocial relationship between fan and celebrity can offer nonthreatening psychological benefits to individuals who are lacking in interpersonal skills

or who have low or easily threatened self-esteem.

In 2002, the National Association of Fan Clubs shut down in the face of the rapid spread of online fansites. Another, more ambitious organization, dating from 1967, remains: the International Fan Club Organization, which more closely matches the international reach of the Internet.

The oldest fan clubs are devoted to memorializing the movie stars of yesteryear. Comedians Abbott and Costello have two clubs, one official, the other not. Jean Harlow, Clara Bow, Betty Grable, Vivian Leigh, Susan Haywood, Ava Gardner, Lauren Bacall, Joan Crawford, Ginger Rogers, Rita Hayworth, and Jayne Mansfield still have active fan clubs. Marilyn Monroe has at least eleven clubs. Elvis has her beat, however. According to the official elvis.com Web site, the late king of **rock** and roll still has somewhere between 350 and 500 fan clubs around the world. Other male stars having clubs include Bing Crosby, Gene Autry, Clark Gable, Errol Flynn, W. C. Fields, and James Dean. A few such clubs have clever names, such as The Marilyn Lives Society, for the late Marilyn Monroe, The Marx Brotherhood, and singer-actress Cher's club, Cher'd Interest.

Like movie stars, many pop singers have fan clubs. Among them are Bruce Springsteen, Elton John, Michael Bolton, and Pat Boone. Madonna has a fansite, as do Pat Benatar, Mariah Carey, Tiffany, Olivia Newton-John, Brandy, and many other singers. **Country** singers by the truckload have their own fan clubs or fansites: George Jones, Garth Brooks (The Garthoholic webpage), LeAnn Rimes, and Shania Twain (The Shania Twain Shrine), for example.

Groups or bands that have their own fan clubs include The Spice Girls (The Spice Shack), The Red Hot Chili Peppers (The Red Hot Temple), the Dave Matthews Band, the Oak Ridge Boys, the Beach Boys, and Nirvana. Broadway music has its own collective Broadway Fan Club. A few television shows have clubs of their own: *The Andy Griffith Show* Rerun Watchers Club, the *Married with Children* Fan Club, and the Official Canadian *Dukes of Hazzard* Fan Club, for instance. The *Star Wars* movies have multiple fan clubs and fansites, and America's best-known **cult film** has the *Rocky Horror Picture* Show Official Fan Site.

Fan clubs for sports teams are everywhere, often in the form of booster clubs, and standout **athletes** such as Tiger Woods, Shaquille O'Neal, and Joe Montana have their own clubs. Quarterback Michael Vick, serving prison time for dog fighting, is temporarily stuck with the Michael Vick Hater Club. A few performing animals have had clubs of their own: the Official Secretariat Fan Club and the Official Lassie Fan Club, for example. Perhaps the most surprising club of them all is the Official Loch Ness Monster Fan Club, a fan club for something that might not exist at all. *See also*: **Comedy**; **Criminals**; **Dream Girls**; **Movies' Role**.

Sam G. Riley

For Further Reading

Dewey, Patrick R. *Fan Club Directory*. 2nd ed. Jefferson, NC: McFarland, 1998.

Logan, Joyce, and Vicki Lovett. *Celebrity Fan Clubs for Fun and Profit*. East Haven, CT: Emporium Pub. Co., 1999.

http://bestoftulas.com/elinks/fan_clubs.

http://countrymusic.about.com/of/fanclubs/ Country_Music_Fan.

www.elvis.com/fan_relations.

www.entsweb.co.uk/cinema/fanclubs.

www.fansource.com/fan_clubs.

www.ifco.org/fanclubs.

www.musicfanclubs.org.

FASHION DESIGNERS

Fashion designers are no strangers to celebrity. Responsible for creating the red-carpet looks worn by Hollywood's elite, designers have oftentimes become household names as a result of the media scrutiny surrounding events like the Oscars; however, this is not a new phenomenon. Designers have been making names for themselves well before gossip columns and entertainment shows were reporting their every move. This entry focuses primarily on those designers who rose through the ranks of stardom after 1950 and highlights only a few of fashion's famous. It is in no way an exhaustive list.

Often thought of as the preeminent celebrity designer, the Italian-born Gianni Versace is credited with being the first to understand the value of the front-row fashion show celebrity, as well as the importance of the **supermodel**. A publicity machine mastermind, Versace placed his front-row fan base of stars in his scandalous advertising campaigns (for example, Madonna, Elton John, Patricia Arquette),

Greatest of all fashion designers, Coco Chanel lounges in her Paris salon, 1954. Courtesy of Photofest.

commissioned his fashion show soundtracks from high-profile musicians, and embraced **tabloid**-favorite celebrities when they created controversy.

Known for his bold prints and over-the-top, hyperglamorous garments, Versace created designs that were not for the faint of heart. British actress Elizabeth Hurley's career skyrocketed when, in 1994, she wore a black Versace gown held together by safety pins to the premiere of then-boyfriend Hugh Grant's movie *Four Weddings and a Funeral*. In 2000, three years after his untimely death, Versace's reputation for making jaw-dropping garments persisted thanks to sister Donatella's daring designs—Jennifer Lopez caused a stir after famously wearing a backless, barely there, green tropical print gown

to the Grammy Awards. Creating a legacy that combined his craft with classicism and pop culture, Versace found inspiration not only in celebrity, but also in pop art, Grecian motifs, Italian Baroque, and **rock** music as well. Although his career spanned just twenty-five years, Versace left his mark on the fashion world, building an empire that was worth $807 million at the time of his death.

But long before media-savvy Versace, there was Paul Poiret. The precursor to the celebrity designer, Poiret was an early 20th-century French couturier best known for liberating women from the corset in or around 1906. Described by Style.com as "the godfather of today's fashion-as-lifestyle" concept, Poiret was a shrewd businessman who expanded his empire to include fragrances and home décor, including furniture. A thoroughly modern designer, Poiret was a master at parlaying the furor over his revolutionary garments into free publicity, brokering celebrity endorsements and throwing lavish and memorable parties—long before it was de rigueur to do so.

Poiret's contemporary, Gabrielle "Coco" Chanel, remains perhaps the world's best-known fashion designer—even, some have argued, the greatest in the first half of the 20th century. Beginning her career in millinery, Chanel dominated the fashion scene in the 1920s and beyond, popularizing chic and comfortable sportswear, costume jewelry, bobbed hair, the tan, and the tweed suit. Best known for her iconic perfume, Chanel No. 5, she built a formidable empire consisting of her fashion house, a textile business, perfumes, and a costume jewelry line. Although she took a fifteen-year sabbatical in the late thirties, her comeback collection debuted in early 1954 and heralded her return as a widely popular designer. Her pervasive influence is still felt—she is often (mis)credited with inventing the little black dress, which today remains a staple in every woman's wardrobe—and her eponymous label, now under the direction of Karl Lagerfeld, is one of the most recognizable names in luxury and haute couture.

Lagerfeld, Chanel's heir, is a German-born couturier, ready-to-wear designer, and all-around Renaissance man. Widely recognized for his work as Art Director at the House of Chanel, Lagerfeld has had a long and illustrious fashion career spanning more than fifty years. Since 1952, Lagerfeld has worked in couture at the houses of Balmain, Patou, and Chanel as well as in ready-to-wear, most notably for Fendi (a label for whom he currently designs) and Chloé. In 1983, he took the reigns at the then-fledgling House of Chanel, and his keen ability to blend street with high fashion turned the already iconic label into one of the most sought after in the world. In addition to designing for Fendi and Chanel, Lagerfeld exerts creative control over his line, the Lagerfeld Collection, which was sold to Tommy Hilfiger in 2005. He also shoots fashion spreads for magazines, owns a bookshop and publishing house, and exhibits his photography in galleries around the world.

With a Warholian appreciation for the cult of celebrity, Lagerfeld has manipulated his signature look of stark white hair, high collar, ascot, and perma-attached fan to transcend the medium in which he worked. As a result, he has become a larger-than-life star with his own following, including celebrity admirers ranging from Lindsay Lohan to Nicole Kidman. His face has been immortalized on everything from pins to t-shirts, further cementing his celebrity status.

Like Lagerfeld, Marc Jacobs is one of today's highly regarded and easily recognizable designers. As head designer of the French fashion house Louis Vuitton, with his Marc Jacobs label and his lower-priced line, Marc by Marc Jacobs, he is often dubbed one of the most influential American designers of the 21st century. He has become as famous for his clothes, however, as he has for his celebrity friends, former wild ways, personal reinvention, and tabloid-worthy relationships. His cavalcade of admirers includes muse Sofia Coppola, Victoria Beckham, M.I.A., and Winona Ryder, all of whom have been featured in his advertising campaign for Marc Jacobs. Jennifer Lopez, Scarlett Johanssen, and Uma Thurman have leant their faces to Louis Vuitton, helping to establish it as a sexy and glamorous label—a departure from the sweet, arty, and somewhat grungy quality of the Marc Jacobs line. The ad campaigns, while polar opposites of one another, offer insight into Marc Jacobs's evolving personality. A graduate of the Parsons School of Design in New York City, Jacobs has transformed himself into a buff, yoga-loving, diamond-earring wearing superstar—a far cry from the designer that he once was: grungy, awkward, overweight, and constantly clad in oversized glasses and dowdy sweaters. Most recently, Jacobs has appeared on MTV's (Music Television) *The Hills* and posed nude on the cover of various magazines like *OUT* and *Arena Hommes Plus*, and in so doing has made his name recognizable to those beyond the fashion industry. Additionally, Jacobs, much like his celebrity counterparts, has made waves with his trip to rehab and his controversial relationships, most notably one with an ex-escort. A self-proclaimed attention seeker, Jacobs has played the modern fame game well, ensuring that he will remain in the public realm at least for his headline-grabbing antics, if not for his clothes.

Almost no other designer embodied the sex- and drug-fueled spirit of the 1970s more than American designer Roy Halston Frowick. A graduate of Indiana University and the Art Institute of Chicago, Halston began his career in fashion as a milliner in that city. Soon, he was making hats for celebrities like Kim Novak, Shirley Booth, Deborah Kerr, and Hedda Hopper, before moving to New York at the age of twenty-five. Despite having designed the pillbox hat that Jackie Kennedy wore to her husband's inauguration, Halston was forced to turn to clothing design in 1966, as women were favoring bouffant hairstyles to hats. Within a few years, Halston had built a company consisting of both couture and ready-to-wear lines, and he became widely known for his use of ultrasuede, an imitation leather material that could be machine washed. As his reputation as a designer grew, so too did his clientele. Personalities such as Liza Minnelli, Elizabeth Taylor, Martha Graham, Bianca Jagger, and Candice Bergen often were seated front row at his fashion shows, and according to the *New York Times*, pop-artist and cultural icon Andy Warhol referred to the shows as "the art form of the '70s." Although Halston was never formally trained in fashion design, he was the master of cut, finishing, and detail, and in addition to the women seated front row at his shows, he dressed luminaries such as Princess Grace (in powder blue ultrasuede, no less), Barbara Walters, Lauren Bacall, and Betty Ford.

He surrounded himself with fame, becoming a fixture at Studio 54, and eventually was hailed King of the New York Nightlife. Thanks to his popularity among the glitterati, Halston garnered a mention in "Big Shot," the 1978 Billy Joel song. His ability to hold celebrities in his sway contributed to his success in getting them to dress as carbon copies—either in fashionable muumuus or his famous model No. 704, a knee-length, belted ultrasuede shirt, which was called the "status security blanket" by the *New York Times*. The herd instinct had become chic, in large part, due to Halston. He died at the age of fifty-seven and is often regarded as one of the first international superstar designers and a symbol of American fashion in the 1970s.

Among other notable designers have been Christian Dior, Hubert de Givenchy, Thierry Hermes, and Yves Saint Laurent in France; Adele Fendi, Giorgio Armani, Guccio Gucci, Miuccia Prada, and Valentino Garavani in Italy; and Bill Blass and Calvin Klein in the United States. *See also*: **Dream Girls**; **International Celebrity**; **Movies' Role**; **News Media Figures**.

Amy Widmayer

For Further Reading

Goblin, Pamela. *Fashion Designers.* New York: Watson-Guptill, 2001.

Kellogg, Ann T. *In an Influential Fashion: An Encyclopedia of Nineteenth- and Twentieth-Century Fashion Designers and Retailers Who Transformed Dress.* Westport, CT: Greenwood Press, 2002.

Milbank, Caroline Rennolds. *Couture: The Great Fashion Designers.* London: Thames and Hudson, 1985.

Steele, Valerie. *Women of Fashion: Twentieth-Century Designers.* New York: Rizzoli International, 1991.

http://fashion.about.com/od/fashion designers/Fashion_Designers.htm.

www.top-fashion-designers.info.

FORMER SPORTS STARS AS MEDIA CELEBRITIES

The public has long elevated **athletes** to objects of hero worship, but media proliferation and scrutiny mean that star athletes' lives can be placed under a stronger microscope, resulting in new dimensions of celebrity. The obvious representation of this trend is O. J. Simpson, the University of Southern California's 1968 Heisman trophy winner, who continued his stellar football career as 1973's National Football League (NFL) Most Valuable Player, and in 1985, was named to professional football's Hall of Fame. Even while playing football, Simpson parlayed his fame into a successful film and television career (*Roots, The Towering Inferno,* and *The Naked Gun* trilogy). He endorsed projects from Hertz and Pioneer Chicken and also served as commentator on *Monday Night Football* and *The NFL on NBC.* But his media celebrity status exploded with his "white Bronco" pursuit, **arrest**, and trial for the 1994 murders of his ex-wife Nicole Brown Simpson and their friend Ronald Goldman. He was acquitted in a highly publicized, televised **criminal** trial. In 2006, he wrote a book called *If I Did It,* a supposed first-person fictionalized retelling of the murders. O. J. achieved media celebrity status in a way that few would desire.

Not all former sports stars attain the type of scandalous celebrity of O. J. Simpson. A lucrative **endorsement** contract also can create media buzz. Interest in sports stars and their lifestyles makes everything they wear, eat, drink, and do part of their celebrity. Football Hall of Fame quarterback Joe Namath became even more of a popular-culture icon after he appeared in television advertisements during and after his playing career, most notably for Noxema shaving cream (he was shaved by a then-unknown Farrah Fawcett) and for the Hanes Beauty Mist Pantyhose he donned in 1973. Michael Jordan, Chicago Bulls guard, became Nike's signature athlete, a global superstar, and a name brand. His signature shoe, the "Air Jordan," remains popular.

Pharmaceutical companies use former sports stars to raise awareness about various medical conditions and products via media tours, **Internet** sites, and advertising campaigns. Dickinson and Co. uses swimming gold medalist Gary Hall, Jr., who has diabetes, to promote its diabetes products. Former Chicago coach and **tough guy** Mike Ditka made discussing erectile dysfunction public with his ads for Levitra. Products of all kinds help to thrust former athletes into media celebrity. In the 1970s, Hall of Fame Yankees centerfielder Joe DiMaggio brought national awareness to the then-revolutionary coffee machine Mr. Coffee. Two-time world heavyweight boxing champ George Foreman made a fortune with his namesake grills, which debuted as an infomercial in 1994. Endorsement deals may be established around athletic prowess and personality, but it is media's **globalization** and expansion that have taken the athlete to celebrity beyond sport.

Former athletic stars do not have to rely on product endorsements to become media celebrities. They can return to their sports as commentators and enjoy a second career. Former quarterbacks Boomer Esiason and Troy Aikman, wide receivers Lynn Swann and Ahmahd Rashad, shortstop Ozzie Smith, and running backs Frank Gifford and Tiki Barber are examples of athletes who have made the successful transition to media celebrity via football commentating. Former coaches Lee Courso, Lou Holtz, and Pat Riley expanded their celebrity when

they became media fixtures. Cincinnati's Johnny Bench worked with CBS (Columbia Broadcasting System) Radio broadcasting the National Game of the Week, the All-Star Game, the League Championship Series, and the World Series. Former forward Charles Barkley is an Emmy Award–winning basketball color commentator. Golfer Ken Venturi, the 2000 President's Cup Captain, is a golf analyst for CBS Sports. Olympians also move into the media spotlight beyond their sports, including Dan Jansen (speed skater), Scott Hamilton (figure skater), Nadia Coamneci (gymnast), and Bela Karolyi (gymnastics coach). Boxing great Ray Charles "Sugar Ray" Leonard had a successful career as a television broadcaster for National Broadcasting Company (NBC), American Broadcasting Company (ABC), Home Box Office (HBO), and the Entertainment and Sports Programming Network (ESPN).

Some former athletes gain celebrity through the entertainment media of television, film, and even books. Among them are football's legendary running back Jim Brown (*The Dirty Dozen*, 1967; *Ice Station Zebra*, 1968; *Mars Attacks!*, 1996; and other movies); defensive tackle Alex Karras (*Blazing Saddles*, 1974; *Porky's*, 1982; *Paper Lion*, 1968; *Victor/Victoria*, 1982; and ABC's *Webster* sitcom, 1983–1989); center Kareem Abdul-Jabbar (*Airplane!*, 1980; *Game of Death*, 1981); and center Shaquille O'Neal (*Blue Chips*, 1994; *Kazaam*, 1996; *Freddy Got Fingered*, 2001; *Scary Movie 4*, 2006). Also included are lightweight champion boxer Ray "Boom Boom" Mancini (*Aces: Iron Eagle III*, 1992; *Amazing Stories: Book Three*, 1991; *Wishful Thinking*, 1997); **martial artist** Chuck Norris (television's

Walker Texas Ranger, 1993–2001; the *Missing in Action* films, 1984, 1985, 1988; and many others); and professional wrestler Dwayne "The Rock" Johnson (*The Mummy Returns*, 2002; *The Scorpion King*, 2002; *Walking Tall*, 2004; *Doom*, 2005). Tennis great John McEnroe has landed television, film, and advertising roles in which he plays off his well-known belligerence.

Reality television has afforded former athletes a new celebrity spotlight: since 2005, ABC's *Dancing with the Stars* has featured numerous former sports stars, extending their celebrity to an entirely new audience. Examples include Misty May-Treanor (Olympics beach volleyball); Evander Holyfield (boxing); Stacy Keibler (wrestling); Jerry Rice and Emmitt Smith (football); Clyde Drexler (basketball); Laila Ali and Floyd Mayweather, Jr. (boxing); Apollo Anton Ohno (speed skating); Helio Castroneves (auto racing); and Monica Seles (tennis). Wrestler Hulk Hogan produced his own family's reality show *Hogan Knows Best* (2005–2007); Jose Canseco starred in *VH1's Surreal Life* (2003–2006). Fullback Larry Csonka hosts and produces outdoor adventure programs. Defensive end Howie Long penned the book *Football for Dummies* (1998). Jose Canseco wrote *Juiced: Wild Times, Rampant 'Roids, Smash Hits, and How Baseball Got Big* (2005). Pitcher Jim Bouton's irreverent and revealing *Ball Four* (1970) was selected by the New York Public Library as one of the "Books of the Century"; he also invented Big League Chew—shredded bubble gum. Newer media also have spawned celebrity. Former Oakland Raider football coach John Madden developed a larger-than-life image through years of network NFL broadcasts plus a long career in commercials, but he became a pop-culture icon with his franchise Electronic Arts "Madden NFL" video game. Launched in fall 2008 with a "Maddenpalooza" at the Rose Bowl with rock acts and video kiosks, the game has been a consistent bestseller and has even spun off television shows on which players compete.

Perhaps the most positive form of media celebrity is achieved by sports stars who become synonymous with important causes long after their athletic success. Tour de France winner Lance Armstrong (LiveStrong: Lance Armstrong Foundation) created one of the most influential organizations of its kind, focusing on the battle against cancer. The iconic yellow silicone wristband, introduced in May 2004 as a fundraising item, has inspired other charities to develop their own wristbands to raise money and awareness. Linebacker Nick Buoniconti created the Miami Project to Cure Paralysis (spinal cord injuries, 1985) in response to his son's football spinal cord accident. In 1991, point guard Earvin "Magic" Johnson set up the Magic John Foundation after he revealed that he had tested positive test for HIV. Heisman quarterback Doug Flutie developed the Doug Flutie, Jr., Foundation for Autism, Inc. (2000) in honor of his son, Doug Jr. Other athletes who developed added media presence through the promotion of their causes include quarterback Boomer Esiason (cystic fibrosis); the late basketball coach Jimmy Valvano (The V Foundation, dedicated to finding a cancer cure); and skateboarder Tony Hawk, whose foundation (2002) supports recreational programs with a focus on the creation of public skateboard parks in low-income communities.

Sports play a leading role in popular culture; the star athletes may symbolize a cultural identity, possess economic importance, and gain fame or notoriety beyond their sport. They acquire fame and celebrity status, sometimes not even because of their former prowess; instead, they become products or inventions of media interpretations. *See also*: **African American**; **Comedy**; **Dancers**; **Dream Girls**; **Humanitarian Efforts**; **Television's Role**.

Beth M. Waggenspack

For Further Reading

Andrews, David L., and Steven J. Jackson. *Sport Stars: The Cultural Politics of Sporting Celebrity*. London and New York: Routledge, 2001.

Coakley, Jay J., and Peter Donnelly. *Sports in Society: Issues and Controversies*. 8th ed. Toronto: McGraw-Hill Ryerson, 2004.

Long, Diane. *He's Just My Dad! Portraits of Celebrity Athletes and Their Children*. New York: Harper Entertainment, 2000.

Smart, Barry. *The Sport Star: Modern Sport and the Cultural Economy of Sporting Celebrity*. London: Sage, 2005.

http://www.athlebrities.com.

http://www.playingfieldpromotions .com/athlete-endorsements.asp.

G

GLOBALIZATION

Since 1945 the world's diverse celebrity cultures, like its **politics** and economies, have been reshaped thanks to globalization, the pattern of which extends economic, political, and cultural processes beyond nation-state boundaries. Globalization has fostered more extensive networks of exchange and communication than ever existed before through international trade pacts, electronic funds transfers, jet-speed travel, the **Internet**, facsimile machines, satellite phones, international cable television systems, multinational entertainment conglomerates, and the like. These transnational connections link distant societies, reduce barriers between and among countries, and turn the world into a cultural supermarket in which the celebrity of entertainment and sports stars transcends national and even regional boundaries. Around the world people speak, with fear or enthusiasm, of the globalization that has clearly benefited some, bringing jobs or attractive new ideas, while harming those who become economically marginalized or see their cultures destabilized. Jobs, people, cultural products, and fame move from one country to another. Societies become more dependent on each other for everything from consumer goods and entertainments to fuels and technological innovations. All around the world, people consume Chinese textiles, U.S. films and sports broadcasts, Persian Gulf oil, and Japanese electronics.

Global forces, symbolized by satellites relaying information and advertising for foreign-made goods around the world, interact with local cultures. As a result, local traditions and products are sometimes replaced, and imported and local cultures blend. The inequitable relationship between the industrial nations and the developing nations has prompted some observers to perceive cultural imperialism, as Western, especially U.S., economic and political power enables their cultural products, entertainments, and celebrity fame to spread widely, sometimes undermining local cultures. Referring to one American consumer icon, some speak of the "Coca-Colazation" of the world. To critics, the United States exports its popular music, disco dancing, skimpy women's clothing, and **sex**-drenched films and publications reflecting American values. Other societies adopt these products, which modify or suffocate their own traditions. For instance, big-budget Hollywood films attract large audiences, whereas local films, with small budgets, cannot compete, often killing the local film industry. To survive, local filmmakers adopt the formulas used by successful Hollywood filmmakers—sex and violence. For decades, Hollywood stars, from John Wayne, Marilyn Monroe, and Elizabeth Taylor in the 1950s to Tom Cruise, Angelina Jolie, and Julia Roberts today, have become huge international celebrities.

Popular culture produced in the United States, enjoyable but also challenging to traditional values, has emerged as the closest thing available to global entertainment. Cable channels worldwide carry American music and sports events. Popular U.S. television programs, including such programs as *Dallas* (a drama series), *The Muppet Show* (a variety show), both in the 1980s, and *Desperate Housewives* and *American Idol* of the 21st century, are broadcast in dozens of nations, often sparking local imitations, such as the immensely popular *Super Girl* singing competition in China in which millions of fans vote for a winner.

American cultural influence, including the prominence of celebrities, is ubiquitous. Hard Rock Cafes have been established as far afield as China's capital, Beijing, and American pop stars such as Elvis Presley, Michael Jackson, and Madonna have sparked imitators and **fan clubs** all over Asia and Europe. Decades after Presley's death, Elvis impersonators still perform in cities around the world. Due to the popularity of the British **rock** group The Beatles, pop music in the 1960s and 1970s was imitated by local musical groups using guitars and drum sets. The music was called "yeah yeah music" after The Beatles' song "She Loves You (Yeah Yeah Yeah)" and was performed in countries as different as Brazil and Malaysia. The exploits of Anglo-American sports stars such as Tiger Woods, Kobe Bryant, Serena Williams, and David Beckham top the sports pages in many nations. At the same time, non-U.S. stars, such as Chinese basketball player Yao Ming and Japanese baseball star Ichiro Suzuki, gain fame and exposure because of their success in U.S. sports leagues.

The popular culture of music, films, fads, foods, fashions, jeans, and sports may be the United States's number-one export. Hence, many more Asians than Americans followed the fanciful, bloody, and imperialistic adventures of Rambo, the American film hero of the 1980s. A million people raced to see *Rambo: First Blood*, within the first ten days of its Beijing opening. In Indonesia, the Rambo Amusement Arcade did a huge business while vendors along the streets offered posters of the film's star, Sylvester Stallone. Later the film *Jurassic Park* and the *Star Wars* series became massive global hits. Versions of Disney World opened in Paris, Tokyo, and Hong Kong, enhancing the celebrity of Mickey Mouse. Cable channels worldwide broadcast American music and sports events.

Some American celebrities and icons, from basketball star Michael Jordan to McDonald's, became symbols of a new global modernity and capitalism. Ads featuring Jordan, with his shaved head and fluid moves on the court, sell athletic shoes and promote McDonald's in more than 100 nations. Not even the Chinese, with one of the world's most admired cuisines, were immune to the appeal of modern U.S. marketing techniques and convenience for harried urbanites. In 1993, a famous roast duck restaurant in Beijing sent its management staff to study the McDonald's operation in then-British-ruled Hong Kong, and then introduced its customers to "roast duck fast food." The restaurant also faced a challenge from the growing number of McDonald's franchises in Beijing.

Still, popular American entertainments and celebrities often face opposition. Governments, from the Islamic clerics running Iran to the more democratic leaders of India, have attempted to halt or control the influx of what they consider destabilizing, immoral pop culture. In 1995, an Islamic political party in Pakistan even demanded, unsuccessfully, that the United States turn over to them American pop stars Madonna and Michael Jackson, so that they could be placed on trial as "cultural terrorists" destroying humanity. Yet, the sudden death in 2009 of Jackson, known equally for his spectacular musical talents and bizarre personal life, illustrated the global influence of U.S. popular culture. His demise and legacy dominated the mass media for weeks, a star-studded memorial tribute was televised around the world, and millions of people bought his recordings and memorabilia.

Anglo-American cultural forms and celebrities are not the only ones to reach a global audience. Mexican and Brazilian soap operas; Indian (Bollywood) films; Nigerian novels; Arab, African, and Caribbean pop music; and Japanese comics, animation, and electronic games have been popular around the globe. For example, thanks in part to the massive popularity of Jamaican singer-musician Bob Marley, reggae music from the Caribbean developed a huge presence in Latin America, Africa, Southeast Asia, Japan, the South Pacific, and on Native American reservations in North America. Hong Kong **martial arts** action films and their stars such as Jackie Chan, Bruce Lee and Jet Li have huge followings worldwide. In North America, Western Europe, and Australia, people have taken up Indian yoga, Chinese *tai qi*, and other Asian spiritual disciplines; patronize Thai, Indian, Chinese, and Japanese restaurants; enjoy Brazilian and African pop music; learn Latin American dances; and master Asian martial arts, such as karate and judo. Many North American universities have student clubs dedicated to Japanese *anime* (animation) and comics. Yet, few Americans revere foreign celebrities unless, like Yao Ming, Ichiro Suzuki, Austrian-born action film star (later California governor) Arnold Schwarzenegger, Canadian rocker Neil Young, and Australian film star Nicole Kidman, they make their careers largely in the United States.

The meeting of global and local cultures fosters hybridization, the blending of two cultures, a process that can be either enriching or impoverishing. Record stores in industrial nations have sections for "world music," popular music originating largely outside of North America that mixes Western influences with local and other traditions. This trend has allowed musicians such as the Senegalese Youssou N'Dour, the South African Johnny Clegg, the Indian film diva Asha Bhosle and the Brazilian Caetano Veloso to build audiences far from their homelands, including in the United States. Meanwhile such Anglo-American pop stars as Paul Simon, Dave Matthews, and Peter Gabriel add world influences to their own music. Through their global celebrity, and using the power of the mass media, Western pop stars mount concerts to address issues such as racism, political prisoners, famine, and African poverty. Bono, the lead singer for the Irish rock band U2, hugely popular worldwide, uses his celebrity to campaign the world's most influential political leaders for such causes as debt relief for poor nations.

A worldwide communications network spurred by technological innovation was a chief engine of celebrity globalization: films and radio in the 1930s, television in the 1950s, personal computers in the 1980s, and music players in the 1990s. By 2008, the world had some 1.4 billion Internet users and 100 million Web sites, all part of a vast information superhighway. Every minute, 20 million e-mail messages are dispatched via computer, some of them sharing jokes or music or celebrity gossip. Anyone with a networked computer or multifunctional handheld mobile phone or other electronic device can access information and entertainment from around the world. Millions download music or films. Most celebrities and their fan clubs have exclusive Web sites. Repressive states seeking to limit information flow, such as Iran, China, and Cuba, have banned satellite dish receivers or have tried to jam access to controversial Web sites, including those used by political dissidents, although these efforts have been only partly successful. Despite these challenges and a mixed record of improving life, globalization will continue to reshape cultures, affect people both in North America and around the world, and foster the internationalization of celebrity. *See also*: **Athletes**; **Hispanic/Latino**; **Humanitarian Efforts**; **Movies' Role**; **Television's Role**; **Tough Guys**.

Craig A. Lockard

For Further Reading

Crothers, Lane. *Globalization and American Popular Culture*. Armonk, NY: Rowman and Littlefield, 2006.

LaFeber, Walter, *Michael Jordan and the New Global Capitalism*. New York: W.W. Norton, 2002.

Mathews, Gordon. *Global Culture/ Individual Identity: Searching for Home in the Cultural Supermarket*. New York: Routledge, 2000.

Taylor, Timothy D. *Global Pop: World Music, World Markets*. New York: Routledge, 1997.

Tomlinson, John. *Globalization and Culture*. Chicago: University of Chicago Press, 1999.

H

HALLS OF FAME

The definition of "hall of fame" typically includes the intent to honor past achievements and to inspire future excellence, as well as some sort of stringent requirements for selection into the elite and a physical location where the public may learn about the organization and its honorees. However, a hall of fame may also be a collection of memorabilia and artifacts and may not have any building or other structure to house it.

It was estimated by American Broadcasting Company (ABC) News in the 1990s that the United States housed about 3,000 halls of fame. The United States clearly seems to host the majority of halls of fame in the world.

America's first hall of fame stands on the campus of the Bronx Community College, The Hall of Fame for Great Americans, a neoclassical colonnade featuring bronze busts of the likes of George Washington, Thomas Jefferson, Booker T. Washington, and Susan B. Anthony as well as the less-remembered Sen. Rufus Choate, actress Charlotte Cushman, and historian John Lothrop Motley.

The Hall of Fame for Great Americans, however, has fallen into financial difficulties and has not elected a class of entrants since 1976. As it has faded into neglect, numerous halls of fame that honor almost every imaginable avenue of popular culture have flourished. Interestingly, one of these is the Hall of Fame for Great American Indians in Anadarko, Oklahoma.

Although halls of fame may be found for the conventional (the Accounting Hall of Fame, housed at Ohio State University) and unconventional (the Quackery Hall of Fame in Minneapolis, which houses bizarre medical equipment), most halls of fame tend to recognize achievements in sports, music, and entertainment.

Perhaps the best-known hall of fame can be found in Cooperstown, New York, where myth tells us that Abner Doubleday invented the game of baseball in 1836. The town, accessible by narrow state roads that wend past farms, hills, and Lake Otsego, presents itself as a throwback to the pastoral era that spawned baseball. The National Baseball Hall of Fame and Museum opened its doors in 1939 and attracts more than 350,000 visitors a year. Thousands come for Induction Day in August.

Other major sports halls of fame also have physical locations linked to the past. The Pro Football Hall of Fame honors the game's Midwestern roots with its Canton, Ohio, location; and the Naismith Memorial Basketball Hall of Fame is found in Springfield, Massachusetts, where in 1891 James Naismith invented the game.

But major sports are hardly the only ones with halls of fame. Consider these examples: the National Midget Auto Racing Hall of Fame, the International Surfing Hall of Fame, the Shuffleboard Hall of Fame, the Billiard Congress of America Hall of Fame, and the Roller Derby Hall of Fame.

The foremost American music hall of fame is much newer. The **Rock** and Roll Hall of Fame and Museum began operations in 1983 in Cleveland, Ohio, where **disc jockey** Alan Freed, who coined the phrase "rock and roll," once worked. The Hall had more than 450,000 visitors in 2007.

Other musical genres are represented throughout the states. The **Country** Music Hall of Fame is located in Nashville, while the Nesuhi Ertegun **Jazz** Hall of Fame in the Lincoln Center in New York City is one of the newest to honor jazz performers, and the American **Classical Music** Hall of Fame is located in Cincinnati. Indicative of the popularity of music halls of fame are at least five halls dedicated to polka music (the National Cleveland-Style Polka Hall of Fame, the San Francisco-Style Polka Hall of

Fame, the National Polka Hall of Fame in Chicago, the Wisconsin Polka Hall of Fame, and the Michigan State Polka Hall of Fame), where honorees are niche celebrities.

The entertainment field's best-known hall of fame is not a hall at all, but rather the Hollywood Walk of Fame. Hollywood pedestrians can walk down Hollywood and Vine and step across more than 2,000 imbedded stars with the names of those selected by the Hollywood Chamber of Commerce. Each pink star has a bronze border and is inlaid into a charcoal square imbedded in the sidewalk.

Those selected for a star must pay a $25,000 fee—usually given by a studio or network—to the Chamber and agree to participate in a public ceremony within five years. An older Hollywood sidewalk tradition is the footprints and handprints in cement outside Grauman's Chinese Theater.

The selection process leads to the interesting and sometimes controversial distinction of "hall-of-famer." The term itself indicates the highest level of success in a field; fans often debate just which players or performers are worthy of inclusion. There is an even higher standard for first-time hall-of-famers—those who are selected to the hall on their first eligible opportunity.

Though the Hollywood Walk of Fame requires an entry fee, most halls depend on a panel of experts to weigh nominees' merits. The Baseball Writers of America, for example, select names from a ballot and those who earn 75 percent of the vote enter the Hall. The Pro Football Hall of Fame uses a panel of thirty-two sports journalists. As many as six finalists per year must earn an 80 percent vote. The Rock and Roll Hall of Fame requires more than 50 percent approval by a panel. Other halls use less transparent methods, simply mentioning that electors will select those who will be inducted. But halls of fame traditionally maintain at least a curtain of secrecy over the process. Individual ballots are usually not made public, unless the voter chooses to do so—and some, like the Pro Football Hall of Fame, punish voters who reveal what went on behind closed doors.

Many halls have published criteria for those to be considered, and, typically, have a period of time in which an individual may be considered. But the halls often have "side doors." Music halls of fame, for example, often have categories for those who did not perform on stage. The Hollywood Walk of Fame has directors, producers, studio heads, and even a wrestling promoter (Vince McMahon) included on the sidewalks. The Baseball Hall of Fame has paths to honor journalists, executives, and others who did not play the game, as well as a Veterans' Committee to select those ignored by the Baseball Writers of America.

The lack of transparency can lead to controversy in the selection process. Author Bill James castigated the practices of the Veterans' Committee, which for years seemed to operate on a personal-friend basis rather than an analytical one. Debates rage among fans about the worthiness of certain players not yet selected.

Yet strictness should be a necessity for selecting honorees. The Rock and Roll Hall of Fame has come under fire for its 50 percent policy that allows "lesser" acts an opportunity to be enshrined. Because the Hollywood Walk of Fame requires its fee, critics do not necessarily consider the honorees to be legitimate hall-of-famers.

Many halls of fame are found at the state level, including a plethora of sports halls: the Texas Sports Hall of Fame is joined by similar halls in Georgia, North Carolina, Oregon, Wyoming, and Hawaii, among others. There are also numerous state aviation halls of fame, including some in Georgia, Utah, Colorado, and Minnesota. Still, the wonder of the hall of fame is that it allows individuals who excel an opportunity to receive special status among their peers. Part of the wonder comes from the incredible array of halls of fame that provide a panorama of popular culture in America (and Canada, which has its share of halls of fame).

Niche celebrity is furthered via the National Jousting Hall of Fame (Mt. Solon, Virginia), the Hall of Fame of Distinguished Band Conductors (Troy, Alabama), the California Social Work Hall of Distinction (Los Angeles), the National Jewish Sports Hall of Fame (Commack, New York), the National Sprint Car Hall of Fame (Knoxville, Iowa), the Mascot Hall of Fame (Newark, Delaware), the Alabama Jazz Hall of Fame (Birmingham, Alabama), the Museum and Hall of Fame of Science Fiction (Seattle, Washington), the National Inventors Hall of Fame (Akron, Ohio), the Circus Hall of Fame (Peru, Indiana), the National Cowboy Hall of Fame (Oklahoma City, Oklahoma), the North Dakota Cowboy Hall of Fame (Medora, North Dakota), and the ProRodeo Hall of Fame (Colorado Springs, Colorado). Remarkably, there is also a Cockroach Hall of Fame (Plano, Texas). *See also*: **Athletes**; **Awards and Ceremonies**.

Randy Miller

For Further Reading

Danilov, Victor J. *Hall of Fame Museums: A Reference Guide*. Westport, CT: Greenwood Press, 1997.

James, Bill. *Whatever Happened to the Hall of Fame? Baseball, Cooperstown, and the Politics of Glory*. New York: Fireside, 1994.

Soderberg, Paul, Helen Washington, and Jaques Cattell Press. *The Big Book of Halls of Fame in the United States and Canada*. New York: R. R. Bowker Co., 1977.

http://web.baseballhalloffame.org.

http://www.rockhall.com.

http://www.seeing-stars.com/Immortalized/WalkOfFame.

HIP-HOP AND RAP

The big-money celebrities of America's hip-hop culture are the rappers, who unquestionably are the most influential poets of the last twenty or thirty years. Hip-hop's less prosperous cohorts are break **dancers** and graffiti artists. In rap, the anger and frustration of America's economically depressed ghettos is expressed in rhythmically spoken rhymes, sometimes prewritten, sometimes improvised, over a thumping beat. Some rap is playful; some has been used for community uplift; but much of it has been raw, angry, and profane. It has often promoted violence, **drugs**, and disrespect for women and for gays. It has been so combative and iconoclastic that by the mid-1980s, white teens found this new musical form exciting and appealing in the same way that 1950s teens embraced **rock** and roll.

Rap is said to have originated in New York's Bronx and Harlem neighborhoods in the 1970s and is thought to have grown out of the work of fast-talking **disc jockeys** and MCs (masters of ceremonies) such as DJ Kool Herc (Clive Campbell), Afrikaa Bambaataa, and Grandmaster Melle Mel (Mel Glover) of The Furious Five. Another associate of that group was Keith Cowboy (Keith Wiggins), said to have coined the term "hip-hop." The work of these early rappers often used a disco-type beat, but that changed as disco music itself fell from popularity. In Philadelphia, DJ Lady D (Wendy Clark) became the first woman to record rap music, and two early rappers

Rapper/actor Ice-T scowls at the camera in his television role as Law and Order's *Detective Fin Tutuola. Courtesy of Photofest.*

who made it big were LL Cool J (James Smith) and Kurtis Blow (Curtis Walker).

Rap became more socially conscious in the 1980s with the work of the groups Public Enemy and Grandmaster Flash (Joseph Saddler) and the Furious Five. Helping bring hip-hop into the mainstream in the 1980s was the group Run-D.M.C.

Rap took on a harder edge in the late 1980s with "gangsta rap" and its glorification of street drug culture. This strain of hip-hop originated partly in Los Angeles with rapper Ice-T (Tracy Morrow) and the group NWA and in part in Philadelphia with such performers as Schooly D (Jesse Weaver), who helped popularize the term "gangsta rap." Rapper Ice Cube (O'Shea Jackson) performed gangsta rap with a political message. Some rappers collaborated with hard-rock groups such as the Beastie Boys, and in California, Hispanic rappers such as DJ Disco Wiz (Luis Cedeno) and Mellow Man Ace (Ulpiano Reyes) gave their rap a Latino sound. Dr. Dre (Andre Young), Snoop Dogg (Cordozar Broadus), and others popularized a slower, funkier West Coast sound in the early 1990s; and in New York, Puff Daddy (Sean Combs), Nas (Nasir Jones), the Wu-Tang Clan (eight new York rappers), and Jamaican American Busta Rhymes (Trevor Smith) became big sellers.

Pimp C (Chad Butler) and the group UGK in Port Arthur, Texas; the jazzy Philadelphia group The Roots; the rap duo OutKast in Atlanta; Nelly (Cornell Haynes) in St. Louis; Common (Lonnie Lynn) in Chicago; and Public Enemy front man Chuck D (Carlton Ridenhour) on Long Island gained celebrity,

and new sounds continued to turn up in the work of groups such as De La Soul and Mos Def.

An unfortunate part of rap's history is its penchant for macho posturing, taunting, and feuding, which has led to violence and occasionally death. Part of the problem has been the East Coast versus West Coast rivalry that is thought to have led to the murders of two highly successful rappers: Tupac Shakur of Death Row Records in Los Angeles and, on the East Coast, The Notorious B.I.G. (Christopher Wallace) of Bad Boy Records. With gun violence came more emphasis on "bling-bling" (expensive jewelry), expensive clothes, and substance abuse. Feuds have continued to spring up among such rappers as 50 Cent (Curtis Jackson), Fat Joe (Joseph Cartagena), Ja Rule (Jeffrey Atkins), and The Game.

Recent rappers have included The Game (Jayceon Taylor), the group A Tribe Called Quest, Coolio (Artie Ivey), Ludacris (Christopher Bridges), Lil Wayne (Dwayne Carter), Kayne West, Young Jezzy (Jay Jenkins), and T.I. (Clifford Harris). African American rappers have had white competition from such performers as Vanilla Ice (Robert Van Winkle), hot-selling Eminem (Marshall Mathers), MC Serch of the group 3rd Bass, and Debbie Harry, formerly with the group Blondie. Other female rappers have been highly successful entertainer Queen Latifah (Dana Owens), Sister Souljah (Lisa Williamson), Lil'Kim (Kimberly Jones), Eve (Eve Jeffers), MC Lyte (Lana Morrer), and English rapper Monie Love (Simone Wilson).

William Shakespeare once asked, what is in a name? Perhaps a rose by any other name would smell as sweet, but a rapper named Bill Smith would not sell nearly so well as if he adopted a suitably "cool" stage name, any more than a major art gallery would smile on the work of an artist named Bubba Gunch. In rap and elsewhere, a name can mean a lot. *See also*: **African American**.

Sam G. Riley

For Further Reading

Chang, Jeff. *Can't Stop, Won't Stop: a History of the Hip-Hop Generation.* New York: St. Martin's Press, 2005.

Keyes, Cheryl Lynette. *Rap Music and Street Consciousness.* Urbana: University of Illinois Press, 2002.

Watkins, S. Craig. *Hip Hop Matters: Politics, Pop Culture, and the Struggle for the Soul of a Movement.* Boston: Beacon Press, 2005.

HISPANIC/LATINO

Hispanics and Latinos constitute the largest minority in the United States, and they have contributed immensely to the nation's culture. Many Hispanics and Latinos have gained stardom through music, film, and sports, and their growth as celebrities tends to involve a complex balance of the culture of their Latino heritage and that of American popular culture, of which they also are a part. Some celebrities gained popularity as Latinos, while others rose to fame with a more assimilated mainstream identity.

Cuba-born musician Desi Arnaz catapulted to stardom as a Latino musician on television with his wife, Lucille Ball, in the popular **comedy** *I Love*

Actress Jennifer Lopez looks elegantly sultry dancing with Richard Gere in Shall We Dance. *Courtesy of Photofest.*

Lucy. Arnaz, speaking with a heavy accent and at times at pains to understand the language and culture of his adopted homeland, conformed to stereotypic portrayals of Latino immigrants, speaking Spanish only on occasion to express exasperation or bewilderment. Nevertheless, the couple founded the Hollywood television powerhouse Desilu Studios, which developed the now-common three-camera method of shooting situation comedies on adjacent sets and shaped the nature of American television programming for decades. Their decision to film the performances and retain the film's rights was a prescient move that enabled the production company to reap a financial windfall from syndication in subsequent decades.

Anthony Quinn, born Antonio Rodolfo Oaxaca Quinn in Chihuahua, Mexico, enjoyed a life-long career on stage and in film, winning two Academy Awards and garnering six nominations. Later in life, in his eighties, Quinn gained commercial acclaim as a painter and sculptor. Unlike Arnaz, Quinn did not rise to fame with a strong Latino identity, although he often was cast in roles in which he portrayed someone from the Mediterranean or Latin America.

Naturally, the use of English has been a key factor in celebrities' fame in mainstream America. Latinos who originally developed their talent in Spanish often have found it necessary to use English to gain acceptance by a wider audience.

Puerto Rican musician José Feliciano, the talented singer-songwriter, is best known for his bilingual hit "Feliz Navidad." He is comfortable performing in both English and Spanish and has consistently embraced his Latino heritage as part of his public identity.

Singer Linda Ronstadt established her career in the 1960s singing in English as an accomplished vocal stylist ranked among the most popular singing acts in the United States. In 1987, though, she recorded *Canciones de Mi Padre*, a well-received album of songs reflecting her Mexican American heritage. The album was certified double platinum, becoming one of the bestselling non-English-language albums in the United States.

Gloria Estefan moved from her native Cuba to Miami, Florida, when she was a toddler. She rose to fame in the 1980s when she became the lead singer for Miami Sound Machine, a group started by the man who would become her husband, Emilio Estefan. Her albums have been wildly popular, certified as multiplatinum, and have supported her rise to international fame. Her first Spanish-language album, the Grammy Award–winning *Mi Tierra*, sold millions of copies around the world and highlighted her Cuban heritage. Since then, Estefan has recorded albums in both English and Spanish.

Puerto Rican singer Ricky Martin, born Enrique Martín Morales, first found the spotlight as a member of the boy band Menudo in the 1980s. Martin began his solo career in the 1990s with Spanish-language albums that were immensely popular in Latin America. An eponymous English-language album released in the United States in 1999 proved to be an instant hit, selling more than 17 million copies. The album's success came at a time when several Spanish-language artists were releasing "crossover" albums in English, following in the wake of Gloria Estefan's mainstream success with Latin-style pop music.

Shakira Mebarak, Colombian singer-songwriter, also burst onto the U.S. pop music scene in 2001, but she, like Ricky Martin, had enjoyed notable success in Latin America for several years. Shakira started a foundation to help Colombian children who were victims of violence and also was named an international goodwill ambassador for UNICEF, the United Nations Children's Fund.

Singer and actor Jennifer Lopez was born in New York to Puerto Rican parents. Lopez began her career as a backup **dancer** but soon landed acting roles in major films, earning critical acclaim for her lead performance in *Selena*. As her career grew, Lopez also recorded successful music albums. Her first, *On the 6*, released in 1999, featured a Spanish-language track. Her first Spanish-language album was released in 2007. Lopez is reputedly one of the wealthiest women in the entertainment industry and also used her success to become the executive producer of various television series ventures.

Mexican American actor Richard "Cheech" Marin rose to fame with Tommy Chong as the comedic duo Cheech and Chong in the 1970s. Marin subsequently established an independent acting career in several television shows, including *Nash Bridges*, and in supporting roles in films, including the *Spy Kids* trilogy. Marin is also known for his extensive collection of Chicano art and actively supports exhibitions of this art form.

Opera tenor Plácido Domingo, born in Mexico to Spanish parents, grew up in a musical home and began his career in opera in Mexico and in the United States in the early 1960s. The acclaimed tenor has more than 120 roles to his credit but is perhaps better known to the general public for his blockbuster performance tours with two other tenors, José Carreras and Luciano Pavarotti, that introduced legions of people to opera. His forays into English-language pop, including a well-received album with John Denver, have demonstrated his musical versatility, but Domingo remains foremost an exemplary operatic tenor. Domingo, who has won nine Grammy Awards and two Latin Grammy Awards, has also helped launch and develop the careers of several opera singers through his Operalia talent-discovery program. Domingo has received the Presidential Medal of Freedom and the Hispanic Heritage Award for Arts for his singular contribution to fine arts.

Mexican comic actor Mario Moreno was famous throughout Latin America and among Spanish-speaking Latinos as Cantinflas. He appeared in more than forty films. His efforts to cross over to English-language audiences were less successful, though, mainly because his style of comedy relied on his rapid-fire gift of gab and plays on words, although he was praised for his role alongside David Niven in *Around the World in Eighty Days* (1956).

Other Latino celebrities have refused to seek fame in mainstream America, among them Puerto Rican heartthrob Chayanne and Colombian singer Carlos Vives. Vives first became known for his roles in Spanish-language soap operas but now is more famous for his catchy fusion of accordion-led *vallenato* music with a tropical beat and **rock** sounds. He won a Grammy for his 2001 album *Déjame Entrar* and a Latin Grammy in 2005 for his album *El Rock de mi Pueblo*. But he, like many other celebrities, is content with his vast fan base among Spanish-speaking audiences.

Vicente Fernández, the king of *ranchera* music, is best known for the iconic scene of a guitar-strumming cowboy in a large sombrero leaning against a fence post under a shade tree. He enjoyed notable success in the United States among Spanish-speaking audiences. He recorded more than fifty albums and appeared in more than twenty Spanish-language movies.

Don Francisco, born Mario Kreutzberger in Chile, pioneered television entertainment in his native country in the 1960s. He copied the format of his wildly successful weekly show in Miami as *Sábado Gigante*, a three-hour variety show that features guest artists, audience-participation games, comedy routines, and human-interest segments. For three decades, Don Francisco has hosted an annual charity telethon in Chile to raise money for that country's disadvantaged children.

Juan Luis Guerra, of the Dominican Republic, took popular *merengue*-style music and added socially conscious lyrics about poverty, corruption, and other social ills. Guerra, who began recording in the 1980s, is known for innovative music and thought-provoking topics. He also started a foundation that provides medical care to poor children in the Dominican Republic.

Not all Latino celebrities rise to fame via music or acting. Roberto Clemente, born in Puerto Rico, was the first Latino baseball player to be inducted into the National Baseball Hall of Fame, an honor he received in 1973. Clemente died when a plane carrying **humanitarian** aid he was taking to earthquake-devastated Nicaragua crashed. His selfless charity work also led baseball Commissioner Bowie Kuhn to create the "Roberto Clemente Award" to recognize the highest levels of sportsmanship and community outreach.

Sammy Sosa, born in the Dominican Republic, is one of the most notable Latino **athletes**. In 1998, he competed with Mark McGuire to be baseball's homerun king, becoming Major League Baseball's first athlete to hit sixty-five homeruns in a single season before he was passed by McGuire, who hit seventy. Both Sosa and McGuire have been named the *Sports Illustrated* "Sportsman of the Year," and Sosa was also voted the National League's Most Valuable Player.

Juan Pablo Montoya, born in Colombia, became the first Hispanic to win a race in NASCAR's Nextel Cup. Montoya, who rose to fame winning the Indianapolis 500 and seven Formula One races, is expected to broaden NASCAR's appeal beyond its traditional base of fans.

A brief look at a few of the many Latino celebrities reveals that they are recognized as masters of their craft, whether it be in the field of music, acting, or sports. In addition, these celebrities vary in the degree to which they project their Latino heritage as part of their public identity, and in the degree to which they use English, but they all are renowned for their excellence and are true celebrities. *See also*: **Awards and Ceremonies**; **Classical Music**; **International Celebrity**; **Movies' Role**; **Television's Role**.

Robert Magee

For Further Reading

Chávez Candelaria, Cordelia, Arturo J. Aldama, and Peter J. García, eds. *Encyclopedia of Latino Popular Culture*. Westport, CT: Greenwood Press, 2004.

Gutiérrez, David G., ed. *The Columbia History of Latinos in the United States Since 1960*. New York: Columbia University Press, 2004.

Suárez-Orozco, Marcelo, and Mariela Páez, eds. *Latinos: Remaking America*. Berkeley: University of California Press, 2002.

HOBBIES AND SPORTS

Like the rest of us, celebrities need diversion from their work and home lives. Some find enjoyment in collecting and amass considerable quantities of whatever objects interest them. Celebrities not bitten by the collecting bug find activities to enjoy as participants, and still others, like their own fans, become fans of activities in which they do not physically take part. Some celebrities' hobbies are of the gentle sort: painting, sculpting, photography, music, or writing. Others are more physically active: rock climbing, hunting, fishing, automobile racing, **martial arts**, tennis, or golf.

The favorite sport of celebrities is golf. According to *Golf Digest* magazine, the most talented golfer-celebrity in Hollywood is actor Dennis Quaid. Others nearly as good at this game are his brother Randy Quaid, Samuel L. Jackson, Craig T. Nelson, Hugh Grant, and Mark Wahlberg. Action hero turned politician Arnold Schwarzenegger and fellow action hero Sylvester Stallone play frequently, while Sean Connery, Clint Eastwood, and Robert Redford golf occasionally.

Many well-known entertainers play in celebrity golf tournaments, a trend that got a long-ago boost from comedian Bob Hope and crooner Bing Crosby. Such tournaments today feature the likes of actors Matt Damon, Matthew McConaughey, George Clooney, Will Smith, Thomas Gibson, Kyle MacLaughlan, and Macaulay Culkin as well as **comedy** notables Jimmy Fallon, Cheech Marin, and Kevin Nealon. Musical celebrities who golf include rockers Meatloaf, Alice Cooper, and Justin Timberlake, plus singers Huey Lewis and Michael Bolton and saxophonist Kenny G. Two examples of women entertainers who play or played golf are Katherine Hepburn, who also played tennis, and Catherine Zeta-Jones.

Football players who golf include Joe Namath, Doug Flutie, Dan Marino, Peyton Manning, Derek Anderson, Roy Green, and Jerry Rice. Basketball's golfers include Michael Jordan, Charles Barkley, Julius Erving, and Spud Webb; and from baseball, Roger Clemens and Yogi Berra. Other **athletes** who golf are tennis greats Roger Federer, Pete Sampras, Andre Agassi, and Michael Chang; former Olympian Bruce Jenner; and professional surfer Kelly Slater.

While so many of their fellow celebrities are on the golf course, actors John Travolta, Clint Eastwood, and Harrison Ford make a hobby of flying. The late actor Christopher Reeve also was an amateur pilot, as well as a skier, scuba diver, sailor, and horseman. Singer Rod Stewart likes working on his model railroad layout; Lee Marvin enjoys fishing for marlin; Tom Cruise prefers rock climbing; and Alfonso Ribeiro likes cart racing. Celebrity military figure Gen. Norman Schwarzkopf hunts, fishes, and shoots skeet; and actors Robin Williams, Ed Burns, and Vin Diesel favor playing video games.

Among celebrities who relax with the fine arts are singer Tina Turner, a watercolorist; Tony Bennett; Angela Landsbury; and macho actors Viggo Mortensen and Jack Palance, both of whom write poetry. Kung fu actor David Carradine both painted and sculpted, **talk show host** Jenny Jones's hobby is nature photography and her competitor Sally Jesse Raphael likes to build picture frames. Clint Eastwood plays **jazz** piano, magician Penn Teller plays the acoustic bass, and radio's Dr. Drew Pinsky sings opera.

Catherine Zeta-Jones, David Arquette, and football great Rosie Greer knit. Bad-guy actor Danny Trejo restores classic cars, singer Isaac Hayes cooks, retired boxer George Foreman rides and breeds horses, and **rock** guitarist Steve Vai is a beekeeper.

Wine is a hobby, and sometimes a side business for many celebrities, including Dan Aykroyd, Robert Redford, guitarist Carlos Santana, racer Jeff Gordon, and French movie star Gerard Depardieu. Among celebrities having business interests in wine are moviemaker Francis Ford Coppola, actors Fess Parker and Raymond Burr, comedian Dick Smothers, singer Sting, and sports figures Peggy Fleming, Greg Norman, Arnold Palmer, Tom Seaver, and Joe Montana.

A similar hobby for many celebrities is fine cigars (a hobby that owes much to England's Sir Winston Churchill), one enjoyed by actor George Burns, said to have smoked as many as twenty cigars a day; comedy's Groucho Marx; and dapper President John F. Kennedy. These dissimilar figures added to the appeal and panache of cigar smoking, and, in recent years, a long list of cigar-loving celebrities have graced the cover of *Cigar Aficionado* magazine. A few examples are Pierce Brosnan, Kevin Bacon, Antonio Bandaras, Alec Baldwin, Gene Hackman, Morgan Freeman, and William Shatner. The cover of this magazine has also featured the comely images of such women cigar smokers as Bo Derek, Susan Lucci, Demi Moore, Claudia Schiffer, Sharon Stone, and Raquel Welch. *See also*: **Authors**; **Dream Girls**; **Tough Guys**.

Sam G. Riley

For Further Reading

http://cbs3.com/slideshows/hobbies. celebrities.stars.

www.accuracyproject.org/hobbies.

www.diynetwork.com/diy/hobbies.

HUMANITARIAN EFFORTS

Celebrity humanitarian activists are devoted to promoting human welfare through social reforms, serve to create awareness about issues, and raise funds to improve the quality of life. Celebrities can place a spotlight on an issue, and they can generate large sums of money.

Celebrities often become identified with specific humanitarian efforts. Former president Jimmy Carter created the nongovernmental organization Habitat for Humanity, building houses for the poor. Paul McCartney and his late wife Linda contributed to animal welfare causes, including groups opposing animal testing and furs and promoting vegetarianism. Tour de France winner Lance Armstrong's foundation unites, inspires, and empowers people affected by cancer. Actor Leonardo DiCaprio is an environmentalist raising awareness of global warming. Oscar-winner George Clooney's efforts have increased attention on genocide in Darfur.

"Celebrity diplomacy" is practiced by individuals who have a worldwide sense of purpose. Often, their commitment has little to do with the reasons for which they achieved celebrity, yet their status allows them to play to the global audience. The historic model for celebrity diplomacy was established in 1954 by actors Danny Kaye and Audrey Hepburn for their work for UNICEF, the United Nations Children's Fund. Irish **rock** band U2 vocalist Paul David Hewson (Bono) is

Cyclist Lance Armstrong inspires the troops in Aviano, Italy, in 2007. Courtesy of the Department of Defense.

increasingly involved in campaigning for debt relief in developing countries, lobbying to make poverty relief a bigger governmental priority, and raising awareness of African issues. British soccer star David Beckham has used his fame to attempt reconciliation of nations. The late Princess Diana transcended royal status by speaking out about land mines, AIDS, and other causes. Actress Angelina Jolie is a goodwill ambassador for the United Nations High Commissioner for Refugees.

Many celebrities serve a humanitarian purpose through philanthropic activity. Elizabeth Taylor founded Macy's Passport, a charity food and fashion auction that raises funds for HIV/AIDS services, prevention, and research. Microsoft founder Bill Gates

and his wife Melinda's Gates Foundation funds worldwide humanitarian efforts to improve health, education, and living conditions. Comedian Jerry Lewis established a twenty-one-and-a-half-hour, star-studded variety show that simultaneously entertains, informs, and raises funds for Muscular Dystrophy Association service and research programs. Actor Danny Thomas built St. Jude Children's Research Hospital (1962), focused on pediatric treatment and research for cancer and other catastrophic diseases. In the mid-1970s, singer Harry Chapin raised money to combat United States hunger, cofounding World Hunger Year. The Oprah Winfrey Foundation empowers and educates women, children, and families around the world. The Barbra Streisand Foundation supports civil liberties, environmental causes, and civil rights organizations dedicated to democratic values. Tennis champion Andre Agassi's charitable foundation is committed to transforming U.S. public education for underserved youth.

Multiple-celebrity telethons and concerts also serve humanitarian purposes. **Comedy** Relief (1986, Robin Williams, Billy Crystal, and Whoopi Goldberg) has raised funds for health care services to United States homeless men, women, and children; in 2006, it raised funds for Hurricane Katrina victims. Farm Aid (1985) keeps family farmers on their land, raising awareness about the loss of family farms. Singers Willie Nelson, Neil Young, and John Mellencamp organized the first Farm Aid concert. Live Aid (1985) was a multivenue rock concert held simultaneously in London's Wembley Stadium and Philadelphia's JFK Stadium, organized by singers Bob Geldof and Midge Ure to raise funds for Ethiopian famine relief. National Broadcasting Company (NBC), American Broadcasting Company (ABC), and Columbia Broadcasting System (CBS) simultaneously devoted one hour of commercial-free prime time for Stand Up to Cancer (2008), involving television, film, sports, and music celebrities raising funds for cancer research. *See also*: **Athletes; Corporate Celebrity; Dream Girls; Movies' Role**.

Beth M. Waggenspack

For Further Reading

Cooper, Andrew F. *Celebrity Diplomacy*. Boulder, CO: Paradigm, 2008.

Holmes, Su, and Sean Redmond, eds. *Framing Celebrity: New Directions in Celebrity Culture*. New York: Routledge, 2006.

http://www.hollywoodreporter.com/hr/search/article_display.jsp?vnu_content_id=1000564256.

http://www.looktothestars.org.

I

INTERNATIONAL CELEBRITY

International celebrities are people who are famous beyond their home country and whose fame transcends language and culture.

Benjamin Franklin is often considered to be America's first international celebrity, known in the United States and Europe for his scientific achievements, journalism, and the publication of *Poor Richard's Almanac*, a compilation of witticisms and proverbs that expressed the values of the common citizen. His achievements earned him the Copley Gold Medal, the most prestigious award of his day, and honorary degrees at the world's leading universities. When he went to France to enlist support for the American Revolution, he cultivated the image of a dignified and forthright Enlightenment man from the New World. Soon, Europeans were copying his simple, yet elegant style of dress; and promotional items, such as rings or watches bearing his likeness, were sold. Poems were written in his honor, and women even had their hair styled to resemble the fur cap he wore. Amazed at his reception, Franklin wrote that his face was "as well known as the man in the moon."

International celebrities in the 19th century include Mark Twain, Oscar Wilde, and Harry Houdini. Twain and Wilde were known for their writing and wit, Houdini for his daring escapes. The rise in the number and nature of such celebrities has accompanied the rise of mass media. Houdini's fame spread through newspaper accounts, and he carefully cultivated relationships with the press to pique public interest in his stage performances. During his wildly popular tour of Europe, for example, Houdini would arrive in town before the show to challenge the local police, with local media present, to lock him in a way that would prevent him from escaping. After appearing to struggle, Houdini would emerge, and the print media would carry elaborate accounts of his formidable escape. Naturally, his shows were sold out.

The advent of radio led to celebrities in music, while the rise of film and

Britain's Princess Diana walks the red carpet, beautifully attired. Courtesy of Photofest.

television contributed to people becoming celebrities for their acting talent. Web sites have also begun to spawn celebrity status for people based on their creativity or niche appeal. More important, though, as the mass media have become international in scope, so have some celebrities acquired an international appeal that transcends language and culture. For most celebrities, this fame is fleeting, but some international stars have learned how to maintain their international appeal. Still others have developed ways to use their star status as a way of changing the world, working, for instance, to end hunger or violence against women.

Star Power and Publicity

A star's worldwide appeal can border on fanatical devotion among fans.

Much of an international celebrity's attraction is due to exceptional talent or excellence. However, some of the apparently "natural" appeal is attributable to shrewd promotion. There were many stage magicians in Houdini's day, for example, but none matched his knack for generating publicity.

Elvis Presley was crowned the King of Rock and Roll. While Elvis certainly had talent and a unique musical style that fused **rock** with rhythm and blues, he generated a great deal of controversy with the way he moved his hips and legs; but this controversy only enhanced his appeal among teenagers. His manager, "Colonel" Tom Parker, always sought ways to shape the singer's public image, and he capitalized on controversy to spark increased interest in the rising star. Elvis, who never toured internationally, was famous worldwide as the leading figure of 1950s rock and roll and inspired other performers, such as The Beatles. Despite the controversy he generated, Elvis proved his talent by setting records for the greatest number of top forty and top ten hits, and the longest tenure of a number-one hit.

Pop star Madonna, no stranger to controversy, has a keen understanding of ways to generate publicity. Her early work trespassed on social mores regarding **sex** and the Catholic Church, as her songs, album titles, and concert imagery were based on sexual double-entendres and religious symbols. The more authorities took offense, the more popular Madonna grew, becoming one of the world's bestselling pop artists of the 20th century.

Controversy is not necessarily a surefire means of generating favorable publicity, though. Rock-and-roll musician

Jerry Lee Lewis had number-one hits with "Great Balls of Fire" and "Breathless," but he faced a backlash among the British public in 1957 when it was discovered that he had married his first cousin once removed, Myra Gale Brown, then thirteen. Lewis was forced to cancel his tour and return to the United States, where his music was pulled from radio. He migrated to **country** music for several years. It was not until a decade later, however, that he released a rock-and-roll album, which was well received around the world. In 1973, he released *The Session*, an album that featured several British rock stars and was the highest-ranked album of his career. Nevertheless, only in the 1990s did he truly regain his international stature as a luminary rock-and-roll figure.

John Lennon invited Paul McCartney to join him in a band known as The Quarrymen. McCartney later pressed Lennon to add George Harrison as lead guitarist, and the musicians went through several drummers before they landed Ringo Starr. The band later changed its name to The Beatles. Their innovative style and new look proved to be a success, although widespread acceptance was not without its **setbacks**. Although the group was popular in Britain, success did not come immediately in the United States. U.S. record labels either did not issue the first singles authorized for the United States, or those that were released did not receive much airplay. However, a news clip of Britain's "Beatlemania" sparked greater interest in the group, and by the time the foursome arrived in America, they were superstars. Masterful songwriting, coupled with innovative sounds formed the foundation of their lasting celebrity. Their tally of number-one singles (twenty) even surpassed Elvis's seventeen. In 1970, Paul McCartney announced he was leaving The Beatles, effectively disbanding the group.

Advertisers have been keen to capitalize on the public's adoration of superstars. By hiring an actress known for her beauty and glamour, for example, a cosmetics company can associate its product line with the star's image, hoping that her beauty will "rub off" on its products in the mind of the consumer. Although stars can earn considerable income from product **endorsements**, some international celebrities hesitate to endorse products in the United States for fear that it might jeopardize their reputation as a serious artist. Nevertheless, these same celebrities can earn considerable cash hawking products in other countries while never endorsing a product in the American market. For example, Arnold Schwarzenegger, movie star and later California governor, has endorsed premium movie channels and a touted potency beverage in Japan, while Harrison Ford has endorsed a Japanese beer. Through these associations, companies are able to harness the stars' persuasive power to promote their product.

Star Power and Social Issues

Much of celebrities' influence stems from the public and mass media attention they command. For example, the decisions by Madonna and Angelina Jolie to adopt orphans from developing countries brought many people's attention to the possibilities of international adoption. Many international celebrities, conscious of their star power, have used their stature to raise awareness of social issues.

Shirley Temple, the Depression-era child film star, soared to fame because of her dancing, singing, and acting talents, coupled with her cherubic features. She continued to act steadily until 1949, and her films were popular around the world. As evidence of her star power, promotional products such as toys and apparel associated with Shirley Temple, like those associated with Benjamin Franklin in France, proved quite profitable. Later in life, her celebrity was an asset in her diplomatic endeavors, whether helping people escape Czechoslovakia when Soviet tanks invaded or as a U.S. ambassador to Ghana and Czechoslovakia.

Plácido Domingo, the acclaimed tenor who grew up in Mexico, has performed in all the world's major opera houses. Domingo began charity work when Mexico City was struck by an earthquake in 1985 and he lost relatives. In the aftermath, Domingo performed several benefit concerts and recorded an album to raise funds for the earthquake survivors and their families. Since then, Domingo has used his talent and star power to raise money for a number of causes, including the plight of victims in Darfur and the rebuilding of New Orleans following Hurricane Katrina.

Comedian and actor Danny Kaye performed benefit concerts and became a goodwill ambassador for the United Nations Children's Fund (UNICEF) in 1954, the first among many celebrities who learned how to use their star power to help underprivileged children around the world.

Actress and fashion icon Audrey Hepburn vaulted to fame in the 1953 film *Roman Holiday*. In the 1980s, she followed in Danny Kaye's footsteps and became a UNICEF goodwill ambassador. Her concern for the plight of children stemmed from her childhood experience of hunger and oppression when Nazi Germany occupied The Netherlands, and that devotion fueled her determination to see children gain access to drinking water and food. She made more than fifty visits to UNICEF projects around the world.

Comedian Jerry Lewis gained popularity with partner Dean Martin as a comedic duo and was popular for his clownish antics. The pair made several popular films for nearly a decade, and then parted ways. Lewis continued to do solo work, insisted on creative control with attention to detail, and ventured into screenwriting, producing, and directing. His physical style of **comedy**, which helped him transcend cultural and language barriers, and his treatment of the absurd made his comedy appeal to fans around the world. In Europe, Lewis received director-of-the-year award eight times. Lewis has enjoyed especially longstanding popularity in France, where he received the French Legion of Honor for his creative achievements. For more than four decades, Lewis has held an annual telethon to raise money for the Muscular Dystrophy Association, which he helped found.

ABBA, the Swedish superstar pop group, enjoyed international celebrity from the mid-1970s until 1982, when the band broke up. The members, Agnetha Fältskog, Anni-Frid Lyngstad, Björn Ulvaeus, and Benny Anderson, were developing individual careers in music when they formed the group, which was named by using the initials of their given names. The group's catchy and unique style capitalized on the popularity of disco and dance music but infused their sound with the lyric and instrumental variety of pop music. ABBA recorded in English, and the group's songs were well received around the world. In 1979, the Year of the Child, the group donated the royalties of their hit song "Chiquitita" to UNICEF. Rather than contribute a cash sum, or raise money through a benefit concert, or help raise awareness as a spokesperson, all of which were more common ways of aiding a charitable organization, ABBA donated half the group's royalties from the sale of the song, which has provided the organization some $2.5 million dollars.

Irish rock band U2 has long been known to address political and social issues in its music. The band's first major foray into social causes came with a benefit performance for Amnesty International's support of human rights. Bono, the group's lead vocalist and lyricist, has also gained acclaim for pushing for concrete action on some of the world's most vexing social problems: AIDS, hunger, and debt relief for impoverished countries, especially those in Sub-Saharan Africa. Bono seeks every opportunity to prod political, business, and religious leaders to tackle such issues. He and colleague Bob Geldof organized the Live 8 international concerts to push for the elimination of the foreign debt burden that the world's poorest countries bear.

Nelson Mandela, South Africa's first democratically elected president, won a Nobel Prize for Peace (with former President F. W. de Klerk) for his efforts toward racial reconciliation. He has used his international reputation to work in support of human rights and racial harmony around the world. South

African singer Miriam Makeba is as famous for her music as for her **humanitarian** work. She was banned from her native South Africa in 1960 for her opposition to apartheid and traveled throughout the world in support of human rights. In 1986, she was awarded the Dag Hammarskjöld Peace Prize. Grammy award–winner Youssou N'Dour, born in Senegal, is known for developing an engaging pop style that fuses African sounds and rhythms with Western styling. The artist, a UNICEF goodwill ambassador, has supported immunization efforts in Africa and performed many benefit concerts for the organization.

Brazilian singer and songwriter Gilberto Gil, loved by many jazz fans in the United States and around the world for decades for his intricate and smooth vocal and guitar technique, was Brazil's minister of culture from 2003 to 2008. The Grammy award–winning Gil also has been a tireless promoter of the U.N. Food and Agriculture Organization (FAO) and its antihunger campaigns and was named a 2001 goodwill ambassador for the organization.

Australian movie star Nicole Kidman became a goodwill ambassador for the United Nations Fund for Women (UNIFEM) to draw attention to the infringement of women's human rights. Of particular concern is violence against women, which afflicts as many as one-third of the world's women. Actress Angelina Jolie, a goodwill ambassador for the United Nations High Commissioner for Refugees, devotes time to raising awareness of the conditions in which refugees live around the world. Puerto Rican pop phenomenon Ricky Martin, a UNICEF goodwill ambassador, uses his fame to draw attention to the plight of children who are victims of the sex trade.

Mexican rock group Maná, with millions of albums sold and sold-out international tours, has enjoyed nearly three decades of unswerving popularity in Spanish-speaking nations. As part of its commitment to improving the conditions in which millions of poor people live, the band started a foundation, Selva Negra, to focus on issues related to sustainable economic development in Latin America. The group also was named goodwill ambassadors for the FAO and has promised to donate $1 from all ticket sales to the U.N. agency's hunger relief efforts.

The phenomenon of international celebrities, though not entirely new, has exploded with the growth of mass media, and as mass media have become more international in scope, so have some celebrities. The power of celebrities, for better or worse, lies in capturing people's attention, and to the degree that they can transcend world's languages and cultures, they can become international stars. *See also*: **Authors**; **Child Celebrity**; **Classical Music**; **Comedy**; **Internet's Role**; **Politics**.

Robert Magee

For Further Reading

Cashmore, Ellis. *Celebrity/Culture*. New York: Routledge, 2006.

Cooper, Andrew F. *Celebrity Diplomacy*. Boulder, CO: Paradigm Publishers, 2007.

Holmes, Su, and Sean Redmond, eds. *Framing Celebrity: New Directions in Celebrity Culture*. New York: Routledge, 2006.

Jackson, David J. *Entertainment and Politics: The Influence of Pop Culture on Young Adults' Socialization*. New York: Peter Lang, 2002.

Turner, Graeme. *Understanding Celebrity*. Thousand Oaks, CA: Sage Publications, 2004.

http://www.biography.com.

http://www.rockhall.com.

http://www.unicef.org/people/people_ambassadors.html.

INTERNET'S ROLE

The advent of the Internet has influenced celebrity careers substantially. Stars can send messages and sell merchandise to their fans using official Web sites, and fans maintain their own online shrines as well. Celebrity news and gossip, spread via the World Wide Web and e-mail newsletters, can help or harm celebrity careers, and social networking sites such as MySpace and Facebook even provide the opportunity for fans to be "friends" with their favorite actor, musician, or **athlete**.

While the Internet has a powerful influence on existing celebrities, it can also have a hand in creating them. Unique aspects of the Internet are particularly amenable to the spontaneous rise of new celebrities. First, it is easy to appear on the Internet. Almost anyone can create a Web site with the potential to be viewed by millions. Second, the Internet allows word of mouth to spread quickly. Interesting Web links, narratives, images, and video can spread rapidly across networks of friends and colleagues through e-mail messages that are passed along with the click of a mouse. Because of this ease of publication and potential for rapid dissemination, the Internet can send someone skyrocketing to fame without the aid of the traditional news and entertainment media typically responsible for celebrities' ascendancy.

Aspiring journalists, authors, filmmakers, and others in media-connected pursuits may find a route to success and renown through diligent work on the Internet (for example, as celebrity **bloggers**). On the other hand, many Internet celebrities, or "Web celebs," are launched to stardom by nothing more than a contagiously interesting, informative, or entertaining Web site, e-mail message, image, or video.

Craig Shergold may hold the distinction of being the first Internet-spawned celebrity. In 1989, nine-year-old Shergold was diagnosed with brain cancer, and his condition was deemed terminal. Cheered by the greeting cards sent to him, Shergold sought to earn recognition in the *Guinness Book of World Records* (since renamed *Guinness World Records*) for the most cards received. The request was spread through local media and also emerged as an e-mail chain letter. Shergold received millions of cards within a year, achieving his goal, and his cancer was also driven into remission by successful brain surgery. The e-mail chain letter, however, continued to travel the world in various forms, and the get-well cards kept coming. Over a decade later, a healthy, adult Shergold had received more than 350 million cards despite his pleas for an end to the deluge.

Turkish schoolteacher Mahir Çağrı has also landed in Guinness's record book, named as the owner of the world's most-visited personal Web site. Çağrı's site, which he later claimed was actually made by a friend without his knowledge, was amateurishly designed and crawling with pictures and friendly broken English phrases such as "I like to be friendship from different country," "She can stay my home" and "I kiss you!" The site drew millions of Web visitors beginning in 1999 and catapulted Çağrı into **international celebrity** that resulted in worldwide media coverage, tours, and a music video release.

In 2005, Canadian Kyle MacDonald used a blog Web site and online community networks to publicize his "One Red Paperclip" project, the goal of which was to obtain something of value in exchange for a paperclip by way of a series of trades with online acquaintances. About a year later, a series of fourteen trades had resulted in MacDonald owning a two-story home in Saskatchewan. MacDonald's trades received substantial media attention along the way, and he later published a book on the endeavor.

The development of social networking Web tools has aided the nascence of Internet celebrities. The MySpace Web site, launched in 2003, allows users to create and customize personalized profile pages, add other users as "friends," who then can share music, video, and commentary. Among the Internet celebrities it has created is purported cofounder and initial president Tom Anderson, who is automatically listed as each user's first "friend" upon account creation. Tila Nguyen, better known as "Tila Tequila," was involved in a career in modeling before creating her MySpace account, but she achieved superstardom by cultivating a network of more than a million "friends" on the site. Nguyen's resulting fame led to a music career, a clothing line, and a reality television show on the MTV (Music Television) network.

Short video clips, shared use of e-mail, and video-sharing Web sites such as YouTube, have also accounted for a number of Internet celebrities. YouTube, created in 2005, allows users to upload video that can be viewed by any Web user. Given that scores of millions of videos have been uploaded to YouTube, not all of the offerings are widely viewed. Some videos, though, lead to fame for their creators. Adam Nyerere Bahner, a University of Minnesota graduate student, uploaded a video of himself performing his song *Chocolate Rain* under the pseudonym Tay Zonday in 2007. Within months, Bahner had appeared on a number of television programs internationally, "Chocolate Rain" had become a profitable mobile phone ringtone, and several popular musicians had covered or parodied his Internet hit. When a series of YouTube videos featuring Dutch teenager Esmée Denters singing popular songs was discovered by a music industry executive in 2006, she was signed to a recording contract with star musician Justin Timberlake's label and was performing on Timberlake's tour within a year. Not all YouTube celebrities found fame via music videos, though. In 2007, Tennessean Chris Cunningham, using the stage name Chris Crocker, uploaded an emotional rant titled *Leave Britney Alone*, in which he tearfully demanded a moratorium of scrutiny directed at troubled celebrity Britney Spears. The clip was replayed in news and entertainment media across the nation, widely parodied, and excerpted in dance music "remixes."

Some Internet celebrities' fame was altogether unintended and undesired, at least initially. In 2002, Quebecois teenager Ghyslain Raza used a borrowed videotape to record himself playing with a golf ball retriever as if it were a light saber from the *Star Wars* movie series. The tape's owner later discovered the video and, with the help of friends, uploaded it to an Internet file-sharing service without Raza's knowledge. Eventually, the "Star Wars" video and various adaptations of it ended up being viewed hundreds of millions of times, and Raza won a substantial settlement in a lawsuit against the video's uploaders.

Unlike Raza, Gary Brolsma deliberately uploaded an Internet video clip of himself dancing and lip-synching to *Dragostea din tei*, a Moldovian pop song. What Brolsma, an office-supply store employee from New Jersey, did not expect was that his playful *Numa Numa Dance* clip would amass hundreds of millions of viewings (estimates place it second only to the Raza clip in terms of total views) and would attract substantial media attention. Although he initially shunned the resulting celebrity, Brolsma eventually embraced his fame with a Web site featuring sequels to the video, purchasable mobile phone ring tones, and a video submission contest featuring a $45,000 cash prize.

Occasionally, an appearance on other broadcast media can be made much more notorious by repeated Internet viewings. Lauren Caitlin Upton was representing South Carolina in the 2007 Miss Teen USA pageant when she badly fumbled her response to a question about Americans' woeful knowledge of geography. Online videos of Upton's gaffe rapidly garnered an online audience that dwarfed that of the original pageant's broadcast, and Upton's subsequent television appearances included a parody of herself at the 2007 MTV Video Music Awards.

A few other Internet celebrities of varying repute include Jay Maynard, whose Web site documenting a homemade *TRON* costume led to some fame as the "Tron Guy"; Hosea Jean Frank (also known as ZeFrank), whose online birthday party invitation featuring comedic dance move examples was originally sent to seventeen friends in 2001 but was soon viewed by millions; Matt McCallister, who uploaded a time-lapse video of himself wearing 155 t-shirts simultaneously; and Andrew Meyer, who was captured pleading, "Don't tase me, bro!" while being subdued by University of Florida police after Meyer had been disruptive during an on-campus visit by U.S. Sen. John Kerry.

The popular-culture influence of "Web celebs" is exemplified by the music video that the alternative rock band Weezer created for their 2008 song "Pork and Beans." The video features scores of Internet celebrities and phenomena, including Bahner, Brolsma, Cunningham, McCallister, Raza, and Upton. Appropriately, the video premiered on the YouTube site. *See also*: **Movies' Role**; **News Media Figures**; **Product Lines**.

James D. Ivory

For Further Reading

Bennett, Jessica. "The Flip Side of Internet Fame." *Newsweek,* March 3, 2008.

"Internet Celebrity Videos." http://www.albinoblacksheep.com/video/celebrity.

MySpace. http://myspace.com.

"The Web Celeb 25." http://forbes.com/webcelebs.

YouTube. http://www.youtube.com.

J

JAZZ AND BLUES

Jazz and blues are two broad categories of American popular music, each with its own rich, complicated history. These dual histories have their roots in pre-1900 black and Southern culture. Both musical traditions blossomed in the first half of the 20th century, especially during the Jazz Age (the 1920s), the Great Depression, and World War II. The black purveyors of the blues in the Mississippi Delta and south side of Chicago would later become legendary, but they were in no way celebrities while they carried on their unadorned tradition of slavery-era origins. Jazz leaders of the Big Band (or Swing) era in the 1930s and 1940s—Duke Ellington, Count Basie, Glenn Miller, and Benny Goodman—rose to stardom with phonograph records selling in the millions, popular radio shows, and dance crazes. Since 1950, however, as **rock** exploded onto the scene, jazz and blues have receded yet continued to evolve into something like an acquired taste for aficionados—including a large number of rock stars who appreciated blues especially as their musical fountainhead.

Defining jazz and blues is a job for poets and fools. Scholars can never quite agree on the genealogies of these musical traditions, for their histories are by nature fluid, extra-institutional, and hybrid. Louis Armstrong, the black jazz trumpeter-singer nicknamed "Satchmo," is not the only jazz celebrity who joked that if you do not know what jazz is, do not mess with it. Certainly African rhythms and New Orleans black band traditions incubated early jazz. But also important were European musical forms and the creativity that came out of other cities, such as Memphis, St. Louis, Chicago, Kansas City, and New York.

Modern jazz stars have been a diverse, multigenerational lot, drawing fans to crowded little nightclubs or giant jazz festivals. Such big names as Dizzy Gillespie, Miles Davis, John Coltrane, Cannonball Adderley, Thelonious Monk, Sonny Rollins, Stan Getz, and Dave Brubeck enjoyed almost religious devotion from their followers but never gained much wealth despite the serious attention a few writers have given them. Singers such as Frank Sinatra and Ella Fitzgerald fused big-band swing with popular melody. The most prominent jazz artists showed up in the annual readers' and critics' polls of *Downbeat* magazine and in *Esquire* magazine's all-American bands (selected by an expert panel starting in 1944). The audience was narrower for atonal and "free" genres that emerged in the 1960s, associated with the likes of saxman Ornette Coleman and pianist Cecil Taylor. Electronic "fusion" and jazz funk, as well as more mellow jazz, continued to inject jazz into the pop mainstream.

The blues, by contrast, changed little from its earliest forms but rose to legendary status from the 1960s, thanks to the respect paid by rock stars and rock critics. Rock's tributes to the blues are endless. For example, "Rolling Stone Blues" by blues giant Muddy Waters is honored by the Rolling Stones in their band's name, by Bob Dylan's "Like a Rolling Stone," and by the title of the magazine of rock, *Rolling Stone. See also*: **African American**.

Douglas Cumming

For Further Reading

Collier, James Lincoln. *The Making of Jazz: A Comprehensive History.* Boston: Houghton Mifflin, 1978.

Ellison, Mary. *Extensions of the Blues.* New York: Riverrun Press, 1989.

Palmer, Robert. *Deep Blues*. New York: Viking Press, 1981.

K

KITSCH

The word *kitsch* describes that which is inferior, imitative, tacky, tawdry, or crassly commercial. Sometimes people's affection for their favorite celebrities overwhelms their judgment and leads them to buy questionable items, bringing joy to the sellers of such merchandise. For some people, "kitsch" implies snobbery and derision of those less fortunate. Others embrace kitsch merrily, regarding it as "campy" or whimsical, perhaps even as a logical extension of entertainment escapism.

The strength of America's celebrity culture is such that even dead celebrities can "make millions" year after year for their heirs and assigns. For singers, most of this posthumous income is derived from the sale of albums and compact discs. But another income source is the sale of novelty items such as t-shirts, sweatshirts, and posters. Some deceased celebrities whose estates rake in the most money include Marilyn Monroe, Kurt Cobain, Tupac Shakur, Steve McQueen, Bob Marley, James Brown, and James

Dean; but the big two, year after year, are Elvis Presley, followed closely by John Lennon. Most of Lennon's earnings are from sales, licensing, and royalties for his music; but Elvis's estate also makes a great deal of money from the sale of an amazing array of Elvis mementos and collectibles. Perhaps the most remarkably tacky of them all is the Alive Elvis singing and talking bust—a reasonably good likeness of the lank-haired, sideburned, leather-clad King of Rock and Roll's head and shoulders. This curious automaton moves its lips, even reproducing Elvis's signature one-sided upper-lip sneer, while singing "Hound Dog" and several other hits of yesteryear. It also makes typical Elvis "moves," slurs "Thankyouverymuch," and tells brief Elvis anecdotes. The Elvis bust even accommodates would-be Elvis impersonators with its Karaoke mode.

Iconic among Elvis kitsch are cheaply framed paintings of the great rocker done on black velvet. To go with this item, the devout fan can select from a mind-boggling range of Elvis dolls, some with guitar, some clutching a microphone. An Elvis nesting doll set is available, as are several variations of Elvis bobble-head dolls. When alive, the King was known for occasionally giving Cadillacs to needy admirers who caught his eye, and his kindness has been commemorated in the Elvis Franklin Mint Cadillac miniature—in shocking pink. If the talking Elvis bust is too costly, one can buy a ceramic Elvis bust, obviously made in Asia, inasmuch as this Elvis looks decidedly Asian. Aspiring **rock** and rollers can purchase an Elvis guitar strap, whittle their own guitar pick with the Elvis Aloha Knife, light a cigarette with the Elvis Zippo, stay on schedule with the Elvis Desk Clock, and relax by reading Elvis comic books. Fans can also swap Elvis trading cards.

Other items of Elvis kitsch include the Elvis watch, necktie, pendant, area rug, pajamas, coffee mug, scented candle, calendar, wallet, baby bib, key ring, collector's plate, Christmas ornament, Christmas stocking, soap dispenser, soap dish, toothbrush holder, shower curtain, waste basket, iPod case, coin purse, tote bag, and salt and pepper shakers. Men who are thoroughly caught up in the Elvis mystique can dress the part, too, in a variety of dreadful jumpsuits, or perhaps just settle for the Elvis cape. One of the most expensive of all these items is the Graceland Box, which is made to resemble Elvis's Memphis home and which holds fifty-four compact discs. Fans can buy an Elvis ring tone for their cell phone, take an Elvis-themed cruise, stay at Memphis's Heartbreak Hotel in one of its Elvis-theme suites, or enter holy matrimony in Las Vegas with an Elvis-theme wedding at the Graceland Wedding Chapel, or any

other of several competing chapels. Another Graceland Wedding Chapel is open for business and is located adjacent to Graceland mansion in Memphis. Although not officially part of the pantheon of Elvis paraphernalia, a wonderfully kitschy "Golden Throne" toilet seat set really should be, inasmuch as the King is known to have died while "on the throne." On this model, the seat and rim are gold colored, and when open, the lid reveals a large, sparkling golden crown. To beg the use of a cliché, Elvis's estate has taken kitsch to a whole new level.

No other dead celebrity even comes close to Elvis's ability to rake in kitsch-cash from merchandise, but doing quite well are deceased **sex** goddess Marilyn Monroe and Western hero John Wayne. To remember the beautiful Marilyn and render unto her the respect due one of our fairest sex symbols, nostalgic fans can buy Marilyn Monroe linen handkerchiefs, scarves, refrigerator magnets, steering wheel knobs (does anyone still use those?), cigarette lighters, metal tote bags, various mugs and shot glasses, cookie jars, trading cards, the Marilyn Monroe Barbie doll, a Marilyn lamp, and an enormous selection of posters and plaques showing the comely star in various stages of undress.

Say the name John Wayne, and people will instinctively mutter "The Duke" in respectful reference to this all-American star, who also is gone but not at all forgotten. Available to remember him by are John Wayne clocks and knives, a John Wayne cigar box, fleece blanket, knife and key chain set, paper cut-outs (an item that seems strangely effete for so manly a figure as Mr. Wayne), Franklin Mint plates and other figures, and even an singularly tawdry John Wayne cookie jar.

Also holding his own from the grave is a handsome young actor who died young, James Dean. Among the usual t-shirts and posters are James Dean bobble head dolls, mugs, refrigerator magnets, salt and pepper shakers, a "Live Fast" metal license plate, floor mats for one's fast car, Christmas ornaments, neckties, pocket knives, wall clocks, wristwatches, a welcome mat, and a tin lunch box. Additional dead celebrities responsible for a respectable amount of kitsch merchandise are Kurt Cobain of the group Nirvana (action figure and a $1 bill with Cobain's likeness in place of George Washington), Grateful Dead leader Jerry Garcia (plush Jerry bear, watch, and neckties, and Anna Nicole Smith (bobble head doll, which sold far more briskly after her death than before). A few more deceased celebrities have Barbies or other dolls to commemorate their acclaim. Examples are former First Lady Jacqueline Kennedy Onassis and television's Lucille Ball, who also is commemorated with a tote bag bearing her likeness.

Live celebrities, of course, inspire kitsch made in their own image as well. Although pop entertainer Michael Jackson's star dimmed prior to his 2009 death, Jackson kitsch sells on in the form of his signature sequin-covered white glove; belt buckles; necklaces with white-glove pendant; lapel pin, also with white glove; Thriller Doll; transistor radio; key ring; trading cards; and handbag mirror. Another kitsch-producing celebrity entertainer is pop singer Cher (nesting dolls, Half-Breed Doll, and earrings), and Farrah Fawcett is fittingly represented by a signature

hair dryer. The Rolling Stones weigh in with ashtrays, mugs, dog tags, and cufflinks; and Britney Spears has her own action figure. Recalling Mr. Spock of *Star Trek* fame, played by actor Leonard Nimoy, plastic Vulcan ears are available. For collectors of entertainment-world figures and dolls, a useful accessory is the **Paparazzi** Play Set, a grouping of nine desperate-looking reporters and photographers; the set comes with a "velvet rope" to keep them away from the celebrities. Rubber bathtub celebrity ducks are also there for the buying—in the likenesses of James Brown, the Blues Brothers (Dan Aykroyd and John Belushi), James Dean, and television's menacing Mr. T (born Laurence Tureaud) of the 1980s television show *The A-Team*.

Sports collectibles and memorabilia are another market for vendors of kitsch, so much so that this form of questionable merchandise suffers from the vending of counterfeit or fake items, such as signed game balls or team posters. In addition to the inevitable, omnipresent t-shirts, sweatshirts, and ball caps, the world of sports offers a rich trove of other kitsch. NASCAR fans can buy watches and jewelry, some specific to drivers such as Dale Earnhart. Most sports greats appear on trading cards, and specialized sets of rookie cards are available. Especially popular are the sports kitsch items connected with athletes who are in legal trouble, witness former football great O. J. Simpson's drink coasters, bumper stickers, knives, and so forth. Baseball's Barry Bonds, accused of steroid use, is commemorated in the form of a bobble head doll. Bobble heads, in fact, are sold for many celebrities of every sort, including Jesse Jackson,

John F. Kennedy, Billy Graham, Bill Clinton, The Three Stooges, and Johnny Depp dressed as pirate Jack Sparrow (also available as an action figure).

The star-struck fans of Hollywood also can purchase kitsch that is not specific to particular celebrities. For example, one can buy his or her very own director's clapboard and megaphone or a facsimile Hollywood Walk of Fame star with stick-on letters to form one's own name. Naturally, one can also buy plastic copies of the Oscar statuette, as well as a coin bank in the shape of a movie camera. *See also*: **Athletes**; **Awards and Ceremonies**; **Criticisms of Celebrity Culture**; **Dream Girls**; **Endorsements**.

Sam G. Riley

For Further Reading

Brown, Curtis F. *Star-Spangled Kitsch: An Astounding and Tastelessly Illustrated Exploration of the Bawdy, Gaudy, Shoddy Mass-Art Culture in This Grand Old Land of Ours*. New York: Universe Books, 1975.

Dorfles, Gilo, and John McHale. *Kitsch; The World of Bad Taste*. New York: Universe Books, 1969.

Gillilan, Lesley. *Kitsch Deluxe*. London: Mitchell Beazley, 2003.

Olalquiaga, Celeste. *The Artificial Kingdom: a Treasury of the Kitsch Experience*. New York: Pantheon Books, 1998.

L

LAWSUITS AND COURT CASES

Until recently, U.S. courts traditionally have shunned cameras because of abuses during the 1935 "Trial of the Century" of immigrant handyman Bruno Richard Hauptmann, executed for kidnapping and murdering the infant son of celebrated trans-Atlantic flyer Charles Lindbergh. Following the American Bar Association's subsequent ban on courtroom cameras, sketch artists did their best to picture real-life legal celebrities, but much better known were fictional lawyers such as *Perry Mason* portrayed by Raymond Burr (1957–1966).

In the late 1980s, most state courts lifted their bans on cameras, subject to discretion of the presiding judge. Soon after, Court TV launched the modern era of legal celebrities. The cable channel became the default pool video feed for a string of celebrity **criminal** trials.

Pre-Television Law

Before television, courtroom stars were known through their legal feats. Best known were thirty-year U.S. Supreme Court Justice Oliver Wendell Holmes and Clarence Darrow, defender of hopeless causes. Darrow saved teenagers Leopold and Loeb from a death sentence in 1924 and Tennessee teacher John Scopes in the so-called Monkey Trial in 1925. Opposing counsel in the Scopes trial was three-time Democratic presidential nominee William Jennings Bryan.

Sensationalized trials created other celebrities: anarchists Bartolomeo Vanzetti and Nicola Sacco (1927); Nazi leaders tried in the Nuremburg war crimes trials (1945–1949); U.S. House of Representatives Committee on Un-American Activities hearings to root out Communists from public life (1949–1954); the Alger Hiss perjury conviction (1950), which catapulted the careers of California Congressman Richard Nixon and Wisconsin Sen. Joseph McCarthy; McCarthy's own witch hunt for Communists (1950–1954); and Julius and Ethel Rosenberg, executed for passing atomic secrets (1953).

In the 1970s, the Vietnam War and the Watergate Scandal caused deepening mistrust of social institutions. Hollywood fed the increased fascination in the law with 103 courtroom dramas for the big screen, from *12 Angry Men* (1957) to *Fracture* (2007).

Prominent political trials penetrating celebrity culture included the "Catonsville Nine" draft protestors trial (1968); the "Chicago Eight" conspiracy trial (1970); the Watergate congressional hearings (1973–1974); the Iran-Contra congressional hearings (1986–1987), and subsequent criminal trials of White House advisors John Poindexter and Oliver North (1989–1990); allegations of sexual harassment in the Senate confirmation of U.S. Supreme Court Associate Justice Clarence Thomas (1991); U.S. House and Senate committee hearings on the Whitewater Scandal (1994–1998); and the House of Representatives' impeachment of President Bill Clinton (1998), followed by the Senate's acquittal of Clinton (1999). Perhaps the most controversial case of all was held behind closed doors: the U.S. Supreme Court's decision in *Bush v. Gore* that gave the U.S. presidency to George W. Bush in the 2000 election.

Media on Trial

A series of U.S. Supreme Court decisions brought the courts into celebrity culture. *Sheppard v. Maxwell* (1966) established trial judges' responsibilities to manage media access. The Sheppard case was fictionalized in a hit television series, *The Fugitive,* later made into a film starring Harrison Ford.

Other Supreme Court decisions protected the media when covering celebrities. *New York Times v. Sullivan* (1964) shifted the burden of proof in defamation cases from the media to government official plaintiffs. *Gertz v. Robert Welch* (1974) extended the libel burden of proof to public-figure plaintiffs, who were defined as either all-purpose celebrities or newsworthy private persons. *Sullivan* and *Gertz* together relieved the news media from the threat of libel suits from public officials or celebrities.

The media got invasion of privacy protection from *Time Inc. v. Hill* (1967), which placed the burden of proof on newsworthy private persons. The case involved the Hill family's kidnapping by escaped convicts. Joseph Hayes based his novel, *Desperate Hours*, on their story. The novel was made into a Broadway play, Hollywood movie (1955), and movie remake (1990). The public figure legal principle was upheld and extended to infliction of emotional distress cases in *Hustler Magazine v. Falwell* (1988), which involved a parody of evangelical minister Jerry Falwell, Sr., and which made girlie magazine publisher Larry Flynt into a celebrity advocate for free expression rights.

Television in the Courtroom

The American Bar Association's anti-camera standard, Canon 35, was expanded in 1952 to prohibit televising courts in all but four states. In 1962, financier Billie Sol Estes gained celebrity due to his fraud conviction in Texas in part because of his ties to Vice President Lyndon Johnson. The U.S. Supreme Court overturned Estes's conviction in *Estes v. Texas* (1965) because cameras and broadcasters had created a carnival-like atmosphere that prevented a fair trial. However, the court held that technological improvements in the future might make televised trials legal.

Florida permanently opened the state's courtrooms to television coverage in 1979, subject to judges' discretion. In *Chandler v. Florida* (1981), the U.S. Supreme Court upheld Florida's right to televise trials, even when the defendants objected. Influenced by the *Chandler* ruling, the ABA amended its anticamera policy in 1982. Soon every state implemented guidelines for televising trials. However, cameras remain banned in federal courts under Federal Rule of Criminal Procedure 53.

Court TV

After New York state approved cameras in the courtroom, Steven Brill pitched a business deal that he described as a cross between C-Span and soap opera, and Courtroom Television Network or Court TV was launched in 1991 (renamed *truTV* in 2008). It carried gavel-to-gavel coverage of the rape trial of political family scion William Kennedy Smith (acquitted), a case that exposed the seedier side of high society. But it was the 1995 murder trial of professional footballer turned movie star O. J. Simpson that most captivated the public. Simpson had the best celebrity defense **lawyers** that money (reportedly $4 million) could buy. Simpson's "Dream Team" included F. Lee Bailey, Johnnie Cochran, Barry Scheck, and Alan Dershowitz.

In 1966, Bailey successfully argued the case of convicted murder Dr. Sam Sheppard to the U.S. Supreme Court and won a retrial and acquittal. Thereafter, Bailey sought other high-profile defendants, including the "Boston Strangler" Albert DeSalvo in 1967 (conviction), My Lai massacre commander Captain Ernest Medina in 1971 (acquittal), and newspaper heiress turned bank robber Patricia Hearst in 1976 (conviction). His vigorous cross-examination of a racist police detective helped to clear Simpson in 1995.

In 1993, Cochran defended singer Michael Jackson against allegations of child molestation and in 1995 became an **international celebrity** as leader of O. J. Simpson's legal defense. In his closing arguments, Cochran held up the murderer's glove, saying, "If the glove doesn't fit, you have to acquit." After the trial, Cochran made frequent television appearances, accepted movie deals, and hosted his own show, *Johnnie Cochran Tonight*, on Court TV.

Simpson "Dream Teamer" Scheck was known for uncovering wrongful convictions. In 1997, he defended nineteen-year-old British *au pair* Louise Woodward in her Massachusetts murder trial and won her release for time served. In 1999, Scheck used DNA (Deoxyribonucleic acid) evidence to exonerate Dennis Fritz and Ron Williamson for rape and murder in Oklahoma.

"Dream Teamer" and Harvard law professor Dershowitz won a dismissal of Claus Von Bülow's 1984 murder conviction. His book, *Reversal of Fortune: Inside the Von Bülow Case,* was made into a movie. Dershowitz led the appeals of numerous other celebrities: Patricia Hearst, porn star Harry Reems, spy Jonathan Pollard, real estate investor Leona Helmsley, movie star son Christian Brando, boxer Mike Tyson, evangelist Jim Bakker, movie director John Landis, car designer John DeLorean, junk bond trader Michael Milken,

Hare Krishna leader Kirtanananda Swami, and fellow lawyers F. Lee Bailey and William Kunstler.

Legally Infamous

Orderly society is preserved by the public prosecution of villains whose terrible deeds and capitulation to justice are memorialized by the mass media. Political assassins turned infamous celebrities include Byron De La Beckwith, murderer of civil rights leader Medgar Evers (1963, convicted 1994); Robert Chambliss, Bobby Frank Cherry and Thomas E. Blanton, Jr., bombers of the Sixteenth Street Baptist Church in Birmingham, Alabama (1963, convicted decades later); Lee Harvey Oswald, accused killer of President John Kennedy (1963); Jack Ruby, Oswald's assassin (1963); Valerie Jean Solanas, attempted assassin of artist Andy Warhol (1968); James Earl Ray, assassin of civil rights leader Martin Luther King, Jr. (1968); Sirhan Sirhan, assassin of U.S. Sen. Robert Kennedy (1968); Arthur Bremer, attempted assassin of U.S. Democratic presidential candidate George Wallace (1972); Lynette "Squeaky" Fromme, former Charles Manson "family" member and attempted assassin of President Gerald Ford, followed seventeen days later by Sara Jane Moore, second attempted assassin of Ford (1975); Mark David Chapman, assassin of pop singer John Lennon (1981); and John Hinckley, Jr., attempted assassin of President Ronald Reagan (1981).

Mass murderers in the media's roll of infamy include David Berkowitz, the "Son of Sam" who terrorized New York City (1977); Theodore "Ted" Bundy, executed murderer of dozens of young women in several states (1978); John Wayne Gacy, executed rapist and murderer of thirty-three boys and young men in Illinois (1978); Ramzi Yousef, mastermind of the first Al Qaeda terrorist attack on the World Trade Center (1993); Timothy McVeigh, executed for killing 168 people when he bombed the Alfred P. Murrah Building in Oklahoma City (1995); imprisoned "Unibomber" Theodore Kaczynski (1998); and Zacarias Moussaoui, imprisoned coconspirator of the second Al Qaeda attack on the World Trade Center that killed thousands (2001).

Media exposure transformed the legacies of some legal cases. Mass murderers Richard Hickock and Perry Smith would have died unknown, except for Truman Capote's bestselling book *In Cold Blood* (1965). Immortalized in Norman Mailer's Pulitzer Prize–winning novel *The Executioner's Song,* was murderer Gary Gilmore, executed in 1977. A magazine article by Mailer in 1981 led to the parole of murderer Jack Henry Abbot, who killed again six weeks after his release. Errol Morris's 1988 nonfiction film *The Thin Blue Line* prompted the overturning of Randall Adams's murder conviction after twelve years in prison. Amid massive, mostly sympathetic news coverage, New York City "subway vigilante" Bernard Goetz served only eight months in jail for shooting four assailants in 1984.

The parade of high-profile legal celebrities on Court TV has included actress Anna Nicole Smith (inheritance plaintiff, 2000–2007); basketball star Kobe Bryant (sexual assault lawsuit settled out of court, 2004); singer Michael Jackson (acquitted of child molestation, 2005); media mogul Martha Stewart (imprisoned for securities fraud, 2004); actor Robert Blake (acquitted of murder, 2005); and music producer Phil Spector (murder mistrial, 2007). Each such case has served as a public referendum on fairness of the U.S. legal system.

Amateur video now plays an important role in spawning case-related celebrities. In 1991, bystander George Halliday videotaped four overzealous Los Angeles policemen tasering and beating Rodney King, Jr. Halliday's video was broadcast across the country and outraged the African American community. When three of the four officers were acquitted of police brutality by a mostly white jury in 1992, riots broke out in several cities. Two of the four officers eventually served prison time for violation of King's federal civil rights. *See also*: **Arrests of Celebrities**; **Athletes**; **Politics**; **Reality Television's Role**; **Television's Role**.

Russell J. Cook

For Further Reading

Cohn, Marjorie, and David Dow. *Cameras in the Courtroom: Television and the Pursuit of Justice*. Jefferson, NC: McFarland and Co., 1998.

Grace, Nancy, with Diane Clehane. *Objection! How High-Priced Defense Attorneys, Celebrity Defendants, and a 24/7 Media Have Hijacked Our Criminal Justice System*. New York: Hyperion, 2005.

Rojek, Chris. "Celebrity and Transgression." In *Celebrity*. London: Reaktion Books Ltd., 2001.

Sherwin, Richard K. *When Law Goes Pop: The Vanishing Line between Law and Popular Culture*. Chicago: The University of Chicago Press, 2000.

Thaler, Paul. *The Watchful Eye: American Justice in the Age of the Television Trial*. Westport, CT: Praeger, 1994.

Court TV. "Famous Cases." http://www.courttv.com/trials/famous.

Linder, Douglas O. "Famous Trials." http://www.law.umkc.edu/faculty/projects/ftrials/ftrials.htm.

LAWYERS

Celebrity is the radiant child of Talent and Chance. Talent, languishing in obscurity, remains unrecognized. Chance, lightly kissing the brow of mediocrity, passes unnoticed. For lawyers, Celebrity is often brought by Chance in the guise of a case having colorful participants, a compelling theme, uncertainty, and drama. One has only to think of Johnnie Cochran, who won acquittal for O. J. Simpson, or Alan Dershowitz, who gained celebrity when he won the appeal that led to the exoneration of Claus von Bulow from a conviction for the murder of his wealthy socialite wife, Sunny.

By the turn of the century, Chance had played a unique role in the rise of two remarkably talented lawyers who rose from humble beginnings to achieve national and international recognition as legal celebrities: David Boies and Gerry Spence.

David Boies

On December 11, 2000, the justices of the U.S. Supreme Court took their seats to hear the case of *Bush v. Gore*. Standing at the lectern before them to present an argument that would decide the presidency of the United States was David Boies, arguably the most celebrated lawyer of his time. By this time, he had been a leading lawyer in virtually every major corporate litigation of the preceding twenty-five years.

Boies's path to legal stardom was far from traditional, however. Diagnosed as severely dyslexic as a child growing up in southern California, he has found reading problematic his entire life. Nonetheless, at an early age, he realized that his retentive memory, competitive spirit, and logical mind would more than make up for his reading difficulties. In high school, he gravitated to the debating team. His dyslexia made it difficult for him to debate using notes, but his memory allowed him to do without them, an ability he found invaluable later in court.

Boies married his high school sweetheart at the end of their senior year, and at her insistence, enrolled at a local college, completing a three-year academic program in two. Chance, in the person of a professor, suggested to Boies that he take the law school admission examination. Boies took the exam, and his scores were so high that he was promptly accepted both at Stanford in California and Northwestern in Chicago. Chance again reached out. Although his wife wanted to remain in California, Boies, with Chance looking on, elected to attend Northwestern, a decision that was to change his life.

Boies loved law school. His mind naturally took to the Socratic method of instruction, and he excelled. The long days of study and nights spent in part-time

jobs took its toll on his marriage, however. At the end of his first year in law school, his wife left with their children and returned to California. Now, for a third time, Chance intervened, introducing Boies to Judith Daynard, a fellow student working with him on the school's law review. A romance ensued, but one not without difficulties, for the object of his affection was the wife of his evidence professor. The situation became so untenable that their dean offered to assist them in relocating to any other law school in the country. A New Yorker, Daynard chose Columbia Law School, and Boies selected Yale, an hour away by train.

Boies graduated magna cum laude, second in his class. He and Daynard had married while in law school, and so when Boies received an offer to join the eminent law firm of Cravath, Swaine and Moore in New York City, he readily accepted. Boies was an odd fit at Cravath from the beginning. It was a firm that prided itself on its "culture," and Boies's eccentricities such as wearing Lands' End outfits or Sears suits and tennis shoes to the office with a cheap wristwatch over his coat sleeve was definitely not part of that cultural pattern. Cravath did recognize, however, Boies's extraordinary brilliance. During his tenure at the firm, he salvaged Texaco from near bankruptcy resulting from a ruling by a Texas court in favor of rival Pennzoil and also fought the federal government to a draw in its long-running suit against IBM.

In 1977, Boies took a sabbatical from Cravath to work in Washington as chief counsel to the Senate Judiciary Committee chaired by Ted Kennedy. Boies's marriage to Daynard had ended, and he had no thought of remarriage. However, Chance, still hovering at his shoulder, had other plans. At a lunch meeting with administrative staffers Boies met Mary Schuman, also a government lawyer. By August 1982, Boies married Schuman, who had left the government for a position with CBS. Less than a month after the wedding, Chance firmly embraced Talent when CBS asked Boies, who had no significant experience with libel or slander cases, to defend CBS against charges brought by General William Westmoreland, the former commander of U.S. forces in Vietnam.

Westmoreland accused CBS and Mike Wallace of *60 Minutes* fame of defaming him by saying that he had misled the public as to the true strength of Vietnamese forces during the war. Boies had the daunting task of arguing that this American hero who had spent his life in the service of his country had been less than truthful. Through a brilliant cross-examination in which he never directly contradicted Westmoreland, Boies used documents prepared by the general to leave an impression with the jury that Westmoreland had indeed made statements that were less than completely accurate. Following the cross-examination by Boies, Westmoreland dropped the suit. Because of the high profiles of Westmoreland, Wallace, and CBS, newspapers and television devoted enormous attention to the case, and to Boies, who became a media hero. For himself, Boies instinctively understood the importance of the press and enjoyed the interplay with reporters, a relationship which was to continue as Boies moved from success to success.

Following the Westmoreland case, Boies left Cravath to form his own firm

and went on to represent clients as large and diverse as the New York Yankees and team owner George Steinbrenner; the U.S. government in its antitrust action against Microsoft, where a withering examination of Bill Gates by Boies again captured national media attention; and celebrities such as Don Imus, Michael Moore, and Hank Greenberg of AIG. By the time he stepped to the podium to argue in *Bush v. Gore*, Boies had been inducted as a popular celebrity into the Vanity Fair Hall of Fame together with the cast of the *Sopranos,* and cyclist Lance Armstrong, and he had been named "Lawyer of the Year" by the *National Law Journal,* which compared his courtroom performances to Michael Jordan on the basketball court.

From the beginning, Chance embraced Boies and led him inexorably to Celebrity. By Chance he had taken the law school entrance exam. By Chance, he had fallen in love with a professor's wife and by Chance had followed her back to New York. By Chance he met his third wife at a casual luncheon, and by Chance, he was given the opportunity to defend a major network in one of the most highly publicized trials of the time.

Gerry Spence

Karen Silkwood's case was the stuff of movies—and indeed was made into a successful motion picture staring Merle Streep as Silkwood. The case pitted the power of a large corporation against a lone individual, nuclear contamination, cancer, conspiracy, and allegations of murder.

In 1972, Silkwood, a twenty-six-year-old mother fleeing from an unhappy marriage, took a job at Kerr-McGee's Cimarron River Plant in Cresent, Oklahoma. The plant manufactured fuel rods containing plutonium for use in nuclear reactors. Silkwood became increasingly concerned about safety measures at the plant, and with the encouragement of union representatives, began to collect information on failures of Kerr-McGee to provide sufficient protection for its employees against radioactive contamination. In November 1974, Silkwood learned that she had been seriously contaminated. When her apartment was tested, it too showed high levels of contamination, leading to suspicions that radioactive material had been planted in her home. On November 13, 1974, Silkwood left a union meeting at the Hub Café in Cresent to drive to Oklahoma City. Before leaving, she had shown a folder to several companions, telling them it contained information from her investigations. She said she planned to deliver the folder to a *New York Times* reporter. Ten minutes after she left, she was found dead in her car in a ditch beside the road. The folder was never found. Although the police ruled her death an accident, groups as diverse as the Oil, Chemical and Atomic Workers Union and the National Organization of Women (NOW) would not accept the death by accident explanation. Silkwood's father filed suit against Kerr-McGee on behalf of Silkwood's three children, alleging that she had been contaminated as a result of Kerr-McGee's negligence in allowing radioactive material to escape from its plant.

Spence was born and raised in Wyoming. By 1977, he was a very successful country lawyer practicing in Casper, Wyoming. Like Boies, he had not come from wealth, had married

before entering law school, and had worked at a variety of jobs. Growing up in what he has described as difficult times, Spence thought practicing law was the road to success in his community, but the idea of leaving Wyoming to study law at Harvard or Yale never crossed his mind. Consequently, Spence attended law school at the University of Wyoming. While Boies enjoyed law school, Spence hated it. He thought the cases he read were sterile, totally devoid of any sense of the human condition. He concluded that the only way out was to graduate, and that to do well, he did not have to think like a lawyer but like a law professor. The result of this theory was that Spence graduated first in his class.

In the years following law school, Spence was remarkably successful as a county prosecutor and at defending insurance companies. Then one day Chance led him to a local store where he met an accident victim he had defeated on behalf of an insurance company. Spence was so moved that he abandoned his prior practice and began to represent only criminal defendants and plaintiffs in civil suits.

In 1977, Spence had never heard of Silkwood. He did not think of himself as a "cause" lawyer, taking on cases for some overriding objective beyond the case itself. The outraged cries of antinuke groups, unions, and feminists who had taken up the Silkwood cause had not resonated with him. Nonetheless, Chance was drawing together the gossamer strands of her web to draw this talented country lawyer to national and international fame.

A year after the Silkwood case had been filed, Spence got a call from Danny Sheehan, the young lawyer originally retained to pursue the case. He had learned of Spence through the most tenuous connection Chance could employ. Sheehan's girlfriend, Sara Nelson, was leading the NOW campaign to publicize the mystery surrounding Silkwood's death. Nelson, by Chance, had met a former ranch-hand who had worked for Spence. The ranch-hand told Nelson that Spence was the best trial lawyer he had ever met, and Nelson promptly dispatched Sheehan to hire Spence.

Spence became intrigued and agreed to enter the case with the understanding that he was interested only in getting money for Silkwood's children, not in espousing antinuclear or feminist causes. As he delved into the case, he grasped the magnitude of the issues and raised the original damage claim from $160,000 to $1.5 million, an eye-catching sum for the time. The 1979 Silkwood trial lasted two and a half months. During the trial, Spence never abandoned his trademark fringed buckskin jacket, boots, and Stetson hat. The issues alone would have attracted national press coverage, but Spence's devastating cross-examination of Kerr-McGee's witnesses and his colorful appearance captivated the media. Referring to the fact that Kerr-McGee could not account for a quantity of deadly radioactive material, Spence, in rhythmic cadences, emphasized again and again to the jury, "If the Lion Got Away, Kerr-McGee Has to Pay"—for the pain and terror Silkwood faced before her death. At the end of the trial, the jury gave Spence an award of more than $10 million. Years later, Spence was invited to defend former football great O. J. Simpson but refused. Simpson was ultimately defended by another celebrity lawyer, Johnnie Cochran, who demanded in a similar vein, "If the glove doesn't fit, you have to acquit."

Following the Silkwood verdict with its attendant publicity, Spence became the prototypical celebrity lawyer. Tall, with graying hair and blue eyes, the brilliant cowboy lawyer, in his trademark outfit, was sought out by famous clients in some of most highly publicized cases in the country, culminating in the successful defense of Imelda Marcos, wife of a former president of the Philippines charged with fraud and deceit by the federal government. In his career, Spence never lost a criminal case and has not lost a civil case since 1969. His aggressive high-profile approach has had a major impact on the practice of trial advocacy.

Perhaps there is no better example of Celebrity arising from the marriage of Chance and Talent, than Chance bringing a singularly talented lawyer to change the nature of his practice and then causing his former ranch-hand to call Spence's formidable Talent to the attention of the feminist supporters of the Silkwood cause. *See also*: **African American**; **News Media Figures**.

Randle B. Carpenter, Jr.

For Further Reading

Boies, David. *Courting Justice.* New York: Miramax Books, 2004.

Cochran, Johnnie L. *Journey to Justice.* New York: Ballantine Books, 1996.

Dershowitz, Alan M. *The Best Defense.* New York: Random House, 1982.

Dershowitz, Alan M. *Reversal of Fortune, Inside the von Bulow Case.* New York: Random House, 1986.

Spence, Gerry, *The Making of a Country Lawyer*. New York: St. Martin's Press, 1996.

Spence, Gerry. *Gunning for Justice*. Garden City, NY: Doubleday, 1982.

LGBT CELEBRITY

While there is evidence of gay, lesbian, and bisexual personalities throughout history, including such famous persons as Aristotle, Michelangelo, Leonardo DaVinci, and King James I of England, the modern meaning and understanding of sexual orientation did not become a publicly acceptable designation until the last half of the 20th century.

A well-known heartthrob who actually was gay was Rock Hudson. Jody Foster came out in 2007 while accepting the Women in Entertainment award when she paid tribute to Cydney Bernard, her partner of fourteen years. Sir Ian McKellen, British actor in both theater and Hollywood, was openly gay from the beginning of his career, but in recent years he has become more politically active and in 2007 launched Gay History Month. Entertainer Ellen DeGeneres "came out" as a lesbian in 1997 during the fourth season of her television sitcom, *Ellen*. Other **talk show hosts** and **comedy** celebrities include show host Rosie O'Donnell and comedians Lily Tomlin and Margaret Cho. The five stars of the Bravo reality show, *Queer Eye for the Straight Guy*, were all gay men: Thom Filicia (design), Ted Allen (food), Kyan Douglas (grooming), Jai Rodriguez (culture), and Carson Cressley (fashion). Other famous gay actors include Raymond Burr, Rupert Everett, George Takei, Wilson Cruz, Richard Chamberlain, and Sigfried (Fischbacher) and Roy (Horn) the famed **magicians** and animal trainers.

Best known among gay journalists is Anderson Cooper, an anchor for Cable News Network (CNN); his CNN colleague Thomas Roberts also is gay. Mike Penner, a sports columnist for the *Los Angeles Times*, transitioned to Christine Daniels and discussed the process in her column. Within the gay community, Paul Schindler, editor-in-chief of *Gay City News*, a weekly newspaper serving the greater New York area, plays a significant role in the coverage of civil rights for lesbian, gay, bisexual, and transgendered (LGBT) people. Leroy F. Aarons, former executive editor of the *Oakland Tribune*, formed the National Lesbian and Gay Journalists Association (NLGJA) in 1990. Representative of other gay journalists are Jeffrey Kofman (ABC news correspondent), Jeffrey Schneider (ABC News senior vice president), Manuel Gallegus (CBS correspondent), David Brown (FOX news producer), and Deb Price (*Detroit News*).

Gay **authors** include humor writer David Sedaris and mystery writer Christopher Rice, son of popular novelist Anne Rice. Russell T. Davies, author of the *Dr. Who* series as well as the Showtime Network show *Queer as Folk*, is a screenwriter whose career began by working on children's programming for the British Broadcasting Company (BBC) and Granada TV in Britain. Patricia Cornwell is a bestselling crime and mystery writer. Rita Mae Brown writes novels that cover a wide range of topics, but of special interest is her series of mystery books featuring

Sneaky Pie Brown, a cat. The successful writer of adolescent novels about gay high school students, Alex Sanchez, is openly gay.

Music, both classical and popular, has been generally open to LGBT performers. **Classical musicians** Leonard Bernstein, Van Cliburn, and Michel Tilson Thomas are gay men. Lesbian performers include Melissa Etheridge, k. d. lang, Sinead O'Conner, Ani DiFranco, and Joan Baez. Gay pop musicians include Johnny Mathis, Freddie Mercury, Chuck Panozzo (founding member of Styx), Rob Halford (Judas Priest), Michael Stipe (R.E.M), Elton John, and Barry Manilow. Music groups with a LGBT identity include the Indigo Girls (Amy Ray and Emily Saliers), Pansy Division, Pet Shop Boys, and Christian musicians Jason and deMarco (Jason Warner and deMarco DeCiccio).

In the world of design, Dolce & Gabbana (Domenico Dolce and Stefano Gabbana) were a couple until 2005, but they remain business partners. Mitchell Gold is the chief executive behind the Mitchell Gold furniture company. Herb Ritts was a renowned fashion and celebrity photographer.

Sports celebrities have been hesitant to be openly LGBT, especially during their active careers, but cracks in the "closet" are beginning to show, and if the number of high school and college LGBT **athletes** is any indicator, the number of "out" athletes will rapidly increase. One of the first athletes to come out was Tom Waddell, who placed sixth in the 1968 Olympic decathlon. In 1976, Waddell and his partner, Charles Deaton, were the first gay men to be featured in the "Couples" section of *People* magazine, and in

1981 Waddell formed San Francisco Arts and Athletics to plan the first "Gay Olympic Games" that took place in 1982. In 1975 David Kopay, a National Football League running back who played for five teams (San Francisco, Detroit, Washington, New Orleans, Green Bay) between 1964 and 1972, became the first professional athlete to come out, but only after having been retired three years. Other football players who came out after retiring from competition were Roy Franklin Simmons, an offensive lineman for the New York Giants and Washington Redskins who came out of the closet in 1992 on the Phil Donahue Show, and Esera Tuaolo, who played for the Carolina Panthers, Jacksonville Jaguars, Minnesota Vikings, Green Bay Packers, and Atlanta Falcons during his career. Esera came out on a Home Box Office (HBO) sports show in 1999. Jerry Smith, who played for the Washington Redskins, never acknowledged that he was gay, but after Smith's death from AIDS, David Kopay described him as his first lover. In 1981 Billie Jean King, tennis champion, was "outed" when Marilyn Barnett sued her for "galimony" after their breakup. The same year, tennis professional Martina Navratilova publicly revealed that she was a lesbian during an interview with the *New York Daily News*, an announcement that cost her **endorsement** dollars. One of the first swimmers to come out was Bruce Hayes, who won a gold medal at the 1984 Olympics. He came out publicly at the 1988 Gay Games where he won seven gold medals. Greg Louganis, four-time Olympic gold medalist in diving who was HIV-positive, came out at the 1998 Gay Games. Matthew Mitcham, an out

Australian diver, won gold at the 2008 Olympics. John Amaechi was the first National Basketball Association (NBA) player to come out, but only after he retired and just before his autobiography was published. Sheryl Swoopes, star basketball player at Texas Tech, and later for the Houston Comets and other WNBA and European teams, came out after divorcing her husband. Glenn Burke, who played for the Los Angeles Dodgers and Oakland Athletics from 1976 to 1979, was the first Major League Baseball player to be out to his teammates and team owners during his professional career. He died from AIDS-related causes in 1995. Billy Bean, who played for the Detroit Tigers, LA Dodgers, and San Diego Padres from 1987–1995, came out in 1999 as a gay man, but, again, only after retiring.

Government officials and politicians are another group that has been slow in publicly admitting their sexual orientation. The first openly gay man to hold a major political position was Harvey Milk, who was elected in 1977 as a member of San Francisco's board of supervisors; in 1978 another supervisor shot and killed both Milk and the mayor of San Francisco. The first openly gay man to serve in the U.S. Congress was Gerry Studds, but Rep. Barney Frank of Massachusetts is America's best-known gay politician. Another member of the House of Representatives is Tammy Baldwin, who was elected in 1998 by Wisconsin voters even though she was openly lesbian. The first gay Republican congress member was Steve Gunderson of Wisconsin, and Jim Kolbe of Arizona was the second. Sexual orientation can be a divisive issue, as demonstrated in the case of former New Jersey governor Jim McGreevey, who resigned his office in 2004 following allegations of a same-sex extramarital affair with an employee. State legislators have been more successful as openly gay or lesbian, with both Massachusetts Rep. Elaine Noble and Minnesota Sen. Allan H. Spear coming out in 1974, after being elected. In 2003, two gay legislators were elected (Ernesto Scorsone of Kentucky and Adam Ebbin of Virginia), with three more in 2004 (Matt McCoy of Iowa, Nicole LeFavour of Idaho, and Julia Boseman of North Carolina), and four in 2006 (Patricia Todd of Alabama, Kathy Webb of Arkansas, Al McAffrey of Oklahoma, and Reed Gusciora of New Jersey).

Even with the "don't ask, don't tell" bias of the **military**, LGBT people do serve in the armed forces. In 1989, Margarethe Cammermeyer, in response to a question during a security clearance interview, disclosed that she was a lesbian. She was honorably discharged from the military in 1992, but she filed a lawsuit against the decision in civil court. In 1994, a federal district court ruled her discharge, and the ban on gays and lesbians serving in the military, unconstitutional. She returned to the National Guard and served as one of the few officially accepted openly gay or lesbian people in the military until her retirement in 1997. Maj. Alan G. Rogers was killed by an improvised explosive device (IED) in Iraq in 2008 and was posthumously awarded both the Purple Heart and Bronze Star. As a result of newspaper stories, he was "outed" and thus became one of the first gay casualties of the war.

Two religious leaders clearly fit the designation of LGBT celebrities.

Bishop V. Gene Robinson was elected as the first openly gay bishop in the Episcopal Church. His election sparked a major discussion and division within the U.S. Episcopal Church as well as the larger Anglican Communion. Mel White was a leading evangelical writer who worked for both Jerry Falwell and Pat Robertson as a ghost writer before coming out and publishing his auto-biography, *Stranger at the Gate*, in which he recounted his long struggle over his sexual orientation. He formed the religious-based gay rights group Soulforce and continues to engage evangelicals in discussion and debate on the issue of homosexuality in the church.

Finally, there are children and rela-tives of famous people who are gay or lesbian, including Mary Cheney (daughter of former U.S. Vice President Dick Cheney), Chastity Bono (daughter of Sonny and Cher), Candace Gingrich (half-sister of former speaker of the house Newt Gingrich), and Daniel J. O'Donnell (brother of lesbian enter-tainer Rosie O'Donnell). *See also*: **Movies' Role**; **News Media Figures**; **Politics**; **Rock and Pop**; **Television's Role**.

Edward H. Sewell, Jr

For Further Reading

Miller, Neil. *Out of the Past: Gay and Lesbian History from 1869 to the Present*. Los Angeles: Alyson Pub-lishing, 2008.

Equality Forum. www.equalityforum.com.

Outsports. www.outsports.com.

Servicemembers Legal Defense Net-work. www.sldn.org.

M

MAGAZINES' ROLE

Walk into any newsstand in America and you will find hundreds of celebrities peering down from the covers of magazines. From sports digests to specialized business periodicals, from women's journals to fanzines, from city and regional monthlies to men's publications, editors rely on celebrities to help sell their product. In turn, these periodicals play a crucial role in the culture of celebrity. Magazines help create new celebrities by running stories and photos focusing on up-and-coming personalities; they increase the buzz around existing notables, thrusting them into superstardom, or accelerate them into a downward spiral with investigative pieces or photo spreads that disillusion readers about their faltering heroes.

The magazine industry's love affair with celebrities is nothing new. In the 19th century, magazines fell under the spell of the "Swedish Nightingale" and helped create P. T. Barnum's phenomenon, Jenny Lind. By the turn of the century, such mass-circulating magazines as *McClure's* and *Munsey's* grew fat on America's insatiable appetite for profiles on entrepreneurs and political figures. By the 1930s, *Collier's*, *Saturday Evening Post*, *Woman's Home Companion*, *Liberty,* and *American*, and a new generation of celebrity reporters, like John K. Winkler, Adela Rogers St. Johns, and Henry F. Pringle, perfected a new form of journalism, one that aimed to give the "real" story behind the movie, music, and sports standouts of the day.

Yet all this seemed but a dress rehearsal for the post–World War II magazine industry. Fueled by an advertising industry that demanded a highly focused audience, a new type of magazine emerged: specialized "niche" publications covering a specific topic, market, or geographic region. The number of U.S. magazines skyrocketed, from 9,657 in 1975 to roughly 30,000 at the end of the 20th century. Central to the editorial focus of these new publications were personality profiles, success stories that focused on the notables in the niche, creating a new class of celebrity, the niche celebrity.

In addition, a whole new genre of niche magazines debuted—celebrity periodicals, whose only aim was to give the inside story about the new, "hot" personalities of the day. But the emphasis on celebrities was not limited to niche magazines. Editors of mass-circulating magazines, especially women's magazines and men's monthlies, discovered that celebrity covers sold well at the newsstand.

Although magazines have long included personality profiles in their editorial mix and thereby did their part in pushing the cult of celebrity forward, the one periodical that has most frequently been credited—or blamed—for fanning the flame of personality journalism in America in the last quarter of the 20th century has been *People Magazine*.

A product of Time Inc.'s Magazine Development Group, *People*—as a concept—had first been suggested by the company's chairman of the board, according to one member of the development group. Eventually the concept was tested in thirteen cities and proved to be a huge seller. The magazine was launched with the March 4, 1974, issue with the young actor Mia Farrow, who was then starring in the season's movie blockbuster, *The Great Gatsby*, on the cover.

The new magazine was under the direction of Dick Durrell as publisher and Richard B. Stolley as managing editor. The DNA of contemporary celebrity journalism—Stolley preferred to call it personality journalism—is found in that magazine. While the magazine dealt with the movie, music, sports, and television personalities of the day, it also profiled everyday heroes, including the wives of Vietnam veterans who

were missing in action. All those personalities were tied together by what Stolley called a return to bedrock reporting about humans and what's happening to them, not as statistics or trends.

The magazine—the first weekly launched in the United States in years—initially was sold exclusively on the newsstand and was an immediate success, profitable within eighteen months. The key to newsstand sales—and profitability—was the right cover selection. Stolley admits it took some time to get the knack of picking the right celebrity and the right photo to bring in the large newsstand sales. *People*'s first million-copy seller was issued July 1, 1974, with bare-chested Telly Savalas, at that time star of the top-rated television detective show *Kojak*. Stolley eventually codified what sells and does not sell as follows: "Young is better than old. Pretty is better than ugly. Rich is better than poor. Television is better than music. Music is better than movies. Movies are better than sports. Anything is better than politics. And nothing is better than the celebrity dead."

Those sentiments have guided *People* for more than thirty years and have influenced the thinking of a generation of magazine editors as they choose just the right celebrity photo for the front cover. Those guidelines also explain the enormous success of *People*'s top-selling issues: the collapse of New York's Twin Towers on September 11, 2001; the death of Princess Diana in September 1997; and the untimely death of John F. Kennedy, Jr., in 1999.

People's success led to the launch of many imitators. *US Weekly* debuted in 1977 as the *New York Times*'s foray into celebrity journalism. The newspaper did not stay long in the niche, selling the property to Macfadden Holdings, which in turn converted it to a biweekly. *US Weekly* was subsequently sold to Wenner Media, owner of *Rolling Stone*. That publishing house converted the magazine to a monthly and then in 2000 relaunched it as a weekly. Today, *US Weekly* has 1.5 million readers, number two in the celebrity magazine field but far behind the behemoth in the niche, *People* magazine, with 3.6 million. *OK!* magazine, the American version of the British celebrity weekly, debuted in 2005 with a different editorial philosophy, unapologetically paying celebrities for their stories. Notwithstanding the controversial "checkbook journalism," *OK!* quickly became a newsstand favorite with 1.3 million readers. The other two main competitors in the celebrity niche are American Media's *Star* magazine, which was started as a **tabloid** in 1972 but was relaunched as a glossy in 2004 with 1.3 million weekly readers, and Bauer Publishing's cheap weekly *InTouch* magazine, with a circulation of 1 million. (Women are the primary readers of all the celebrity magazines.)

The genre's success has led to cutthroat competition for the latest celebrity gossip, and especially photos, the mainstay for all magazines in the celebrity niche and most magazines generally. Newborn babies and weddings seem to bring the largest dollar amount. In 2008, photos of the newborn twins of actors Angelina Jolie and Brad Pitt set a record when sold to U.S.'s *People* and Britain's *Hello* for $14 million. Stories reported that all proceeds went to charity. Up until then, the largest amount paid for a celebrity photo had

been $4.1 million, for another baby picture—of Shiloh Nouvel Jolie-Pitt, first born of the Jolie and Pitt union, in 2005—to *People*. To date, *OK!* has paid the largest amount for wedding pictures: $3 million for the photos of the marriage of actors Demi Moore and Ashton Kutcher in October 2005 and $2 million for pictures taken at the union of professional basketball player Tony Parker and *Desperate Housewives* star Eva Longoria in July 2007.

Babies and weddings cannot possibly fill all these magazines nor can they quench the never-ending demand for celebrity photographs. Editors of celebrity magazines engage in a pitched battle for exclusive photos of superstars and notables in the news. For these photos, editors rely on celebrities; their representatives, families, and friends; and both professional photographers (**paparazzi**) and amateur shooters lucky enough to come upon a celebrity. Prices for candid shots of elusive celebrities and exclusive photos of newsworthy moments can bring in hundreds of thousands of dollars. According to *Forbes* magazine, *InTouch* paid a reported $400,000 for a photo of celebrity Anna Nicole Smith with her son hours before his death, and *US Weekly* paid an estimated $500,000 for a picture of actors Brad Pitt and Angelina Jolie simply out for a stroll on an African beach. Most photos taken by paparazzi, however, do not bring such astronomical prices.

Celebrity magazines represent only one small part of the magazine industry. Nonetheless, they have had a tremendous influence on the entire field. Week after week, celebrity magazines have demonstrated that the face of a personality on the front cover can sell an issue on the newsstand and can grab the attention of the news media across the country, further publicizing (and increasing the marketability) of the issue. For example, the news of *People* magazine's "Sexist Man Alive" issue is regularly covered on television, cable, the Internet, newspapers, and even some other magazines. This lesson has not been lost on the editors of niche and mass magazines, who must compete to get an A-list celebrity for their own covers.

In today's competitive magazine market, celebrities clearly have the upper hand and often extract demands from editors who wish to feature them in their periodicals. According to a *New York Times* survey of three dozen editors, writers, publicists, and Hollywood executives, publicists and magazines most commonly negotiate about which writers and photographers will be assigned to write the story or photograph the celebrity. But demands from publicists often reach beyond that—to photograph selection, approval of quotes, and even review of the feature before publication. Negotiations between magazines and publicists often become what the *New York Times* calls a "dance of mutual self interest." For example, in one "dance," *Rolling Stone* wished to partner with superstar Madonna. The magazine wanted to feature the diva on its thirtieth anniversary cover on the women of rock and roll. Madonna refused unless she had approval of layout and photographs and copyright ownership of all pictures that featured her likeness. *Rolling Stone* got the dance but had to relinquish control of photograph approval and copyright ownership of such pictures.

The "dance of mutual self interest" can bring enormous wealth and notoriety to magazine editors themselves. Of course, there is nothing new about editors becoming celebrities. Harold Ross of *The New Yorker,* Samuel S. McClure of *McClure's,* and Edward W. Bok of the *Ladies' Home Journal*—to name but a few—were iconic figures in publishing and American culture in their day. But their fame seems to pale in comparison to the best-known magazine editors of the late 20th and early 21st centuries. Hugh Hefner, who founded *Playboy* magazine, has both created celebrities and become a celebrity himself. Early playmates like deceased reality star Anna Nicole Smith and actor Pamela Anderson began their journey to celebrity in the centerfold of *Playboy* magazine. For decades, Hefner himself has been a celebrity as the pipe-smoking symbol of the *Playboy* lifestyle. His business exploits, his profits and losses, but mostly his marriages, divorces, and liaisons have all been fodder for gossip columns in newspapers and magazines over the decades. Now in his eighties, Hefner has achieved a kind of supercelebrity status, as the editor of the nationally circulated magazine, architect of a multimillion dollar entertainment kingdom that includes the cable television reality program, *The Girls Next Door.* Paparazzi and gossip columnists keep track of Hefner, his lovers, and any salacious details they can uncover about the legendary Playboy mansion or its inhabitants. Hefner is perhaps the most extreme example of the editor as celebrity. Tina Brown, former editor of *Vanity Fair* and *New Yorker* and founder of the online magazine *The Daily Beast*; Helen Gurley Brown, former editor of *Cosmopolitan*; Kate Young, current editor of that magazine; Gaylord Carter, editor of *Vanity*

Fair; and Jann Wenner, founder of *Rolling Stone,* are but a few who have gained celebrity status through their connections with magazines.

Editors as celebrities are only one side of the magazine picture. Another side is the celebrity as magazine editor. In the early days of the 21st century, several celebrities tried their hands at magazine publishing. A look at just two illustrates the potential and the problems associated with celebrities putting out their own magazines. Both celebrities were popular daytime **talk show hosts**. Both had the financial backing of major publishing houses. One succeeded and the other failed.

Oprah Winfrey, "the queen of day-time talk," launched her magazine *O: The Oprah Magazine* in April 2000. A collaborative venture of Winfrey's Harpo Entertainment and the Hearst Corporation, a major U.S. media company, *O*, which always features Oprah on the front cover, was an immediate success. The magazine reflected Oprah's talk show personality, attitudes, and concerns. Designed to celebrate women's lives, the magazine offered everything from success stories to celebrity profiles and how-to pieces, amid lots of advertising. Circulation capped at 2.7 million and now hovers at 2.4 million. Rosie O'Donnell, "the queen of nice," soon tried her hand at publishing, with quite different results. In a collaborative venture between KidRo Productions, O'Donnell's production house, and Gruner + Jahr, an international publishing house based in Germany, Rosie agreed to transform *McCall's*, a long-time women's magazine with a circulation of 4.2 million, into her magazine voice. Unfortunately, O'Donnell was not able to successfully transfer her television persona into print. *Rosie: The Magazine with Personality* had a darker edge than *O*. When Rosie gave up her television talk show, the readership that Gruner + Jahr had hoped for melted away. The publication faltered. O'Donnell, who contended she had been denied editorial control, walked away; and Gruner + Jahr, claiming breach of contract, sued. But *Rosie* (aka *McCall's*) folded, and a piece of magazine history was lost.

Throughout American history, magazines—and much of the nation's public—have been fascinated with celebrities. But since World War II, and especially since 1974, that fascination has become a fixation. Magazines and the celebrity have developed a complex relationship, where the power now often rests with the publicists. *See also*: **Divas**; **Dream Girls**; **Famous for Being Famous**.

Kathleen L. Endres

For Further Reading

Gamson, Joshua. *Claims to Fame: Celebrity in Contemporary America.* Berkeley, Los Angeles, and London: University of California Press, 1994.

Johnson, Sammye. "Magazines and the Celebrity Culture: Oprah and Rosie and Martha, Oh My!" *Journal of Magazine and New Media Research* Spring (2002): 1–15, http://aejmc magazine.bsu.edu/journal/archive/Spring_2002/sjohnson%204-1.htm.

Ponce de Leon, Charles L. *Self-Exposure: Human-Interest Journalism and the Emergence of Celebrity in America, 1890–1940.* Chapel Hill:

University of North Carolina Press, 2002.

Rose, Lacey. "The Most Expensive Celebrity Baby Photos." *Forbes Magazine*, August 4, 2008, http://www.forbes.com/home/2008/08/04/pitt-jolie-celebrity-biz-media-cx_lr_0804babypix.html (accessed October 1, 2008).

MAGICIANS

Common knowledge has it that prostitution was the first profession, but some magicians claim that their craft should enjoy that distinction. In either case, the practice of magic has been around in various forms for untold centuries. In 1950, stage magic was practiced mainly in theaters and auditoriums scattered about the nation. Some of its practitioners became at least minor celebrities, but by the year 2000, thanks to the entertainment demands of television and Las Vegas hotels and casinos, a few outstanding magicians found themselves working in a golden age of magic, capable of becoming extremely well known and exceedingly wealthy. Glitzy and spectacular, the shows put on by performers such as David Copperfield, or by recently retired stars such as Doug Henning, or the combined magic and animal act of Siegfried and Roy, are expensive to mount, but they can result in enormous financial rewards. Siegfried once remarked that the most certain way to please an audiences is with magic, which appeals to people of all ages and circumstances.

Many illusionists, mentalists, and escapologists have performed as magicians, but of America's early

Greatest of all magicians and escape artists, Harry Houdini appears ready to make another escape. Courtesy of Photofest.

practitioners, the most renowned by far was Harry Houdini, born Ehrich Weisz in Budapest, Hungary. He took his stage name from Parisian clockmaker, builder of lifelike automatons, and magician Eugene Robert-Houdin, who died in the 1870s. Houdini's most popular feats were extracting himself from straightjackets, handcuffs, and other shackles; his signature feat was escaping from what he called the Chinese Water Torture Cell, in which the shackled performer would be suspended upside down. The great escape artist died in 1926. Hundreds of stage magicians have come and gone, but among the better known of those who performed in the early 1900s were Harry Kellar, whose vanishing birdcage and vanishing lamp illusions were seen all over the world; card trick specialist Howard Thurston; Claude Alexander, who dressed in Oriental garb and used a crystal ball; William Mozart Nicol, who performed as Nicola the Great until all his props were lost at sea; and Harry Jansen, who headed a large troupe and performed as Dante. Of the elegant school of magicians, those who affected capes, top hats, and canes, examples include Richard Pitchford, whose stage name was Cardini, and Leon Mandrake, who inspired the popular comic strip *Mandrake the Magician*, which was introduced in 1934 by comic artist Lee Falk. Close-up magic specialist Slydini was born Quintino Marucci in Italy, and seventh-generation Indian magician Sorcar was known for his flying carpet illusion and his Indian rope trick. The Great Blackstone was Harry Blackstone, Sr., known for "sawing women in half"; he was succeeded by his son, Harry Blackstone, Jr., who appeared on television shows and elsewhere in the 1970s and 1980s. All these magicians were well known, yet none other than Houdini could be said to have been celebrities in the modern sense of generating enormous interest in the individual's private life and commercial exploitation.

The same might be said of Carl Ballantine, despite his many appearances spanning four decades on *The Ed Sullivan Show*, *The Garry Moore Show*, *The Andy Williams Show*, *The Dean Martin Show*, *The Tonight Show,* and many other programs; Banachek (born Steven Shaw), a mentalist who also creates new tricks for other magicians; The Amazing Randi (James Randi), who both performs and debunks others' claims of having paranormal powers; and The Amazing Jonathan (John Szeles), who combines magic and comedy by intentionally having some of his tricks fall flat. Somewhat better known is The Amazing Kreskin (born George Kresge, Jr.), a mentalist who had enjoyed the *Mandrake* comic strip as a boy and who went on to do his own television series, *The Amazing World of Kreskin,* in the early 1970s, as well as appearing on *Late Night with David Letterman.*

Major celebrities of stage magic have been the duo of Siegfried and Roy (Siegfried Fischbacher and Roy Horn), who came to the United States from their native Germany where Horn had been an animal trainer and Fischbacher a magician. In the early 1970s, the two men combined their considerable talents in a Las Vegas show at the Mirage Hotel, where they very profitably remained until a tragic accident in 2003, which caused them to retire after performing more than 5,000 shows. The pair had worked with many kinds of big cats over the years, the most popular of which were white tigers, raised from cubs by Horn. One of the tigers apparently became confused and began to drag Horn off the stage. Stagehands intervened, and in the confusion, Horn was critically injured by the cat but eventually recovered. During their long career in Las Vegas, the men were among the highest-paid performers of any kind in the nation. Another pair of celebrity magicians are Penn and Teller (born Penn Jillette and Raymond Teller), who also have performed magic together since the 1970s. Their act is more comedic, and the duo has appeared on several television shows as well as in their own off-Broadway show. They also have published a number of books about magic and have done what few magicians care to do: explain how some of their tricks work.

A major celebrity of stage magic who died in 2000 was Doug Henning, who looked like a 1970s flower child with his wildly-colored outfits, excess of hair, childlike enthusiasm, and big goofy smile. The Canadian performer, who did levitation and vanishing acts, first came to public attention on Broadway in *The Magic Show*, after which he brought his annual special, *Doug Henning's World of Magic,* to U.S. television starting in 1975. A proponent of transcendental meditation, Henning had plans to team with The Beatles' spiritual advisor, Maharishi Mahesh Yogi, in building a Himalayan theme park, but the highly successful magician died in his early fifties of liver cancer. The biggest moneymaker of all contemporary magicians has been illusionist David Copperfield (born David Kotkin). Copperfield, who took his stage name from Charles Dickens's novel, was a prodigy of magic. At twelve, he became the youngest ever inductee of the Society of American Magicians, and before turning twenty, he taught magic at a university and had his own act at a Honolulu hotel. A handsome, casually dressed performer, Copperfield has preferred working in front of live audiences and has specialized in illusions of grand scale, such as "dematerializing" the Statue of Liberty or making a jet plane "disappear." Magic has given him a net worth into the hundreds of millions of dollars, and his celebrity was enhanced by his six-year engagement to German **supermodel** Claudia Schiffer. He has used some of his personal fortune to collect all kinds of paraphernalia having to do with magic, and his collection, housed in Las Vegas, is called the International Museum and Library of the Conjuring Arts. In 2006, the flamboyant Copperfield announced that he had located the Fountain of Youth at Musha Cay in the Bahamas. In the following year came more controversy when the Federal Bureau of Investigation began investigating him for alleged sexual misconduct. The charges caused him to cancel shows, which resulted in breach of contract suits. Despite these setbacks, Copperfield has won a record number of awards, including twenty-one Emmys, and he has his own star on the Hollywood Walk of Fame.

Two other men who have gained celebrity via stage magic are David Blaine (born David Blaine White) and Lance Burton, one of the few magicians who works under his actual name. Blaine has specialized in spectacular stunts and escapes, such as being encased in ice for roughly five days at Times Square and living in a "fish bowl" at Lincoln Center. Burton, whose leading-man looks have contributed to his success, has had a highly lucrative contract since the mid-1990s to perform in Las Vegas, where his Lance Burton Theatre is located. Finally, the sole female celebrity magician in what has been largely a man's field is the beautiful, shapely Melinda (Melinda

Saxe), who for a short while was married to Lance Burton. Her spectacular Las Vegas show features her in bikinis and strapless gowns, prancing about as she flirts with audience members, makes horses and even automobile race driver Al Unser "disappear," and performs lavishly staged levitation tricks. *See also*: **International Celebrity**; **One-Name Celebrity**; **Television's Role**.

Sam G. Riley

For Further Reading

Blackstone, Harry, Charles R. Reynolds, and Regina Reynolds. *The Blackstone Book of Magic and Illusion*. New York: Newmarket Press, 2002.

Christopher, Milbourne, and Maurine Brooks Christopher. *The Illustrated History of Magic*. Portsmouth, NH: Heinemann, 1996.

Fleischman, Sid. *Escape! The Story of the Great Houdini*. New York: Greenwillow Books, 2006.

Gibson, Walter B. *The Master Magicians: Their Lives and Most Famous Tricks*. Garden City, NJ: Doubleday, 1966.

Krull, Kathleen, and Eric Velasquez. *Houdini: World's Greatest Mystery Man and Escape King*. New York: Walker & Co., 2005.

Steinmeyer, Jim. *Hiding the Elephant*. New York: Carroll & Graf, 2003.

www.magicnook.com/forum.

MARTIAL ARTS

The term "martial arts" covers a lot of ground. This treatment of the topic will be restricted to hand-to-hand, weaponless fighting. The term itself was derived from Mars, the Roman god of war, and for most of U.S. history, American fighting traditions came mainly from those of the Europeans, principally boxing and wrestling. Then came the two world wars, plus Korea and Vietnam, in which many American troops came into contact with Asian combat traditions, which are remarkably many and which involve a range of striking with open or closed hands, knees or elbows, kicking, throwing, and pinning. The Asian martial arts, whether devoted to offensive or defensive use, offered Americans something new: an exotic, mystique-laden kind of combat that often had religious, philosophical, and even medical tie-ins. Some native practitioners of these arts came to America and began offering instruction in toughening the body, learning systems of moves, and cultivating inner confidence and focus. Judo and jujitsu gained early popularity among Americans, as eventually did karate. Many of the countless Americans who have received at least some instruction in these techniques have done so as a means of feeling safer on mean city streets; others, to compensate for lack of size or brawn; and still others, for the enjoyment of organized competition.

The appeal of learning these skills also was furthered by the U.S. mass media, especially television and the movies. U.S. television viewers were captivated in 1972 by the series *Kung Fu*, in which David Carradine, an American actor who had not competed in any of the martial arts, played a Shaolin master—half white, half Chinese—who rambled inscrutably about the 19th-century American West defending the helpless and embarrassing the bad

Martial arts expert and actor Chuck Norris prepares to entertain the troops at Ramstein Air Base in Germany, September 2007. Courtesy of the Department of Defense.

guys. Around that same time began an outpouring of movies starring Asian talent, highly skilled individuals who had actually competed successfully in the various forms of the martial arts. Probably the greatest of them all was Bruce Lee, born Lee Jun-Fan. Lee was a child actor in Hong Kong, China, and by age eighteen had been in roughly twenty movies. Coming to America, he played Kato on *The Green Hornet* television series in 1966 and 1967, appeared in such action shows as *Marlowe* and *Longstreet*, and in 1972 found movie success in the action films *Fist of Fury*, *The Chinese Connection*, and *Way of the Dragon*. Lee died suddenly a year later shortly after filming *Enter the Dragon*, leaving behind an iconic legend and adding to America's growing stock of conspiracy theories. It is thought that his death was

caused by a reaction to painkillers and other drugs.

The next Asian martial arts star to gain celebrity in America was skilled, likeable Jackie Chan, who combined acrobatic kung fu fighting and slapstick humor in the coming-of-age film *Drunken Master* (1978). This Chinese actor also has enjoyed a successful singing career and has made at least twenty albums. His path to stardom began as a stuntman in Bruce Lee films. Another of Chan's movies, also in 1978, was the underdog story *Snake in the Eagle's Shadow*. In 1979 a third such star, Jet Li, was introduced to movie viewers in the revenge movie *The Shaolin Temple*. Li, a Wushu champion in China, was born Li Lianjie in Beijing. His first U.S. film role, in 1988, was in *Lethal Weapon 4*.

An important boost to the popularity of Asian martial arts in the United States was the blockbuster movie *The Karate Kid* (1984), with Ralph Macchio as the slight but determined Daniel, picked on by a bully but schooled to success by veteran actor Pat Morita, playing the elderly but megaskilled Mr. Miyagi. Untold numbers of American youths immediately signed up for lessons at their nearest *dojo* (instructional studio), although few made it past the first year's lessons. By this time, such terms as *dojo*, *sensei* (master teacher), *gi* (the outfit worn), and *kata* (system of moves to be practiced alone or with a partner) had become well known to most Americans. *Dojos* sprang up in strip malls and elsewhere across the nation, offering instruction in many Asian combat forms, the most popular of which include judo, jujitsu, karate, kung fu, aikido, tae kwon do, and tai chi.

Speaking broken English, overweight, but loveable as a teddy bear is Hong Kong–born martial artist Sammo Hung, who had worked with Bruce Lee and had appeared in movies such as *Pedicab Driver* (1989) for years before his celebrity-creating role in the humorous detective series *Martial Law* (1998–2000).

Meanwhile, some U.S. actors—actual martial arts practitioners and otherwise—began to capitalize on Americans' newfound admiration for the fast-moving skills of Asian fighting systems. An early example, *The Born Losers* (1967) and *Billy Jack* (1971), was actor Tom Laughlin, who played the character Billie Jack, half white, half Native American; a hapkido master; and a former Green Beret. Chuck Norris, who actually was part Cherokee and who had learned tangsudo in South

Korea while serving in the Air Force, acted with Bruce Lee in *Way of the Dragon* in 1972, appeared in *Good Guys Wear Black* in 1978, and came into his own in 1980 in *The Octagon*. He is an eighth-degree black belt grand master in tae kwon do and is best known as the character Cordell Walker on the television series *Walker, Texas Ranger*, which opened in 1993 and seems destined to live forever in reruns. Rounding out the short list of major homegrown martial arts celebrities is large, imposing Steven Segal, a seventh-degree black belt in aikido and the first American to own and run a *dojo* in Japan. Segal gained stardom in 1992 in the action film *Under Siege,* playing Casey Ryback, Navy SEAL. Another action movie star well known to U.S. movie audiences is handsome Belgian Jean-Claude Van Damme, successful European karate champion, bodybuilder, and actor. Van Damme's career-defining role was in 1988 in the movie *Bloodsport.*

Among other martial artists who enjoy some level of celebrity is ninth-degree black belt in Kajukenbo Eric Lee, whose credits include *Killer Elite* (1975), a Sam Peckinpah film that starred Robert Duvall and James Caan. Women, too, have worked in martial arts films. One of the first was Yu So Chow, who appeared in more than 150 movies, mainly in the 1950s and 1960s. Others include Michelle Yeoh of *Supercop* (1996) and *Crouching Tiger, Hidden Dragon* (2000), and Cynthia Rothrock of *Yes, Madam* (1985) and *Martial Law* (1990), holder of five black belts. Finally, a karate champion who has made an unusual contribution to society is Billy Blanks, who has become more of a celebrity for his video-marketed tae bo exercise program than for the career accomplishments he has derived from having earned a seventh-degree black belt in tae kwon do.

It is perhaps unfortunate and ironic that the popularity of these disciplines has been lessened in the early 21st century by the popularity of mixed martial arts competitions. Variously called cage fighting or ultimate fighting, very nearly anything goes and injuries are frequent. In these contests, the grace and elegance of the required skills seem lost, and the contests sadly resemble human dog fighting. *See also*: **African American**; **Asian American**; **Comedy**; **Movies' Role**; **Television's Role**; **Tough Guys**.

Sam G. Riley

For Further Reading

Corliss, Richard. "Alive and Kicking." *Time*, April 21, 2008, 73.

Crompton, Paul H. *The Complete Martial Arts*. New York: McGraw-Hill, 1989.

Donohue, John J. *Warrior Dreams: The Martial Arts and the American Imagination*. Westport, CT: Bergin & Garvey, 1994.

Goldenberg, Linda. *Women in the Martial Arts*. New York: Dodd, Mead, 1983.

Goodman, Fay. *The Ultimate Book of Martial Arts*. New York: Lorenz Books, 1998.

Green, Thomas A., and Joseph R. Svinth. *Martial Arts in the Modern World*. Westport, CT: Praeger, 2003.

Johnson, Willie, and Nancy Musick. *The Complete Martial Artist*. Champaign, IL: Human Kinetics, 2001.

Reid, Howard, and Michael Croucher. *The Fighting Arts: Great Masters of the Martial Arts*. New York: Simon and Schuster, 1983.

MILITARY CELEBRITY

U.S. military figures generally shun publicity, but some gain celebrity by their deeds or because they seek the limelight to pursue civilian politics. The two 20th-century world wars produced many American heroes. Five-star Gen. George C. Marshall won the Nobel Peace Prize in 1953 for his plan to reconstruct war-torn Europe. Five-star Gen. Douglas MacArthur was an unapologetic glory seeker whose feats lived up to his ego. His dismissal for disobeying presidential orders during the Korean War ended his chances for a political career. In his farewell to Congress, MacArthur famously said, "Old soldiers never die; they just fade away." The enormously popular five-star Gen. Dwight D. Eisenhower was elected president in 1953 and is identified with the interstate highway system launched during his administration. Highly decorated and handsome, war hero Audie Murphy had a successful career as a movie actor and country music songwriter.

In 1958, pop singer Elvis Presley was drafted into the U.S. Army and served for two years under close media scrutiny. Other major celebrities who served in the military before Elvis include Jimmy Stewart, Henry Fonda, Humphrey Bogart, Ronald Reagan, Lee Marvin, and Johnny Carson.

The Cold War produced numerous military celebrities. In 1960, Air

Four-star General "Stormin'" Norman Schwarzkopf, Jr., does a little verbal stormin'. Courtesy of Photofest.

Force/Central Intelligence Agency pilot Francis Gary Powers became a reluctant celebrity when the Soviet Union shot down his spy plane and paraded him before news cameras. In 1967, President Lyndon Johnson brought his commander in Vietnam, four-star Gen. William C. Westmoreland, to the states for a public relations tour. But even Westmoreland could not explain away the enemy's audacious Tet Offensive in 1968, which convinced Johnson to decline to seek reelection. A 1982 Columbia Broadcasting System (CBS) television documentary accused Westmoreland of manipulating casualty figures. Westmoreland brought a $120 million libel suit, which was settled out of court, with lasting damage to CBS's credibility.

Westmoreland's Vietnam replacement, four-star Gen. Creighton

W. Abrams, Jr., was criticized by Massachusetts Sen. Edward Kennedy for needless sacrifice of soldiers and marines at "Hamburger Hill" in 1969. Abrams also was accused of having had a hand in covering up the My Lai massacre of civilians in 1968. Convicted of murder, platoon commander William Calley, Jr., became the poster boy for misguided U.S. policy in Southeast Asia. Calley was released from prison in 1975.

The Vietnam War's end and conversion to an all-volunteer force made the military less popular, but occasional scandals and wars created more celebrities. Vietnam veteran and Marine Lt. Col. Oliver H. North became a household name in 1987 when he testified to Congress about the Iran-Contra scandal. Resulting criminal convictions were dismissed, and North became a conservative radio and cable **talk show host**.

Vietnam veteran Colin Powell became a four-star general, served in three presidential cabinets, and engineered the U.N. coalition victory in the Persian Gulf War (1990–1991). The U.S. ground commander, four-star Gen. H. "Stormin'" Norman Schwarzkopf, Jr., became a worldwide celebrity by conducting his own televised news conferences, in which he boasted of duping the news media to fool the enemy. *See also*: **Politics**; **Rock and Pop**.

Russell J. Cook

For Further Reading

Kennedy, William V. *The Military and the Media: Why the Press Cannot Be Trusted to Cover a War*. Westport, CT: Praeger, 1993.

www.historynet.com.

MOURNING CELEBRITIES

In a song that swept the musical charts in 1971, Don McLean lamented "the day the music died." The verses of "American Pie" reminisced about the deaths of musicians Buddy Holly, Ritchie Valens, and J. P. Richardson, Jr. (the Big Bopper). On February 3, 1959, a small plane carrying the three musicians from Mason City to Clear Like, Iowa, crashed, killing all three musicians on impact.

In the almost fifty years since "the day the music died," these three performers have been memorialized and honored by devoted fans. There are at least two guitar-shaped monuments to them, and the scene has been recreated

in the films *The Buddy Holly Story* and *La Bamba*. Singer Paul McCartney has paid tribute to Buddy Holly and has purchased the rights to Holly's songs. More than three decades later, McLean's tribute remains popular on classic-**rock** stations.

From movies, television, music, sport, **politics**, even civic life, celebrities touch our everyday lives. Fans celebrated when Brad Pitt and Angelina Jolie had new twins and cheered when Joe Namath or Eli Manning won the Super Bowl. People across the country were glued to the trials of Michael Jackson and O. J. Simpson, and they donned yellow rubber bracelets to fight cancer because Lance Armstrong said to wear them in support of cancer survivors everywhere. Americans also cried when Heath Ledger was found dead in his New York apartment and when Anna Nicole Smith was found dead only months after her young son died.

In a sense, Americans form a bond with celebrities, absorbing them into everyday life, joining their **fan clubs**, wearing t-shirts, even following them from venue to venue. In life, celebrities become part of the family. Consequently, people mourn the death of a favorite celebrity the way they mourn the death of a member of their biological family.

In her classic 1969 book *On Death and Dying*, Elisabeth Kubler-Ross identified distinct stages of grieving when a loved one dies and suggested that these stages apply to any loss. People feel denial ("this can't be happening"), anger ("no, it's not fair"), and depression ("I can't believe she's gone") when a favorite celebrity dies. They bring flowers to their graves, attend annual celebrations of their lives, and continue to love them. In the 21st-century **Internet** era, deceased celebrities are memorialized with Web sites and **blogs** that keep their memories alive. The deaths of celebrities are covered as part of the 24/7 news cycle.

Carolyn Kitch, in her book *Pages from the Past: History and Memory in American Magazines* (2005), wrote that the celebrities we remember and commemorate most often are those whose life stories are like our own. Usually, these celebrities have risen from humble beginnings on their way to stardom. She wrote that when celebrities die, fans wallow in a "virtual grief" that is a "media-orchestrated empathy" bordering on voyeurism. Fans know what to do when celebrities die—they pile flowers on doorsteps, light candles in vigils, and gather in silence on the doorsteps of homes, hoping to have their own grief assuaged by the public assemblage of others who feel the same pain.

Kitch examined magazine coverage of the deaths of twenty celebrities over forty years, noting that through media coverage, audiences come to believe they really know the celebrities they admire and thus can fully mourn them. She notes that anthropologists acknowledge a rite of passage in three steps, beginning with separation and ending with reincorporation into society. Through the media, people move through the mourning process until they have made peace with the death.

Americans' interest in celebrity has always been recognized in such magazines as *Time*, *Life,* and *Newsweek*; and this interest began to grow exponentially with the March 1974 debut of *People* magazine. Magazines also have published "special reports" and "extra" issues to commemorate the deaths of beloved celebrities.

An enormous American public outcry over the death of a celebrity came on August 16, 1977, with the death of Elvis Presley, the King of Rock and Roll. Elvis was found dead in the bathroom of his Graceland mansion in Memphis, Tennessee. That night and the next day, newspaper headlines screamed, "The King Is Gone," a sentiment later reflected in a song by Elvis impersonator Ronnie McDowell.

Since his death, however, Elvis has become the focus of not one but two annual commemorations—one the week of his birth in January, and a second in August marking the anniversary of his death. Every year, hundreds of thousands of people visit Graceland, which opened to the public in 1982. Elvis's widow, Priscilla, and his daughter, Lisa Marie, continue to run Elvis Presley Enterprises, a multimillion dollar a year endeavor.

Some celebrities remain popular far longer than they were in the public spotlight in the first place, as with young movie star James Dean, who died on September 30, 1955. Dean's star in Hollywood was rising, and the handsome star of *Giant* (1956), *East of Eden* (1955), and *Rebel Without a Cause* (1955) was a frequent headliner in celebrity magazines. Only twenty-four when he died in a head-on collision on a California Highway, Dean is celebrated with an annual festival in his hometown of Fairmont, Indiana. For the four days leading up to the anniversary of his death, fans of the actor, who starred in only three films in his entire career, gather to exchange memories. The official Web site www.Jamesdean.com hosts a list of at least twenty-three officially sanctioned tribute sites. Songs like "American Pie" by Don McLean, "Rock On" by David Essex, and "James Dean" by the Eagles also mention Dean. The character of "the Fonz" on *Happy Days* (1974–1984) was designed as a tribute to Dean, and the character Fonzie hung Dean's picture on his wall.

Young Norma Jean Baker was not all that special when she married James Dougherty in 1942, but at age sixteen, she wanted to be a star. Americans came to know her as Marilyn Monroe, whose fourteen-year movie career included films like *The Seven-Year Itch* (1955), *Gentlemen Prefer Blondes* (1953), and *Some Like It Hot* (1959).

America's fascination with Marilyn Monroe is as strong almost fifty years after her death in August 1962 as it was in her lifetime. Her image embellishes suitcases, t-shirts, and purses. Rock star Elton John wrote the haunting "Goodbye, Norma Jean," in memory of the troubled star. While details of her death are still debated, Monroe is seen as a beautiful yet tragic symbol of Hollywood excess.

Another beautiful celebrity having a huge international following was mourned in 1997 when she was killed in a car accident. In an outpouring of affection that stretched worldwide, Diana Spencer, the Princess of Wales, was mourned in a public funeral carried in the world's news media.

Diana was called "The People's Princess" from the day she became engaged to Prince Charles, heir to the British throne. In June 1981, Americans awoke at 6:00 a.m. to watch her wedding on television and continued to idolize her throughout her rocky marriage to her prince.

Diana's death at age thirty-six spawned countless Internet sites, books, and even a song, "Goodbye, England's Rose." Singer-composer Elton John revised his tribute to Marilyn Monroe to honor Diana and sang it at her funeral.

Another enormous outpouring of public grief occurred after the June 25, 2009, death of entertainer Michael Jackson from cardiac arrest. For two nights, the 6:30 national television news was almost exclusively devoted to his death, to the exclusion of news about America's two wars, its economic problems, and other important issues.

The Kennedy name is synonymous with U.S. **politics**, and the deaths of members of this family have received celebrity treatment. Scholar Barbie Zelizer has examined how journalists devoted themselves to covering the assassination and death of President John F. Kennedy on November 23, 1963. For five days, television and radio stations covered every detail of the president's funeral; newspapers and magazines devoted issue after issue to the topic. Famous images from the president's funeral—carefully planned by his widow, Jacqueline—are pervasive even today: Kennedy's young son, John, saluting as the caisson passed; a riderless horse, boots facing backward, moving through the streets of Washington.

Just five years later, the assassination and death of presidential candidate Robert F. Kennedy—John's younger brother, Bobby—received similar treatment. *Time*, *Life,* and *Newsweek* were among the magazines that devoted covers to Kennedy's death, which also was covered round-the-clock by network television.

This celebrity attraction, in fact, extended thirty-one more years into the future to John Kennedy, Jr., and his wife, Carolyn Bissett Kennedy, who died together in a plane crash off Martha's Vineyard in July 1999. Media coverage of the search for their missing plane spanned several days and was punctuated by photos of heaps of flowers laid at the door of their New York apartment. Interspersed with the tribute was an aging photo of "John John" Kennedy, taken thirty-six years earlier. *See also*: **Dream Girls**; **Early Deaths**; **International Celebrity**; **Magazines' Role**; **Television's Role**.

Ginger Carter-Miller

For Further Reading

Denenberg, Barry. *All Shook Up: The Life and Death of Elvis Presley.* Oxford and New York: Oxford University Press, 2003.

Kitch, Carolyn L. *Pages from the Past: History and Memory in American Magazines.* Chapel Hill: University of North Carolina Press, 2005.

Zelizer, Barbie. *Covering the Body: The Kennedy Assassination, the Media, and the Shaping of Collective Memory.* Chicago: University of Chicago Press, 1992.

MOVIES' ROLE

Celebrity has been an inextricable part of motion pictures since their inception. Movies created a galaxy of stars, and stars, in turn, furnished the medium with a mechanism of popular appeal to large audiences. Stars emerged quickly in film history. In 1915, one year after his first appearance in films for the Keystone studios, Charles Chaplin was earning $670,000 per year, with $10,000 bonuses for each short comedy that he made. These exorbitant sums were premised on the simple fact that Chaplin was the most popular movie star in the world, and moviegoers went to the theater based in large part on the stars who were in the movies. Chaplin's presence in a comedy guaranteed a huge audience of paying customers, and the film industry rewarded him accordingly.

While the era of silent film had plenty of stars—Rudolph Valentino, Douglas Fairbanks, Mary Pickford, Lillian Gish—it was the Hollywood studio system in the 1930s and 1940s that represented the golden age of celebrity in American film. Each of the major studios had numerous celebrity actors under long-term contract, and these personalities epitomized an age of glamour, beauty, and sophistication in film that has been unmatched since that time. Myrna Loy, Irene Dunne, Bette Davis, Clark Gable, Spencer Tracy, William Powell, John Wayne, and scores of other major stars personified the movies as the era's most vibrant and exciting form of popular culture. Sound, which came to the movies in the late 1920s, created a new intimacy between movie celebrities and their audiences, and henceforth the sound of an actor's voice and the way that he or she spoke were essential ingredients of celebrity appeal. James Cagney's fast, clipped street patter and the sultry smokers' voices of Lauren Bacall and Lizabeth Scott helped make them stars.

In that era, the film studios were in the business of creating stars. Players were nurtured through appearances first

Major Hollywood stars Brad Pitt, Matt Damon, and George Clooney (left to right) share a laugh in December 2001. Courtesy of the Department of Defense.

in small roles and then were launched as leading actors in major pictures. Each studio maintained departments of publicity and promotion whose jobs were to keep the stars in the public eye and, on occasion, to whisk them discretely away when scandal threatened to break. (Sometimes scandal could work for a star. Robert Mitchum's marijuana bust in 1948 cemented his rebel image.) Stars represented the most visible form of the industry's capital investment in motion pictures. The industry viewed them as a form of production value, increasing the revenue returned by the pictures in which they appeared. And, in turn, folklore, mythology, and legend entwined Hollywood's stellar performers, at least in the eyes of the public. Cary Grant was not Archibald Leach, relatively unschooled and uneducated, but the personification of elegance, wit, and

gentlemanly demeanor. John Wayne epitomized the contradictions between life and the movies that stars often embodied. In private life, he was bookish and an avid reader. On screen, he was a patriotic tough guy who fought in World War II throughout Europe and in the Pacific. In fact, he avoided military service during the war for the sake of his film career. The industry perpetuated its myths about celebrity grandeur, disseminating these myths through fan magazines and industry-produced public relations shorts that showcased the stars and through such archetypal films as *A Star Is Born*, which Hollywood produced three times (1937, 1954, 1976). And sometimes reality was close enough. Lana Turner's legend has her discovered as an unknown in Schwab's Drugstore and elevated to stardom. True to fact, she was a high school kid skipping class and hanging out with a soda at the Top Hat Café when she was recruited for the movies.

In the old days, movie stars could establish themselves across a huge body of work. In the 21st century, fewer movies are made because they are more expensive, and thus contemporary stars, looking back at the end of long careers, will inevitably find that they have been in far fewer films. Bette Davis made more than 100 films from 1931 to 1989. During the 1930s, she appeared in from three to six films per year, a rate of output that no star today matches. Jean Arthur made more than ninety films in her career, Joan Fontaine nearly fifty, and Ingrid Bergman more than fifty. Myrna Loy made more than 130, Joan Crawford nearly 100, and John Wayne more than 150. Much of what made these stars so great and imposing was the longevity of their careers and the sheer number of films in which they appeared. No 21st-century actor matches this record.

By the 1950s, cracks had begun to appear in the arranged marriage between studios and stars. The studio system was breaking apart under the onslaught of television and a Supreme Court antitrust decision that forced the studios to relinquish their movie theaters. These developments changed the prevailing relationship in which actors were treated as long-term employees of studios, which controlled the films in which they appeared and the details of their on-screen personas. Several stars broke free of long-term studio contracts by forming their own production companies. Seeking greater control over their work, Burt Lancaster and Cornell Wilde were among the first Hollywood stars to launch their own companies. Lancaster formed Norma Productions

in 1948, which subsequently became Hecht-Hill-Lancaster Productions, and Wilde formed Theodora Productions in 1955. John Wayne formed Batjac Productions in 1952, and Clint Eastwood formed Malpaso in 1968. In the 21st century, it is fairly common for stars to operate as producers.

The 1950s brought other changes, most notably in terms of a new generation of stars whose on-screen personas were more tangled, troubled, brooding, and neurotic than had been the norm in Hollywood's golden age. This was partly the result of Method Training, but it also made them accessible to what would be an increasingly important adolescent audience. Marlon Brando, James Dean, Montgomery Clift, and Paul Newman brought a more psychological and internalized acting style to the screen, and their performances in *On the Waterfront* (1954), *Rebel Without a Cause* (1955), *A Place in the Sun* (1951), *Hud* (1963), and other films revolutionized performance on the American screen. Moreover, Dean's key role in *Rebel Without a Cause* had tremendous popular impact on a generation of young film viewers. When he shouted at his parents in an early scene, "You're tearing me apart," the film's young viewers knew exactly what he meant. While earlier Hollywood movies had portrayed troubled adolescents, *Rebel* was the first film to present its story from their point of view rather than from that of adult authority figures. As such, the film represents a key shift in the demographics of celebrity in American movies. The adolescent stars of 21st-century films all are traceable back to Dean and his trend-setting performance, and it was a short leap from Dean in the 1950s to the rebel heroes beloved of youth audiences in the 1960s. Warren Beatty and Faye Dunaway played the scruffy country gangsters, Bonnie and Clyde, as if they were glamorous movie stars in Arthur Penn's 1967 film, and Peter Fonda and Dennis Hopper achieved **international** stardom in *Easy Rider* (1969) after careers that had stalled in the previous decade. The sullen, angst-ridden teen stars that populate so many contemporary movies are descendents of these rather more imposing progenitors.

The biggest change that now separates contemporary film from the Hollywood period of earlier decades lies in the fact that actors now are free operatives, not bound by long-term contracts to one studio. They are represented by talent agencies that act to broker deals with production companies, and the talent agent takes a percentage of the salary that he or she negotiates for a star. This has driven up the price of celebrity talent to the point that the fee taken by a Tom Cruise or a Julia Roberts will often be the biggest single production expense in the making of a movie. The practice of taking points also demonstrates the power of stars in Hollywood. A point is a percentage of a film's box office gross sales, and top directors and stars are routinely awarded a number of points. *Mission Impossible III* (2006) grossed $400 million in worldwide markets, and every point that Tom Cruise may have taken in his contract would have been worth $4 million.

Not surprisingly, studios and production companies have found ways of getting around the economic pitfalls represented by the huge cost of employing stars. Many of today's biggest box office films have been successful without big stars. The *Harry Potter* (2001–2011) and *Lord of the Rings* (2001–2003) film series hired no major stars, and this made them more profitable ventures for their studios because they did not have to pay huge star salaries or bestow points on performers. *The Chronicles of Narnia* (2005) and *Superman Returns* (2006) were without major stars, as was *Batman Begins* (2005). These films appealed to audiences because of their clever stories and eye-popping special effects, not on the basis of sheer star power. The implications of successful film franchises without stars are intriguing, and this commitment to engineering expensive film series or franchises has taken Hollywood to a kind of post-star period. The industry prefers to launch an expensive film series with relative newcomers or unknowns as performers in the lead roles. Moreover, few stars can be relied on to carry a hit film. Will Smith has been successful; his pictures, which include *Hitch* (2005), *I Am Legend* (2007), and *Hancock* (2008), have been extremely popular in world markets. But many established stars have shown a poor box office track record in recent years. These include Nicole Kidman, Harrison Ford, Tom Cruise, and Robert Redford.

But if Hollywood is in a poststar period, it is in a postcelebrity period? Celebrity is a bigger category than is film stardom and, at the same time, is often a more trivial and ephemeral one. The greatest of Hollywood's stars have endured and, in their day, enjoyed long careers. Tom Hanks is probably the best example of a classic Hollywood star—terrifically talented, charismatic, and retaining a screen personality with which audiences enjoy spending time.

Gene Hackman is another contemporary star who has had the kind of career longevity and the range of roles that were more typical of the classical Hollywood period. In contrast, celebrities come and go quickly, sometimes enjoying only a fraction of their fifteen minutes of fame. On occasion, a celebrity may mutate into a star, but this is relatively uncommon. Leonardo DiCaprio was a celebrity based on his appearance in the cult film *The Basketball Diaries* (1995) and on a series of smaller roles in other pictures. He became a star based on his ability to take the enormous visibility granted him by his lead role in *Titanic* (1997) and use it to establish and sustain a career with major filmmakers in A-list pictures: Steven Spielberg (*Catch Me If You Can,* 2002), Martin Scorsese (*The Departed,* 2006), and Ridley Scott (*Body of Lies,* 2008).

The film industry today, like popular culture in general, is loaded with celebrities. Jessica Alba, Dwayne "the Rock" Johnson, Jennifer Aniston, and Britney Spears have all made movies, but they are not movie stars. Carmen Electra has appeared in more than fifty movies and television shows and is probably best known for a parody scene in *Scary Movie* (2000) in which she is attacked in her underwear by a masked killer who succeeds only in impaling a breast implant. The parodic and juvenile nature of this scene suggests that one difference between film stars and film celebrities involves issues of substance, measured by such things as the quality of the work and the level of performing talent on display. Another difference between film stars, especially from Hollywood's golden age, and 21st-century movie celebrities is

that one can easily envision sitting down with the latter and having pizza and a beer. But would one do this with Cary Grant? Or Irene Dunne? Or Joan Crawford? Or Clark Gable? The answer is no—a gulf of status and prestige separated fans and stars in the old days. Contemporary celebrities are like the average citizen except that they are richer and are caught more often by "flashbulbs." The movies will always have stars and will always have a bevy of celebrities. The two mix and intertwine, especially on **awards** shows, but the industry depends on them because they supply the human touch in a medium that otherwise is heavily so dependent on machines that record image and sound. Cinema is an intensely personal medium for its audiences, and stars and celebrities are at the heart of its ability to reach these audiences with strong emotional appeals. *See also*: **African American**; **Comedy**; **Divas**; **Dream Girls**; **Tough Guys**.

Stephen Prince

For Further Reading

DeAngelis, Michael. *Gay Fandom and Crossover Stardom: James Dean, Mel Gibson, and Keanu Reeves.* Durham, NC: Duke University Press, 1991.

Basinger, Jeanine. *The Star Machine.* New York: Knopf, 2007.

DeCordova, Richard. *Picture Personalities: The Emergence of the Star System in America.* Champaign: University of Illinois Press, 2001.

Dyer, Richard. *Heavenly Bodies: Film Stars and Society.* New York: Routledge, 2003.

Access Hollywood. http://www.access hollywood.com/topic/celebrities.

MURDERS OF CELEBRITIES

In 1995, twenty-three-year-old Mexican American singing sensation Selena was on her way to becoming a crossover star when the president of her **fan club** killed her. The major networks covered her death, the *Globe* ran her autopsy photographs, *People* dedicated an entire issue to her, and a 1997 biopic about her launched Jennifer Lopez's movie career.

When a celebrity like Selena is murdered, a barrage of grocery-store **tabloids**, television crime shows, fan-based Web sites, newspapers, magazines, books, made-for-television movies, and films perpetuate the victim and perpetrator's celebrity, making famous people larger than life and minor celebrities even more famous. For instance, starlet Sharon Tate might not be remembered today had Charles Manson's followers not viciously murdered her in 1969. Murder victims from six-year-old beauty queen JonBenét Ramsey to national leaders, such as Martin Luther King, Jr., John F. Kennedy, and Robert Kennedy can be fair game for a media onslaught. The media also turn celebrities' family members (Bill Cosby's murdered son) and unknown murderers (Susan Smith and Scott Peterson) into instant celebrities. And the murders of famous people in a variety of fields (Dian Fossey, zoologist, and Gianni Versace, **fashion designer**) can receive as much attention from the media as do entertainers and **athletes**.

However, slain actors (Sal Mineo in 1976, *Rebel Without a Cause*; Haing S. Nor, 1996, *The Killing Fields*; Dominique Dunne, 1982, *Poltergeist*; and Adrienne Shelly, 2006, *Waitresses*) always attract media attention. The same is true of television stars. Bob Crane (*Hogan's Heroes*) was found bludgeoned to death in 1978 in a motel room in Scottsdale, Arizona. Phil Hartman (*Saturday Night Live*) died in 1998 when his wife, Brynn, shot and killed him. High on margaritas, cocaine, and Zoloft, she later committed suicide at their home. Her estate sued her psychiatrist and Pfizer, the manufacturer of Zoloft.

Of all entertainers, musicians seem to have had more than their share of sensational coverage. For example, rhythm-and-blues legend Marvin Gaye's minister father killed him on April 1, 1984, a day before his forty-fifth birthday. Gaye, a drug addict, was having money and mental problems and was staying at the home he had bought his parents in the Crenshaw district of Los Angeles. Marvin and his father, an alcoholic, had always had a strained relationship. One day, the older man verbally abused Gaye's mother, and Gaye defended her. In a scuffle, he pushed his father to the ground. The seventy-year-old went to his room, returned with a gun Gaye had bought him and killed his son.

Gaye's hero, soul singer Sam Cooke, was also shot. Bertha Franklin, manager of a motel in South Los Angeles, said she shot Cooke, thirty-three, in self-defense. On December 11, 1964, Cooke had come to Franklin's motel with a woman, who allegedly escaped with his money and clothes. In a rage, Cooke broke into the manager's

Civil rights leader the Rev. Martin Luther King, Jr., addresses a multitude lining the Mall in Washington, D.C., from the vantage point where, in 2008, Barack Obama would become the nation's first African-American president. Courtesy of Photofest.

apartment, wearing only his suit jacket and one shoe. Accusing the manager of being the woman's accomplice, he started grappling with her. Franklin broke free, went for her gun and shot Cooke.

Contemporary murders include two of rap's biggest stars—Tupac Shakur (also known as 2Pac) and Christopher Wallace (The Notorious B.I.G.). Shakur, also an actor, was shot on the evening of September 7, 1996, in Las Vegas after leaving a Mike Tyson–Bruce Seldon fight. Shakur was in a BMW driven by Marion "Suge" Knight, chief executive of Death Row Records, when he was shot. He died six days later. Many people say Shakur's death was the result of a feud between East Coast and West Coast rappers. Six

months afterward, The Notorious B.I.G., in Los Angeles recording a video, was gunned down in a drive-by. Both murders remain unsolved.

John Lennon's murderer, on the other hand, waited at the crime scene reading *The Catcher in the Rye* until he was arrested. On the evening of December 8, 1980, unstable fan Mark David Chapman shot Lennon, forty, in front of the New York City apartment where Lennon lived with his wife Yoko Ono and son Sean. Chapman, who had gotten Lennon's autograph earlier that day, shot Lennon four times in the back. Due to Ono's efforts, Chapman has been denied parole five times.

Instead of being a victim, drug addict and Punk superstar Sid Vicious (John Ritchie) was a perpetrator.

Vicious, a member of the English band The Sex Pistols, stabbed Nancy Spungen, his twenty-year-old girlfriend, on October 12, 1978. She died in a room they shared in New York's Chelsea Hotel.

Bandleader Spade Cooley, known as the "King of Western Swing," also killed his significant other. In the early days of television, he had a popular **country and Western** variety show in Los Angeles. Some of his guests included Frank Sinatra and Bob Hope. In 1961, Cooley, who thought his wife was having an affair with Roy Rogers, beat her to death in front of his fourteen-year-old daughter Melody.

Like Cooley, well-known singer Andy Williams had a popular television variety show (1962–1971). He was not a victim or a perpetrator, but was drawn into a murder trial. Williams had met his French-born wife, showgirl Claudine Longet, when her car broke down on a Las Vegas road and he stopped to help her. Married in 1961, they divorced in 1975. A year later, Longet, thirty-four, shot her boyfriend, Olympic skier Vladimir "Spider" Sabich. Williams supported the mother of his three children throughout her trial. Longet made the cover of *People*, Mick Jagger wrote a song about her, and a skit, "The Claudine Longet Invitational," appeared on the first season of *Saturday Night Live*. As skiers raced down ski slopes in this skit, they wiped out when Longet "accidentally" shot them. Longet was a minor celebrity, but the publicity was due to her ex-husband.

Movie star Lana Turner, like Williams, was not victim or perpetrator, yet her life was dramatically changed by two murders. Her father was murdered when she was ten, but it was a later murder that brought unwanted media attention. Turner, a top box office draw, met Johnny Stompanato, small-time gangster, in spring 1957. When she learned of his ties to gambler Mickey Cohen, she unsuccessfully tried to break up with him. That fall Stompanato, suspicious she was having an affair with costar Sean Connery, followed Turner to England where she was filming. He came onto the set waving a gun, but Connery punched him and took away his gun.

The couple reunited after her return to California. On the evening of April 4, 1958, they argued in Turner's Beverly Hills home. The star's fourteen-year-old daughter, Cheryl Crane, thought Stompanato was going to hurt her mother, so she grabbed a butcher knife, ran to her mother's defense and stabbed Stompanato in the abdomen. The inquest, which resulted in a verdict of justifiable homicide, was a media sensation. Reporters said Turner's testimony at the inquest was one of her best performances.

The same has been said about Marlon Brando's testimony at his son's 1990 murder trial. Christian Brando had murdered his half-sister Cheyenne's fiancé, Dag Drollet. The focus of the trial coverage, however, was on Marlon Brando, not his children. Christian Brando's name came up again in a later celebrity murder trial. Robert Blake, former child actor (*Our Gang* comedies), television star (*Baretta*), and movie star (*In Cold Blood*), was accused of arranging the murder of his wife, Bonny Lee Bakley. During the trial, it was rumored that Christian Brando, not Blake, was the father of Blake's daughter Rose and that

Christian Brando had murdered Bakley. Blake, whose paternity was proven, eventually was acquitted.

The most famous celebrity accused and acquitted of murdering his wife was O. J. Simpson. His murder trial changed the face of celebrity reporting, but Simpson wasn't the only star of the trial. The media turned Marcia Cross, the prosecutor; Johnnie Cochran, Simpson's main defense attorney; and others into minicelebrities. Cross's love life was reported during and after the trial, and when Cochran later died, his funeral was covered extensively. Brian "Kato" Kaelin, an important prosecution witness who lived in the Simpsons' guesthouse, gained the most notoriety. An aspiring actor, Kaelin's involvement resulted in many career opportunities.

Other **athletes** besides Simpson have been caught up in murder. An intruder shot twenty-four-year-old Sean Taylor, a safety for the Washington Redskins, on November 26, 2007, at his Miami-area home. He died the next day. Wide receiver Rae Carruth of the Carolina Panthers was convicted of conspiracy to commit murder. His pregnant girlfriend and one of his unborn twins were murdered. The other twin survived, but had severe physical problems. On June 25, 2007, World Wrestling Entertainment wrestler Chris Benoit murdered his wife, Nancy, and their seven-year-old son, Daniel, and then committed suicide. There is speculation that repeated concussions contributed to Benoit's unstable mental state.

Advances in victims' rights may be the only upside to extensive coverage of celebrity murders. On May 28, 1998, a **stalker** killed twenty-one-year-old Rebecca Schaffer (*My Sister Sam*, 1986–1988) on the porch of her Los Angeles home. Because of her death, stalking is now a felony in California. The Sharon Tate murder also changed California law. Tate's mother, Doris, and others pushed for passage of the Victim's Rights Bill (1982), which allowed family members to make a statement at parole hearings. *See also*: **Criminals**; **Fashion Designers**; **Hip-Hop and Rap**; **Lawsuits and Court Cases**; **Lawyers**; **Temporary Celebrity**.

Victoria Gof

For Further Reading

Crane, Cheryl, and Cliff Jahr. *Detour: A Hollywood Tragedy My Life with Lana Turner, My Mother*. New York: Arbor House/William Morrow, 1988.

Lull, James, and Stephen Hineman, eds. *Media Scandals: Morality and Desire in the Popular Culture Marketplace*. New York: Columbia University Press, 1997.

N

NEWS MEDIA FIGURES

For nearly 200 years most news stories were produced anonymously in America. There were no bylines. Readers relied on the veracity of eyewitness accounts. The story was the story, not the person writing it. The "committees of correspondence" nationally syndicated stories, eventually urging separation from England. The Stamp Act of 1765 further radicalized editors, who had been bankrupted by their opposition to imperial control. Benjamin Franklin, America's first celebrity editor, published a famous illustration in the *Pennsylvania Gazette* of a snake divided into sections, arguing the colonies would perish separately unless they united in common cause against King George. On the eve of the Revolution, Franklin's achievements as an **author**, publisher, statesman, and man of science had made him the best-known American on both sides of the Atlantic.

In the early Republican period, a partisan press was financed by political factions. James Gordon Bennett achieved a certain celebrity as publisher of the *New York Herald*, starting in 1833, when his widely imitated penny paper attracted a wide readership by promising firsthand up-to-the minute accounts on sensational events. Suddenly, city hall, cops, and the courts became major beats regularly patrolled by a straggle of underpaid, ill-trained, and largely anonymous reporters in major cities across the country. Richard Adams Locke developed a fan-like following when he admitted he had written a series of tall tales in 1835 for the *New York Sun*, claiming there were blue unicorns and winged batmen on the moon.

Civil War reporting could be equally hyperbolic. Civil War reporters were a bohemian brigade of men on the make, snooping around military camps and spreading rumors. Whitelaw Reid of the *Cincinnati Gazette*, often writing under the name "Agate," was perhaps the most widely read and respected reporter of the period, following his eye-witness accounts of the battles of Shiloh and Gettysburg. Sam Wilkeson's story in the *New York Times* about the fighting at Gettysburg was unsurpassed in its poignancy. Wilkeson's nineteen-year-old son, Bayard, had fallen in the fighting.

In 1869, British-born Henry M. Stanley began two years of reporting on the hunt for David Livingston, a missionary thought lost in Africa. The nationally syndicated story became a sensation and made Stanley a star. Further African explorations were jointly financed by the *New York Herald* and London's *Daily Telegraph* and became the basis of Stanley's highly successful book *Through the Dark Continent*. His growing reputation as an explorer and adventurer made him an emissary of Belgium's King Leopold II and, in 1895, a member of the British Parliament.

Elizabeth Cochrane became a Gilded Age celebrity through her twin talents in stunt reporting and self-promotion. In 1887, the twenty-three-year-old was already a seasoned reporter for the *Pittsburgh Dispatch* and had been kicked out of Mexico for denouncing the Diaz regime for its attacks on a free press. That year she landed at Joseph Pulitzer's *New York World*, auditioning for a job by going undercover to reveal how sane women were driven to madness at the Women's Lunatic Asylum on Blackwell Island, New York. The stories, published under the pseudonym Nellie Bly, were a bombshell. Two years later, more than 1 million readers predicted whether Bly could beat Phileas Fogg's fictional record of going *Around the World in Eighty Days*. Bly made it in seventy-two days, six hours, eleven minutes, and fourteen seconds and was welcomed back in New York by legions of adoring fans, many who saw her as a symbol of women's independence. Bly was making an unprecedented $25,000 annually when she married a millionaire in 1894. She would later be seen at the Eastern Front, reporting the Great War (World War I) for the *New York Evening Journal* and reporting ringside at the Jazz Era jousts of the Manassa Mauler, Jack Dempsey.

Richard Harding Davis was bigger than any newspaper when he covered the German advance on Brussels in 1914. He was his generation's Gibson Man, tall and well-turned, decked out in a foppish bowler, studded collar, cane, and trademark gloves. Teddy Roosevelt considered the college-educated writer and reporter "as good an American as ever lived" and made him an honorary Rough Rider. Davis's autobiographical accounts of the Spanish-American and Boer wars, bestselling books involving the crime-solving Gallegher, and long-running Broadway plays made him in Booth Tarkington's view as big a celebrity as a president. He settled into a Massachusetts mansion, had movies made of his best-known books, and became the 20th century's template of reporter-celebrities who hit it big.

If Davis demonstrated a skilled reporter's multimedia reach, his contemporary Stephen Crane became the prototype of the self-indulgent celebrity reporter who cracks up. Crane was only twenty-three when his big break came with his *Red Badge of Courage,* which was first serialized in half a dozen American newspapers. *McClure's* magazine hired him to write on working conditions in Pennsylvania coal mines, followed by five pieces on Civil War battle sites. His feature stories on the West made Sunday supplements across

America by the end of 1895. A **sex** scandal sullied Crane's reputation but his reporting on the Cuban rebellion reestablished it. Fired by Joseph Pulitzer, he was hired by William Randolph Hearst. Although promoted by the literati of his day—Joseph Conrad, Henry James, H. G. Wells, William D. Howells, and Hamlin Garland—Crane died from tuberculosis at age twenty-eight, deeply in debt.

The Progressive period in American history was made for investigative journalists whose detective work dominated the pages of highly competitive and widely read news magazines and gave them a national following. Chief among them was the star-making *McClure's*. The magazine's self-conscious certainty in creating a more moral civil society was launched by Ida Tarbell's year-long investigation of America's wealthiest man, John D. Rockefeller, and his Standard Oil Trust. Tarbell's series of stories revealed the role of the Cleveland Plan in driving Rockefeller's competitors into bankruptcy. Tarbell discovered that Rockefeller received illegal kickbacks from the railroads that shipped his oil to market at rates his competitors could not match. Rockefeller had not played fair, Tarbell wrote, and that fact harmed his reputation. The man who foresaw the coming of the Industrial Revolution did not appreciate the significance of the press and celebrity reporting in the information revolution. Rockefeller chided "Ida Tarbarrel" on her muckraking without realizing her reporting was mobilizing public opinion nationwide against Standard Oil's predatory practices. In 1911, the pressure led to the Supreme Court ruling ordering the break up of Standard Oil.

Several of Tarbell's colleagues at *McClure's* also became celebrities. William Allen White from Emporia, Kansas, became the nation's quintessential small-town editor. Ray Stannard Baker accompanied Woodrow Wilson to Paris and became the president's official biographer. Upton Sinclair's undercover work in the Chicago stockyards led to publication of *The Jungle* and the creation of the Food and Drug Administration to oversee the nation's food supply. Sinclair became a leader in the Socialist movement and the party's candidate for California governor. Fellow socialist Lincoln Steffens was also a *McClure's* alum. His indictment of graft in municipal government led communities to clean up political patronage.

Steffens was reviled for his celebrity reporting, but David Graham Phillips was killed for his. Phillips was **stalked** and shot near his Gramercy Park apartment by a reader convinced the Indiana native had slandered his sister. Phillips had honed his craft under Charles Dana and Joseph Pulitzer before coming into the orbit of William Randolph Hearst. His 1906 series for *Cosmopolitan* called "The Treason of the Senate" argued that certain senators had advanced the financial interests of a favored few over the interests of the public and won Phillips national admirers. Bestselling books followed. Phillips's face and four-inch collars became nationally known. When he died on January 23, 1911, a day after suffering six gunshot wounds, that face covered front pages in newspapers across the country.

"I was hatless and my hair was matted with blood," wrote headline-hunter Floyd Gibbons from a military hospital in Bezu le Guery. The *Chicago Tribune* foreign correspondent, who had accompanied Pancho Villa's fight for freedom in 1916, was aboard the RMS *Laconia* when it was torpedoed by a German submarine off the Irish coast in February 1917. Sixteen months later he accompanied the Fifth Marine Corps forces into the Battle of Belleau Wood, where he was badly wounded. Gibbons recovered and was awarded the Croix de Guerre with Palm, France's greatest honor. His war memoir *And They Thought We Wouldn't Fight* (1918) was widely read and moved Gibbons on to the celebrity circuit. *Time* called him one of early radio's "fair-haired boys" for commentaries covering Italy's attack on Ethiopia and Japan's advance on China. He also was honored with a star on the Hollywood Walk of Fame.

Ernest Hemingway was an unconventional war reporter who rose to celebrity status through his writing. Hemingway's seven-month stint as an eighteen-year-old at the *Kansas City Star* made him a convert to the cause of simple declarative sentences. He was a Red Cross ambulance driver when wounded in July of 1918 at the Italian Front. He recovered to cover the Greco-Turkish War for the *Toronto Star* before becoming their foreign correspondent in Paris. *In Our Time* (1925), *The Sun Also Rises* (1926), and *A Farewell to Arms* (1929) were semi-autobiographical works that made Hemingway his generation's most famous and frequently imitated writer.

Hemingway originally filed his stories under the pseudonym Ring Lardner, Jr., to pay homage to celebrity sportswriter Ring Lardner. H. L. Mencken and F. Scott Fitzgerald shared Hemingway's certainty that no writer was more gifted than Lardner in the use of vernacular.

Lardner led Jazz Age sportswriters who grew bigger than the papers they wrote for, and sometimes bigger than the events they covered. Grantland Rice became the dean of American sportswriters in the tall tales he told about of sports legends Jack Dempsey, Babe Ruth, Ty Cobb, Bobby Jones, and Bill Tilden. Rice nicknamed Red Grange "the Galloping Ghost" and Notre Dame's backfield "the Four Horsemen of the Apocalypse." Celebrity sportswriter Damon Runyon also had a way with words. His forays into Lower Broadway produced a memorably nefarious cast of characters—Good Time Charley, Nathan Detroit, Dave the Dude, Harry the Horse, Little Miss Marker, Apple Annie, and Little Pinks. Runyon's popular plays changed the nation's vocabulary. The nose became a snoot, heads noggins, knives shivs. Women became tomatoes or broads. Guns were called equalizers. Runyon's "running mate" Walter Winchell showed a similar strategy. At his peak, one American in three read Winchell's nationally syndicated gossip column and millions more heard his Sunday night broadcasts on National Broadcasting Company's (NBC's) Blue Network. Winchell slid around the libel laws by reporting that a couple in love was "Adam and Eveing it." To get married was to be "welded" or "merged." Expectant parents were "getting storked." Those planning divorce had gone "phfft."

Radio became a star factory for journalists. Edward R. Murrow invented broadcast journalism with his reporting on the Battle of Britain in the summer of 1940. Columbia Broadcasting

System (CBS) listeners heard eye-witness accounts of nightly bombing raids by Adolf Hitler's Luftwaffe over East London. "This is London," Murrow would report, followed by detailed description of scene. For Murrow's generation, hearing, not seeing, was believing, which is why British Prime Minister Winston Churchill believed Murrow's reporting greatly boosted American support of the British war effort.

Radio network commentators Hans V. Kaltenborn and Raymond Gram Swing developed devoted followings of their own. In print, no one surpassed Ernie Pyle of Scripps-Howard in telling the story of "G.I. Joe." A movie based on Pyle's reporting was opening in theaters across America in the spring of 1945, when word came that Pyle had been killed on an island off Okinawa during an American advance in the waning weeks of the war.

Murrow and Walter Cronkite, a war correspondent with United Press, were among the first celebrity journalists of the television age. Murrow's *See It Now* show on CBS in 1954 was memorable for its attack on Wisconsin's Red-baiting Sen. Joseph McCarthy. Cronkite anchored the first half-hour nightly network news program in 1963 and across two decades became famous for his reporting on the space race and the Vietnam War. He was voted the most trusted man in America during the 1970s at the peak of his powers. Chet Huntley and David Brinkley, both print reporters with modest reputations, were sensations as coanchors of *NBC Nightly News*. Brinkley, more than anyone, developed the terse vocabulary and clipped cadence that came to characterize network news reporting.

Uncovering scandals solidifies reputations for celebrity reporters, none more so than the June 1972 break-in at the Watergate Hotel in Washington, D.C. When evidence pointed to President Richard Nixon's complicity in the crime, Brinkley famously commented that the American people will put up with a great deal but do not tolerate anyone who claims to be above the law.

The Pulitzer Prize–winning work of *Washington Post* city reporters Bob Woodward and Carl Bernstein kept the Watergate story before the American people, later leading to Nixon's resignation and their elevation to celebrity status. The two collaborated on the bestselling *All the President's Men* (1974), and in 1976 a motion picture by that name became an Academy Award winner. Woodward went on to write a series of bestselling books chronicling the coming crises of successive presidents.

Barbara Walters, who first came to the attention of network viewers on NBC's *Today Show*, became famous as a celebrity journalist who liked interviewing other celebrities. She led a coterie of highly paid performers who were more popular than the stories they covered. The faces of Diane Sawyer, Mike Wallace, Jane Pauley, and Sam Donaldson became as familiar to tens of millions as members of their own families, promising large ratings in the news magazine shows that dominated prime-time viewing in the 1980s and 1990s.

Internet schmoozer and **blogger** Matt Drudge in 1998 broke the Monica Lewinsky story that led to the impeachment of President Bill Clinton on charges he had obstructed justice by coaching a White House intern to lie about their sexual affair in testimony she gave under oath. The story was characteristic of news in the new millennium as new media outpaced old in setting the agenda for the day. The days when the *New York Times* and the *Washington Post* and the news networks could decide the major news of the day were rapidly coming to an end. The end of the analog era was the high water mark for news celebrities. Tom Brokaw at NBC, Peter Jennings at ABC (American Broadcasting Company), and Dan Rather at CBS comforted the nation after terrorist attacks on September 11, 2001, but the end of their extraordinary influence was in sight.

Cable produced digital celebrity, including Bill O'Reilly, Sean Hannity, Chris Matthews, and Keith Olbermann, who took positions and argued their cases. Critics carped that the new breed of celebrity reporters were not reporters at all, but entertainers. Many acknowledged that late 20th- and early 21st-century journalism had seen a withering wall of separation between the advocacy of integrated marketing and the social responsibility of journalists. The former saw citizens as consumers who needed to be colonized. The latter attempted to serve citizens with news they needed to know that makes democracy and self-governance possible. In this new media environment, William F. Buckley, followed by conservative commentators Rush Limbaugh and Laura Ingraham, went on to fame and fortune across major media platforms. Liberal listeners turned to Bill Maher and Steven Colbert.

The Internet has democratized information and created a cast of celebrity journalists largely known to their niche.

Most Americans cruise multiple sites in getting their news of the day. For others, Jay Leno, David Letterman, and Conan O'Brien were as likely to frame the day's news as any journalist who traveled the webbed world. The signs of the times are clear—the future will unveil more celebrity journalists than ever before, but they may not be known beyond their niche and they may not be widely known as journalists. *See also*: **Criminals**; **Newspapers' Role**; **Talk Show Hosts**; **Television's Role**.

Bruce J. Evensen

For Further Reading

Cronkite, Walter. *A Reporter's Life*. New York: Random House, 1996.

Goldberg, Robert, and Gerald Jay Goldberg. *Anchors: Brokaw, Jennings, and Rather*. Seacaucus, NJ: Carol Publishing, 1990.

Jeal, Tim. *The Impossible Life of Africa's Greatest Explorer*. New Haven, CT: Yale University Press, 2007.

Kroeger, Brooke. *Nellie Bly: Daredevil, Reporter, Feminist*. New York: Times Books, Random House, 1994.

Lubow, Arthur. *The Reporter Who Would Be King: The Biography of Richard Harding Davis*. New York: Scribners, 1992.

Smith, Jeffrey A. *Printers and Press Freedom: The Ideology of Early American Journalism*. New York: Oxford University Press, 1988.

NEWSPAPERS' ROLE

On January 9, 1910, the *New York Times* had on its front page a story celebrating the arrival at Grand Central

Station of Florence Lawrence, a Universal Pictures official said to have been killed in St. Louis by a trolley. Carl Laemmle, head of Universal Studio, knew better. Reports of Lawrence's passing had been passed by Laemmle, who hoped to gin up public support for Lawrence's "final feature." The strategy succeeded beautifully. The 5,000 fans who greeted the studio system's first star made sure neither Laemmle nor the *Times* would be disappointed. The attention exceeded that elicited by President William Howard Taft, who had appeared in town the day before and reflected on an evolving ethos of reciprocity involving the entertainment industry and its puffers in the press. Silent screen stars Mary Pickford, Charlie Chaplin, and Douglas Fairbanks soon became the most familiar faces on the planet.

Celebrity has long seemed to assign symbolic significance in our new nation. Dolly Madison's White House dinners offered abundance and the promise of prosperity. This early First Lady became fodder for early Republican papers seeking to stimulate circulation among women readers. Frontier explorer Daniel Boone appeared in the pages of national newspapers, and Tennessee congress member Davey Crockett followed, played up as the quintessential backwoodsman. Tales of his exploits flowed to the press from the pen of publicist Thomas Chilton. Capitalizing on growing readership in the industrializing East, penny publications on pulp paper and Crockett almanacs pushed the legend along. Crockett appeared on Broadway as Nimrod Wildfire, King of the West, a character loosely based on his life. Crockett's constituents were unimpressed. He lost reelection and went to Texas, where he died defending the Alamo, a final curtain that only enhanced his legend.

Samuel Clemens went West hoping to strike it rich. In Nevada, he salted a few mines and got out before the boom went bust. Much of his frontier reporting was one part fact, two parts fiction, and nearly all of it was done in the interest of personal publicity. When he reported on a celebrated jumping frog named Dan'l Webster from Calaveras County, his flirtation with California folklore won him a national reputation, launching his career as America's most celebrated 19th-century writer.

Behind every iconic celebrity there is a publicist, as with Buffalo Bill Cody, presented to the nation through the fertile imagination of hack writer Ned Buntline, who knew a good deal when he saw one in the rise of the *Sunday Supplement*. Sabbatarians seethed when Sundays became days when the unrepentant slept in and opened their newspapers to read of Buffalo Bill's exploits against Indians who savagely stood in the way of Manifest Destiny. Buffalo Bill was aided by trick-shot artist Annie Oakley and eventually Chief Sitting Bull, who had settled his score with Gen. George Armstrong Custer before making appearances in Bill's Wild West Show.

Nationally syndicated stories told how Wild Bill Hickok backed by Calamity Jane shut down Deadwood before Hickok was shot in the back. The James Brothers pulled bank jobs and other robberies yet were portrayed in the press as modern-day Robin Hoods, taking from the rich and giving to the poor. Wyatt Earp ingratiated himself with frontier editors, who pictured him as an incorruptible marshal.

In real life, Earp took his cut from crooked card games and brothels. The way the press played his life created the legend that later gave him posthumous celebrity through film and television.

The manufacture of celebrity by the national press extended to men of science. Thomas Edison carefully cultivated the brand of "the Wizard of Menlo Park" in publicity that celebrated his invention of the electric light, the phonograph, and the motion picture camera. Reporters would go to Edison's laboratory in West Orange, New Jersey, and would find themselves pushing his latest products before they left his laboratory. He himself was the greatest of all his inventions.

Both the secular and the sacred were fodder for journalists in Edison's era. It took many ingredients to sell newspapers in an increasingly competitive marketplace, and editors did their best to provide sensation and sentiment as a survival strategy. In religion, D. L. Moody, a lay evangelist and revivalist with a fifth-grade education, was touted as God's man for the Gilded Age. At the close of his campaigns, other towns would bid for his future services, and everything would be sold to fan followers, from Moody's towel down to his wash basin. Moody was a businessman who knew it was better to advertise than preach to empty pews and worked closely with the local press. As a result, Moody's revival meetings drew record crowds no single church could hold. Billy Sunday and Billy Graham followed Moody's methods and became celebrity evangelists in the century that followed.

Sport joined spirituality in conferring celebrity in an industrializing America. Baseball was billed in the sporting press as "the national pastime"; and the hard-drinking, hard-hitting Mike "King" Kelly was its first star. "Slide, Kelly, Slide" became an early hit for Edison's phonograph. In saloons, Kelly's picture was posted above the bar. He wrote an autobiography, took his act to vaudeville, and was one of the first Americans to be asked for his autograph. His highly publicized death at thirty-six only enhanced his legend. Cy Young, Christie Mathewson, and Walter "Big Train" Johnson became heroic pitchers through the box score developed by baseball writer Henry Chadwick. Cap Anson, Ty Cobb, Rogers Hornsby, and Tris Speaker earned rich contracts when all the men who played the game were white. Meanwhile, Josh Gibson, James "Cool Pap" Bell, John "Buck" O'Neill, and Satchel Paige became baseball legends in the Negro League, promoted in the historically black press.

Babe Ruth and Lou Gehrig propelled the Yankees to a series of world championships as Jazz Age sportswriters saw circulations soar. The interwar era was a golden age for sports. Red Grange and Knute Rockne in football, Bobby Jones in golf, Bill Tilden in tennis, and Johnny Weissmuller and Gertrude Ederle in swimming made the sports section the most read part of a newspaper. No one outpointed heavyweight champ Jack Dempsey in stimulating circulation while inventing hefty personal appearance fees. His title defenses were cultural spectacles and coincided with the creation of National Broadcasting Company (NBC) in 1926 and Columbia Broadcasting System (CBS) in 1927. The "Manassa Mauler" was portrayed as a latter-day

Neanderthal, whose crowd-pleasing punching struck a blow on behalf of every reader ever tempted to redress a grievance by taking matters into his own hands.

The Wright Brothers' first powered, heavier-than-air flight was witnessed by only five people at Kill Devil Hills on the Outer Banks of North Carolina on December 17, 1903. A famous photograph captured the first moment of manned flight. Six years later, Wilbur Wright, the man in that photo, piloted a plane that circled the Statue of Liberty, watched by roughly a million onlookers. The Wrights were welcomed by royalty in Europe, their success anticipating the public adulation that would follow Charles Lindbergh's first solo crossing of the Atlantic in May 1927. Ticker-tape parades signaled the twin seductions of advanced technology when wedded to a narrative of personal courage.

Publicity encouraged Lindbergh imitators but also had unintended consequences when Lindbergh's twenty-month-old son was kidnapped on May 1, 1932, and later was found dead. On the five-year anniversary of Lindbergh's flight, Amelia Earhart became the first woman to fly solo across the Atlantic, becoming America's new celebrity aviator. She married publisher George Putnam, edited *Cosmopolitan,* and touted Active Living Wear for Macy's and Lucy Strike cigarettes. Her attempt to circumnavigate the globe ended when her plane disappeared in the central Pacific on July 2, 1937.

A single-engine plane carrying Maj. Glenn Miller disappeared over the English Channel on December 15, 1944, as the nation's number-one band leader was flying to Paris to prepare a concert for American forces who had just helped liberate that city. The eagerly awaited nationwide broadcast showed the cooperative significance of newspapers, network radio, and the recording industry in promoting celebrity to a leisure culture that had time on its hands and money in its pocket.

A massive publicity apparatus joined by cooperative newspapers and fan magazines helped support five major and three minor studios and make Hollywood a dream factory with "more stars than there are in the heavens." Hedda Hopper and Louella Parsons were nationally syndicated gossip columnists who wrote celebrity tittle-tattle, and fans grew up and grew old with their favorite stars. Stars were typecast in carefully cultivated screen personas, ensuring big box office hits. Some of these celebrities crossed media platforms to radio and later television.

Newspapers and the newer media conferred status. Media separated the somebodies from the nobodies at a time in which Americans lived at greater distances from their roots. The birth of Lucille Ball's baby in January 1953 was bigger news for many than the inauguration of President Dwight D. Eisenhower. Milton Berle, Steve Allen, Jack Paar, Sid Caesar, Jackie Gleason, and Johnny Carson were television's first and second generation of heavy hitters. Jack Benny became an enormous success on radio and television, impeccably playing the part of a cheapskate. Newspapers got in on the excitement by publishing personal profiles of actors and actresses on television's top ten shows, as they long had done for movie stars. Publicists of popular music kept pace. **Rock** and roll was a mid-1950s phenomenon, launching Elvis

Presley into super stardom and stimulating the growth of the U.S. youth culture. The Beatles, the Rolling Stones, and Michael Jackson would follow, giving newspaper writers a steady supply of fodder.

Martin Luther King did not live to see the day when his dream of a color-blind society would be realized, but his widely publicized nonviolent campaign to bring the nation to its senses made him an inadvertent celebrity in the press and made the press an eventual ally in the struggle for a just society. The historically black press continues its presence, serving African American readers, and the Hispanic-Latino press in America has grown tremendously. In the 21st century, the campaign for the presidency by Barack Obama might not have been possible without the transformative power of the press in orchestrating a national dialog on what it means to be an American. *See also*: **African American**; **Athletes**; **Comedy**; **News Media Figures**; **Politics**; **Publicity**.

Bruce J. Evensen

For Further Reading

Czitrom, Daniel J. *Media and the American Mind: From Morse to McLuhan*. Chapel Hill: University of North Carolina Press, 1982.

Evensen, Bruce J. *God's Man for the Gilded Age: D. L. Moody and the Rise of Modern Mass Evangelism*. New York: Oxford University Press, 2003.

Evensen, Bruce J. *When Dempsey Fought Tunney: Heroes, Hokum, and Storytelling in the Jazz Age*. Knoxville: University of Tennessee Press, 1996.

Klapp, Orrin E. *Heroes, Villains and Fools: The Changing American Character*. Englewood Cliffs, NJ: Prentice-Hall, 1962.

Mandell, Richard D. *Sport: A Cultural History*. New York: Columbia University Press, 1984.

Rojek, Chris. *Capitalism and Leisure Theory*. London: Tavistock, 1985.

NICKNAMES

Perhaps nicknames are in part a reflection of Americans' predisposition toward informality. The bestowing of a nickname provides its recipient a "biography in extreme miniature" in that often such names have a long shelf life because they influence how individuals are remembered long after their death. Certainly the nickname is no stranger in the world of celebrity. Some such names are leftovers from childhood, such as Buzz for astronaut Edwin Aldrin, whose nickname came from "buzzer," the way his younger sister pronounced "brother." Basketball guard Vernell Coles was given the moniker Bimbo at an early age; actress Mary Elizabeth Spacek was dubbed Sissy by her siblings; filmmaker Shelton Jackson Lee's mother nicknamed him "Spike"; and prominent politicians Henry M. Jackson and Thomas O'Neill are also known by their childhood nicknames, Scoop and Tip. Harry Lillis Crosby, crooner, was nicknamed Bing after "Bingville Bugle," a comic strip he enjoyed as a child. Operatic soprano Beverly Sills's nickname, Bubbles, also dated from her youth. Others are self-bestowed, as was the case when boxer Mohammad Ali dubbed himself "The Greatest."

Most nicknames, for celebrities and for the public, are signs of affection for those we like or think we would like if we knew them. President Woodrow Wilson was so proper and formal that one would be hard pressed to imagine that anyone had ever endearingly called him Woody. A few nicknames, however, work in the negative, as when British fans of entertainer Michael Jackson took note of his increasingly bizarre behavior and began calling him Wacko Jacko. Among his loyal fans, the second part of that nickname began being used alone. Another negative nickname is Dubya, a derisive moniker for former celebrity-in-chief President George W. Bush. Even more condescending was the nickname Texas columnist Molly Ivins gave him: Shrub. A third such unwanted nickname, the president brought upon himself in a speech: The Decider. In this way, Mr. Bush follows in the footsteps of a Republican predecessor, President Richard "Tricky Dick" Nixon as well as those of his Democratic predecessor Bill "Slick Willie" Clinton.

Another term used in place of "nickname" is of French origin: sobriquet. Although the two terms tend to be used interchangeably, one might think of the Babe in George "Babe" Ruth as his nickname and The Bambino or The Sultan of Swat as sobriquets. Similarly, football great Harold Grange was nicknamed Red, and he enjoyed the added sobriquet The Galloping Ghost. Both the simpler nickname and the longer sobriquet are rich in connotative meaning and offer the public a feeling of shared cultural knowledge. Mention the name of singer Bruce Springsteen, and people will reflexively mutter "The Boss." The same is true for Elvis Presley, The King, and actor John Wayne, The Duke. Similarly, mention The Godfather of Soul and most Americans of sufficient age will make the connection to singer James Brown or would know that The King of the Cowboys was Roy Rogers. It is possible that a good nickname or sobriquet can lift a person who has achieved some fame to the level of true, commercially exploitable celebrity, or keep him or her at that level long after death or retirement.

People from all walks of life who have risen above the crowd have been given nicknames, but most of all in sports. This has been true for a long time, and the "labels" provided by these nicknames help keep the players' memories fresh: Ted Williams, The Splendid Splinter; Pete Rose, Charlie Hustle, a sobriquet given him by another baseball star, Mickey Mantle. How many people today can tell you the identity of Joseph Jefferson Jackson? But mention Shoeless Joe Jackson, and memory is stirred, as would also be the case with Elroy "Crazylegs" Hirsh, whose nickname immortalized the unusual way he ran with the football.

In sports and in the other parts of U.S. celebrity culture, nicknames originate in a variety of ways. Probably most numerous are those based on a person's physical appearance. Blond hair has accounted for golfer Greg Norman being known as The Great White Shark, halfback Paul Hornung as The Golden Boy, and pitcher Edward Ford as Whitey. Hair plus size and success made golf's Jack Nicklaus The Golden Bear. Size was responsible for William Perry's nickname, The Refrigerator; coach Paul Bryant is remembered as Bear; and pool hall great Rudolf

Wanderone "adopted" the descriptive nickname of a movie character based on him: "Minnesota Fats." Musician Thomas "Fats" Waller got his nickname for obvious reasons, as did 6'9" football player Ed "Too Tall" Jones. In a more color-conscious era, boxer Joe Louis was called The Brown Bomber, and hockey great Gordie Howe was called Blinky because he actually blinked a lot. Frank Sinatra was known as Old Blue Eyes, comedian George Gobel was Lonesome George thanks to his woebegone expression, and **country** singer Johnny Cash was The Man in Black due to his customary wardrobe. Entertainer Jackie Gleason was known as The Great One not for his girth, but for his intelligence.

Many other celebrities' nicknames came from the way they acted or performed. Intimidating football star Dick Butkus was The Animal; straight-at-you boxer Joe Frazier was Smokin' Joe; great batter Joe Dimagio was Joltin' Joe or The Yankee Clipper; long-ago boxer James J. Corbett was Gentleman Jim for his dress and comportment; and Joe Green of football fame was Mean Joe. Pooch-cheeked **jazz** trumpeter John Gillespie is remembered as Dizzy; variety show host Ed Sullivan, The Great Stoneface; acid-tongued comedian Don Rickles, Mr. Warmth; and laid-back singer Perry Como, Mr. Relaxation. Running back Walter Payton was known as Sweetness because of his gentle nature off the field; soft-spoken golfer Benjamin Crenshaw is called Gentle Ben. The personal elegance of pianist and composer Edward Ellington accounts for his nickname, Duke, and William "Count" Basie received his nickname for the same reason. Football player

turned Supreme Court justice Byron White was Whizzer in his playing days; football's Raghib Ramadian Ismail was called Rocket for his speed; and Earvin Johnson was Magic due to his seemingly effortless skills on the court. Pistol Pete is how we remember basketball player Pete Maravich, and Little Sure Shot was allegedly applied to markswoman Annie Oakley by Apache chief Geronimo. Crooner Mel Torme was known as The Velvet Fog for his singing style, and Clarence "Frogman" Henry for his gravelly voice. Comedian Clerow "Flip" Wilson was so named due to his zany demeanor (always flipped out). Western sidekick actors George "Gabby" Hayes and Lester "Smiley" Burnette were so known, one for his constant chattering, the other for his permanent grin. Dr. Jack Kevorkian, celebrity physician who, until his arrest and conviction assisted in many voluntary suicides, was Dr. Death. Joe Namath's nickname, Broadway Joe, came not so much for his actions on the football field as for his ability to retain the limelight in other settings. What he frequently said rather than what he did made baseball's Willie Mays The Say Hey Kid. In Hollywood, the voice of Bugs Bunny, Porky Pig, and scores of other cartoon characters was Mel Blanc, The Man of a Thousand Voices.

Some nicknames are simply variations on or abbreviations of the person's birth name, as in the cases of basketball players Meadow George "Meadowlark" Lemon and Julius "Doctor J" Erving, track star Florence Griffith "Flo-Jo" Joyner, or former football standout O. J. (Orenthal James) "Juice" Simpson. Golfer Frank Urban Zoeller's nickname, Fuzzy, stemmed from his initials; singer-actress Bette Midler is The Divine Miss M; and actor Humphrey Bogart was Bogey. A name base produced tennis star's Nasty (Ile Nastase). Others rhyme, as with basketball's "Wilt the Stilt" Chamberlain or baseball's "Stan the Man" Musial. Still others are alliterative, as with pitcher Dizzy Dean (Kay Hanna Dean) or the aforementioned Whizzer White. Still others are designed to be provocative, as was Gorgeous George, an early wrestler, Raymond Wagner, who adopted a deliberately lush, jeer-producing ring persona.

Especially in sports, animal nicknames are fairly common: Reese "Goose" Tatum—the nickname came from his ability to leap or "fly"; Raging Bull for boxer Jake LaMotta; and football's Bronislau "Bronko" Nagurski. Less used in our present era of greater cultural sensitivity are nicknames tied to one's ethnicity, such as those of two Hispanic tennis competitors, Pancho (Richard Alonzo) Gonzales and Pancho (Francisco) Segura. Also, largely outmoded are geographic nicknames such as The Georgia Peach, for baseball great Ty Cobb, or The Manassa Mauler, for boxer Jack Dempsey.

People with nicknames and sobriquets may be found in all walks of celebrity life. Father and son Haitian dictators Francois "Papa Doc" Duvalier and his successor Jean-Claude "Baby Doc" Duvalier became known for their misdeeds, as did a long succession of U.S. celebrity mobsters: George "Machine Gun" Kelly, Jack "Legs" Diamond, Charles "Lucky" Luciano, "Scarface" Al Capone, Peter "Horseface" Licavoli, Antonio "Big Tuna" Accardo, Benjamin "Bugsy" Siegel, Carmine "The Snake" Persico, Antonio "Tony the Ant" Spilotro, John "The Dapper Don" or "The Teflon Don" Gotti, and Salvatore "Sammy the Bull" Gravano.

Nicknames given in surprising ways are Baba Wawa for newswoman Barbara Walters, who was parodied as such on *Saturday Night Live*, and Julian "Cannonball" Adderly, whose enduring nickname was derived from its childhood version, Cannibal, for his voracious appetite. *See also*: **African American; Athletes; Comedy; Criminals; Rock and Pop**.

Sam G. Riley

For Further Reading

Frommer, Harvey. *Sports Roots*. New York: Atheneum, 1979.

Phillips, Louis, and Burnham Holmes. *Yogi, Babe, and Magic: The Complete Book of Sports Nicknames*. New York: Prentice Hall, 1994.

Shankle, George Earlie. *American Nicknames*. New York: H. W. Wilson Co., 1955.

Sifakis, Carl. *The Dictionary of Historic Nicknames*. New York: Facts on File, 1984.

"Underworld Nicknames." www.onewal.com/maf-nick.

O

ONE-NAME CELEBRITY

Some celebrities have chosen to market themselves using a single name. Singers Madonna (birth name Madonna Louise Ciccone Ritchie), Sting (Gordon Matthew Thomas Sumner), and Prince (Prince Rogers Nelson); rappers Ludicris (Christopher Brian Bridges) and Eminem (Marshall Bruce Mathers III); retired soccer great Pele (Edison Arantes do Nascimento); wrestler Chyna (Joan Marie Laurer); models Fabio (Fabio Lanzoni) and Vendela (Vendela Maria Kirsebom Thomessen); **fashion designer** Valentino (Valentino Clemene Ludovico Garavani), and a host of others have found it advantageous to be known by a single name. Most do so to be distinctive, to stand out from their many competitors. Others use one name because their birth name is long, or plain, or foreign-sounding to the American ear; and some up-and-comers use one name because it is easier for fans to remember. Still others use a single name that promises to give them the kind of image they desire.

Most contemporary noncelebrities use both a family name (surname) and a given name (first name), and many have a middle name as well. Such was not always the case, however. The earliest people required to have family names, around 2850 B.C.E, were the Chinese, who used multiple names, but among the ancient Greeks and Romans, single-name usage was common. Greeks such as general and statesman Pericles; historian Herodotus; and philosophers Socrates, Plato, and Aristotle were celebrities of their time in the 400s and 300s B.C.E. Most Romans during the early decades of the Roman Empire also used a single name, but later the trend in Rome was to use multiple names. The Roman philosopher we remember as Cicero was Marcus Tullius Cicero, for example. As Rome's power began to decline, use of one name again came into fashion, a trend that continued throughout the early part of the Middle Ages. Eventually a geographic place name was appended as a further identifier, as in Francis of Assisi. Also, use of a single name was common during the early centuries of Christianity.

Among the early predecessors of today's one-name celebrities were kings and queens, such as England's Canute, Scotland's Macbeth, and France's long succession of monarchs named Henry, Louis, Philip, and Charles. Some royalty went by one name followed by a descriptive byname or epithet, such as Alexander the Great, Ethelred the Unready, or Edward the Confessor, a practice echoed by modern performers such as the late wrestler Andre the Giant (Andre Roussimoff).

In more recent times, a few writers have worked for at least part of their careers under a single name: the French essayist Voltaire (Francois-Marie Arouet) in the 1700s; English essayist Charles Lamb as Elia, French novelist Marie-Henri Beyle as Stendhal, and English novelist Charles Dickens as Boz in the 1800s; and short-story great Hectror Hugh Munro as Saki in the early years of the 1900s.

Similarly, a small number of actors have preferred a single stage or screen name, although in 21st-century Hollywood, one-name celebrity is rare. A celebrity in the Europe of the mid-1800s was French actress Rachel (Elisabeth Rachel Felix). A popular Hollywood star in the 1930s–1950s was Mexico-born Margo (Maria Marguerita Guadalupe Teresa Estrela Bolgado Casilla y O'Donnell), wife of actor Eddie Albert. Tahitian actress Tarita, Marlon Brando's third wife, was another. Using the screen name Cantinflas, Mexican actor Mario Moreno Reyes acted in two U.S. films; known mainly for his portrayal of Teyve in "Fiddler on the Roof" was Israeli performer Topol (Chaim Topol). Remembered

for her classical beauty is the late French movie star Capucine (Germaine Lefebvre). Although almost all the performers who played the vaudeville music halls used full names, Australian dancer Saharet (Clarissa Rose) and Californian trapeze performer and strongwoman Charmion (Laverie Vallee Cooper) used only one, as did Virginia-born tapdancer Bojangles (Bill Robinson).

By the same token, only a few of America's many comedians have worked under one name. One of the first was Troja, a singing comedienne before and after 1900. Spanish singer, guitarist, and comic Maria del Rosario Pilar Martinez Molina Baeza Rasten became known to U.S. television audiences as Charo, the self-described "coochie-coochie girl," and the imposing David Adkins has done his comedy act as Sinbad.

Many a stage **magician** has used a single name. An early example was Alexander (Claude Alexander Conlin), who in the early 1900s used a crystal ball and wore a turban. One of the last vaudeville magicians performed simply as Thurston (Howard Thurston). Mandrake (Leon Mandrake), in his top hat and cape, inspired a comic book and comic strip by the same name, which in turn inspired George Joseph Kresge, Jr., to perform a magic act as Kreskin. Other one-name stage magicians of the elegant school were Blackstone (Harry Blackstone), Cardini (Richard Pitchford) from Wales, and Dante (Harry August Jansen) from Denmark. Slydini was born Quintino Marcucci in Italy. More recent practitioners are Steven Shaw, a mentalist who performs as Banachek, and perhaps the most famous one-name magicians of recent years have been two illusionist teams: Penn and Teller (Penn Jillette and Raymond Joseph Teller) and Siegfried and Roy (Siegfried Fischbacher and Roy Horn) from Germany.

Only a few celebrity fashion models have chosen to use one name. Veruschka (Countess Vera von Lehndorff-Steinort) of Germany, Dutch Wilhelmina (Wilhelmina Behmenburg), and England's Twiggy (Lesley Hornby) were big in the 1960s; and more recent examples are Iman (Iman Abdulmajid) from Somalia and Sasha (Sasha Pivovarova) of Russia, who also works as an artist.

Bursting into prominence in the early years of television was flamboyant pianist Liberace (Wladziu Valentino Liberace), and a much more recent one-name piano performer is Dino (Dino Kartsonakis). Versatile instrumentalists Yanni (Yiannis Hrysomallis) of Greece, Australian Flea (Michael Peter Balzary), and rock guitarist Slash (Saul Hudson) also used one name in their work.

Where the greatest number of one-name celebrities can be found, however, is among the ranks of singers of various kinds. One of the earliest was the elegant cabaret singer Hildegarde (Hildegarde Loretta Sell), whose partially French theme song was "Darling Je Vous Aime Beaucoup" even though she was born in Germany and grew up in Milwaukee. Most blues musicians avoided the single stage name, with the exception of the versatile Leadbelly (Huddie William Ledbetter), who performed in the early 1900s. Among **rock and pop** singers, the handsome Fabian (Fabiano Anthony Forte) could barely carry a tune when he began performing in the 1950s to the adoring squeals of

teenage girls. Another performer who dates from the 1950s was Dion (Dion DiMucci), whose pop and doo-wop work was best known when he sang with The Belmonts. Two very different one-name singers who started in 1965 were the Scottish folk-rock performer Donovan (Donovan Philips Leitch) and the megacelebrity Cher (Cherilyn Sarkisian LaPierre), whose singing covered a range of musical styles.

After Cher, the one-name choice became more popular, and new arrivals were Sting (Gordon Mathew Thomas Sumner), whose music went all the way from rock to **classical**; lead singer for the Irish rock group U2, Bono (Paul David Hewson); and pop icon Madonna (Madonna Louise Ciccone Ritchie). An American original was Jon Bauman, who sang bass as Bowzer with the group Sha-Na-Na. Prince (Prince Rogers Nelson) started singing under a single name, then became a "one-name celebrity once removed" by declaring that he wished to be known as "The Artist Formerly Known as Prince."

More recent singers who cover a range of musical genres include Pink (Alicia Moore), Thalia (Ariana Thalia Sodi Miranda), Omarion (Omari Ishmael Grandberry), Seal (Seal Henry Olusegun Alumide Adeola Samuel), Aaliyah (Aaliyah Dana Haughton), Brandy (Brandy Rayanna Norwood), Usher (Usher Raymond IV), Bjork (Bjork Guomundsdottir) from Iceland, Enya (Eithne Patricia Ni Bhraonain) from Ireland, and many others. Fantasia (Fantasia Monique Barrino) parlayed a 2004 win on television show American Idol into a career on Broadway.

The related musical genres in which the great preponderance of singers use one name are **hip-hop and rap**.

Standouts include Ciara (Ciara Princess Harris), Ashanti (Ashanti Shequoiya Douglas), Res (Shareese Renee Ballard), Nelly (Cornell Haynes, Jr.), Ludacris (Christopher Brian Bridges), Chingy (Howard Bailey, Jr.), Coolio (Artis Leon Ivey, Jr.), Nas (Nasir Jones), and Eminem (Marshall Bruce Mathers III). Having performed as Puff Daddy and then P. Diddy, rapper Sean John Combs finally shortened his stage name in 2005 to, simply, Diddy.

Although they, too, are entertainers, many celebrity **athletes** have avoided using one name. Probably inspired by the great Brazilian player Pele, however, a modest number of soccer players have followed suit: Adriano (Adriano Leite Ribeiro), Deco (Anderson Luis de Souza), Garrincha (Manuel Francisco dos Santos), Romario (Romario de Souza Faria), Ronaldo (Ronaodo Louis Nazario de Lima), and others. In the United States, these players enjoy celebrity status only among avid soccer fans, but in parts of the world where this game predominates, they are major celebrities.

In America, the one sport that has produced the greatest number of one-name performers is professional wrestling. One of the most famous is a woman: the now-retired Chyna (Joan Marie Laurer). Another woman recently retired from the ring wrestled as Madusa (Debra Ann Miceli). Quite a few other such women grapplers have come from the United Kingdom: Minx (Sarah Jones), Skye (Shirley Edwards), Nakita (Katarina Walters), and others. Male one-name wrestlers include Ruckus (Claude Marrow), Iceman (King Parsons), Abyss (Chris J. Parks), Homicide (Nelson Erazo), and Onyx (Kyle McNeely). Two men have wrestled as Apolo: Puerto Rican German Figueroa and Mexican Jose Munoz. Boxers and those who compete in mixed martial arts almost always use their real, full names. *See also*: **Authors**; **Circus Celebrities**; **Comedy**; **Dancers**; **Hispanic/Latino**; **International Celebrity**; **Jazz and Blues**; **Movies' Role**.

Sam G. Riley

For Further Reading

Shoumatoff, Alex. *The Mountain of Names: A History of the Human Family*. New York: Simon and Schuster, 1985.

Dame Cateline de la Mor la Souriete. "A Brief Introduction to the History of Names." www.sca.org/heraldry/laurel/names/namehist.

"Origins and Meaning of Names." www.mayrand.org/meaning.

"Celebrities 'Officially' Known by One Name." www.wanderlist.com/OneWordCelebName.

"Celebrities With Only One Name." www.associatedcontent.com/article/389264/celebrities.

P

PAPARAZZI

The paparazzi so familiar to consumers of 21st-century media are merely the contemporary representatives of a fundamental element of human nature that has been around presumably as long as society itself: the often prurient interest of the "common man" in the activities, particularly those of a scandalous nature, of his or her social superiors and those who are in the public eye. This curiosity about the goings-on of the great has been given a modus operandi by the coming together in the post–World War II era of several factors: technological advances such as the ease and speed of mobility, the advanced development of photography, and spread of media into such areas as television and the **Internet**; the increasing popularity of and growing audience for **tabloid** journalism accompanied by the willingness of the media to pay handsomely for material to feed the almost insatiable demand of the public for sensational stories); and the modern cult of celebrity, perhaps a permanent feature of society but much enlarged and enhanced by the increasing place of mass entertainment and the resulting creation of a class of celebrities whose lives are endlessly fascinating to the public.

The term "paparazzi" first appeared in the sensational Federico Fellini film *La Dolce Vita* in 1959, coined by Fellini as the name of a character in the film, Paparazzo—a proper name meaning something like "darting insect" (plural form paparazzi)—who pursued celebrities in the film seeking candid photos of their activities. By 1966, the word had entered the English language to mean those who, for financial motives, pursue celebrities seeking to capture them on film in unguarded moments.

The paparazzi made their modern appearance in Rome on the Via Veneto, the center of fashionable shops and clubs in the 1950s. In previous eras, the public had been fascinated with celebrity culture and had an appetite for its reporting. Particularly noteworthy in this regard was the media frenzy surrounding the Lindbergh baby kidnapping, murder, and trial—perhaps the first of what would be a succession of "trials of the century." In postwar Rome, the end of the repressiveness of the fascist era and recovery from the war led to a period of exuberance captured by Fellini's films. The single event most responsible for the emergence of the paparazzi was the death in 1953 of Wilma Montesi and the subsequent trial in which the sensational circumstances of her death were investigated and two well-connected young Italian men brought to trial for her murder. They were never convicted, and the particulars of her death have never been determined. What did occur was a continuing saga of charges, counter-charges, sexual innuendo, involvement of Italian celebrities, and sensational candid photographs of the two defendants in the case by Tazio Secchiaroli, the first and perhaps greatest of the paparazzi. A frequent companion of Fellini, Secchiaroli was the model for Paparazzo in *La Dolce Vita* and reportedly was even considered for the role before Fellini decided to cast a professional actor.

The essential elements for the emergence of the paparazzi were present in Rome of the 1950s and 1960s. The existence of a highly visible cadre of celebrities, particularly stars of the renowned Italian films of the period (Marcello Mastroianni, Sophia Loren, Anita Ekberg, and others) and occasionally political figures (most notably ex-King Farouk of Egypt) provided subject matter for a public eager to know more about such people's private lives. The growth of tabloid journalism in the newspaper *L'Europeo* and its competitors demonstrated that profits could be made by meeting that public demand, and that papers would pay

well for such material—the racier the better. The ubiquitous motor scooters, Vespas and Lambrettas, provided paparazzi with the mobility to surprise their quarry as they entered or left night clubs, restaurants, or apartments. And, of course, the flash cameras of the period made possible the candid photographs that appeared in the tabloids. The paparazzi phenomenon spread from Rome to become a universally recognized if roundly condemned aspect of modern life and fascination with celebrity. Many imitators of the paparazzi of 1950s and 1960s Italy plied their trade in the major cities of the Western world, particularly Paris, London, New York, and Los Angeles. An especially noteworthy successor to Secchiaroli and probably his most famous follower was Ron Galella, whose pursuit of Jackie Onassis in New York resulted in a restraining order against him in 1972 and more than 4,000 photographs of Onassis during her lifetime.

In essence, the relationship of the paparazzi and the celebrities they pursue is that of battle: the celebrities are like besieged fortresses seeking to protect themselves against frenzied, manic attacks by an enemy, the paparazzi. In addition to the necessity of the subjects being persons of significance, celebrities, three other elements motivate the paparazzi: **sex**, violence, and scandal. The most fertile grounds for the paparazzi will embrace all three of these, but at least one is usually a necessity. Almost any candid shots of celebrities in unguarded moments, especially if the celebrity is publicity-resistant, are marketable as well. Where a posed photo of a movie star or sports hero may be worth a few hundred dollars to the photographer, one taken without the subject's knowledge, or even better, over his or her objections, can be worth much, much more. A photograph of actress Lindsay Lohan passed out in a car, for example, sold for $100,000, and a photograph of Britney Spears after she had all of her hair cut off sold for $500,000. To deter such excessive payments for paparazzi, some celebrities negotiate contracts directly with publications such as *People* or *OK* for the first photos of their celebrity wedding or of their newborn.

In penetrating the barriers erected by celebrities against invasions of their privacy, contemporary technological advances have greatly assisted the efforts of the paparazzi. Telephoto lenses allow photographing unsuspecting subjects from great distances. Miniature cameras and camera phones are easily secreted. Helicopters enable shots from above, taken by paparazzi at celebrity weddings to which they had not been invited. Added to these aids are the incentives provided by developments in the media. In addition to the tabloids that provided the standard outlet for the paparazzi of the 1960s and 1970s are more recent media that are eager for material to fill their voracious appetite. Such popular television programs as *Hard Copy* and *Entertainment Tonight* and news channels telecasting twenty-four hours a day need stories to supplement "hard" news, and news and photographs of celebrity activities and missteps find a ready audience. On the Web, the hugely popular site TMZ.com offers nonstop access to celebrity photographs, video clips, and stories. Its Web site even features a Paparazzi Photo category to which photos of celebrities caught unaware can

be submitted and viewed. In short, the 21st-century environment for the paparazzi is more congenial and fertile than ever. Never has it been easier for anyone to profit from paparazzi-style photographs.

The single event most telling for the current view of the paparazzi was the death of Diana, Princess of Wales, in Paris on August 31, 1997. The facts of the tragedy are well known: Diana, her companion Dodi Fayed, her bodyguard, and the driver of her car were speeding through Paris surrounded by motorcycle-riding paparazzi attempting to get shots of the couple. The chase ended when the car bearing Diana and the others crashed, killing the princess, her companion, and the driver. Immediately, the paparazzi were blamed for the tragedy. Public condemnation of their intrusiveness was universal, the outcry against them overwhelming. Subsequently, it was revealed that her driver was legally drunk (over three times the blood alcohol content acceptable) and perhaps the paparazzi were, if not blameless, only contributory factors. In spite of this, the public attitude toward the paparazzi, whose activities in the final analysis depended on the public's demand for details about celebrities, changed drastically from viewing them as almost comic manifestations of modern media to seeing them as vicious and venal parasites.

Whether viewed benignly or malignantly, it seems clear that the paparazzi are here to stay. The cult of celebrity, the insatiable media demands for material, and public fascination with the prurient and scandalous show no signs of decreasing. Clearly there is a demand for the stories and photographs of the paparazzi, and fundamental economics dictate that where there is demand, the products that can supply that demand will be forthcoming. *See also*: **Drugs and Alcohol**; **International Celebrity**; **Movies' Role**; **Privacy and Publicity Rights**; **Television's Role**.

Tamara Baldwin and Henry Sessoms

For Further Reading

Foerstel, Herbert N. *From Watergate to Monicagate: Ten Controversies in Modern Journalism and Media.* Westport, CT: Greenwood Press, 2001.

Mormorio, Diego. *Tazio Secchiaroli, Greatest of the Paparazzi.* Trans. Alexandra Bonfante-Warren. New York: Harry N. Abrams, Inc., 1999.

http://www.tmz.com.

PARANOIA

Paranoia is an unreasonable fear of being harmed. It is an internal human problem that involves doubt and hurt, and the feelings of persecution it engenders usually imply uncertainty about the source of the perceived persecution.

In an August 1988 *Seattle Post-Intelligencer* book review, Edith Lederer looked at Erich Segal's latest novel, *Doctors*. She wrote that Segal regarded his earlier novel *Love Story* as his youthful Camelot, but believed that *Doctors* would bring him serious critical acclaim. Segal is not alone in such dreams. One emotion that celebrities often seem to share is the strong desire for serious critical acclaim. It is as if the celebrity does not have much respect for the masses who buy the

records and attend the movies and read—or at least buy—the books. What can they know, the star seems to ask, if they fell for my shtick so fast and so fully? In a classic example of questionable self-esteem, this individual asks that nagging question: How can I respect you if you love me when I know what a phony I am? Segal, a professor of classics at Harvard University, must have found his popularity difficult to justify among his learned colleagues. Do we really respect the opinions of the masses? In a democracy, we should, but do we really?

How many television actors long to be in movies? Is it for the money? Hardly. Film stars simply have a higher level of critical esteem than television personalities. Television, regardless of the number of university courses that study the medium, remains a low rung on the ladder of critically respected art forms, somewhat ahead of comic books and pornographic novels, but not by much. And how many film stars long to perform on Broadway in a serious role? Film legitimizes the television actor; theater legitimizes the film star. If not going on stage, then directing. "What I really want to do is direct" has become a one-line joke (with variations) because it has been heard so often. How many genre writers—Stephen King comes to mind, but it is clear with others as well—long to be accepted as so-called serious **authors**? King has responded by brilliantly analyzing and explaining his genre, providing substance to the writing of horror, and he has indeed received some serious critical attention. Others—Danielle Steel, James Patterson, Dean Koontz—are not as fortunate. They seem in fact to be ones who have given up, so to speak, who have decided to take the money and run, to laugh all the way to the bank, begging the use of two clichés.

Such concerns elicit one of two common responses from celebrities: (1) I really do not care what the critics say since it is the fans, the people, the common folk who really count (*the critics are out of touch with reality*); or (2) I'm going to do what I want to do regardless of what anyone thinks, and my popularity gives me the freedom, the power, and the independence to break out. Of course, the artist who changes his or her "style" risks the loss of a fan base. What if no one likes the new work? What if this time not only do the critics hate me, but the fans hate me as well? This is the stuff of paranoia.

Consider the case of Woody Allen, an example of the second response. Perhaps the film that best illustrates this issue is *Stardust Memories* (1980), a movie about a moviemaker whose most persistent question from the fans and the press is, "When will you make another **comedy**?" Allen is a celebrity-artist who became hugely popular as a stand-up comedian, then as a maker of comedies, starting with *Take the Money and Run* (1969), which is about as silly as it gets. Clearly this was not enough for him. For a variety of reasons, Allen wanted to make movies that dealt with serious philosophical issues, even if he did so with—at first—a humorous touch. In doing so, he risked his popularity, and indeed he has seen it wane. Even so, he has changed audaciously and seems now to be much less concerned with audience and more interested in examining philosophical truths, particularly truths of right and wrong, guilt and innocence. The critics have

not necessarily applauded his new work any more than have his fans. Nonetheless, he persists.

Another of this ilk is Bob Dylan. Contrast Dylan's career—seemingly self-managed—with Elvis Presley's. Both started out as groundbreakers in a particular genre of popular song, but Dylan went on to try new things in spite of attacks by fans and critics alike. When Dylan "went electric," he was broadly criticized, and some fans felt he had deserted them. Every time he changed—going from protest songs to folk songs to country to **rock** to gospel, and so on—he left fans behind. Presley, on the other hand, never really challenged his fan base. The Colonel (Tom Parker, his manager) would not allow it. Parker had such great control over Presley's career that he made decisions that often ran directly counter to Presley's own desires. Presley also wanted to be a serious movie actor. He idolized James Dean and Marlon Brando, but he really was not allowed to stretch himself. Once he got into the niche of musicals, he simply stayed there. The same was true of his music. He really did not go far outside his roots—rock, gospel, a touch of blues.

George Clooney is a further example of this category. After his success as a heartthrob on television's *E.R.* (1994–2009), Clooney broke out of this niche and chose to work in movies. Clearly he's done several fluff pieces on film—the *Oceans* series, for instance—but he's also done his best to develop his own voice and to bring better-quality movies to modern audiences not only as an actor but also as a producer and director.

Jack Olsen, called "the dean of true crime writing" by the *New York Times*, has asked his publisher never to show him any negative reviews, since they send him into a kind of frenzy and he is unable to do any other work for weeks thereafter—even though the rest of the reviews are positive. The response to negative **criticism** can be a powerful force.

Rod McKuen is a poet who simultaneously craved and eschewed critical attention. Anyone who remembers him has to recall the beating he took from the critics. Academics looked at him the way contemporary academics look at Paris Hilton, perhaps, or Britney Spears: all fluff with no real substance. When McKuen first broke onto the stage with his collection *Stanyan Street and Other Sorrows*, published in 1967, he claimed that he was not a poet at all but "a stringer of words." Shortly thereafter, he proclaimed in an interview that, yes, he is a poet.

That shift was significant. Any modesty he felt at the beginning of his career seemed to disappear once he was faced with critical attacks. He moved from the defensive to the offensive. This is a typical response by popular artists to serious criticism. McKuen was roundly and soundly attacked by critic after critic, perhaps none more than Karl Shapiro, who lumped McKuen and Bob Dylan together in his vitriolic judgments. When Shapiro's book *The White-Haired Lover* was released, he became the target of McKuen's poem "The White-Haired Loser."

McKuen, however, pales in terms of paranoia next to Tom Laughlin, better known as Billy Jack, his signature role in the mid-1970s. Laughlin had the reputation of being an up-and-coming star in Warner Brothers movies in the late 1960s and early 1970s, but when he created the character of half-breed Indian Billy Jack—defender of the weak, philosopher-warrior—he broke out of any previous mold. Suddenly Laughlin was a star, and his movie—he wrote it, directed it, and starred in it—became a major cult hit in the few years after its 1971 release.

But there was a problem: The critics hated *Billy Jack*. They hated its sequel, *The Trial of Billy Jack*, even more. In 1975, Laughlin came out with the wildest response to critics since the Spanish Inquisition. He published a three-page advertisement in *Variety*, the *New York Times,* and the *Los Angeles Times* announcing an essay contest in which individuals could win huge prizes by writing in response to the question: "Why is it that critics are so totally out of touch with the audiences they are paid to review for?" The contest offered a first prize of $25,000 cash, a second prize of $10,000, a third prize of $7,500, and dozens of lesser prizes, all of which totaled $100,000.

Laughlin went on to fill a page with his own essay. In this response, he attacked critics for missing the significance of films—and plays, by the way, since he addressed the critical versus popular response to Shakespeare, as well. He suggested that in Hollywood films sometimes are cut to avoid a critic's condemnation. He argued that critics who attacked *The Trial of Billy Jack* actually revealed their own ignorance and their own peculiar psychological hang-ups. He called their work a Rorschach test. The critic who called the film "opinionated" wrote an opinionated review; the critic who thought it was "simple-minded" wrote a "simple-minded review"; and the critic who felt it was long-winded ended up with an extremely lengthy review.

He suggested that newspapers should run *two* reviews of each movie, one by a reviewer who disliked the film and another by a second reviewer who liked it, thus giving audience members a chance to decide for themselves. He listed the top ten films chosen by nine of America's major critics, none of which, by the way, included his film, and then asked the ad's readers how many of those films they were dying to rush out and see.

It may be that gaining too much popularity too fast leads one to be suspicious of one's base. Real art, a celebrity could be thinking, takes time and study. If celebrity came quickly, perhaps it is not "real." And how do we know if it is real? Critics, of course. Professional and academic acceptance. Popularity produces a need to be legitimized. Time is a great "legitimizer," but does one really have time? Celebrities certainly do not have the centuries that seem to provide serious "proof" of worthiness. No, most celebrities have a few years, at best. They want to know their greatness—and to show the world—now. *See also*: **Movies' Role**; **Television's Role**.

Jack Estes

For Further Reading

Kantor, Martin. *Understanding Paranoia: a Guide for Professionals, Families, and Sufferers*. Westport, CT: Praeger, 2004.

Landrum, Gene N. *Paranoia and Power*. New York: Morgan James, 2007.

Melley, Timothy. *Empire of Conspiracy: the Culture of Paranoia in Postwar America*. Ithaca, NY: Cornell University Press, 2000.

Siegel, Ronald K. *Whispers: The Voices of Paranoia*. New York: Crown, 1994.

www.freud.org.uk/paranoia.htm.

PARODIES

Parodies ludicrously imitate well-known authors, celebrities, movies, or books. A master of parody, Mel Brooks, created spoofs of cultural sacred cows in *Blazing Saddles* (1974), which contrasted racism with the mythic conventions of Westerns; in *Young Frankenstein* (1974), a tour de force of horror films that cast outsiders in a zany light; and in *High Anxiety* (1977), a celebration through laughter of Alfred Hitchcock's films. Perhaps being the target of parodies emphasizes a celebrity's artistic achievements. Performing successful parodies increases celebrities' fame, and flops at least teach them lessons about comedic methods.

Leslie Nielsen, who was already famous, segued from drama to **comedy** in the 1980s with the *Airplane* movies and the original *Naked Gun*, the 1990s with the *Naked Gun* sequels, *Mr. Magoo* in 1997, and the *Scary Movie* twists on horror classics in the 2000s. Nielsen also appeared in a great many television programs. Parodies endear fans to celebrities by touching on the incongruities inherent in human existence.

For eleven years (1967–1978), *The Carol Burnett Show* amused audiences with parodies of commoners, like the tight-skirted secretary Mrs. Wiggins (Burnett) or the slowest old man on earth (Tim Conway). Besides Burnett, the ensemble cast included Harvey Korman, Vicki Lawrence, Lyle Waggoner, and (after Waggoner left) Tim Conway who created parodies of soap operas (*As the Stomach Turns*) and movies (*Gone With the Wind*). Burnett's Scarlet O'Hara wore a gown made from drapes and the curtain rod. Video stores rent the series as *Carol Burnett and Friends*. In 2007, the queen of funny spoofs lost her copyright, trademark, **privacy, and right of publicity** lawsuit against 20th Century Fox's caricature of her charwoman character on *Family Guy*.

Some television variety shows mix political or cultural commentary into parodies. *That Was the Week That Was* debuted in the United States on January 10, 1964, and ended on May 4, 1965. Television satirist David Frost served as emcee during the second season. Tom Lehrer wrote biting songs about racism, nuclear power, and other political topics. The juxtaposition of music and images in his parodies, such as "The Vatican Rag," often upset censors.

The Smothers Brothers Comedy Hour (1967–1969) featured guitar strumming, impetuous Tom and his older, sober sibling (Dick, a string bass player). In *Television Myth and the American Mind* (1984), Hal Himmelstein praises the duo's clever use of laughter to comment on the Vietnam War, the civil rights movement, and various social issues. Columbia Broadcasting System (CBS) watchdogs clipped controversial segments from the program. Then, in June of 1969,

Hee-Haw, a hillbilly version of National Broadcasting Company's (NBC's) hit, *Rowan & Martin's Laugh-In*, replaced the *Comedy Hour*. From January 22, 1968, to May 14, 1973, Dan Rowan and Dick Martin's forty-plus ensemble blended slapstick with catch phrases such as "Here comes da judge," and "Sock it to me."

Saturday Night Live began in 1975 with George Carlin as the guest host and in 2009 continues to amuse viewers with wacky parodies performed by many celebrities: Chevy Chase, Steve Martin, Dan Aykroyd, John Belushi, Jane Curtin, Garrett Morris, Laraine Newman, Gilda Radner, Chris Farley, Gary Weis, Peter Corbett, Al Franken, Conan O'Brien, Pamela Norris, David Spade, Adam Sandler, Eddy Murphy, Mike Myers, Bill Murray, Billy Crystal, Martin Short, Nancy Dowd, and Paula Dixon. *See also*: **Movies' Role**; **Television's Role**.

Paulette D. Kilmer

For Further Reading

Himmelstein, Hal. *Television Myth and the American Mind*. 2nd ed. Westport, CT: Praeger, 1994.

King, Geoff. *Film Comedy*. New York: Wallflower Press, 2002.

www.imdb.com/title/tt0072562/fullcredits.

www.nndb.com/people/158/000023089.

PHYSICIANS

Physicians are often respected community members, and many experience some degree of local fame or even celebrity. But national recognition, especially beyond the medical community, is unusual. Even so, celebrity physicians have heavily influenced public opinion regarding health issues.

Some of the most well-known physicians are thought of as "diet doctors." Robert Atkins and Arthur Agatston (the South Beach diet), are known for their diets more than for their personalities. The famous Scarsdale diet appeared in 1979. Although the book was a success, the author, Herman Tarnower, achieved greater fame after his lover murdered him in 1980. The story became a made-for-television movie in 1981 and again in 2006.

Mehmet Oz, coauthor of several health-related and weight-loss books, is probably best known for his appearances on the *Oprah* show and *Discovery Health*. Along with Oprah's endorsement, frequent appearances on national television have made him a household name in the late 2000s.

Robert Rey also capitalized on the desire to improve one's body. He, however, is a plastic surgeon. Beginning in 2003, his appearances on the E! reality show—*Dr. 90210*—made him an instant celebrity. Rey also cocreated a line of body-shaping undergarments frequently featured on the Home Shopping Network.

Perhaps the country's most iconic physician is Benjamin Spock, whose books encouraged a more relaxed approach to parenthood. Spock's celebrity physician status garnered him even more public attention as he protested the Vietnam War and ran as the People's Party presidential candidate in 1972. The party platform called for public health care and the legalization of homosexuality and abortion.

C. Everett Koop, the U.S. Surgeon General from 1982 until 1986, played perhaps the most notable role in public health policy. His controversial platform included sex education, AIDS, and smoking. The media welcomed the consequent uproar and encouraged his celebrity.

Jack Kevorkian made the acceptance and legalization of assisted **suicide** his life's mission and put the issue on the national agenda. Kevorkian frequently appeared in media and was influential in passing the 1994 Death with Dignity Act in Oregon. After a 1998 Columbia Broadcasting System (CBS) *60 Minutes* appearance that included a taped assisted suicide, Kevorkian served eight years in prison.

Another celebrity physician, Robert Jarvik, initially achieved celebrity status in the early 1980s for his contributions toward the artificial heart. In 2006, Jarvik's celebrity was reignited after controversy surrounding television ads for pharmaceuticals raised questions about his credentials and contributions.

Although not always a woman, Renee Richards is perhaps medicine's most celebrated female. An ophthalmologist, professional tennis player, and since 1975, a transwoman, Richards appeared on news and talk shows throughout the 1970s. Her fight to play tennis as a woman as well as the newness of sex-change surgery itself attracted a great deal of media attention. Richards has since written two autobiographies, one in 1986 and a second in 2007. *See also*: **Athletes**; **Authors**; **Lawsuits and Court Cases**; **Setbacks and Obstacles**; **Television's Role**.

Vanessa Murphree

For Further Reading

Nicol, Neal, and Harry Wylie. *Between the Dying and the Dead: Dr. Jack Kevorkian's Life and the Battle to Legalize Euthanasia*. Madison: University of Wisconsin, 2006.

Richards, Renee. *No Way Renee: The Second Half of My Notorious Life*, New York: Simon & Schuster, 2007.

PLASTIC SURGERY

The term "plastic surgery" is often used to describe cosmetic surgery procedures. While plastic surgery is used primarily for correcting a body's function (for example, to repair a deviated septum), cosmetic surgery is performed to enhance a person's aesthetic appearance (for example, a rhinoplasty, or "nose job," to slim the tip of the nose).

The United States is increasingly infatuated with cosmetic surgery, and it is estimated that in 2006 more than 10 million cosmetic procedures took place in the United States. Some of the most common cosmetic enhancements include abdominoplasty ("tummy tuck"), blepharoplasty ("eyelid surgery"), mammoplasty ("breast enlargement"), rhinoplasty, rhytidectomy ("face lift"), suction-assisted lipectomy ("liposuction"), and collagen, fat, or other tissue filler injections (such as botulinum toxin, "Botox"). The procedures range in price from a $200 Botox injection to a $5,000 breast enlargement or nose job.

Critics are wont to place blame for America's cosmetic surgery explosion squarely on the sculpted shoulders of our culture's glorified celebrities, who yearn to appear both flawless and youthful. Examples of these procedures are readily found among the famous. Dolly Parton and Pamela Anderson are walking advertisements for mammoplasty, while the taut faces of Kenny Rogers and Joan Rivers exemplify the effects of rhytidectomy. Similarly, Michael Jackson and Ashlee Simpson's evolving profiles demonstrate rhinoplastic work, Melanie Griffith and Donatella Versace's lush pouts suggest a not-so-subtle hint of collagen, and Nicole Kidman and Janice Dickinson's creaseless foreheads imply Botox injections. Sometimes celebrities, such as comedic queen Phyllis Diller, acknowledge their cosmetic work, and other celebrities, for instance Lindsey Lohan, deny any physical enhancements.

But media backlash against celebrity cosmetic surgery is plentiful. For example, when Priscilla Presley judged an episode of television's *Dancing with the Stars* in 2008, her appearance created a stir within nationwide gossip columns. When the New York City newspaper the *Daily News* asked a former president of the American Society for Dermatologic Surgery to comment on Presley's appearance, the doctor stated, "Her chin is too masculine and wide. It's too big of an implant. It looks manly. Her eyes are smaller. It looks like someone used too much filler around them." Other reports claimed Presley had attended an "injection party," where a group of friends gather and have a doctor perform filler injections into their skin.

Regardless, negative press surrounding these enhancements does not appear to be derailing the cosmetic surgery industry. In fact, it is now almost commonplace to hear stories about teenage girls receiving mammoplasty or rhino-plasty for their sixteenth birthdays. So long as U.S. culture continues to place precedence on a flawless and youthful appearance, the upsurge of cosmetic enhancements will undoubtedly con-tinue. *See also*: **Criticisms of Celeb-rity Culture; Movies' Role; Physicians; Television's Role**.

Elizabeth Hendrickson

For Further Reading

Blum, Virginia L. *Flesh Wounds: The Cul-ture of Cosmetic Surgery.* Berkeley: University of California Press, 2003.

Haiken, Elizabeth. *Venus Envy: A His-tory of Cosmetic Surgery.* Baltimore, MD: The Johns Hopkins University Press, 1997.

Pitts-Taylor, Victoria. *Surgery Junkies: Wellness and Pathology in Cosmetic Culture.* Piscataway, NJ: Rutgers University Press, 2007.

Austrian American action star and California Governor Arnold Schwarzenegger strikes a macho pose at a San Diego football game in 2007. Courtesy of the Department of Defense.

POLITICS

Politicians have always aspired to fame. However, the advent of broadcast televi-sion and modern advertising techniques in the 1950s made politics an integral part of celebrity culture. Politicians became what Daniel Boorstin has called human "pseudo-events"—commodities crafted for mass consumption. Emphasis on celebrity and appearance over sub-stance of ideas and actions has trans-formed the political process.

Politicians invest so much time and money to get reelected that the cam-paign cycle consumes the entire term of office. Incumbents must raise funds to support continuous campaigning, which reduces time for their elected duties. Expensive television advertising balloons campaign budgets, even in local races, which heightens the influ-ence of big campaign contributors on the political process. Television's strength is in conveying surface impres-sions and immediacy, whereas complex issues are avoided. This media bias to-ward the candidates' personal qualities and away from party affiliation has weakened the major political parties and added to the independent block.

Media-Driven Politics

The declining importance of print news accelerated the transition to celebrity politics. Population centers that had been served by numerous daily newspapers saw most dailies fold or be absorbed by competitors and ownership chains. Readers who used to confirm their opinions by reading openly partisan newspapers came to expect the one remaining daily to provide nonpartisan, balanced reporting. The newspapers' shareholders expected bigger profit margins, and unpopular editorial stands became bad business. While newspaper ownership concentrated, the large-circulation picture magazines succumbed to competition from television, and the magazine industry fragmented into thousands of titles addressing narrow special interests.

Before broadcasting, the vast majority of citizens relied on newspapers and magazines to learn about politics. Consequently, politicians worked hard to maintain good relations with the press, which gave journalists considerable influence on public opinion. Radio changed things by bringing the politicians' voices directly into voters' homes, bypassing journalists. An early demonstration of radio's powerful yet intimate appeal was President Franklin Roosevelt's reassuring voice in his "fireside chats," which gave the nation courage to overcome the Great Depression and to unite against global foes.

Television transformed politicians into celebrities by personalizing them for their constituents, effectively removing intermediaries such as journalists and political parties, which previously had controlled political dialogue. The following is a brief survey of milestones in the evolution of politicians as television celebrities:

- In 1952, Republican vice presidential candidate Richard Nixon faced accusations of corruption by appealing directly to the public in a televised national address, later nicknamed his "Checkers" speech, after the family dog he lovingly mentioned.

- In 1954, Sen. Joseph McCarthy of Wisconsin went into rapid decline after Edward R. Murrow's *See It Now* news program on Columbia Broadcasting System (CBS) gave many Americans their first close-up view of the anti-Communist demagogue.

- In 1960, the first live presidential debate, between Richard Nixon and John Kennedy, revealed television's emphasis of style over substance and presaged the medium's determining role in elections.

- In 1961, Kennedy's first live presidential press conference put the White House in control of the news agenda and pace. The Kennedy presidency was nicknamed "Camelot" for its fairytale-like celebrity status, which for Jacqueline Kennedy survived her husband's assassination and her remarriage to Greek shipping magnate Ari Onassis.

- In 1968, president-elect Nixon established the White House Office of Communication, which symbolized the chief executive's primary concern in controlling information.

- In 1979, amid a recession and energy crisis, President Jimmy Carter appealed earnestly but unconvincingly to a national television audience that the country faced a crisis of confidence, his so-called "Malaise" speech.

- In 1981, the inauguration of Hollywood actor Ronald Reagan as U.S. president became the role of a lifetime and set a high performance standard for the office.
- In 1991, President George H. W. Bush announced the Desert Storm coalition attack on Iraq to a world television audience.
- In 1992, presidential candidate Bill Clinton and wife Hillary appeared on CBS's *60 Minutes* to refute Gennifer Flowers's claim of an extramarital affair. Bill later referred to himself as the "Comeback Kid."
- In 2003, President George W. Bush appeared in an aviator's flight suit in front of a "Mission Accomplished" banner aboard the USS *Abraham Lincoln*. His speech for television cameras later proved premature.
- In 2008, primary opponents belittled charismatic presidential candidate Barack Obama as a mere "**rock** star"; nevertheless, with astute use of television, Obama became the first African American to win the U.S. presidency.

The **Internet** has had a democratizing effect on politics by increasing the access and influence of ordinary voters on election campaigns, counteracting the importance of television and influence of major campaign contributors. As home Internet access proliferated in the late 1990s, campaigns began to reach out online to voters and donors. Citizen **blogs** grew in number and influence, further undercutting professional political reporters and television pundits.

In 2004, the upstart candidacy of Vermont Gov. Howard Dean for the Democratic presidential nomination, while ultimately unsuccessful, demonstrated the potential of the Internet for grassroots campaigning and fundraising. The major candidates in the 2008 presidential campaign raised millions of dollars in donations through their Web sites. Democratic nominee Obama set new records for small donations over the Internet, which supported his identification as a populist candidate representing the interests of middle-class voters. The special appeal of high-tech campaign strategies to younger, more technologically savvy voters promises to increase their participation in civic affairs.

Celebrity Politicians

Celebrities have the advantage of name recognition in political races, though fame alone has not guaranteed success. Celebrity **athletes** who have won political office include baseball stars Wilmer Mizell and Jim Bunning; basketball stars Morris "Mo" Udall, Bill Bradley, and Tom McMullen; football stars Steve Largent, Steve Kemp, J.C. Watts, Tom Osborne, Alan Page and Pat Swilling; Olympic competitors Jim Ryun, Bob Mathias, and Ben Nighthorse Campbell; and professional wrestler Jesse Ventura. Football star Byron White is an associate justice of the U.S. Supreme Court. Entertainers who have won elective office include radio star Wilbert "Pappy" O'Daniel; singers Jimmie Davis and Sonny Bono; and actors Helen Gahagan Douglas, Sheila

Kuehl, George Murphy, Fred Grandy, Ben Jones, Clint Eastwood, Fred Thompson, and Arnold Schwarzenegger. Celebrities in other professions who became politicians include author Clare Booth Luce, astronauts John Glenn and Harrison Schmitt, social activist Tom Hayden, and businessman Michael Bloomberg. Jerry Springer was mayor of Cincinnati before becoming a television host.

Coincidentally most celebrities seeking political office have affiliated with the Republican Party. Republican Ronald Reagan was the most famous and successful celebrity politician. After three decades of Hollywood acting and political activism, Reagan won the governorship of California and then two terms as U.S. president. His genuine, relaxed demeanor televised well and earned him the nickname "Great Communicator."

Celebrity Diplomacy

Some celebrities seeking to make a difference in society pursue diplomacy rather than elected office. Billionaire Bill Gates and wife Melinda use their celebrity and major gifts to promote several worldwide causes. Television's Oprah Winfrey and golfer Tiger Woods support education through their foundations. Singer Barbara Streisand supports civil and women's rights causes. Actors Brad Pitt and Angelina Jolie use their celebrity to aid refugees. Television's Rosie O'Donnell promotes community development. Actor Nicolas Cage supports Amnesty International. Cyclist Lance Armstrong supports cancer research. Singers Bob Geldof and Bono organize benefit concerts, make appearances, sit on international panels, and

cajole heads of state to support famine and disease relief for Africa. Bono's diplomacy has won many international **awards**, including nomination for the Nobel Peace Prize.

Some politicians use their celebrity to pursue social causes after leaving office. Former President Jimmy Carter promotes human rights through his Carter Center. His several diplomatic missions with and without U.S. government approval won him the Nobel Peace Prize in 2002. Former President Bill Clinton's foundation supports HIV/AIDS research and treatment, nutrition, and environmental causes. Clinton and former president George H. W. Bush announced joint philanthropies responding to several global natural disasters, and former vice president Al Gore won the Nobel Peace Prize in 2007 for his personal campaign to raise awareness about the dangers of global warming. *See also*: **African American**; **Corporate Celebrity**; **Humanitarian Efforts**; **Power**; **Presidential**; **Television's Role**.

Russell J. Cook

For Further Reading

Fitzgerald, Terence J., ed. *Celebrity Culture in the United States. Reference Shelf Series*. Vol. 80, no. 1. New York: H. W. Wilson, 2008.

Marshall, P. David. "The Embodiment of Affect in Political Culture." In *Celebrity and Power: Fame in Contemporary Culture*. Minneapolis: University of Minnesota Press, 1997.

Schickel, Richard. "The Politics of Illusion." In *Intimate Strangers: The Culture of Celebrity in America*. Chicago: Ivan R. Dee, 2000.

Schultz, David, ed. *It's Show Time! Media, Politics, and Popular Culture.* New York: Lang, 2000.

Cillizza, Chris. "The Fix's Grab Bag of Celebrity Politicians." http://voices.washingtonpost.com/thefix/2006/01/the_fixs_grab_bag_of_celebrity.html.

POWER

Social celebrity, the "frenzy of renown," has been much studied. The literature on celebrated objects of social attention and recognition provides knowledge of the dimensions of fame, but there has been less consideration of the larger consequences of a celebrity class. If we continue the habit of deference to a separate class of luminaries deemed worthy of celebration, what will be the eventual outcome? Indeed, what would a future be like in which celebrities are increasingly dominant and powerful?

The late scholar Dan Nimmo developed the intriguing thesis of "media luminocracy." A luminocracy is a consequence of mediated **politics** wherein politicians and mediators adapt to the interests of each other rather than to the "body politick," acting as luminous "stars" in a spectacle that makes citizens into consumers of celebrity, displacing political rule. Power claims are either exploited or ignored, and popular interests are diverted toward the frivolous, the short-term, the clear-cut, or the controversial, focusing attention on recurrent trivial aspects of popularity. This results in luminocracies, which thrive on celebrity marketed as reality wherein fame begets more fame and caters to entertainment wants rather than to practical needs. Such a focus restricts the public to the immediacy of the moment, the sensationality of the event, and the luminosity of the popular personages on display, doing little for serious governance. In a luminocracy, we witness the astounding development of celebrity status and attributes as the core criterion of leadership, dimming concern with practical governance but glowing in the limelight of star power. Through the dramatics of luminaries, citizenries are transformed into audiences.

If contemporary social systems are becoming luminocracies, students of celebrity culture should consider how such an exclusive class of celebrated personages became a social principle of hierarchical dominance. Even as "human pseudo-events," their very vacuity and superficiality qualifies them for the spotlight of popular mediation. It is true that social honorifics in recognition of exclusive status, either exalted by notable achievement or denigrated by infamy, are ancient and ubiquitous, but in the age of popular media, this recognition has changed into a plethora of attention sites. The transition from hero to celebrity, for instance, expanded the category of notable figures of popular curiosity, changing the bases of admiration so that one can achieve fame without merit. The powerful and wealthy were subject to the same transformation, becoming celebrities at the expense of their dignity and privacy. Economist Thorstein Veblen made sport of the "leisure class," the idle rich of immense wealth and privilege who seemed to live in an Elysian field of carefree play. The upper class evoked envious emulation among the populace, becoming a "radiant body" of stylistic and hedonistic mimesis. A leisure class becomes famous for the popular fantasy of vain exhibitionism it offers the many outside the enchanted garden, with the decadent allure of a life of opulent delight, encouraging such popular practices as conspicuous consumption and pecuniary emulation.

The next "socio-logical" step was the popular consumption of the conspicuous via interest in the famous themselves. Attention to exhibitory personages was democratized in the creation of those classes of the willingly and accessibly famous, such as movie stars, sports heroes, and "café society." The principle of celebrity—that social prominence includes the mantle of fame—became a core feature of ascendance into elite realms. Even the hardworking chief executive or ambitious senator is not only a figure of seriousness but also of play: success depends in part on a reputation of having an almost magical quality that illuminates one's status as a radiant body with extraordinary powers and exclusive rights. In an age of popular mediation, the wealthy and powerful have found that they are also creatures of fame, and that their exalted status can be enhanced and extended by communicating a reputed aura. Executives featured in glowing terms in the financial media or politicians magnified by capital-city pundits enjoy celebrated luminocity, although events may burst the bubble of their reputations, turning their status to infamy and thus loss of wealth or power, but apparently never their fame. They may be masters of the rhetorical or expository gifts of literacy, but they must also accommodate themselves to the spectacular imagery of mediacy.

By the time of postmodernism, celebrity constituted a vast media enterprise, complete with cultural conventions and dramatic expectations that required aesthetic sophistication and histrionic skill among the celebrated. The Warholian Imperative impels people to seek their moment of fame, even if it is the ignominious status of criminal outrage. The will to power and the will to wealth become superseded by the will to fame. The pathologies of megalomania and kleptomania become less important socially than exhibitionism. Ambitious people are less interested in being obeyed or rewarded and would rather be seen and recognized, preferring to be a big name rather than a big power or big dealer. If this movement is expansive and ascendant, then the fullest consequence of mediacy may be the creation of an elite, wherein the radiant body of society is the celebrity, the individual skilled at prestigious self-display and popular reputation.

A luminocracy—the rule of the celebrity—would be unprecedented, so we can only imagine what such a social order would be like. This eventuality might occur in the wake of the delegitimation of the state and the market: if the state comes to be seen as the province of military and corporate power, and the economic system as the property of financial plutocrats, their very exclusivity condemns them to be seen as inaccessible and uninteresting, fiefdoms run by megalomaniacs and kleptomaniacs in realms that are self-referential and self-beneficial. A luminocracy would be popular rule with legitimacy based in magical status, playing on our attraction to and admiration for iconic beings who are a species of demotic god, familiar yet exotic, human yet numinous, fanciful yet immortal. The aura of leadership ultimately would be rooted in idolatry, the extent to which we see celebrated leaders as mortal gods. The radiant glow of figures like Princess Diana (the Fairytale Princess, the Wronged Woman, the Lady Bountiful, and so on) fulfills mythic needs that scientific rationality and even political religiosity cannot satisfy. If political and economic systems become less meaningful, the idols who head these crumbling superstructures will become fallen gods, to be superseded by new gods drawn from the luminocracy. We would have returned to a very old form of idolatry, worshipping the image and the imaginary life of magical kings as if they were sacred beings capable of superhuman powers rather than simply lucky mortals. Their leadership would fill a void in a carnival of misrule, but as Nimmo warned, rule of the celebrated might be entertaining yet lack serious prudence by refocusing attention on the trivial theater of momentary squabbles over symbolic incidents, providing ritual play for audiences.

Familiar celebrities could be utilized as spokespersons hired to defend the indefensible for restive populaces; Ronald Reagan and others were accused of being reassuring "mouthpieces," spectacular distractions for major interests. But if a luminocracy were to triumph, luminaries would not only have to represent themselves as charmed beings with virtually shamanistic powers of magical potency, but also as Homeric poets conducting a mythic narrative. The 21st century could well see such figures retelling old, old stories of ancient golden ages and the humble origin of kings and courageous knights and martyred princesses and wise sages and evil villains and peace restored to the realm. In a country whose "City on a Hill" turns out to be Las Vegas, such an old story might seem far-fetched. But the celebrated could conceivably become celebrants of new quests and new faiths and new ways of living, rooted in the mythic heritage of epochs past. The mundane quests of capitols and stock exchanges cannot compare to Holy Grails, the tales which speak to the deep yearning for stories that play out the way we expect. In a world dominated by luminaries, the famous could move from an entertainment class that exists for providing amusement, to a leisure class that exists to justify exclusive privilege, into a bardic ruling class wherein fame or celebrity confers the right to rule by retelling again the old stories. The tale told could be rooted in the ancient story of the mother-goddess who brings spring fertility and tender care to suffering humanity. Or it could be a story of the eternal child who presides over a summer feast of joyful youth and pagan play. Or last, it could be the wintry narrative of the father-king, the warrior god of wrath, who leads us in holy war, smiting endless enemies. It will depend on what myth we want illuminated and enacted. *See also*: **Criticisms of Celebrity Culture**.

James Combs

For Further Reading

Worth, Dean, Ph.D. [Dan Nimmo]. Chapter III and Chapter IV in *The Body Politick*. Unpublished manuscript.

Veblen, Thorsein. *The Theory of the Leisure Class*. New York: Funk & Wagnall's, 1899.

PRESIDENTIAL

The celebrity watch for the modern American presidency was born in a national tragedy. On the morning of July 2, 1881, James A. Garfield had been in office for less than four months when he was gunned down by a disgruntled office seeker in a Washington, D.C., railway station. An "accurate rendering" of the moment appeared in *Frank Leslie's Illustrated Newspaper* and preceded intense summer-long scrutiny of Garfield's critical condition. When probing doctors could not find the bullet that made the president's chest wound, they were editorially excoriated. Lengthy letters to the editor poured in, offering advice. Readers rushed herbs, teas, home remedies, and nostrums to the White House. An elaborate air-conditioning system required 100 pounds of ice hourly to keep the president cool.

On September 6, Garfield was transported by train on a special spur built to a seaside home in Long Branch, New Jersey. When he died less than two weeks later, each rail spike sold briskly in the market place. Even the tile in the Baltimore and Potomac Rail Station where the president was felled became a collector's piece. Garfield's surviving son donated the tile to the Smithsonian in 1909.

Secretary of War Robert Todd Lincoln led the honor guard that took Garfield's remains on a mournful rail route to Cleveland. The symbolic significance of the presidency was not lost on

President Ronald Reagan and wife, Nancy, work the crowd at a 1981 gala. Courtesy of the Department of Defense.

Lincoln, who had accompanied his father's remains to Springfield sixteen years before. The image of a log-splitting, truth-telling "Honest Old Abe" had largely been a creation of Republican Party press backers Joseph Medill and Horace Greeley.

Wars remain the best basis for the creation of celebrity presidents. George Washington carefully cultivated the prototype of the reluctant servant drawn to national responsibilities. The father of his country had no children of his own, but many celebrated presidents can be considered his "offspring." To Andy Jackson, nicknamed "Old Hickory," it did not matter that the War of 1812 was already over when the Battle of New Orleans was won. News of the settlement had not crossed the Atlantic, but Jackson's reputation as an American "everyman" was made. The basis of presidential celebrity ever since has been the balancing act between the ordinary and the extraordinary. A president is one of the public, yet can achieve great things, implying everyone in the new nation had the opportunity to do the same.

William Henry Harrison portrayed himself in the Log Cabin Campaign of 1840 as a man of the people who defeated Tecumseh in the Indian wars; he was actually one of America's wealthiest men and a relentless self-promoter. Ulysses S. Grant fit the celebrity formula. He had been a failed farmer, bill collector, and leather shop salesman, but achieved celebrity status as a Civil War general. His presidency, however, was stricken by scandal and economic panic.

Theodore Roosevelt self-consciously sought publicity as a Western cattle rancher and newsreel Rough Rider who beat the Spaniards at San Juan Hill. Cartoonists pictured him similarly dispatching robber barons and the trusts. Roosevelt used the presidency as a bully pulpit he took to the people while preaching progressive reform. He befriended William Allen White and like-minded editors, built a White House West Wing to accommodate reporters, hired a secretary to field their questions, and encouraged Americans in his writing to live a hearty life. When Brooklyn toy dealer Morris Michtom read that Roosevelt refused to shoot a badly bruised bear on a Mississippi hunting trip, the huggable Teddy Bear was born.

Twentieth-century celebrity extended to presidential family members, as Teddy's niece Eleanor found out, when she married distant cousin Franklin. Franklin Roosevelt used radio during the Great Depression to pitch the New Deal to Depression-era audiences. In 1933, the first of his thirty "fireside chats" evoked 1 million letters from listeners, many of whom thought they knew Roosevelt as well as a member of their own family. Eleanor traveled 40,000 miles in her first year as First Lady, keeping a daily diary syndicated in the nation's newspapers and held weekly press conferences. She wrote a regular column for *Women's Home Companion* and later *Ladies' Home Journal*. At times, her popularity exceeded that of her four-term husband, thanks in part to her weekly radio show sponsored by the Simmons mattress company.

John and Jacqueline Kennedy's photogenic First Family delighted the first generation of television watchers. Jackie Kennedy received an Emmy for hosting network viewers on a tour of the redecorated White House. A record 56 million Americans watched the program on the nation's three networks. Cover stories in *Life* and *Look* magazines captured candid images of Caroline and John Jr., the youngest children to live in the White House in the 20th century. At forty-three, Kennedy was the youngest man ever elected to the White House, and the fortunate outcome of the Cuban missile crisis and his charge that America land a man on the moon by the end of the decade pushed his popularity to a nearly unprecedented 76 percent. His assassination in November 1963 after only a thousand days in office created a national trauma, ending what would later be venerated as a kind of Camelot.

Harry Truman recognized that the modern American presidency was evolving into an exercise in the performance arts; he remarked that future presidents would be "glorified public relations men." Ronald Reagan had, in fact, been a movie actor before becoming a politician, a skill that served him well as one of the nation's most popular presidents.

There was an estimated six-fold increase in the number of photo opportunities developed by Michael Deaver in the Reagan White House than had been manufactured in the Kennedy era. Deaver was a master at realizing that the images he constructed would outlast whatever was written about the president. This was particularly true at a time when three-quarters of all Americans got all or most of their news from nightly network news packages that portrayed Reagan as a latter-day Marlboro Man, out chopping wood on his ranch or riding his horse along the open range. Even the Iran-Contra scandal that rocked Reagan's second term

failed to permanently affect public affection for him.

America's next celebrity president, Bill Clinton, styled himself as the second coming of Kennedy. He donned dark glasses and played the saxophone on *The Arsenio Hall Show* and admitted to one viewer that he wore boxers, not briefs. Clinton shared Kennedy's enthusiasm for adulterous affairs, but unlike Kennedy, the world of twenty-four-hour cable and the **Internet** brought to light what might otherwise have remained hidden. News that Clinton had had a sexual relationship with a twenty-two-year-old White House intern and possibly coached her to lie about it to a grand jury was reported by an Internet gossip columnist on January 17, 1998. The year that followed was a media free-for-all with the public devouring every delicious detail, including a **sex**-filled report by independent counsel Ken Starr on September 9, 1998, that caused many Internet sites to crash. On December 19, 1998, Clinton was impeached on charges of perjury and obstruction of justice. His twenty-one-day Senate trial led to his acquittal.

At a time when fame and infamy often strolled hand in hand, Clinton and Starr shared *Time*'s Man-of-the-Year award. The digital landscape in which their stars shown was made to order for celebrity presidents and those who came close to their reflected glow. Clinton was the first celebrity president of the new era. Conditions were beautifully prepared for others to follow, and, in 2008, Barack Obama stepped gracefully into the role. *See also*: **Criticisms of Celebrity Culture**; **Internet's Role**; **Magazines' Role**; **Murders of Celebrities**; **Politics**.

Bruce J. Evensen

For Further Reading

Farnsworth, Stephen J., and S. Robert Lichter. *The Mediated Presidency.* Lanham, MD: Rowman & Littlefield, 2006.

Grossman, Lawrence K. *The Electronic Republic: Reshaping Democracy in the Information Age.* New York: Viking Press, 1995.

Hallin, Daniel C. *The Presidency, the Press, ands the People.* San Diego: University of California, San Diego, 1992.

Streitmatter, Rodger. "The Rise and Triumph of the White House Photo Opportunity." *Journalism Quarterly* 65 (Winter 1988): 981–985.

Ward, Hiley H. "The Media and Political Values." In *The Significance of the Media in American History*, ed, James D. Startt and William David Sloan, 129–146. Northport, AL: Vision Press, 1994.

PRIVACY AND RIGHT OF PUBLICITY

In the legal systems of the United States and certain other industrial nations, such as England, Canada, and Australia, privacy is a legally protectable right; but some individuals are better protected than others. On the short end of privacy protection in the United States are celebrities and other public figures. In theory, the law affords them less protection than ordinary private citizens because, to achieve the acclaim that results in heightened public curiosity about a person, that individual has voluntarily thrust him- or herself into the limelight. In so doing, according to legal reasoning, the celebrity-public figure has forfeited a large measure of the expectation for personal privacy that the less prominent person enjoys. In most kinds of privacy actions, as well as in defamation law, the celebrity-public figure plaintiff must meet a more stringent burden of proof to win a suit. In defamation law, in the landmark case of *New York Times v. Sullivan* (1964), this stiffer burden of proof was first placed on elected or appointed public (government) officials, then shortly thereafter on nonpolitical public figures as well. *Times v. Sullivan* was first applied to privacy actions in the 1967 case of *Time v. Hill,* bringing privacy law in line with defamation law in that these decisions made it harder for public figures to win a suit of either type.

U.S. privacy law, although of recent origin, goes back a lot further than the 1960s. America's new tort action of privacy invasion dates roughly from the turn of the 20th century, but sentiment in favor of curtailing freewheeling journalism had been percolating for some years before that. Newspapers' interest in the lurid had received an early boost in the 1830s penny press era, when newspapers were first hawked on the street as opposed to being sold by subscription, thus encouraging the use of more sensational headlines, illustrations, and crime and gossip content to reach a broader audience. The next major popularization of the newspaper press came in the late 1800s era described as the time of the yellow press, which often targeted the skullduggery of the wealthy and elite. With the turn of the new century came the muckraking era, in which certain magazines exposed the enormities of America's titans of business and industry. This intensified emphasis on investigative journalism helped break up various monopolies and reinvigorate competition. All these media developments took place in an America that thought of itself as respectable, orderly and God-fearing. As more and more stories appeared that delved into the private lives of the mighty, and as more press attention went to human interest in general, some observers began to think that the press needed to be brought to heel and made to respect the sanctity of home and private life. Gossip has always been part of human interchange, of course, but by the late 1800s, it had become a commercially valuable commodity. At that time, however, America's celebrity culture was still in its future, and the press's target of choice tended to be the nation's social and political elite.

It was in this atmosphere that two Boston **lawyers** wrote what is often described as the single most influential law review article ever published, in that in its wake appeared a new tort action: privacy invasion. The two authors were aristocratic Bostonian Samuel D. Warren and his former law school classmate and law partner Lewis D. Brandeis, who in 1916 became the first Jewish justice to sit on the U.S. Supreme Court. Warren, who appears to have been the article's instigator, had been upset when a news photographer took unwanted shots of Warren's baby in its carriage, and over "society coverage" of some of Warren's relatives, including one brother who was a nudist and another who was gay. The article argued that the law should offer more protection from the prying press.

At that time, a number of other legal provisions had already been made to further privacy. Trespassing on private property was a well-established stricture, and other laws discouraged eavesdropping, wiretapping, and the sordid activities of the Peeping Tom. The Fifth Amendment freed Americans from self-incrimination, another kind of privacy consideration; and also enjoying protection were communications between lawyer and client and the right of spouses not to have to testify against one another.

Adding to those existing protections, Warren and Brandeis laid out four varieties of privacy invasion that they contended were in need of legal attention. These four areas were (1) intrusion into one's solitude, or right to be left alone in one's private life; (2) disclosure of nonlibelous yet embarrassing facts about one's private life; (3) placing one in a false position in the public eye; and (4) unauthorized appropriation for commercial purposes of one's name or picture. In 1903, thirteen years after the appearance of Warren and Brandeis's *Harvard Law Review* article, the state of New York enacted a statute that recognized commercial appropriation as the basis for a tort action, and in 1905, the Supreme Court of Georgia made that state the first to rule in a plaintiff's favor in an appropriation case. Soon a number of other states passed privacy statutes or began recognizing the right to privacy in case law. The result was that these states came to regulate privacy more or less in accordance with what Warren and Brandeis had suggested in 1890.

As movies, radio, and television came along and made possible America's celebrity culture, entertainment celebrities, like government public figures, found it difficult to win cases in the first three areas of privacy law but were the natural beneficiaries of the fourth type, commercial appropriation. Very nearly the only "celebrity" plaintiffs to win in the first three types of privacy action have been temporary celebrities, people who, voluntarily or involuntarily, are thrust into the public eye for a limited period of time.

The classic exception in the intrusion-type privacy action, in which a megacelebrity actually won, is *Galella v. Onassis* (1972). In this case, **paparazzi** photographer Ron Galella had been so outrageous in his zeal to photograph the world's most famous woman of that time, Jacqueline Kennedy Onassis, that a sympathetic federal court found in her favor, ordering Galella to stay certain distances from her, her home, and her children at all times. Other celebrities have not had much luck in curtailing the rapacious paparazzi, although the tragic death of Britain's Princess Diana spurred efforts to deal with the problem. Courts have also shown increasing displeasure with media use of hidden cameras or recorders, directional microphones, and other high-tech means of surreptitious news gathering. Also, prosecution of this kind of privacy invasion suit is sometimes tied in with trespassing, entrapment, or other means of seeking legal relief.

Celebrities likewise have had little success in cases involving the publication of embarrassing facts. In *Bilney v. Evening Star* (1979), six University of Maryland basketball players sued their campus newspaper and the *Washington Star* for having published stories revealing that they were in academic trouble. The university's *Diamondback* had even published the players' grade-point averages. Noting the national prominence of Maryland's basketball program, the Maryland Court of Special Appeals took the position that the players were celebrities and could receive no relief in that their grades were newsworthy. Few celebrities bring such suits, knowing the likely outcome, yet some minor celebrities and temporary celebrities have brought suit. Mike Virgil was a fairly well known "surfer dude" who was profiled in *Sports Illustrated* magazine. The story not only covered his actual surfing, but also delved into his more eccentric proclivities, such as diving down flights of stairs. In *Virgil v. Time Inc.* (1975), the plaintiff lost. A truly sad case involved a temporary celebrity, husky ex-Marine Oliver Sipple, who very likely saved then-president Gerald Ford's life in 1975 by deflecting the handgun held by a deranged woman who was attempting to shoot the president. The media soon discovered that Sipple was a closet gay, and upon the urging of San Francisco's gay community, that fact was soon revealed. Sipple lost his job and most of his family connections. He brought suit, but despite his heroic act, the California Court of Appeal ruled against him in *Sipple v. Chronicle Publishing Co.* (1984) on the basis that his homosexuality was newsworthy. Sipple died in 1989, alone and broke. The embarrassing matter of President Bill Clinton and his 1995–1996 sexual relationship with White House intern Monica Lewinski produced considerable blather about the need to separate a public figure's public life from his or her private life where media coverage is concerned, but "Zippergate" produced no concrete changes to privacy law enforcement. More recently, actress Jennifer Aniston brought suit in 2005 over the use of a camera's telephoto lens to take topless photos of her; the matter was settled out of court the following year.

Some states have refused to recognize the third variety of privacy invasion: false light. In those states that do recognize it, getting a win for the plaintiff is an uphill battle, especially after the Supreme Court's ruling in the celebrated case of *Time v. Hill* (1967). The home of the James Hill family outside Philadelphia had been taken over by a group of escaped convicts in 1952. The Hills' plight was followed all over the nation, making them temporary celebrities. After their release unharmed, their experience was described in a novel, a Broadway play and a movie. In 1955, *Life* magazine, with the Hills' permission, did a photo-essay story, using actors to play the parts of the Hills and the convicts. *Life* embellished the story here and there, and the Hills brought a privacy suit, claiming that the magazine had cast them in a false light. Their lawyer, Richard Nixon, might well have won for them had it not been for the U.S. Supreme Court's decision to apply the standards of the *Times v. Sullivan* libel decision to privacy law, thereby making it extremely difficult for a public figure of any kind to win this variety of privacy action.

Of the four varieties of privacy invasion, the one that has sparked the greatest number of suits, and the one area in which celebrities have been able to sue and often win, is commercial use without consent. This makes sense, inasmuch as the celebrity's name or picture is especially valuable. For many years,

the motivation for such suits lay primarily in protecting human dignity; plaintiffs went to court to prevent a continued use of their name, picture, or image that they found objectionable. In the 1970s, boxing champ Mohammad Ali successfully sued the magazine *Playgirl* over a drawing of a nude black boxer with the caption "the Greatest" (*Ali v. Playgirl*, 1978). Late-night host Johnny Carson, in *Carson v. Here's Johnny Portable Toilets* (1983), was able to stop the obvious reference to him in the marketing of port-a-potties. *Wheel of Fortune* card-turner Vanna White, in *White v. Samsung Electronics America* (1992), stopped that Korean corporation from using a spoof ad that showed a squat robot dressed to resemble her; and singer Cher won in *Cher v. Forum International* (1982) when that magazine ran an ad that implied her **endorsement** of it.

Eventually it became clear that some appropriation suits were being brought not so much to prevent a use of someone's name or likeness, but to realize income from that use. Motivation for such suits was not predicated on protecting dignity, but on pecuniary considerations. Generally regarded as the first recognition of this difference in motive was *Haelan Laboratories v. Topps Chewing Gum* (1953), a successful suit involving the use of players' images and information on baseball cards. Another celebrity suit was *Lugosi v. Universal Studios* (1983), in which the heirs of actor Bela Lugosi wished to participate in profits from licensing of the late Mr. Lugosi's image as Dracula. From such cases was born a new tort: right of publicity, which has been important to celebrities and their estates. Not surprisingly,

California led the way, in 1984, in recognizing this right. With this new tort came two major changes. First, this right gave protection not just to an individual's name and picture, but also to his or her image, as in an actor's portrayal of a character. The second change concerned descendability. In privacy law, the assumption has been that a person's privacy dies with him or her, but in publicity law, rights to a celebrity's image can be willed to heirs or assigns just as tangible property can. Today, a deceased celebrity's image is very likely to have been licensed, and anyone wanting to use that image for a commercial purpose must get written permission or risk suit. Today, nineteen states have adopted right of publicity statutes, although six of those statutes say nothing about image as an inheritable right. In the other thirteen states, rights in a deceased person's image may be exclusive to his or her heirs for lengths of time that vary from 10 to 100 years. An additional eleven states have no statute, but have recognized right of publicity in case law. Celebrities who have made use of this new tort action include Bette Midler, Woody Allen, Joe Montana, Kareem Abdul-Jabbar, Tom Waits, Clint Eastwood, and the heirs of Rudolph Valentino, Groucho Marx, Janis Joplin, Elvis Presley, Marilyn Monroe, and Fred Astair. No federal law addresses right of publicity, but pressures appear to be building in that direction, and in some right of publicity cases, copyright and trademark law also come into play.

In sum, where personal dignity is concerned, the celebrity is not as well protected by law as is the ordinary American, but where money is at issue, the celebrity now enjoys far more protection than once was the case. Meanwhile, celebrities cope with their goldfish-like lives as best they can. They employ bodyguards—sometimes several at a time, buy sophisticated burglar alarm systems for their homes, tint the windows of their cars, buy vicious dogs to patrol their grounds at night, and even resort to wearing disguises. When faced with legal trouble, some celebrities, such as entertainer Michael Jackson, have been able to get sympathetic judges to seal transcripts or other court records. Radio celebrity Garrison Keillor went so far as to move to Denmark, in part to reclaim some of his lost privacy, but he soon returned to the United States. Surely most celebrities realize that a generous measure of privacy is simply something they must give up in exchange for the adulation of the masses and the enormous wealth that can go with it. *See also*: **International Celebrity**; **Lawsuits and Court Cases**; **Magazines' Role**; **Newspapers' Role**; **Paparazzi**; **Talk Show Hosts**.

Sam G. Riley

For Further Reading

Caudill, David. *Protecting Celebrities: the Right of Publicity in the US and Australia*. Melbourne: Centre for Media and Communication Law, 2004.

Gaines, Jane. *Contested Culture: the Image, the Voice, and the Law*. Chapel Hill: University of North Carolina Press, 1991.

LaMay, Craig L. *Journalism and the Debate Over Privacy*. Mahwah, NJ: Lawrence Erlbaum, 2003.

Lumby, Catherine. *Gotcha: Life in a Tabloid World*. St. Leonards, NSW: Allen & Unwin, 1999.

McCarthy, J. Thomas. *The Rights of Publicity and Privacy*. 2nd ed. St. Paul, MN: West Group, 2000.

http://ilt.eff.org/index.php/Right_of_Publicity.

http://library.findlaw.com/1998/Feb/1/130405.

www.ncsl.org/programs/lis/privacy/publicity04.

PRODUCT LINES

Since before actress Lana Turner's glistening blonde waves appeared in photos advertising Lustre Cream shampoo in the 1950s, advertisers have known the power of celebrity to attract customers. Indeed, research has found that celebrities are the most effective endorsers of brands, and the history of advertising is rich with effective campaigns involving celebrities hawking products. The successful formula for corporations and celebrities alike was simple: Find a suitable celebrity to tout your brand and pay him or her a hefty fee for doing so. But in the next few decades, the relationship between products and celebrities would get more complicated as the concept of "branding" grew in sophistication.

Perhaps a defining moment in that transition came in the mid-1980s when a struggling shoe manufacturer, Nike, found itself bidding for the endorsement of a reluctant Michael Jordan. The National Basketball Association (NBA) rookie signed on after Nike offered the unusual enticement of making "Jordan" the most prominent name on the product, launching one of the most successful celebrity product lines to date—the Air Jordan athletic shoe.

At approximately the same time, actress Jaclyn Smith of *Charlie's Angels* television fame took a calculated risk by associating her elegant image with Kmart—a department store better accepted by consumers for its auto parts, warehouse food items, and cheap imports than for high style. But Smith's line of women's clothing caught the attention of Kmart shoppers and became a staple. Smith has estimated that annual sales have reached as high as $600 million.

What Nike, Kmart, and now many other companies figured out is that celebrities are not simply agents receiving financial compensation to back a product. Even as endorsers, they are essentially a cobrand with the product. Just as Jordan did with Nike, a celebrity can help catapult a company to prominence even if the company name takes a back seat. Or, as Smith did with Kmart, a celebrity can add cache and style to a merchant not known for either.

Branding Breaks Out

During the 1990s, **hip-hop** artists took product lines to a new level. Declining to wait for formal corporate courtship, they launched their own retail companies to capitalize on their personalities and style. Def Jam Records founder Russell Simmons launched Phat Farm in 1992, eventually turning it into a multimillion-dollar company. In 1998, Sean Combs unveiled the Sean John clothing line, which became a major player in menswear and brought in $400 million in retail sales by 2003.

In 1999, Jay-Z and Damon Dash introduced the popular Rocawear, which carries a number of celebrity-designed lines, including that of Victoria Beckham.

In 2000, a single appearance by a celebrity in a singularly distinctive dress eventually helped lead to a new era for products bearing the stamp of celebrity ownership. When the up-and-coming music artist and actress Jennifer Lopez presented an award at the Grammys wearing a filmy green frock with a neckline that ended below her navel, marketers knew they had what Hollywood publicist Michael Levine called an "exciting, unpredictable personality." Lopez's subsequent career as a singer, musician, actress, and marketer of clothing, perfume, jewelry, and other products made her a brand in her own right and helped set the stage for an avalanche of celebrity branding.

Perfume

One of Lopez's biggest product line successes was her first scent, Glow, proving in 2002 that she could follow in the footsteps of the queen of celebrity perfumes—1950s and 1960s film icon Elizabeth Taylor. Taylor's launch of White Diamonds in 1991 had been considered an exceptional success and, despite her long absence from movie screens, she stood virtually alone at the top of the celebrity fragrance heap for more than a decade.

After Glow, celebrity scents became a craze, introducing a new generation to a formerly dormant industry. Three years following Glow's launch, celebrity and celebrity-endorsed brands represented 23 percent of the top 100 women's fragrances in the United States, up from 10 percent in 2003, according to market researcher NPD Group. From Britney Spears and Paris Hilton to romance novelist Danielle Steel and even shock rocker Marilyn Manson, those with recognizable names were finding a platform behind the perfume counter.

As of 2006, celebrity fragrances were the fastest-growing segment of the $2.9 billion perfume market. As of the beginning of 2008, more than 100 celebrity perfumes were available. Even established brands such as Chanel and Guerlain were turning to Hollywood for more star power as new products became increasingly expensive to launch. But some experts warned that the sweet scent of success was souring due to market saturation, and the life span of new launches was shrinking steadily. Some perfume manufacturers were starting to get picky about which celebrities they worked with, while consumers began finding that many scents smelled almost alike and questioned whether big names were sometimes tacked onto a slightly altered fragrance as an afterthought.

Not All Celebrity Brands Are Created Equal

Those involved in marketing say the biggest successes occur when celebrities and their product lines mesh in a way that turns an intangible asset, such as a celebrity's name, reputation, or image, into something real in a specific product. In the decade since the turn of the century, celebrities have become adept at applying these types of corporate marketing techniques to their images, with their individual product lines as a major part of the process.

They, and the companies that help manufacture the lines, know that consumers have an emotional bond with the celebrities they favor and therefore will invest emotionally in celebrity products as well—as long as there is also trust. The buzz phrase for celebrity product associations by summer 2008 was "authenticity counts."

For example, skateboarder Tony Hawk achieved brand status via several platforms, including a video game, a book deal, a television production deal, and a line of skateboarding products. His multimillion-dollar success came through maintaining his core audience and not venturing into what his agent called "extreme commercialism."

Another celebrity who has taken a cautious, longer-view approach to growing her reputation as a brand is Oprah Winfrey, who has built a multimedia empire with her name on it but without selling specific consumer goods.

Others who have launched multimillion-dollar product lines and have been able to convey a bestselling message include Mary-Kate and Ashley Olsen with videos, books, music, and apparel; Paul Newman with Newman's Own brand of organic food products; former boxer George Foreman with the George Foreman Lean Mean Grilling Machine; home improvement guru Ty Pennington with his brand-name home goods at Sears; Heidi Klum, Paula Abdul, Brad Pitt, Pamela Anderson, and Patti LaBelle with jewelry; and Beyonce Knowles, Nicky Hilton, and Gwen Stefani with clothing—all of whom have been deeply involved in their clothing design lines and have been repeatedly seen and photographed wearing their own brands.

When Reputations and Economies Falter, So Do Brands

Getting in trouble, such as Martha Stewart and her insider-trading scandal, can sully not only a celebrity's name but also his or her cache in the marketplace. Major advertisers pulled out of Stewart's signature magazine, and in August 2003, Stewart's company, Martha Stewart Living Omnimedia, announced an earnings drop of more than 85 percent. However, sometimes even bad publicity cannot hurt a beloved brand. By 2007, the Martha Stewart Collection component was part of Macy's largest brand rollout in the retailer's history.

It was not just in Stewart's case that media attention was a double-edged sword. Even branding pioneer Lopez became overexposed in the eyes of some licensing agents in the wake of her much-publicized failed relationship with actor Ben Affleck, though she continued to debut products. Both she and Jessica Simpson were criticized for not being seen actually wearing their clothing lines, with Simpson in 2006 facing a $100 million breach-of-contract lawsuit accusing her of failing to promote her brands, Princy and JS by Jessica Simpson.

Some celebrity names have high recall or ad awareness by consumers, but in a negative light. The NPD Group, a retail information company, reported that Bryant, Donald Trump, Spears, Hilton, and the late Anna Nicole Smith all fit that bill, meaning their association with a brand could backfire among consumers.

Conversely, retailers whose fortunes falter can tarnish the names of the celebrities whose product lines they sell. In July 2008, for example, Steve & Barry's faced dire financial difficulties, jeopardizing its exclusive clothing lines by such celebrities as Sarah Jessica Parker, Stephon Marbury, tennis star Venus Williams, golfer Bubba Watson, actress Amanda Bynes, surfer Laird Hamilton, and basketball star Ben Wallace.

Celebrity Lines Are Here to Stay

Despite the pitfalls, celebrity product lines have become a staple of retailing and are likely to remain so in the new marketing environment known as branding. The lines between celebrity and branding are likely to become even more blurred, with celebrities creating brands and brands, such as designers and independent or specialty retailers, creating celebrities. It is also likely that no products will be off limits.

For example, in a recent development, rapper 50 Cent began marketing one item with which celebrities had heretofore not associated—condoms. But the effort appeared to meet the requisite trust and authenticity hurdles. Proceeds were to go to benefit HIV awareness. Singer-songwriter Elton John, too, joined the trend of product lines for good causes by putting the proceeds from his Elton John Fireside Home Fragrance Collection toward the Elton John Aids Foundation. *See also*: **Athletes**; **Awards and Ceremonies**; **Corporate Celebrity**; **Criticisms of Celebrity Culture**; **Dream Girls**; **Hip-Hop and Rap**; **Lawsuits and Court Cases**; **Talk Show Hosts**.

Danna L. Walker

For Further Reading

Levine, Michael. *A Branded World: Adventures in Public Relations and the Creation of Superbrands*. Hoboken, NJ: Wiley, 2003.

"Celebrity Branding." www.thr.com; "Celebrities as Brands." www.brandchannel.com.

"Opportunity Jocks." www.nytimes.com (accessed September 22, 2002).

PSEUDONYMS

Many celebrities have chosen to perform using names other than those they were given at birth. Writers may use a pen name (*nom de plume*); actors and musical performers, a stage or screen name; some wrestlers, a ring name. Their motivations for doing so have differed somewhat over time and by category.

Pen Names

In earlier, more male-dominated times, some women who became celebrity writers used a pen name to obscure their gender and thereby promote acceptance by publishers and reading public alike. French feminist novelist Amantine Aurore Lucile Dupin, Baronne Dudevant, used a much shorter male name: George Sand. The three English Bronte sisters, Charlotte, Emily and Anne, wrote as Currer, Ellis and Acton Bell. English Victorian novelist Mary Ann Evans used George Eliot, Philadelphia novelist Louisa May Alcott wrote as A. M. Barnard, and Danish writer Karen Dinesen used Isak Dinesen. Obscuring gender is less often the reason for using a pen name in the 21st century, yet the bestselling writer of recent decades, J. K. Rowling (born

Joanne Rowling) of *Harry Potter* fame, also took this old-fashioned approach.

Truly outmoded for contemporary celebrity would be the reason the Rev. Charles Lutwidge Dodgson wrote *Alice's Adventures in Wonderland* in the mid-1800s under the name Lewis Carroll: to avoid unwanted attention. American short-story great William Sydney Porter disguised his identity by writing as O.Henry because he was in prison for embezzlement when he began freelancing to magazines. Englishman Eric Arthur Blair (George Orwell) wrote his two great novels under his pen name to separate his writing from his teaching, and his countryman, espionage writer David John Moore Cornwell, began writing as John le Carre while still a secret agent with M16.

English crime fiction writer Agatha Christie wrote six novels as Mary Westmacott for a different reason— because she was trying out a different genre, romance. Princeton professor and writer Joyce Carol Oates has used the pen names Roasmond Smith and Lauren Kelly when writing mystery novels, and U.S. suspense writer Dean Koontz has used a long list of pen names for his work.

Some pen names are chosen to impart a desired image. Alekesy Maksimovich Peshkov of Russia selected Maxim Gorky, because it was shorter and because Gorky means bitter, which matched his angry writing. Pearl Zane Gray, popular writer of Western novels, understandably dropped his first name, and former investigative reporter John Bloom not only took on the name, but assumed the redneck persona of Joe Bob Briggs, critic of b-movies. On a more humble scale, what Bloom has done resembles the grander accomplishment of Samuel Clements, who "became" Mark Twain, one of America's early celebrities.

In rare instances, a writer such as horror great Stephen King will use a pen name (Richard Bachman and John Swithen) as a check on the quality of his writing to see whether his name or his talent was selling books. In equally rare cases, when books are written by collaboration, fictitious pen names may be used. As a prank to demonstrate how far American reading taste had fallen, twenty-four New York writers led by *Newsday* columnist Mike McGrady each wrote a chapter for a novel intended to be as poorly written as humanly possible. McGrady's sister-in-law posed for photos as the 1969 book's "author," Penelope Ashe, and the book was provocatively titled *Naked Came the Stranger*. Sadly, it made the *New York Times* Best Seller List. More recently, the 2005 book *Atlanta Nights* was attributed to Travis Tea (a play on the word travesty) and also was written by committee to embarrass a vanity-press publisher.

Stage and Screen Names

Writers who have used pen names have been eclipsed in number by actors, singers, and other entertainers who have done likewise, and their reasons for using a pseudonym have differed considerably. Entertainers appeal to a much broader, less sophisticated public than do writers. The biggest reason for using a stage or screen name has been the perceived need to sound less foreign. Vaudeville singer Al Jolson was born Asa Yoelson; comedian Jack Benny, Benjamin Kubelsky; and Italian screen heartthrob Rudolph Valentino,

Rudolfo Alfonso Raffaello Piero Filiberto Guglielmi, a name that would have required an extra theater marquee.

Dancer, singer, and actor Fred Astaire was Frederick Austerlitz; Greta Garbo, Greta Lovisa Gustafsson; Joan Crawford, Lucille Fay LeSueur; and Karl Malden, Mladen George Sekulovich. Some entertainers chose their own stage names, while others had them mandated by studios or agents. Amos Alphonsus Muzyad Yaqoob would have been difficult for the average American; Danny Thomas was easier. The same was true for Issur Danielovitch (Kirk Douglas), Margarita Carmen Cansino (Rita Hayworth), Volodymyr Palahnyuk (Jack Palance), Charles David Buchinsky (Charles Bronson), and Doris Mary Ann von Kappelhoff (Doris Day). Some stage names still sounded vaguely foreign, yet shorter and more glamorous, such as Vic Damone (born Vito Rocco Farinola) or Sophia Loren (Sofia Villani Scicolone); but most performers chose names as mainstream as possible: Anne Bancroft (Anna Maria Louisa Italiano), Joan Rivers (Joan Sandra Molinsky), Robert Blake (Michael James Vincenzo Gubitosi), Bobby Darin (Walden Robert Cassotto), and Natalie Wood (Natalia Nikolaevna Zakharenko).

Most, however, adopted less ethnic pseudonyms. Edward G. Robinson was born Emanuel Goldenberg; George Burns, Nathan Birnbaum; Peter Lorre, Laszlo Lowenstein; Victor Borge, Borge Rosenbaum; and sportscaster Howard Cosell, Howard William Cohen. Joesph Abraham Gottleib became Joey Bishop; Arthur Leonard Rosenberg, Tony Randall; Jacob Cohen, Rodney Dangerfield; and Bernard Schwartz, Tony Curtis. Melvin Kaminsky achieved celebrity as Mel Brooks, Joseph Levitch as Jerry Lewis, Jerome Silberman as Gene Wilder, Allen Stewart Konigsberg as Woody Allen, Robert Allen Zimmerman as Bob Dylan, and Winona Laura Horowitz as Winona Ryder.

Another reason for using a stage name was to achieve a desired image the new name suggested. One of the first such performers was escape artist Harry Houdini, born Ehrich Weisz; and English horror film great William Henry Pratt found that Boris Karloff had a more suitable aura of menace. Cowboy actor Alfred LaRue adopted the more dashing Lash LaRue, Norman Eugene Walker chose the less accountant-like Clint Walker, and country singer Lecil Travis Martin became Boxcar Willie. Short-lived rock and roll singer Jiles Perry Richardson performed as the Big Bopper, ukulele-playing warbler Herbert Khaury as Tiny Tim, Donald Eugene Lytle as Johnny Paycheck and beefy rocker Marvin Lee Aday as Meatloaf. Hard-rock singer Vincent Damon Furnier found more suitable the name Alice Cooper, which he borrowed from a band; Steveland Hardaway Judkins became Stevie Wonder; wrestler Terry Gene Bollea achieved celebrity as Hulk Hogan; John Joseph Lydon took the rebellious name Johnny Rotten; androgynous singer George Alan O'Dowd became Boy George; rock musician David Howell Evans performs as The Edge; Brian Hugh Warner chose Marilyn Manson; and hard rock musician Robert James Ritchie became Kid Rock.

Some screen names have been chosen simply because they are shorter, "catchier" and perhaps more alliterative than one's birth name. Examples include Theda Bara (Theodosia Burr Goodman),

Dale Evans (Frances Octavia Smith), Ginger Rogers (Virginia Katherine McMath), Marilyn Monroe (Norma Jean Mortenson), Tab Hunter (Arthur Andrew Kelm), Michael Caine (Maurice Joseph Micklewhite), Vanna White (Vanna Marie Rosich), Cheryl Ladd (Cheryl Jean Stoppelmoor), and Tom Cruise (Thomas Cruise Mapother IV).

Similarly, some stage names replaced birth names that sounded less distinctive or glamorous. Mary Pickford was born Gladys Louise Smith; Charleton Heston, John Charles Carter; Richard Burton, Richard Walter Jenkins; Morgan Fairchild, Patsy Ann McClenny; Patti Page, Clara Ann Fowler; Brenda Lee, Brenda Mae Tarpley; and Conway Twitty, Harold Lloyd Jenkins. Loretta Lynn, invariably introduced as Lovely Loretta Lynn, was born Loretta Webb, and Faith Hill began life as Audrey Faith Perry McGraw. Bo Diddley stood out more than Ellas Otha Bates, Ringo Starr more than Richard Starkey, and David Bowie more than David Robert Jones. Whoopie Goldberg chose a screen name shorter than her birth name, Caryn Elaine Johnson, but that also was purposely more ethnic, and Arnold George Dorsey borrowed use of the name of a German composer, Engelbert Humperdinck.

During the civil rights protest era of the 1960s and 1970s, a few African American entertainers followed the example of Nation of Islam leader Malcolm Little, who had adopted the name Malcolm X. Ferdinand Lewis Alcindor became Kareem Abdul-Jabbar, running back turned sportscaster Robert Earl Moore became Ahmad Rashad, and boxing great Cassius Marcellus Clay became Muhammad Ali.

A few celebrities have had a different reason take a stage name: the less than fortunate connotation of a birth name. Cary Grant was Archibald Leach; Roy Rogers, Leonard Slye; dancer Cyd Charisse, Tula Illice Finklea; Judy Garland, Frances Ethel Gumm; and Diana Dors, Diana Mary Fluck. Rocker GG Allin had too much to live up to under his birth name: Jesus Christ Allin.

Also, a few celebrities have changed their name to disassociate from their families for one reason or another. President Gerald Ford, born Leslie Lynch King, changed his name due to an abusive father; country comedienne Minnie Pearl, born Sarah Ophelia Colley Cannon, came from a socially prominent family; and Nicholas Cage, born Nicholas Kim Coppola, took Cage so as not to trade on the success of the Coppola name. *See also*: **African American**; **Authors**; **Comedy**; **Country and Western**; **Dancers**; **Dream Girls**; **International Celebrity**; **Rock and Pop**; **Tough Guys**.

Sam G. Riley

For Further Reading

Clarke, Joseph. *Pseudonyms: The Names behind the Names*. Nashville, TN: T. Nelson, 1977.

Room, Adrian. *Naming Names: Stories of Pseudonyms and Name Changes With a Who's Who*. Jefferson, NC: McFarland, 1981.

Smith, Stephen. *An Inkwell of Pen Names*. Philadelphia, PA: Xlibris, 2006.

Hoffman, Ivan. "Pen Names." www.ivanhoffman.com/pennames; "Stage Names." www.fiftiesweb.com/dead/real-names.

PSYCHOANALYSIS

Sigmund Freud's idea that the human unconscious could be plumbed through a technique of free association called psychoanalysis had a profound impact on 20th-century popular culture. His notion that actions, dreams, and unfiltered thoughts could reveal one's deepest memories and darkest truths understandably captured the imagination of writers and directors in Hollywood. He is even credited with helping to foster the Western preoccupation with the self—a hallmark of celebrity and celebrity culture.

Freud's influence was reflected in film, particularly in the work of director Alfred Hitchcock. Hitchcock's *Spellbound* (1945), for example, starred Ingrid Bergman as a trainee psychiatrist who tried to uncover a patient's traumatic past. It marked what historians have called the golden age of psychiatry.

By the 1950s and into the 1960s psychoanalysis became the treatment of choice for a well-heeled Western intelligentsia and those within its circle, including celebrities. For example, famed psychiatrist Ralph Greenson, author of *The Technique and Practice of Psychoanalysis,* which served as the bible for generations of analysts, treated such patients as philanthropist Lita Annenberg Hazen and actors Vivian Leigh, Mario Lanza, Vincent Minnelli and, most famously, Marilyn Monroe. Greenson is said to have visited the emotionally fragile movie star in the hours before she died in August 1962 of what the coroner determined was an overdose of prescription drugs. Monroe's mental state and the role of

psychoanalysis in her treatment has been the subject of much publicity, as has the tendency of some psychoanalysts during this period to become closely involved in their patients' lives. Greenson reportedly consulted with Monroe at least seven times a week, and Monroe may have lived at Greenson's residence for a while.

The mystery of the psychoanalytic doctor-patient relationship and the potentially dark side of psychoanalysis have been the subject of many a Hollywood film. Among classics often cited by the psychiatric community are 1975's *One Flew Over the Cuckoo's Nest* starring Jack Nicholson as a rebellious mental patient, 1980's *Bad Timing* starring Art Garfunkel as a psychoanalyst in Vienna, *House of Games* (1987) with Lindsay Crouse as a psychiatrist who gets involved in the underworld, *Girl Interrupted* (1999) starring Winona Ryder as a sane asylum resident, and *Running with Scissors* (2006) in which Joseph Cross plays the real-life Augusten Burroughs, a boy from a dysfunctional family who ends up living with his psychiatrist.

But few in Hollywood have made their psychoanalytic history so much a part of their public biography as actor-director Woody Allen. Allen, with his persona as a New York Jewish intellectual with nebbish tendencies, has mentioned psychoanalysis often in films and in personal interviews. His character in *Annie Hall* claimed to have undergone fifteen years of psychoanalysis, while in real life, Allen admitted to spending eight years "on the couch" before ending his treatment with few self-revelations. The *Journal of the American Academy of Psychoanalysis* called Allen's 1985 film, *The Purple Rose of Cairo,* starring Mia Farrow as a Depression-era wife looking for romance, a perfect allegory for the psychoanalytic experience.

Psychoanalysis has declined in popularity in both reality and in film since the 1970s, but it still plays a part in the cultural zeitgeist. For example, the American Psychoanalytic Association, fretting over its practitioners' declining image, gave actress Lorraine Bracco a special award for her sympathetic portrayal of Dr. Jennifer Melfi, the television psychiatrist of one of America's best-known psychically troubled characters—Tony Soprano of the fictional Soprano crime family. The spectacularly popular Home Box Office (HBO) series *The Sopranos* went off the air in 2007. *See also*: **Classical Music; Comedy; Criticisms of Celebrity Culture; Dream Girls; Early Deaths; Movies' Role; Television's Role.**

Danna L. Walker

For Further Reading

Kirsner, Douglas. "'Do As I Say, Not As I Do': Ralph Greenson, Anna Freud, and Superrich Patients," *Psychoanalytic Psychology* 24, no. 3 (2007): 475–486.

Steinem, Gloria, and George Barris. *Marilyn.* New York: MJF Books, 1997.

PUBLICITY

Contemporary America is fascinated with all things celebrity. U.S. culture readily creates celebrities out of just about any profession, including chefs, chief executive officers, **athletes**, **talk show hosts**, **authors**, musicians, comedians, and, of course, actors and actresses. As the successful reality television show *Dr. 90210* demonstrates, plastic surgeons are also part of our celebrity spectacle. While modern America is captivated with celebrity, corporate America is an old friend of the celebrity pitchman.

Celebrity endorsements are ubiquitous features of modern public relations and advertising campaign strategies. In fact, estimates of the use of celebrities in advertising reveal that as much as 25 percent of all commercials feature a celebrity. Celebrity **endorsements** have demonstrated ability to benefit products, brands, and causes by generating media attention, increasing awareness, raising contributions, improving sales, heightening credibility, attracting new consumers, and changing public perception about a company or its goods and services. Celebrities are especially successful because they are generally perceived by consumers as believable, influential, honest, and likeable.

However, celebrity endorsements are not guaranteed to have a positive influence on products or brands. For success, celebrities must demonstrate expertise, trustworthiness, and compatibility, or fit, with the product they endorse. The meaning transfer model is a common theory used to explain the influence of celebrities on products and brands. Ideally, in this model, image attributes of celebrities as portrayed by media or personified through characters a celebrity plays are transferred to the endorsed products. When audience members identify with a celebrity, they are more likely to see how the benefits of a product or brand could translate favorably to their lives. Meaning transfer is more likely to occur when consumers see the celebrity as a valid communicator for a product. In addition to believability and trustworthiness, attractiveness of the celebrity plays an important role in the effectiveness of the celebrity endorsement. Generally, the more attractive the celebrity to consumers the more likely the endorsement will have a favorable impact.

Another important consideration in the effectiveness of product endorsements is the consumer's evaluation of the fit between the celebrity and the product. In other words, consumers should be able to make a connection between the celebrity and the product or cause being endorsed. For example, athletes are a natural fit with sporting goods and sports beverages. Tiger Woods and Michael Jordan are among the most credible, and successful, celebrity endorsers. The success of Woods and Jordan is evidenced in Nike's willingness to develop and extend their brand identity through products carrying the names of their leading celebrity endorsers (for example, Nike Air Jordan shoes). The power of a celebrity's fit also is observable in cause-related promotions. The death of *CBS Evening News* anchor Katie Couric's husband, Jay Monahan, from colon cancer in 1998 positioned her as a powerful and credible spokesperson for the importance of colon cancer screening. Couric's on-air colonoscopy in 2000 resulted in the "Couric Effect," which significantly increased the number of colonoscopies performed across the country that year.

While many products, brands, and causes enjoy benefits from their pairing with celebrities, celebrity endorsements are not a panacea for all companies. In fact, celebrity endorsements are a double-edged sword. Failure on the part of companies to choose celebrities wisely may actually cost the product or brand through a large payday for the celebrity and no significant effect on consumer sales. Although Tiger Woods continues to enjoy golfing success and remains one of the top celebrity endorsers for a wide range of products and services, there could be danger if Woods becomes overexposed through endorsements. Woods is clearly a fit with sporting industry products, yet his celebrity extends to the many products aiming to capitalize on his remarkable sportsmanship, dedication, and continued leadership in his sport. Brands seeking endorsements from Woods need to be cautious of the possibility of overexposure, which could translate to diminished credibility for Woods and the products he endorses. Endorsements from Woods could backfire if consumers question whether Woods's motivation to endorse products stems from his genuine regard for the product or from personal economic motivation.

Even though the celebrity-product relationship does not always produce huge gains for brands, the real danger results when a paid celebrity receives bad publicity, loses star quality, or gets in trouble with the law. There are many recent examples where celebrity endorsements have caused public relations problems for brands. In the case of Martha Stewart, where the celebrity was synonymous with the Martha Stewart brand, her imprisonment for insider trading had a devastating, albeit short-lived, impact on the brand. While her brand recovered shortly after

Stewart's release from prison, TrimSpa was not so fortunate. TrimSpa became a household brand when former model and reality television celebrity Anna Nicole Smith made headlines after dropping a reported seventy pounds by using the dietary supplement. Smith's death from combined drug toxicity led to fears and speculation about whether TrimSpa contributed to her demise. Her tragic death had grave, lasting consequences for the brand.

Nevertheless, public relations and advertising remain powerful channels for celebrity endorsements of products, brands, and causes. As celebrities make their way around the evening and daytime talk show circuit or grace the pages of magazines dedicated to exploiting their celebrity, consumers pay close attention to the brands and products associated with them. Promoters are getting more savvy in their strategies aimed to benefit from celebrities. With a little creative talent, brands can have the benefits of celebrity without the huge price tag associated with their endorsements.

Public relations and marketing agents use a range of techniques to get products in the hands of celebrities. Product seeding involves planting your products in locations, such as Hollywood, where celebrities live, work, or vacation. The hope with product seeding is that a celebrity will be photographed using the seeded product.

Product seeding is particularly effective when celebrities genuinely develop a liking for a product and espouse its benefits. For example, seeding Oprah and her staff could result in great success, especially if Oprah endorses the product by placing it on her annual holiday "my favorite things" show. In fact, books selected for Oprah's book club almost always become bestsellers. Products contained in the high-priced gift bags, usually provided to celebrities attending events like the major Hollywood award shows, are usually part of a company's gifting strategy. Like product seeding, gifting strategies are aimed at getting products into the hands of celebrities. Additionally, savvy promoters can entice celebrities through barter agreements by which celebrities agree to provide endorsements as a quid pro quo for big-ticket items like exclusive vacation packages or sports cars.

It is unlikely that the use of celebrity endorsements will slow any time soon. In the diversified media landscape, celebrities have the power to gain viewers' attention and cut through the otherwise cluttered advertising environment. *See also*: **Corporate Celebrity**; **Criminals**; **Criticisms of Celebrity Culture**; **Product Lines**.

John C. Tedesco

For Further Reading

Burtonshaw, Ken, Nik Mahon, and Caroline Barfoot. *The Fundamentals of Creative Advertising*. Lausanne, Switzerland: AVA Publishing, 2006.

Rein, Irving, Philip Kotler, Michael Hamlin, and Martin Stoller. *High Visibility: Transforming Your Personal and Professional Brand*. New York: McGraw-Hill, 2005.

Ries, Al, and Laura Reis. *The Fall of Advertising and the Rise of PR*. New York: HarperBusiness, 2004.

R

REALITY TELEVISION'S ROLE

The reality television genre features "regular" people instead of professional actors and offers glimpses into dramatic, humorous, or life-changing and supposedly unscripted circumstances. Cast-member participants are put in strange situations, exotic locations, or challenging dilemmas. Stylistic conventions include soundtrack music, after-the-fact confessions or commentary recorded by cast members that serve narration of events, event manipulation through editing, and other postproduction techniques and even off-screen coaching to ensure drama.

Types of Reality Television

Hoax

Debuting in 1948, Allen Funt's *Candid Camera* (American Broadcasting Company [ABC] and later Columbia Broadcasting System [CBS]) broadcast unsuspecting ordinary people reacting to pranks, creating the type of hoax that hidden-camera reality shows aimed at to create fright, panic, confusion, or humiliation among its unsuspecting participants. Later shows that emulated Funt's antics are *America's Funniest Home Videos* (ABC 1989), *Girls Behaving Badly* (Oxygen 2002), and *Punk'd* (Music Television [MTV] 2003). *Scare Tactics* (Sci-Fi Channel 2003) puts unsuspecting dupes into terrifying situations, usually involving movie-style special effects and makeup. *Celebrity Paranormal Project* (Video Hits 1 [VH1] 2006) featured five celebrity participants in an allegedly "haunted" location. Sometimes in hoax reality shows, the entire season is a drawn-out prank played on duped cast members, who know they are in a reality show, but its actual purpose is hidden from them. The first such show was *The Joe Schmo Show* (Spike 2003).

Relationship

The first contemporary "relationship" reality show, the 1973 sociodrama *An American Family* (Public Broadcasting Service [PBS]), showcased the impact of divorce on the Loud family of Santa

Barbara, California. The show was both controversial and innovative; discussion of the family's trials became part of the lexicon. Production eliminated documentary narration, opting for the voices of the Louds. A technical precedent began when stand-alone cameras and microphones were replaced by portable cameras and wireless microphones.

Intimate family situations were profiled on such shows as *A Baby Story* (TLC, a couple's experiences from the final weeks of pregnancy through the first weeks after birth); *An Adoption Story* (Discovery Health 2003, the adoption process); and *Intervention* (A&E 2005, a person suffering from an addiction or other problem is confronted by family or friends). *Marriage 911* (Fox 2005) offered marriage therapy to troubled couples. *Bridezillas* (Fox 2003, WE 2004) followed the lives of engaged couples.

Unusual family situations were profiled on shows like *Jon and Kate Plus 8* (Discovery 2007), focused on the Gosselins, a family with a set of fraternal twins and sextuplets, showing the challenges of raising so many children. *Little People, Real World* (TLC 2006) features the Roloff family, with parents and son who are little people and three other average-size children. Two families, usually of different social classes, swap wives for a week to share how others live in *Trading Spouses: Meet Your New Mommy* (Fox 2004) and *Wife Swap* (ABC 2004). Bravo focused on women and their families who live lavish lifestyles with *The Real Housewives of Orange County* (2007), *New York City* (2008), and *Atlanta* (2008). *Who's Your Daddy* (Fox 2005) courted controversy by combining competition with

helping an adopted woman meet her biological father.

The Real World (MTV 1992) credited *An American Family* as the inspiration for their show about diverse strangers brought together in a unique environment for a long time, recording their real-life soap opera dramatics. *Road Rules* (MTV 1995) stripped cast members of all of their money, put them on a recreational vehicle and sent them traveling across the land. *Laguna Beach: The Real Orange County* (MTV 2004) and its spin-off *The Hills* (MTV 2006) document the lives of California teenagers.

Dating-based or matchmaking competition shows follow a contestant selecting a mate from a group of suitors. These include *Who Wants to Marry a Multi-Millionaire?* (Fox 2000), *The Bachelor* (ABC 2002), its spin-off *The Bachelorette* (ABC 2003), *For Love or Money* (NBC 2003), *Boy Meets Boy* (Bravo 2003), *Average Joe* (NBC 2003), and *Farmer Wants a Wife* (CW 2008). *Temptation Island* (Fox 2001) tested couples' relationships by placing them in situations with members of the opposite sex. There are also prize-offering matchmaking competitions. *Joe Millionaire* (Fox 2003), a hoax-based dating show, featured a "millionaire" bachelor looking for a bride. Contestants' greed and morality were tested as they dated the "millionaire" in exotic locales, only to learn at the end that he was a construction worker. On the social experiment *Beauty and the Geek* (WB, now CW 2005), a team of "beauties" and a team of "geeks" paired up to learn more about each other, with the winning couple sharing $250,000.

Professionals Working

By the late 1980s, computer-based non-linear editing allowed for hours of video to be quickly edited, something that could not be done with film. *COPS* (Fox, 1989) featured on-duty police officers apprehending criminals; the audience felt they were riding along. COPS had no narrator or music; the officers wore wireless mikes and the you-are-there feeling was emphasized by handheld cameras. Two basic formats exist: in the first, there is no apparent outside involvement of filmmakers, judges, or experts. The earliest example is *COPS*, but more recent additions include *Miami Ink* (tattooing, TLC 2005), *American Chopper* (customizing motorcycles, Discovery 2003), *Deadliest Catch* (Bering Sea fishing, Discovery 2005), *Dog the Bounty Hunter* (A&E 2004), and *Ice Road Truckers* (History Channel 2006). Sometimes outside experts are brought in, either to provide help or to judge results, such as the Food Network's various challenges (*Sugar Showdown*, *Bartender Battle*) and property shows such as *Flip This House* (A&E) and *The Real Estate Pros* (TLC).

Competition

Another format that offers a voyeuristic tone is reality competition, where participants live together in a confined environment, being removed (often by vote) until only one person or team remains to claim a prize. In the early 2000s, *Survivor* (CBS 2000) established the "survival of the fittest" competition aspect of reality television. Strangers were cast to live together in a remote, exotic location, all with the goal of the final survivor winning a large monetary prize. Twists added by the production company included tribal members voting others off; luxury-item rewards; challenges involving eating exotic, stomach-turning food; and secret alignments among cast members. Similar shows were *The Amazing Race* (CBS 2001), which pitted teams in a race around the world, and *The Mole* (ABC 2000), featuring a double agent who tried to sabotage contestants. Named for George Orwell's 1949 novel, *Nineteen Eighty-Four*, in which Big Brother is all-seeing, all-controlling, *Big Brother* (CBS 2000) groups strangers who live together full-time for three months in the Big Brother House, isolated from the outside world but under the continuous gaze of television cameras. Housemates try to win a cash prize by avoiding periodic evictions from the house, voted on by television viewers. A notable aspect is that viewers can also watch a continuous, twenty-four-hour feed from multiple cameras on the Web.

Job Search

Competition reality can also center on a contestant's skill, judged by a panel of experts. The format is usually developed as a job search, where the prize is a contract in that field. *America's Next Top Model* (UPN 2003) helps young women to launch a modeling career. *Hell's Kitchen* (Fox 2005), *The Next Food Network Star* (Food Network 2005), and *Top Chef* (Bravo 2006) center around chefs. Design is represented by Bravo's *Project Runway* (2004, clothing) and *Top Design* (2007, interior design). *Last Comic Standing*

(National Broadcasting Company [NBC] 2003) offered comedians a development contract. *The Shot* (VH1 2007) gave the winning photographer a magazine spread. *So You Think You Can Dance* (Fox 2005) offered dancers a chance at fame. *Project Greenlight* (Home Box Office [HBO] 2000) focused on amateur filmmaking. Bravo's *Shear Genius* (2007) featured hair styling. *The Contender* (NBC 2005) put boxers in an elimination-style competition. *The Apprentice* (NBC 2004), now a worldwide franchise, has contestants competing in an elimination-style competition to become an apprentice to real estate magnate Donald Trump.

Self-Improvement and Makeover

Another reality genre observes people improving their lives, either over a season or in one episode. *A Makeover Story* (TLC 2000) focused each week on two friends or family members ready for a personal makeover. Similar programs were *The Biggest Loser* (weight loss, NBC 2004), *Queer Eye For The Straight Guy* (style and grooming, Bravo 2003), *Supernanny* (child-rearing, ABC 2005), and *What Not to Wear* (fashion and grooming, TLC 2003). *The Swan* (Fox 2004) offered average-looking women a three-month-long "extreme makeover," including **plastic surgery**, dentistry, therapists, trainers, and a life coach, ending in a beauty pageant competition.

People are not the only subjects featured in makeover shows; their property is, too. *Trading Spaces* (TLC 2000) used designers helping neighbors to redecorate a room in each other's house. *Designed to Sell* (HGTV 2004) cosmetically renovates houses on the market on a $2000 budget. On Clean

Sweep (TLC 2003), renovations occurred while homeowners decluttered. *Extreme Makeover: Home Edition* (ABC) creates entirely new homes for deserving families; although it is not a do-it-yourself show, it features design tips. *Pimp My Ride* (MTV 2004) and *Overhaulin'* (TLC 2004) rebuilt vehicles. Failing restaurants are transformed in *Restaurant Makeover* (Food Network 2005) and *Ramsay's Kitchen Nightmares* (Fox 2007).

Talent Shows

If reality involves "real people" placed in life-changing experiences, then talent shows fit the category. The earliest variety show performer showcases were *Arthur Godfrey's Talent Scouts* (CBS 1946), choosing winners with an audience applause meter, and Ted Mack's Original Amateur Hour (DuMont Television Network 1948) where viewers called in to select the winner. *The Gong Show* (NBC 1976) featured performers (most with dubious talent), judged by a celebrity panel. *Star Search* (syndicated 1983) categorized talent into comedy, vocalist (male and female), young performer, and spokesmodel. *American Idol* (Fox 2002) seeks to discover the best singer through a series of auditions and competitions. Judged initially by three judges, stage competitions involve viewer call-ins. Using a similar judging matrix, *America's Got Talent* (NBC 2006) is modeled after the original variety-show types, where singers, **magicians**, **dancers**, and specialty acts participate.

"Celebreality"

Reality television offers a glimpse of the lives of ordinary people, and "celebreality," as VH1 coined the term, focuses on the lives of B- and C-list celebrities. Celebreality began when Ralph Edwards hosted *This Is Your Life* (NBC 1952). With celebrities sitting on center stage in front of a live audience, biographies were told, and they would reunite with family and old acquaintances.

Shows that supposedly pictured celebrities living their daily lives include *The Osbournes* (MTV 2002), *The Anna Nicole Show* (E! Entertainment 2002), *Newlyweds: Nick and Jessica* (MTV 2003), *The Simple Life* (Fox 2003), *Breaking Bonaduce* (VH1 2005), *Hogan Knows Best* (VH1 2005) and its spin-off *Brooke Knows Best* (VH1 2008), and *Gene Simmons Family Jewels* (A&E 2006). E! Entertainment network offered shows like *The Girls Next Door* (2005), about Hugh Hefner and his *Playboy* girlfriends (2005), and *Keeping Up with the Kardashians* (2007), featuring former Olympic decathlete Bruce Jenner and his socialite family.

Other celebreality shows parallel more typical reality fare. Talent shows with weekly eliminations include *Dancing with the Stars* (ABC 2005), which mixes ballroom dancing and celebrities paired with professional dancers, and *Celebrity Duets* (Fox 2006), which combined celebrities with professional singers. In *The Surreal Life* (VH1 2003), an odd mix of celebrities was housed together, competing in challenges and attempting to get along interpersonally. It spawned several successful VH1 sequels, including *Strange Love* (2005), the *Flavor of Love* (2006), *My Fair Brady* (2005), and *I Love New York* (VH1 2007) in which the star attempted to find a mate. *Rock of Love* (VH1 2007) featured a former rock star

searching for romance. *Flavor of Love Girls: Charm School* (VH1 2007) and *Rock of Love Girls: Charm School 2* (VH1 2008) attempted to impart manners to the women who had "lost" on their previous dating shows. *Celebrity Fit Club* (VH1 2007) featured overweight celebrities as they tried to achieve a target weight-loss goal. *Celebrity Rehab* (VH1 2008) chronicled celebrities attending a **drug and alcohol** treatment program. *I Love Money* (VH1 2008) brought together cast members of other VH1 shows (*Flavor of Love, I Love New York,* and *Rock of Love*) in a Big Brother–type competition situation, providing the cast with an extra few minutes of fame.

Why Reality Television?

The choice to be on reality television may be explained by basic human motivations: the desire for prizes or instant celebrity. *American Idol* has created music stars; *Survivor* has launched media careers; *The Surreal Life* has resurrected careers and established others. For the audience, reality television satisfies the need to see others in dire situations, to enjoy another's humiliation, to feel superior to choices others make, to experience catharsis in human drama. For the producers, reality television usually costs much less than scripted programming. Advertisers increase sales through product placement; *The Apprentice* creates competitions around top sales of item (Pontiac Solstice, Hanes t-shirts).

The standard question to be asked of these shows is, "Is this really reality?" Many are partially scripted, with producers casting the contestants and designing the environment and activities. Editing reality shows allows narrative to be arranged to present a selective point of view to enhance the drama, emotion, or humiliation. Nevertheless, reality programs play an important role in contemporary television. The Academy of Television Arts and Sciences gave its first Primetime Emmy Award for Outstanding Reality-Competition program in 2003 (*The Amazing Race*) and in 2008 presented awards for Outstanding Host for a Reality Show or Reality Competition. *See also*: **Awards and Ceremonies**; **Divorces**; **Television's Role**.

Beth M. Waggenspack

For Further Reading

Andrejevic, Mark. *Reality TV: The Work of Being Watched*. Lanham, MD: Rowman & Littlefield, 2003.

Biressi, Anita, and Haather Nunn. *Reality TV: Realism and Revelation*. New York: Wallflower Press, 2004.

Holmes, Su, and Deborah Jermyn, eds. *Understanding Reality Television*. London; New York: Routledge, 2004.

Hill, Annette. *Reality TV: Factual Entertainment and Television Audiences*. London and New York: Routledge, 2005.

Reality-TV-online.com. "History of Reality TV." http://www.reality-tv-online.com/articles/history-reality-tv.html (accessed August 27, 2008).

Rowan, Beth. "History of Reality TV." Infoplease. http://www.infoplease.com/spot/realitytv1.html (accessed August 27, 2008).

Slocum, Charles B. "The Real History of Reality TV" or, "How Alan Funt Won the Cold War." Writers Guild of America, West. http://www.wga.org/organizesub.aspx?id=1099 (accessed August 27, 2008).

ROCK AND POP

There have been two principal eras of mainstream popular music in the United States, each with its own set of celebrities. The first era, stretching from 1900 into the 1950s, was dominated by the songwriters and publishers of Tin Pan Alley and, by the 1950s, pop singers like Frank Sinatra, Bing Crosby, Perry Como, Nat King Cole, Patti Page, Rosemary Clooney, and Doris Day. The career of Sinatra, a former big-band singer known to adoring fans as "Old Blue Eyes," stretching from the 1930s into the 1990s, was that of a superstar celebrity, famed for dozens of albums and films. As late as 1958 Sinatra was voted America's most popular male singer. Other singers such as Perry Como, Andy Williams, and Dinah Shore had their own weekly television programs. Tin Pan Alley's audience was mostly white and middle class, while separate record industries catered to rural white (**country and Western**) and black (rhythm and blues) audiences.

The second era began with the emergence of **rock** and roll in the early 1950s. Tin Pan Alley appealed to all ages, but rock was targeted at teens. Rock and roll began when musicians mixed black rhythm and blues with white country and gospel music. This new interracial music, fast and

Singers Dean Martin (left) and Frank Sinatra perform at the 1985 Presidential Inaugural gala in Washington, D.C. Courtesy of the Department of Defense.

performance and singing styles, enhancing his game, and his fame.

The first true rock superstar, Elvis, revered by fans as "The King," had forty-five gold records. His 107 top forty singles still hold the record (The Beatles are second with forty-eight). His early recordings defied the record industry's rigid division into white and black music. With vast **sex** appeal to girls, Presley became a hero to repressed white teenagers, not least because most adults despised him. Marketing accelerated his impact. His managers used television, film, **fan clubs**, and t-shirts, inventing mass market pop music commercialization. Media saturation meant appearing on the immensely popular weekly Ed Sullivan television show, but censors prohibited any camera shots of Elvis from the waist down. Even today, decades after his death, innumerable men and even a few women work as Elvis impersonators worldwide.

American rockers also achieved celebrity status in Britain and Europe. The Beatles chose their name after Buddy Holly's group, the Crickets, and another British band, the Hollies, adopted its own version of his name. The death of Holly and two other rock stars in a plane crash in 1959 symbolized the end of an era and was later memorialized as "the day the music died" in the 1970 song "American Pie." For several years white middle-class teen idols such as Frankie Avalon and Ricky Nelson as well as girl groups such as the Chiffons and Shirelles dominated pop music, joined soon by the slickly produced crossover soul music of Motown talents, including the Supremes, Temptations, and Smokey Robinson, appealing to both blacks and

danceable, helped to spark a cultural revolution among youth. The first blasts of rock and roll defied the era's puritanical emphasis on social and political conformity, alarming adults and challenging sexual and racial taboos.

White musicians—Bill Haley, Elvis Presley, Jerry Lee Lewis, Buddy Holly—and black musicians—Chuck Berry, Little Richard, Fats Domino— created rock and roll. Haley and his band, the Comets, took rhythm-and-blues songs such as "Shake Rattle and Roll" and reconfigured them for a white audience. Berry invented the distinctive rock guitar style while Holly introduced the basic guitar–drum set combination. Presley, known as "Elvis the Pelvis" because of his suggestive, hip-swinging gyrations, adopted black whites. In the 1960s and 1970s, the soul music of such artists as James Brown and Aretha Franklin conveyed a message of black self-respect and unity parallel to the civil rights and black pride movements of the era.

Rock and roll evolved into harder-edged rock in the early 1960s and became the heart of the youth movement of that era. American society became divided over the war in Vietnam and the movements against racism and sexism. In 1963 the popular British group The Beatles, with moptop hair, toured the United States, beginning a "British Invasion" of groups, including the Rolling Stones and the Kinks, that electrified American audiences and reenergized rock music. "Beatlemania," as their impact was called, reached around the world, spawning local rock groups and spreading new fashions in clothing and hair length. In countries as far apart as Brazil and Malaysia, guitar-based rock became known as "yeah yeah" music, after The Beatles song: "She Loves You (Yeah Yeah Yeah)."

The Beatles, revolutionizing rock, matured from pop songwriters to musical philosophers, infusing many of their later albums with deeper meaning. The Beatles' 1967 album, *Sgt. Pepper's Lonely Hearts Club Band,* became the prototype of the concept album. The Beatles, especially John Lennon and Paul McCartney, wrote their own songs. No longer did songs come chiefly from writers in Tin Pan Alley. Increasingly they came from the musicians themselves and often dealt more directly with social realities. Because of their momentous impact on Western culture and hence global culture, the Beatles became perhaps the most potent musical force in history.

Singer-songwriter Bob Dylan was the other seminal rocker of the 1960s. He began as a folksinger but then adopted the electric guitar, inventing the folk rock idiom. His poetic songs exploring the human experience showed that music could do more than entertain. Dylan's "Blowing in the Wind" became the anthem of youthful dissent against bigotry and injustice. Although reclusive in his personal life, Dylan remained hugely influential and toured regularly into the 21st century, with such international celebrity that there are religious shrines devoted to him in Japan.

Dylan and The Beatles inspired other rockers in the 1960s. The Byrds blended rock with country and folk music, and the Beach Boys expanded the audience of Southern California–based surf music. In San Francisco, Janis Joplin, the Jefferson Airplane, and others, inspired by drug experiences and the era's "flower child" lifestyle, created psychedelic music. Innovative guitarist Jimi Hendrix laid the foundation for what later became heavy metal music. The merging of rock music, political protest, and the counterculture of disaffected youth culminated in the "Summer of Love" in 1967, when more than 100,000 fans congregated in San Francisco, and in the Woodstock Rock Festival of 1969, when 300,000 fans crowded a New York farm to hear rock music. The mass media publicized rock music and its celebrities, who all aspired to be on the cover of *Rolling Stone* magazine, as a popular song proclaimed.

In the 1970s, the music scene and celebrities changed. The Beatles had broken up, rock icons Hendrix and Joplin had died tragically, the war in

Vietnam wound down, protest movements faded, and a more conservative social and political environment emerged. In 1980 John Lennon was assassinated by a mentally ill fan. New styles of rock emerged. Punk music, loud and fast, appealed to working-class youth with a frontal assault on prevailing social and political values. The Clash, the Sex Pistols, and the Ramones reflected alienation more than protest and disdained celebrity. The angriest form of rock, heavy metal, with its deafening guitars, flourished on the margins, often obsessed with sex and violence. Escapist new dance music such as disco had a huge following, featuring stars such as the Bee Gees and Donna Summer.

But some rock musicians addressed social and political issues in their music. In the 1980s Bruce Springsteen criticized U.S. foreign policy and the neglect of the working class and poor. Springsteen's bitter antiwar anthem, "Born in the U.S.A.," about a disillusioned Vietnam veteran and his tribulations, was mistakenly adopted by President Ronald Reagan as an affirmation of the American dream. Mixing rock with folk music, Springsteen remains an influential celebrity, known widely as "The Boss." In the 1990s, punk and heavy metal were combined to form grunge, led by Seattle groups such as Nirvana and Pearl Jam. The **suicide** of Nirvana's lead singer, Kurt Cobain, in 1994 generated widespread angst among his huge fan base. Rap, an eclectic mix of soul, rhythm and blues, and Caribbean traditions, became the most politicized pop music, the songs reflecting the tensions of urban black youth while making millionaires of Public Enemy, Queen Latifah, Tupac

Shakur, P. Diddy, Jay-Z, and many other rappers.

Even so, the rockers and rappers had a smaller audience than theatrical pop megastars such as Michael Jackson, Madonna, and Prince, whose ascendancy was aided by the help of music videos and cable channels, especially MTV (Music Television). Jackson, known as the "King of Pop" to his millions of fans but "Wacko Jacko" to his detractors because of his bizarre personal behavior, made several of the bestselling albums in history. Both Madonna, who extolled sexuality and material values in dance-oriented songs, and Prince, who mixed pop and rock, sold millions of records by flouting social conservatism. By the 1990s, romantic pop stylists Celine Dion, Mariah Carey, and Whitney Houston achieved celebrity by appealing to a huge audience base. Boy bands such as the Backstreet Boys and N'Sync, as well as girl groups such as the Spice Girls, soared to the top of the charts, with huge teenage followings. Soul-influenced singers such as Beyonce Knowles and Alicia Keys transcended racial divisions. By the early 21st century young pop singers—Britney Spears, Christina Aguilera, Ashlee Simpson, and Justin Timberlake—used sex appeal to attain celebrity, while the Jonas Brothers and television personality Miley Cyrus made millions of fans in the ten to sixteen age-group. Spears, like Michael Jackson, was famous as much for her dysfunctional life as for her music. The sudden death of Jackson in 2009 illustrated the global reach of U.S. popular music. Today, celebrities compete for fans as pop and rock music fragment into many niches, compact disc sales and major record companies decline, and stage shows draw smaller crowds, while more fans access music through digital downloads from the **Internet**, often via handheld electronic devices. Yet, as a Sonny and Cher hit song from the 1960s asserts, "The Beat Goes On." See *also*: **Criticisms of Celebrity Culture; Early Deaths; Fads; Hip-Hop and Rap; Magazines' Role; Movies' Role; Television's Role.**

Craig A. Lockard

For Further Reading

Anderson, Simon V. *Pop Music USA*. New York: Simon and Schuster, 1997.

Friedlander, Paul. *Rock and Roll: A Social History*. 2nd ed. Boulder, CO: Westview, 2006.

Gregory, Hugh. *A Century of Pop*. New York: A Cappela Books, 1998.

Starr, Larry, and Christopher Waterman. *American Popular Music: From Minstrelsy to MTV*. New York: Oxford University Press, 2003.

Szatmary, David P. *Rockin' in Time: A Social History of Rock-and-Roll*. 6th ed. Upper Saddle River, NJ: Pearson Prentice Hall, 2007.

S

SETBACKS AND OBSTACLES

The history of celebrity is replete with stories of setbacks and obstacles overcome—either before or after celebrity was attained. As is true for all people, these challenges to success come in many forms. Some of Hollywood's older leading men and **tough guy** actors had to recover from war wounds. Lee Marvin was shot at Saipan during World War II, and James Arness was wounded at Anzio. Cliff Robertson was on a ship that was bombed by the Japanese, and both Clint Eastwood and Jack Palance were hurt in wartime plane crashes. Peacetime automobile accidents were serious setbacks for Montgomery Clift; Sammy Davis, Jr.; Jason Robards; Stevie Wonder; Lucille Ball; and Mark Hamill. Before he achieved celebrity, Yule Brenner was badly hurt in a trapeze accident.

Many celebrities have had to bounce back from illnesses or other medical problems. Olympic sprinter Wilma Rudolph, actor Mel Ferrer, and singer Dinah Shore had childhood polio. Peter Falk has a glass eye due to removal of a malignant tumor when he was three, football star O. J. Simpson suffered rickets during his childhood, and mystery writer Dashiell Hammett had tuberculosis as a young man. Actors Tom Cruise and Henry Winkler were dyslexic, and Stacy Keach had multiple operations to correct his harelip. Writer Jack Kerouac was once diagnosed as schizoid, and suffering various psychological problems were writer Norman Mailer and actresses Paula Prentiss and Roseanne Arnold. Comic actor Tony Randall suffered from severe insomnia, and Paul Hogan (Crocodile Dundee) had a cerebral hemorrhage from weightlifting. Television host and interviewer Barbara Walters has succeeded in her chosen field despite a speech impediment that causes her "r's" to sound like "w's." In fact, her fame appeared to increase when a *Saturday Night Live* skit dubbed her "Baba Wawa." Stuttering had to be overcome by civil rights activist Louis Farrakhan; James Earl Jones, now known for his stentorian voice; and **talk show host** Jack Paar. **Country** singer Mel Tillis is able to sing without stuttering but still stutters when speaking. Obesity at times during their lives has plagued such celebrities as Oprah Winfrey, Raymond Burr, exercise guru Richard Simmons, opera star Maria Callas, chef Paul Prudhomme, television personality Star Jones, and actresses Lynn Redgrave and Kirstie Alley.

A major stumbling block for many celebrities has been substance abuse. Alcohol abuse has been a problem for Montgomery Clift, Jackie Gleason, Morgan Freeman, Robert Morse, Nick Nolte, John Larroquette, Jerry Lee Lewis, and Alice Cooper. Cocaine was the **drug** of choice for Little Richard, Ray Charles, Joe Louis, Chevy Chase, Drew Barrymore, Truman Capote, Nell Carter, Kirstie Alley, and many other celebrities. **Jazz** trumpet great Miles Davis and singers Boy George and James Taylor became addicted to heroin, and Yul Brynner was addicted to opium.

Academic slackers and slow starters might find solace in knowing that the great physicist Albert Einstein did poorly in his early schooling. Andy Griffith failed fourth grade, English mystery writer Agatha Christie was a poor speller, short-story writer Truman Capote failed high school math, and singer Billy Joel did not get his high school diploma until he reached his forties. Humphrey Bogart was expelled from Phillips Academy and never went to college, and Marlon Brando was expelled from **military** school. It is ironic that conservative talk radio's Rush Limbaugh flunked speech communication in college. Writer Kurt Vonnegut failed out of Cornell, Harrison Ford from Ripon College, and Ted Danson from Stanford. Chevy Chase

was expelled from high school and later from Haverford College; Katherine Hepburn from Bryn Mawr; Efrem Zimbalist, Jr., from Yale; and Woody Allen from New York University.

Probably one of the most severe personal setbacks of all is attempted **suicide**, and here the list of celebrities is long indeed. Fans and admirers often find this fact odd and assume that a celebrity "has it all" and should, by all rights, be happy. It is plain, however, that celebrity has its difficulties. An old saying points out that nobility implies responsibility, to which one might add that in contemporary America, celebrity implies pressure. It also seems that some unhappy or driven individuals feel enormous pressure before becoming a celebrity. Something within all of us makes us wonder what it would be like to be a celebrity, but perhaps we should take care lest we get our way. *See also*: **African American**; **Athletes**; **Classical Music**; **Comedy**; **Culinary**; **Divas**; **Drugs and Alcohol**; **Hip-Hop and Rap**; **Movies' Role**; **News Media Figures**.

Sam G. Riley

For Further Reading

Lucaire, Ed. *Celebrity Setbacks: 800 Stars Who Overcame the Odds.* New York: Prentice Hall, 1993.

Sparks, Alicia. "Celebrities and Suicide." www.mentalhealthnotes.com.

SEX AND SCANDAL

Americans revel in the "sexy." Except in the realms of comedy and politics, sex appeal and celebrity seem often to

Former President Bill Clinton eulogizes Admiral William Crowe in October 2007. Courtesy of the Department of Defense.

years after her death. Marilyn Monroe was involved in one of the first sex scandals of the 1950s when her nude photo appeared on a calendar. Rather than denying that she had posed for the photo, Monroe admitted that she had done so because of poverty. She then became a sympathetic and more intriguing character, enhanced by her 1953 appearance as the first *Playboy* centerfold. Her career was alternately boosted and marred by her status as a sex symbol. People still speculate about the impact of her alleged affairs with both John F. Kennedy and Robert Kennedy, and some conspiracy buffs have suggested that their supporters were involved in her untimely death.

Hollywood Scandals

A sex scandal generally has two main characters, a villain and a victim. The victim might be someone enticed into sex with the villain; or, as in the case of "America's sweetheart" Debbie Reynolds, it might be someone left behind while the villain engages in an affair. Reynolds and husband Eddie Fisher were viewed as Hollywood's perfect couple in the 1950s—until it was revealed that Reynolds's friend Elizabeth Taylor was sleeping with Fisher. The marriage fell apart and Fisher married Taylor. Reynolds eventually married three times, Fisher five, and Taylor eight, adding to Hollywood's sometimes-scandalous image. Interestingly, another actress also known as "America's Sweetheart" had become enmeshed in scandal decades earlier, though in that case Mary Pickford was the one cheating on her husband, with actor Douglas Fairbanks.

be inextricable. Yet while fans love their celebrities, they also love to see those celebrities falter. Americans fawn over the sexy and the titillating, fascinated by those who go beyond sexiness to sexually indecent. Impropriety of this sort became the lifeblood of such publications as *Confidential* in the 1950s and later the *National Enquirer*.

Celebrity sex scandals existed long before the 1950s, with the 1920s case of Roscoe "Fatty" Arbuckle having been one of the most famous and tragic. Accused of raping and killing a starlet, Arbuckle was acquitted but his career was ruined. And though the 1960s are known as the era of the "sexual revolution," the staid 1950s actually provided that revolution's launching point—thanks in part to an actress who remains a pop-culture icon more than forty-five

Another actress caught cheating was Ingrid Bergman, who while married to another man gave birth in 1950 to the son of Italian director Roberto Rossellini. The U.S. Senate chastised her for the affair. Coincidentally, a few years earlier Bergman's costar in "Casablanca"—a film famously revolving around a conflict between love and a more noble choice—had been Humphrey Bogart, who left his own wife for much younger actress Lauren Bacall.

Other scandals involving real or perceived "wronged spouses" include those of Spencer Tracy, who carried on a decades-long affair with Katharine Hepburn; actress Halle Berry, cheated on by baseball star David Justice; actor-comedian Robin Williams, who left his wife for their child's nanny; basketball star Kobe Bryant, accused of rape; Jennifer Aniston, divorced from Brad Pitt, who soon married Angelina Jolie; and—reflecting Americans' fascination with royalty—England's Princess Diana, whose husband Prince Charles carried on an affair with Camilla Parker-Bowles.

The case of Woody Allen involved both kinds of victims. Allen's longtime girlfriend, Mia Farrow, found nude photos he had taken of her twenty-one-year-old adopted daughter, Soon-Yi. Though decades younger than Allen, Soon-Yi was clearly an adult. The same was not true of many other youngsters who became involved in scandals. Popular singer Jerry Lee Lewis married his cousin—his third marriage although he was not yet twenty-two—in 1957, when she was thirteen. **Rock** music pioneer Chuck Berry, who a few years earlier had produced a hit titled "Sweet Little Sixteen," spent time in prison after a 1959 arrest for his involvement with a fourteen-year-old girl. Convicted in 1979 of

the statutory rape of a thirteen-year-old, movie director Roman Polanski fled to France, where he later became involved with fifteen-year-old actress Nastassja Kinski and remains technically a fugitive from justice. Actor Rob Lowe was sued and became tabloid fodder after a videotape showed him having sex with a sixteen-year-old in 1988. Rap music star R. (Robert) Kelly was accused of sex with several underage girls. Though he denied the claims, Kelly settled at least two civil suits before a 2002 videotape allegedly showed him engaged in sex acts with a fourteen-year-old. He faced charges of producing child pornography in Florida, where the charges were dropped, and in Illinois, where in 2008 a jury found him not guilty. An even more popular singer, Michael Jackson, settled a civil lawsuit for $22 million in 1994 after being accused of molesting a thirteen-year-old boy. Incidentally, later the same year Jackson married the daughter of Elvis and Priscilla Presley. The two had begun living together in 1963 when she was seventeen and he was a decade older; they had been dating since she was fourteen.

Some "scandals" have no clear victims. In one of the most sensational, 1984 Miss America Vanessa Williams resigned after nude photos of her were found; the photos, taken five years earlier, appeared in *Penthouse* magazine. Famed pianist and showman Liberace won settlements in two 1950s lawsuits against publications that suggested he was gay, and he actively disputed allegations of homosexuality for most of his life before his 1987 death from AIDS. Long-time Hollywood leading man Rock Hudson hid his own homosexuality until shortly before he died of AIDS in 1985. Rock performer George

Michael was arrested in 1998 for public lewdness in a restroom.

British actor Hugh Grant was arrested with a Hollywood prostitute in 1995. Comedian-actor Eddie Murphy faced similar charges two years later, though in his case the prostitute was also a transvestite. At that time Jerry Springer hosted one of the sleaziest shows on television, but his own prostitution scandal occurred earlier, in 1974, when as a Cincinnati councilman he paid for sex with a personal check. Paul Reubens (Pee Wee Herman), host of a popular children's television show, was arrested for masturbating in an adult movie theater in 1991, seriously damaging his career while giving comedians a multitude of jokes based on the name of his program, *Pee-wee's Playhouse.*

News media figures are not immune to scandal. National Broadcasting Company (NBC) sportscaster Marv Albert lost his job in 1997 after being charged with sodomy and plead guilty to assaulting a woman with whom he had been having an affair. Popular radio show and Fox News host Bill O'Reilly was accused of harassing a female producer, who allegedly taped explicit phone calls. He settled the case in 2004. A year later, other sexually explicit phone calls—from Pat O'Brien, cohost of the program *Insider,* to an unknown woman—were recorded and played on television shows and the **Internet**.

Sex, Religion, and Politics

A popular saying states that three topics should not be discussed in polite company: sex, religion, and **politics**. But combining two of those elements with celebrity creates the type of scandal

that people cannot stop talking about. Televangelism turns some religious figures into celebrities, and some of these well-known individuals have been caught up in sexual scandals. In 1987, Jim Bakker's ministry collapsed under revelations of fraud and his relationship with church secretary (and future *Playboy* model) Jessica Hahn. A year later televangelist Jimmy Swaggart tearfully resigned from his ministry after being photographed with a prostitute. In 2006, pastor Ted Haggard, a frequent critic of homosexuality, resigned after another man alleged that Haggard paid him for sex.

Perhaps the first "celebrity president," John F. Kennedy, had numerous sexual liaisons, and numerous presidents before and since also engaged in extramarital affairs. Fortunately for most, their activities occurred at a time when the press generally turned a blind eye to the sexual adventures of America's leaders. That inattention began to change dramatically in the 1970s. Many Americans cannot name their own members of Congress, but at various times most of them have known something about the likes of Wilbur Mills, Wayne Hays, Dan Crane, Gerry Studds, Brock Adams, Barney Frank, Bob Packwood, Gary Condit, Mark Foley, and Larry Craig. All gained notoriety not for legislation but for sex scandals.

When Mills, chairman of the House Ways and Means Committee, had his car stopped by police in 1974, a stripper ran from the car and jumped into the Washington Tidal Basin. Reelected to Congress a month later, Mills was again spotted in the company of the same woman before performing what has become a common act of contrition for celebrities enmeshed in personal scandal: seeking treatment for alcoholism. Two years later Hays resigned over a well-paid secretary who told reporters, "I can't type. I can't file. I can't even answer the phone." The House of Representatives censured Crane and Studds in 1983 for engaging in sexual activities with teenage congressional pages. Crane, an Illinois Republican involved with a seventeen-year-old girl, lost his next bid for reelection. Studds, a Massachusetts Democrat involved with a seventeen-year-old boy, was reelected six more times. Another Massachusetts Democrat, Frank was reprimanded in 1989 after a man he had hired as a personal assistant was caught running a gay escort service out of Frank's basement. Frank, too, did not suffer politically and has been reelected in every election since. Illinois Democrat Mel Reynolds also was reelected in 1994, despite his indictment in August of that year for the sexual assault of a sixteen-year-old campaign volunteer. Convicted on **criminal** charges, he resigned the following year. Washington Republican Adams gave up his Senate seat after one term, weakened politically by allegations that he drugged and raped one woman and engaged in sexual misconduct with others. Oregon voters elected Republican Packwood to the Senate five times, but he resigned in 1995 after the Senate Ethics Committee recommended his expulsion over multiple claims of sexual abuse and assault. Democratic Congressman Condit had an affair with former intern Chandra Levy, who disappeared in 2001 and later was found to have been murdered. Though never implicated in Levy's death, Condit lost his bid for reelection.

In other political sex scandals, married New Jersey Gov. Jim McGreevey resigned in 2004 after disclosing an affair with another man; U.S. Rep. Mark Foley lost a 2006 election after exchanging sexual e-mails with congressional pages; and Sen. David Vitter asked for forgiveness in 2007 after his phone number turned up among a Washington madam's records. Idaho Sen. Larry Craig pleaded guilty to disorderly conduct and declined to run for reelection after his arrest for allegedly soliciting sex in an airport restroom. New York Gov. Eliot Spitzer resigned in 2008 after becoming caught up in a prostitution ring, and Detroit Mayor Kwame Kilpatrick was sentenced to jail the same year after lying about a sexual relationship with his former chief of staff.

Except for Ronald Reagan, Bill Clinton was the biggest celebrity politician of his time, playing his saxophone on the *Arsenio Hall Show* while running for president. Even before Clinton was elected in 1992, however, Gennifer Flowers told a supermarket tabloid that she and the former Arkansas governor had a twelve-year affair. After his election, Clinton faced—and settled—a sexual harassment lawsuit brought by former Arkansas state employee (and future *Penthouse* model) Paula Jones. Then the most dramatic sexual scandal of the 20th century developed due to revelations about Clinton's White House affair with intern Monica Lewinsky. Independent prosecutor Kenneth Starr produced a 445-page report, and numerous newspapers and Internet sites carried part or all of the sexually graphic report. Clinton was impeached by the House of Representatives, though there was virtually no chance the Senate would vote him out of office. The controversy also exposed the sexual indiscretions of some of

Clinton's congressional critics, including Bob Livingston, Newt Gingrich, Henry Hyde, and Helen Chenoweth. The Clinton-Lewinsky case preoccupied the country during most of Clinton's second term, and probably contributed to Vice President Al Gore's loss of the 2000 election.

Gore's presidential hopes may have been destroyed by Clinton's sexual impropriety, but in 1987 Democratic primary frontrunner Gary Hart sabotaged his own chances through his involvement with a Miami model. Another more recent affair, involving 2004 Democratic vice presidential nominee John Edwards, was less dramatic—largely because it became known after he had lost his 2008 primary bid for the White House. Former New York mayor and 9/11 hero Rudy Giuliani ran for the Republican nomination at the same time, though some voters disliked the fact that he had an affair with this third wife while still married to his second. The much older news that John McCain had a relationship with his second wife while married to his first did not prevent him from becoming the 2008 Republican nominee.

Even the Supreme Court, representing the third branch of American government, has not gone untouched by sexual scandal. During televised 1991 Senate confirmation hearings for Clarence Thomas, former coworker Anita Hill testified that Thomas had sexually harassed her when they worked together. Thomas, who referred to the hearings as a "high-tech lynching," was confirmed by a 52–48 vote.

Celebrity through Scandal

Proctor & Gamble was embarrassed when in 1972 its model for the Ivory Snow box became porn star Marilyn Chambers. In recent years, however, the popularity of sexual content in various media has changed the nature of sex scandals. Many women who started out as the subject of news stories decided to keep themselves in the public eye by posing for men's magazines. Porn stars have become mainstream celebrities, and instead of being ruined by sexual impropriety, some 21st-century stars have used sex "scandals" to enhance their recognition, if not their reputations. Singer Madonna produced a photo book titled *Sex* in 1992. Later Pamela Anderson and Paris Hilton became as well known for their sexually explicit home movies, downloaded on the Internet, as for their limited acting abilities. More troubling are the accidental celebrities, such as sixteen-year-old "Long Island Lolita" Amy Fisher (who in 1992 shot her older lover's wife and became the subject of three movies); Lorena Bobbitt, who cut off her husband's penis in 1993 (he and his reattached member later starred in an adult film); and a number of male and female teachers in recent years who have gained attention for their sexual affairs with students.

Perhaps in part because of changing attitudes about sex, many celebrities involved in sexual scandals either suffered no significant harm to their careers or were forgiven by audiences and made comebacks. Those figures include Ingrid Bergman, Jerry Lee Lewis, Chuck Berry, and Vanessa Williams. Americans may love sexual scandal, but they also appreciate talent. *See also*: **African American**; **Comedy**; **Divorces**; **International Celebrity**; **Jazz and Blues**; **LGBT Celebrity**; **Movies' Role**; **News Media Figures**;

Talk Show Hosts; **Temporary Celebrity**.

James Brian McPherson

For Further Reading

Apostolidis, Paul, and Juliet A. Williams, eds. *Public Affairs: Politics in the Age of Sex Scandals*. Durham, NC: Duke University, 2004.

Collins, Gail. *Scorpion Tongues: Gossip, Celebrity, and American Politics*. New York: William Morrow, 1998.

Fowles, Jib. *Star Struck: Celebrity Performers and the American Public*. Washington, DC: Smithsonian Institution, 1992.

Hall, Ann C., and Mardia J. Bishop. *Pop Porn: Pornography in American Culture*. Westport, CT: Praeger, 2007.

Holmes, Su, and Sean Redmond, eds. *Framing Celebrity: New Directions in Celebrity Culture*. London: Routledge, 2006.

Sabato, Larry J., Mark Stencel, and S. Robert Lichter, *Peepshow: Media and Politics in an Age of Scandal*. Lanham, MD: Rowman & Littlefield, 2000.

CBS2Web page. http://cbs2.com/entertainment/entertainmentslideshows/Celebrities.Sex.Scandal.20.596927.html?rid=0 (accessed September 6, 2008).

SIDEKICKS

A secondary yet enduring celebrity is the sidekick: someone who is a companion to the main character or hero in a book, movie, or television show. One might be tempted to think that a sidekick enjoys only reflected acclaim, yet who is to say this idea rings true when one considers that daft old Don Quixote in the novel of the same name "played the lead," whereas his faithful companion Sancho Panza was easily the more sane of the two. The character Huckleberry Finn was introduced by Mark Twain as sidekick to Tom Sawyer, but Huck eventually became the more interesting of the two. By the same token, the actors playing grizzled old coot sidekicks of our Western movie and television heroes often enjoyed careers longer than those of their leading men, who, like everyone else, inevitably aged. Also, some actors introduced as sidekicks have become big celebrities in their own right, as in the case of tiny Herve Villechaize, who scurried up a watchtower and cried, "De plane, boss, de plane," playing the role of Tattoo in television's *Fantasy Island* (1978–1984) opposite suave Ricardo Montalban as Mr. Roarke, host of a Pacific island where people came to live their fantasies. To qualify as a sidekick celebrity, a person would have to play a role that required him or her to spend a good deal of time with the lead character, and sidekicks are usually, but not always, of the same gender as the main character. Not considered sidekicks are actors who play "love interest" roles opposite the leading character of the movie or show.

Sidekicks are encountered in many parts of U.S. celebrity culture but have been most prevalent in Westerns, crime movies and shows, and situation comedies. In the Western movies of the 1930s and 1940s, sidekicks were sometimes referred to as "saddle pals"; most were grizzled old geezers. Raymond

Michael Richards as Cosmo Kramer (center) does a scene with Jerry Seinfeld (right) and Jason Alexander (left), 1998. Courtesy of Photofest.

Hatton was sidekick to Randolph Scott in the 1930s, and in the 1940s, sidekicks proliferated. Cliff Edwards, the voice of Disney's Jiminy Cricket in the song "When You Wish Upon a Star," played opposite cowboy hero Tim Holt; Dub "Cannonball" Taylor provided comic relief with star Tex Ritter, then later with Russell Hayden's Hopalong Cassidy; George "Gabby" Hayes began his sidekick career in the 1930s as Windy Halliday, saddle pal of William Boyd, another actor who portrayed Hopalong Cassidy. Hayes later gained lasting fame under his own name as sidekick to Roy Rogers; and portly Andy Divine was another Roy Rogers sidekick, "Cookie Billfincher." Foghorn-voiced Divine's most memorable role was "Jingles P. Jones," Guy Madison's sidekick in the 1950s *Wild Bill Hickok* series. Like Gabby Hayes,

Lester "Smiley" Burnette was sidekick to more than one Western hero. In the 1930s, he played alongside Charles Starrett, the Durango Kid, and later teamed up with Gene Autry.

Western actor-singer Tex Ridder had 6'8" Lloyd "Arkansas Slim" Andrews as his saddle pal into the early 1950s, and Clayton Moore as The Lone Ranger had his "faithful Indian companion" Tonto, played by Jay Silverheels, a Canadian Mohawk whose birth name was Harold J. Smith. Another popular Western hero was the Cisco Kid, played by a variety of actors. Cisco's first sidekick was called Gordito, acted by Chris-Pin Martin; in the 1950s television series, he was known as Pancho, played by Leo Carrillo. In a made-for-television Cisco Kid movie in the 1990s, Pancho was actor Cheech Marin. Even more sidekick variety existed in the radio and television versions of *Gunsmoke*. In radio, sidekick Chester Proudfoot was played by actor Parley Baer; in the even more popular television series, Marshall Matt Dillon's assistant, Chester, was played with a limp by Dennis Weaver. When Weaver left the show, he was replaced by a new sidekick, brave but illiterate Festus Haggen, played by Ken Curtis. Surprisingly, Curtis himself had moved as he aged from Western hero to sidekick. In his leading-man days the 1940s, he had his own grizzled sidekick, played by Shug Fisher.

In detective fiction, the prototypical sidekick is Dr. John Hamish Watson, who shared 221B Baker Street with Arthur Conan Doyle's great detective Sherlock Holmes. Both Holmes and Watson have been played by innumerable actors, but the Watsons who have had the greatest celebrity have been Nigel Bruce, whose doddering, maundering persona was delightful; and later, in the 1980s television series, Edward Hardwicke, whose less obtuse Watson was more true to the character Doyle created. In the 1930s, fictitious Chinese American detective Charlie Chan's sidekick was his eldest son, known simply as Number-One Son. The Green Hornet, a masked crime fighter in a 1930s urban setting, had an Asian sidekick, Kato. The name was borrowed in the 1960s, this time spelled Cato and played by Burt Kwouk, a sidekick for Peter Sellers's comic detective Inspector Jacques Clouseau in the *Pink Panther* movies (1963–2009).

In the 1950s television series *Perry Mason*, lawyer Mason's sidekick was Paul Drake, private eye, played by William Hopper. The first hour-long television detective show, *77 Sunset Strip*, was launched in 1958 with dual leads played by Roger Smith and Efrem Zimbalist, Jr. Their shared sidekick, Edd Byrnes, portrayed the character Gerald Kookson, or Kookie, who talked in "cool" street slang and was often pictured combing his hair. A year later, in *Hawaiian Eye*, another pair of detective heroes shared comic sidekick Poncie Ponce, cab driver (Kim Quisado). Making two runs on television in the 1950s and 1960s was *Dragnet*, in which the sidekick was Officer Bill Gannon (Harry Morgan). Another show set in the islands was *Hawaii Five-O*, which appeared in 1968. In it, star Jack Lord's sidekick was James MacArthur, playing Danny Williams. In many episodes, when the crooks were caught, Lord would utter the stock line, "Book 'em, Danno." Michael Thomas, playing Ricardo "Rico" Tubbs, was sidekick to Don Johnson in the 1980s hit *Miami Vice*.

Two British detectives became popular in the 1980s on British Broadcasting Company's (BBC's) *Mystery Theatre*: Hercule Poirot and Miss Jane Marple. Poirot, a short, portly, fastidious Belgian living in England, was portrayed by David Suchet alongside Watson-like sidekick Arthur Hastings, played by Hugh Fraser. The 1980s run of Miss Marple, starring Joan Hickson, often appeared without sidekick, but an earlier version in England starred the mumbling, huffing Margaret Rutherford, whose sidekick was her own real-life husband, James Stringer Davis. A later BBC detective show with a sidekick was *The Inspector Linley Mysteries*, in which the supporting role of working-class Sergeant Havers is acted by Sharon Small, playing off the aristocratic Inspector Lynley (Nathaniel Parker). The use of sidekicks in crime shows is most prevalent in those having one lead character and a single plotline, as opposed to the more complex multiplot shows and films popular during the late 20th and early 21st centuries.

The same can be said of sidekicks in situation comedies. These programs originated in radio, where the best-known sidekick was Jack Benny's hoarse-voiced valet, Rochester, played by former vaudeville actor Eddie Anderson. Double sidekicks in early television appeared on *The Jackie Gleason Show*, in which Gleason (Ralph Kramden) and Audrey Meadows (Alice Kramden) had sidekicks Art Carney as Ed Norton and Joyce Randolph as Norton's wife, Trixie. Similarly, in *I Love Lucy*, Lucille Ball and Desi Arnaz played opposite sidekicks Vivian Vance and William Frawley as Ethel and Fred Mertz. Another use of dual sidekicks was in the *Star Wars* adventure films, where Luke Skywalker's sidekicks were robots: R2D2 and C3PO. On *The Andy Griffith Show*, Sheriff Andy Taylor worked opposite the nervous, bumbling Deputy Barney Fife (Don Knotts). On *The Mary Tyler Moore Show*, Mary's sidekick was Valerie Harper as Rhoda, until that character was spun off to begin her own show.

In *I Dream of Jeannie*, astronaut Tony Nelson (Larry Hagman) had the suspicious sidekick Major Roger Healey (actor Bill Daily); *Get Smart*'s comic secret agent Maxwell Smart (Don Adams) had actress Barbara Feldon, known only as Agent 99, even after the character was rewritten from sidekick to wife; and Hawkeye Pierce (Alan Alda) of *M*A*S*H* pulled pranks with Trapper McIntyre (Wayne Rogers). One of the best comic sidekick

roles ever was Flo, a diner waitress played to perfection by Polly Holliday on the show *Alice*. *Three's Company* star John Ritter as Jack Tripper had sideman Richard Kline as his pal, Larry Dallas. *Seinfeld*'s (1989–1998) protagonist Jerry Seinfeld, playing himself, had dual sidekicks: Michael Richards as scatter-brained Cosmo Kramer and Jason Alexander as serial loser George Costanza. Squeaky-voiced Megan Mullally played sidekick Karen Walker opposite Debra Messing's Grace on *Will and Grace*; Zach Braff as Dr. J. D. Dorian swaps pranks and insecurities with best friend Dr. Christoper Duncan Turk (Donald Faison) on *Scrubs*; and a new dumb standard was set on *My Name Is Earl* by Ethan Suplee, playing Earl's brother Randy opposite Jason Lee in the starring role. Late-night shows have had sidekicks, too, such as Ed McMahon on *The Johnny Carson Show* or Paul Shaffer on the *Late Show with David Letterman*.

Movie comedies sometimes have sidekicks. One of the best was Marty Feldman's Igor, deranged assistant to the good doctor in Mel Brooks's *Young Frankenstein*. Although sidekicks might be viewed as "back-burner celebrities," many actors who have played such roles have done very, very well for themselves. *See also*: **Authors; Comedy; Hispanic/Latino; Movies' Role; One-Name Celebrity; Television's Role**.

Sam G. Riley

For Further Reading

Cameron, Ann. *Sidekicks in American Literature*. Lewiston, NY: Edwin Mellen Press, 2002.

Tibbals, Geoff. *The Boxtree Encyclopedia of TV Detectives*. London: Boxtree, 1992.

"Greatest Sidekicks." www.ew.com/ew/article.

"Saddle Pals and Sidekicks." www.b-westerns.com/pals.

STALKERS

Stalking is any persistent, unwelcome attempt to contact another person, to include following, repeatedly approaching, entering the property or home of, loitering near, or repeatedly telephoning or sending letters, e-mails, or faxes. Individuals of all kinds can find themselves victims of a stalker, but by virtue of being constantly in the public eye, celebrities are especially likely to fall prey to this potentially dangerous problem. Some stalkers are neurotic, others psychotic. Not all are alike in motivation. The most dangerous individuals stalk with the aim of sexually attacking or killing their victim. Some are infatuated with their celebrity "target" and have convinced themselves that their feelings of love are reciprocated. Other stalkers have unreasonable feelings of resentment due to perceived affronts or a feeling of having been rejected or otherwise harmed by the celebrity, despite the fact that the two people have never met. This social problem has become increasingly frequent in recent decades and has resulted in the passage of antistalking laws in every state.

The seriousness of stalking has been recognized for years. An early case in point inspired the 1984 Robert Redford baseball film *The Natural*. In 1949, real-life Philadelphia Phillies player Eddie Waitkus was shot and almost killed by a pretty but deranged nineteen-year-old named Ruth Ann Steinhagen, who had fixated on Waitkus for three years and who told him when she shot him that if she could not have him, no one else would either. A fatal shooting by a stalker was the 1968 assassination of civil rights leader Martin Luther King, Jr., by escaped convict James Earl Ray. That Ray was able to succeed in killing King and that he escaped the country and managed to remain at large for two months has resulted in multiple conspiracy theories about the case. In 1980, delusional dropout Mark David Chapman, hearing voices and obsessing about the book *The Catcher in the Rye*, briefly stalked and fatally shot former Beatle John Lennon. Chapman did it, he later said, to get attention for doing something big. The following year, a wealthy young man named John Hinckley, Jr., tried to assassinate President Ronald Reagan. He had been inspired to imitate the plot of the 1976 presidential assassination movie *Taxi Driver*; became obsessed with actress Jodie Foster, who played a child prostitute in that film; and initially planned to impress her by killing President Jimmy Carter. Hinckley was arrested while stalking Carter and after treatment for depression, chose as his next target the new president, Ronald Reagan. The president was hit by a ricocheted bullet, but his press secretary, James Brady, and two officers were hit directly and were more seriously injured. Hinckley was found not guilty by reason of insanity and remains in psychiatric care.

In 1983, Louisiana man Michael Perry, who had stalked singer Olivia Newton-John, was prevented from camping at her home. Returning to Louisiana, Perry killed his parents and other family members. In the following year, deranged man Ralph Nau also obsessed over Newton-John. When unsuccessful at having contact with her, he beat his own stepbrother to death; Nau also had stalked performers Cher and Shana Easton. In the late 1980s, actor Michael J. Fox received several thousand letters over a span of two years from an unbalanced middle-age woman, Tina Marie Ledbetter. When Fox married actress Tracy Pollan, Ledbetter's letters became ever more violent and contained death threats.

The celebrity whose stalking and 1989 murder led to the first state anti-stalking law, in California, was sitcom actress Rebecca Schaeffer, who costarred in *My Sister Sam* (1986). She was stalked and shot to death by deranged nineteen-year-old Robert Bardo, who had written letters to her and had tried unsuccessfully to meet her at her television set. He killed her after he viewed a bedroom scene she did in the movie *Scenes from the Class Struggle in Beverly Hills* (1989), which he apparently interpreted as behavior unfaithful to him. California's stalking law was passed in 1990, after which all other states followed suit. Also in 1989, singer Rod Stewart had to physically fend off a woman who had a delusional love-hate obsession with him. Perhaps the most stalked of all celebrities has been late-night host David Letterman. Of all the unwanted attention Letterman has received, his most persistent stalker has been Margaret Ray, who stole his Porsche in 1988 and, when arrested, claimed to be his wife. She continued to fantasize that she and

Letterman were romantically involved, was arrested for trespassing at the entertainer's home, and spent time in prison. This incident prompted Connecticut to pass a stalking law similar to that of California. In 1998, Ray wrote a suicide note to her mother, knelt on the tracks in front of a freight train, was struck, and died instantly. Only a short time later, another delusional woman, Nellie Shirley, was taken into custody at Letterman's home, and in 2005, yet another adoring fan, Colleen Nestler, claimed that Letterman was sending her suggestive coded messages on his show and, in an ironic turn of fate, got a judge to issue a restraining order against the late-night host. Following a dose of publicity, the judge rescinded his order.

A deranged man named Eric Keene was captured in 1991 in the attic of horror story writer Stephen King's home. King also had been stalked by a man named Steve Lightfoot, who somehow held King responsible for the shooting of John Lennon. In 1993, Guenther Parche, who had developed an obsessive love for and stalked tennis star Steffi Graf, stabbed and nearly killed her rival player Monica Seles. At the time of the stabbing, Seles was leading Graf in a match. Seles recovered, but her stellar tennis career did not.

In 1995, a deranged homeless man, Robert Hoskins, was arrested for making threats against pop star Madonna. Hoskins claimed that she was his wife and threatened to cut her throat and kill her bodyguards. Hoskins climbed a wall at Madonna's fortress-like home, which had once belonged to gangster Bugsy Siegel, and was shot and wounded by a bodyguard, then arrested.

In 1997, **supermodel** Elle Macpherson's home was broken into by stalker Michael Mischler, and in that same year, a serial killer on the Federal Bureau of Investigation's Ten Most-Wanted List stalked and killed **fashion designer** Gianni Versace in Miami, Florida. The man, Andrew Cunanan, previously had murdered four other victims. Cunanan chose **suicide** rather than arrest. In the following year, a husky young man was arrested in possession of handcuffs, a boxcutter, duct tape, and an album of photos of film director Steven Spielberg. The man, Jonathan Norman, was charged with stalking. In 1999, a young actress, Athena Rolando, was arrested in the Hollywood home of heartthrob actor Brad Pitt. Rolando, who earlier had left multiple letters for Pitt at the star's front gate, was arrested wearing items of Pitt's clothing. In 2000, a middle-age pizza delivery man, Michael Soiu, was placed in a mental hospital after repeated efforts to contact actress Gwyneth Paltrow; and a New Jersey accountant, Mark Baily, was placed on probation for sending threats to actress Brooke Shields. In 2001, Gary Benson, who had stalked comedian Jerry Lewis over a period of years, died in his cell while awaiting trial for having threatened Lewis's life. Also in 2001, Croatia-born architect Dubravko Rajcevic was sentenced to two years in prison for having stalked and repeatedly sent letters to Australian tennis star Martina Hingis, and actress Nicole Kidman got a restraining order against stalker Matthew Hooker.

Movie leading men such as Richard Gere want women to find them desirable, but not to the extent of phoning them 1,000 times or showing up

uninvited, as did Ursula Reichert-Habbishaw, a middle-age woman from Kassell, Germany. She was arrested for stalking in 2002 but was allowed to return to Germany. Four more high-profile stalking cases occurred in that year. Japanese fan Masahiko Shizawa was deported to Japan for trying to break into two of singer Britney Spears's homes, but not before he brought suit for emotional distress against Spears and two of her bodyguards. Singer Gloria Estefan turned having been stalked into a song, "Famous." Would-be actor Juan Carlos Diaz had appeared in two of Estefan's music videos. Estefan got a restraining order against the thirty-three-year-old man. A third stalking case of the year was that of stalker-plagued director Steven Spielberg, who was granted a restraining order against Diana Napolis, who claimed that Spielberg and his wife, actress Kate Capshaw, had implanted a satanic microchip in her head. Sadly, Napolis transferred her stalking and delusions of persecution to a new celebrity, actress Jennifer Love Hewitt. Napolis pled guilty after having spent time in a mental facility. The fourth case involved German supermodel Claudia Schiffer, who was stalked by Agostino Pomata, a mentally ill Italian who claimed that the Pope had told him to marry Schiffer. She had the same problem two years later, when Canadian Louis Brisette sent letters and made uninvited visits to her home.

Calling singer Sheryl Crowe his "spiritual twin," thirty-eight-year-old Ambrose Kappos, a former Navy diver who claimed to converse with God, was brought to trial in 2004 for stalking Crowe. Actress Halle Berry had her own stalker in 2004, a man named

Greg Broussard, who, like Kappos, claimed to be a Navy SEAL. Broussard apparently thought he and Berry were engaged and claimed she spoke to him in his dreams. A third case that year involved Dawnette Knight, age thirty-two, who attempted sleeping-pill suicide in her cell after having been arrested for stalking actress Catherine Zeta-Jones. Knight was infatuated not with Zeta-Jones, to whom she had sent threatening letters, but with the actress's husband, actor Michael Douglas. Ironically, Knight had been a psychology student.

Another tennis star, beautiful Anna Kournikova, was stalked, and in 2005 William Lepeska swam nude across Miami's Biscayne Bay to the tennis player's house. He claimed that she had left a door unlocked for him. The troubled Lepeska, who had an "Anna" tattoo on one arm, was found mentally unfit to stand trial. Also in 2005, a restraining order was issued against forty-six-year-old Robert Gardner, who had stalked singer Janet Jackson for nine years; buxom actress Pamela Anderson got a restraining order against a homeless Englishman, William Peter Stansfield, who, among other things, had demanded to be hired as Anderson's manager; and vagrant Zack Sinclair got three years in prison for stalking actor and director Mel Gibson. Actress Hilary Duff got a restraining order in 2006 against eighteen-year-old Russian immigrant Maksim Myaskvskiy, who had repeatedly threatened her life; and in 2008, Emily Leatherman, a transient woman in her early thirties, was arrested for violating a restraining order that had been issued in 2006 to keep her from harassing actor John Cusack.

Stalking is a frequently occurring and dangerous problem. It appears that in a culture heavily fixated on celebrity, entertainment figures will continue to find stalking a strange bedfellow of fame and a major threat to their well-being. *See also*: **African American**; **Athletes**; **Criticisms of Celebrity Culture**; **Movies' Role**; **Murders of Celebrities**; **Talk Show Hosts**.

Sam G. Riley

For Further Reading

Brewster, Mary P. *Stalking: Psychology, Risk Factors, Interventions, and Law*. Kingston, NJ: Civic Research Institute, 2003.

Gallagher, Richard. *I'll Be Watching You: True Stories of Stalkers and Their Victims*. London: Virgin, 2001.

Gross, Linden. *To Have or to Harm: True Stories of Stalkers and Their Victims*. New York: Warner Books, 1994.

Harvey, David. *Obsession: Stalking Celebrities*. Dublin, Ireland: Merlin, 2003.

Mair, George. *Star Stalkers*. New York: Kensington, 1995.

Mullen, Paul D., Michele Pathe, and Rosemary Purcell. *Stalkers and Their Victims*. Cambridge: Cambridge University Press, 2000.

Ritchie, Jean. *Stalkers: How Harmless Devotion Turns to Sinister Obsession*. London: HarperCollins, 1994.

SUICIDES

The truth of the adage "All that glitters is not gold" is borne out by more than ninety suicides of celebrities, major and minor, since 1950. Some of these deaths of individuals who ostensibly "had it all" probably were due to clinical depression, others to the pressures that come with renown, still others to an inability to hang onto the celebrity one had earlier in one's career. A few other instances of celebrities taking their own life came about due to love problems or money troubles, and a few more because the individuals wished to avoid the long, slow ravages of a terminal illness.

The most famous suicide in the early years of America's history was that of Meriwether Lewis in 1809; some believe that the great explorer of our continent in the Lewis and Clark expedition was actually murdered. Many high-profile deaths of celebrities,

Rocker Sid Vicious gives the camera "the eye" in 1986. Courtesy of Photofest.

usually those involving overdoses of pills, are disputed as to whether they were accidental or suicide. Marilyn Monroe was found dead of an apparent sleeping pill overdose in 1962; in her case, conspiracy theories about murder abound. Judy Garland's 1969 death and Italian actress Pier Angeli's death in 1971 involved overdosing on barbiturates, and in 1982 Austrian movie star Romy Schneider died of a combination of sleeping pills and alcohol.

Overwhelmingly, the leading method of male celebrity suicide has been death by self-inflicted gunshot, although musicians have often chosen to overdose instead. An especially stupid way to die by gunshot is by playing Russian roulette, which brought about the early demise of singer Johnny Ace (born John Alexander, Jr.) in 1954 and **rock** musician Terry Kath in 1978. Overdosing and hanging tie for second place for male celebrity suicides. Women celebrities usually choose overdosing, with gunshot suicides a distant second. Third for both men and women was asphyxiation by gas or carbon monoxide, and fourth was jumping to one's death. One celebrity, former *Saturday Night Live* comedian Charles Rocket (born Charles Claverie), committed suicide in 2005 by slitting his own throat, and National Football League player Terry Long died in that same year from drinking antifreeze.

The two most widely publicized celebrity suicides of the 1950s were those of Edwin Armstrong, father of FM radio, who jumped from a building in 1954, and early television's Superman, George Reeves, who apparently shot himself. In the 1960s, the first major celebrity suicide was that of writer Ernest Hemingway, who shot himself in

1961. Deaths by overdose of one kind or another included Clara Blandick, who had played Auntie Em in *The Wizard of Oz*, in 1962; actor Alan Ladd (1964); Nick Adams, who had appeared in *Rebel Without a Cause* and starred in the television series *The Rebel* (1968); and rhythm-and-blues singer Frankie Lymon (1968).

Actor George Sanders overdosed in 1972 as did both Sex Pistols bassist Sid Vicious and actress Jean Seberg in 1979. Puerto Rican comedic actor Freddie Prinze died by self-inflicted gunshot in 1977, and in 1978, actor Gig Young shot and killed his wife, then himself. In the 1980s, suicides by gunshot included Don "Red" Barry, who had starred in the *Red Ryder* westerns (1980); television host Dave Garroway of the *Today Show* (1982); and actor Walter Slezak (1983). Musician Chet Baker leaped from a hotel balcony in 1988, and in 1989, colorful 1960s political activist Abbie Hoffman ended his life by phenobarbital overdose.

The 1990s was an especially active decade for celebrity suicides. Rusty Hamer, who had been a child star on Danny Thomas's show *Make Room for Daddy*, shot himself in 1990, as did actor Dennis Crosby, son of famous crooner Bing Crosby, in 1991; tiny *Fantasy Island* actor Herve Villechaize (1993); Nirvana lead vocalist Kurt Cobain (1994); Hugh O'Connor, adopted son of actor Carroll O'Connor and a detective on the series *In the Heat of the Night* (1995); **country** singer Faron Young (1996); and actor Brian Keith of *Family Affair* (1997). Former host of the game show *Family Feud* Ray Combs hanged himself (1996), and suicides by overdose in that decade included model and actress

Margaux Hemingway (1996); Milli Vanilli lip sync "singer" Rob Pilatus (1998); and actress Lois Hamilton of *Three's Company* and *The Dukes of Hazzard* (1999). In the first decade of the new century, suicides by gunshot included Richard Farnsworth, known for his role in the 1982 movie *The Grey Fox* (2000); country singer Gary Stewart (2003); "gonzo" journalist Hunter S. Thompson (2005); and comedian Richard Jeni (2007). Suicide by overdose ended the life of Glenn Quinn, who had played Mark Healy on the series *Roseanne* (2002).

Among suicides by **athletes**, professional wrestlers fared worst: Eddie Graham in 1985; three brothers—Mike Adkisson in 1987 (the actual family name was Von Erich), Chris Adkisson in 1991, and Kerry Adkisson in 1993; and Chris Benoit in 2007.

While the suicides of celebrities are highly regrettable in and of themselves, the greater fear is that susceptible, suggestible, and unhappy fans might use a favorite celebrity's suicide as a template and engage in copycat suicides. Upon the death of any major celebrity, people's preoccupation with death appears to be heightened, and with celebrity suicide, the "contagion factor" may be especially high. *See also*: **Comedy**; **Hispanic/Latino**; **International Celebrity**; **Talk Show Hosts**.

Sam G. Riley

For Further Reading

Coleman, Loren. *The Copycat Effect: How the Media and Popular Culture Trigger the Mayhem in Tomorrow's Headlines*. New York: Paraview Pocket Books, 2004.

Frasier, David K. *Suicide in the Entertainment Industry*. Jefferson, NC: McFarland, 2002.

Maris, Ronald W., et al. *Comprehensive Textbook of Suicidology*. New York: Guilford Press, 2000.

www.ezinearticles.com/?Celebrity-Suicides-And-Deaths.

www.glamorati.com/celebrity.

SUPERMODELS

Modeling has had a long and storied history, beginning in 1852, when Maria Vernet Worth, a Parisian shopgirl and wife of couturier Charles Frederick Worth, became the first fashion model, acting as house mannequin in her husband's shop. And though other models, like Hannah Lee Sherman, Dinarzade, and Edwina Prue became relatively well known in their time, models—for the most part—long remained anonymous, pretty faces that graced fashion spreads. That all changed with the advent of the supermodel.

Supermodels, those icons of fashion for whom last names are not required, are known the world over for their beauty, hyperglamorous lifestyles, and antics both on and off the catwalk. The supermodel phenomenon, which reached a fever pitch in the late 1980s, actually has it roots in the 1930s; however, the term was not coined until 1943, when Clyde Matthew Dessner, owner of a small agency, used it in his book *So You Want to Be a Model*. Post–World War II, models were fast becoming celebrities, mostly because, according to the *New York Times*, fashion's influence was steadily expanding from high society to society in general.

It is difficult to name the world's first supermodel, but several women have had that honor bestowed upon them: Anita Colby, Lisa Fonssagrives-Penn, Suzy Parker, and Parker's sister Dorian Leigh. Colby, who appeared on the cover of fifteen magazines in one month, began her career in the 1930s in New York. She was the first model to receive $100 an hour for her work. Swedish-born Fonssagrives-Penn, wife of famed *VOGUE* fashion photographer Irving Penn, had a career that lasted well into her forties. Over the course of twenty years, from the 1930s to the 1950s, she was a favorite of *VOGUE* magazine, appearing on its cover more than 200 times. Parker, sometimes referred to as America's first internationally known supermodel, was the first model to make more than $100 an hour and $100,000 a year. She inspired Audrey Hepburn's role as a fast-talking beatnik in the 1957 fashion satire film *Funny Face*, in which she made a cameo appearance. Her sister Dorian Leigh, called the best model of her time by famed modeling agent Eileen Ford, was one of the most-photographed women in fashion history. Because of her many torrid love affairs, Leigh was a gossip column favorite and was even rumored to have inspired friend Truman Capote's famous heroine, Holly Golightly, in *Breakfast at Tiffany's*.

The 1960s ushered in the waifish model—a far cry from the curvaceous and womanly figure of earlier decades. Twiggy was arguably the most famous of the 1960s models, although others, such as Jean Shrimpton, Veruschka, Wilhelmina, Penelope Tree, and Lauren Hutton, were also well known. In the

Supermodel Claudia Schiffer does a scene with Mike Tyson in Black and White, *2000. Courtesy of Photofest.*

1970s, women such as Marisa Berenson, Rene Russo, Cheryl Tiegs, Janice Dickinson, and Beverly Johnson, the first African American to grace the cover of *VOGUE*, were in demand on the runway and in fashion spreads.

In the 1980s and early 1990s, the supermodel phenomenon exploded. In the beginning of the decade, Brooke Shields, Christy Brinkley, and Gia Carangi made headlines for their romances, racy advertisements and, in the case of Carangi, **drug** use. They all eventually took a back burner to the "supers": Christy Turlington, Linda Evangelista, Naomi Campbell, Cindy Crawford, and Claudia Schiffer—some of whom, as was said of Evangelista, "wouldn't get out of bed for less than $10,000 a day." *VOGUE* editor Sally Singer has

remarked that these women were a cadre of wild-living bons vivants whose shenanigans, combined with their professionalism, changed modeling from a niche concern to a global spectacle.

Owing to the grunge movement, glamour died, taking the supermodel spectacle with it. In its place sprang up a new crop of models, most notably Kate Moss, who made headlines with her so-called heroin chic look. The waifish model was soon replaced by the celebrity cover girl—likeable and relatable women like Jennifer Aniston and Sarah Jessica Parker. Though the celebrity model is still popular among magazine editors and the general public alike, models—old and new—are making an early 21st-century comeback, particularly in print ads and on magazine covers. *See also*: **Dream Girls**; **Magazines' Role**.

Amy Widmayer

For Further Reading

Gross, Michael. *Model: The Ugly Business of Beautiful Women.* New York: HarperCollins, 1995.

Liaut, Jean-Noel. *Cover Girls and Supermodels, 1945–1965.* London and New York: Marion Boyers, 1996.

http://supermodels.nl.

T

TABLOIDS' ROLE

"Tabloid" usually refers to a half-size newspaper that features sensational coverage of murders, natural disasters, curiosities, and famous people. Some tabloids, like the *Chicago Sun*, focus on short, significant news stories accompanied by huge photos, but national tabloids, like the *National Enquirer*, the *Sun*, the *National Examiner*, the *Globe*, or glossy weekly magazines, cover celebrities. Racks near supermarket checkouts provide a natural venue for these amalgamations of rumor and reality, plus the free publicity essential for maintaining celebrity. Tabloids cloak lore in gossip that echoes cultural values. They showcase cultural heroes whose example may light the path, and they provide escape from reality's troubles.

Tabloids Tell Fractured Fairy Tales

A constant tabloid theme explores what makes someone noble. Power and status alone do not win respect. Instead, like Prince Charming who proves himself worthy by trying the glass slipper on all the maiden's feet in his kingdom, modern royalty (political leaders, movie stars, and **athletes**) must earn fans' adulation. For example, President George W. Bush resolved a crisis cunningly, according to the *Globe* headline: "Bush Ditches Condi to Save His Marriage! He wants Rice to run as McCain's vice president." The lesson: Domestic tranquility trumps political expediency; furthermore, even the chief executive deals with problems, like envy, that confront all humans.

A few pages later, in the same issue of the *Globe*, the British royal family laughs off humiliation. Accompanying a photo of Queen Elizabeth's eighty-seventh birthday is a caption that begins, "ROYAL STINKER," regarding Prince Philip having passed gas. The caption adds that while others hid their mirth behind their hands, Prince Philip smiled, trying to look innocent—but fooled nobody. Like Aesop's frog physician who could not heal himself, aristocrats as well as commoners must suffer the ugly indignities of being human.

Sisters—One Good, One Bad

Tabloids grew out of storytelling as old as humanity. In the 21st century, window-peeping coverage of celebrities and scandals echoes timeless morals, and some motifs surface repeatedly. In fairy tales, contests between good and bad siblings reveal virtue. Likewise, the tabloids contrasted two sisters: the star of the teen television sitcom, *Zoey*, "Jamie Lee" Spears, and her older sister Britney Spears, flamboyant singer. The scoops involved the out-of-wedlock birth of Jamie Lynn's daughter. *The Enquirer* accused Britney of acting like a big baby while the newborn struggled to survive. "Jamie Lynn Has the Daughter Britney Always Wanted," *In Touch Weekly* declared. *US* magazine claimed that Britney ducked out to smoke cigarettes and to draw attention away from her seventeen-year-old sister. *Life and Style* concluded that losing custody of her two infant sons had cast Britney into depression. *The Globe* repeated the jealously motif but emphasized that Britney was afraid their mother would raise the baby without Jamie Lynn's consent.

Nevertheless, these divergent views tell the same story: Britney's **drug and alcohol** abuse broke her heart and separated her from her little sister. Yet, the tabloids promise, Britney's example will prevent Jamie Lynn from ruining her own life. Thus, the timeless archetype (a pattern repeated over the ages)—the next generation learning from elders' errors—is expressed in tell-all photos and catty prose. Only *People* magazine explained that Britney flew home to Los Angeles soon after the birth to see her own children.

Paragons of Something?

The Spears sisters—one childless because of addiction, the other an unwed mother—show the consequences of choosing bad role models. While heroes abound in mythology and historical legend, tabloids warn that emulating fools brings dire consequences. For instance, the tabloids explained that seventeen Gloucester, Massachusetts, high school girls who idolized Jamie Lynn got pregnant after making a pact to raise their babies together.

In Touch Weekly scolds another unreliable paragon, Brad Pitt, with "Runs Off Again While Pregnant Jolie Is Stuck at Home." Fans who copy Pitt's alleged carousing during Angelina Jolie's last months of bed rest with twins might lose their happy homes. In the same vein, Sen. Ted Kennedy's brain tumor inspired the *National Examiner* to say the alleged one-time cheater longed for forgiveness from first wife Joan. A miracle vaccine might give the seventy-six-year-old head of the Kennedy clan time to restore order in his universe, the *Globe* suggested.

The tabloids mix folk wisdom with facts and falsehoods to tell stories readers want to believe. For example, the *National Examiner* describes a parrot screaming "Uta!" (the name of a philanderer's girlfriend), which simultaneously alerted the wife and warned that womanizers face ruin. Likewise, in Hollywood's divorce wars, the *National Enquirer* said that to prevail in court, **country** singer Shania Twain dug up dirt about her husband, Robert "Mutt" Lange's affair. Christie Brinkley offered her husband $25 million to just go away after he had chased teenagers and committed adultery, the *Enquirer* said.

Often, in tabloids, heroes suffer. Paul Newman, who stayed married to Joanne Woodward for fifty years, battled leukemia bravely. Actress Reese Witherspoon learns from her first hasty, unhappy marriage, *US* infers. This time before planning a wedding, Whitherspoon is building a relationship (that includes her children) with Jake Gyllenhaal, whom she met in 2007 while filming *Rendition*. Businesswoman Elon Bomani scraped her way up from a homeless single mom to a multimillionaire in eighteen months by buying property with credit cards, the *National Enquirer* noted.

In a *Country Weekly* "CW EXCLUSIVE," Faith Hill, Josh Gracin, Ronnie Dunn, Sara Evans, Keith Urban, Josh Turner, Trace Adkins, Jimmy Olander, Garth Brooks, and Gretchen Wilson recall one day that changed their lives forever. They struggle with the same problems that beset other human beings. On the other hand, their answered prayers, bouts in rehab, survival of car crashes, and second chances offer hope and inspiration.

The *Globe* commends Elizabeth Smart for turning her pain into positive action. A lunatic and his first wife kidnapped Smart hoping to force her into a polygamist marriage, but she was rescued nine months later from "the twisted fiend" who had planned to wed forty-nine wives and sire hundreds of offspring in Utah, the *Globe* said. Smart helped write a pamphlet, *You're Not Alone,* for abduction survivors. Ergo, Smart not only lives up to her name, but she also demonstrates that courage combined with family love overcomes evil,

an ancient folklore theme. Tabloids convert plucky victims into celebrities without their seeking fame and sometimes even despite their protests.

Unfortunately, love eludes many celebrities. The *National Examiner* declares that Camilla's shrewish ways have driven Prince Charles to the brink of divorcing her. A medical crisis reunites Oprah Winfrey with Stedman Graham, her twenty-year love interest. The *Enquirer* explains that Oprah excels materially but fails interpersonally. Although money cannot buy happiness, Jennifer Aniston may spend $100,000 on a breast augmentation and tattoos to impress musician John Mayer, who prefers young, voluptuous women, the *Star* laments. Since she is thirty-nine, nearly ten years older than Mayer, Aniston has broken the cultural taboo against women loving young men; therefore, the *Star* suggests, she will have to learn that money cannot prevent heartbreak.

On the other hand, the *Star* avoided the stigma long aimed at same-sex couples. Instead, after noting that the California Supreme Court has ruled bans against homosexual marriages unconstitutional, the weekly featured Ellen DeGeneres and Portia de Rossi in the "Star Shot Moment of the Week." The photo depicts DeGeneres, who won her fourth consecutive daytime Emmy in June, pointing to the ring she gave de Rossi, whom she intends to marry.

US magazine includes a picture of DeGeneres and de Rossi with shots of other **talk show hosts**: Regis Philbin, Jimmy Kimmel, and Tyra Banks. *OK* ran a two-page spread, "Who Will Be First to Wed?" that featured DeGeneres with de Rossi, Melissa Etheridge (singer) with Tammy Lynn Michaels ("Supermom"), Cynthia Nixon with

Christine Marinoni ("a Big Apple–based duo"), television actor Neil Patrick Harris with Broadway actor David Burtka, and actor T. R. Knight with Mark Cornelson, a student sixteen years younger than Knight. *OK* mentions DeGeneres's request to hold the nuptials at the Bush family's Texas ranch. President George W. Bush's daughter, Jenna, who was a guest on DeGeneres's talk show said, "Sure!" according to *OK*. The tabloids always reinforce cultural mores, but sometimes emphasize one over another. In this case, they perhaps stress true love over rigid definitions of family.

The Dead Remain Alive via Tabloids

Like legends, tabloids keep the memory of cultural heroes alive. For example, *OK* chastises Spice Girl singer Victoria Beckham for imitating Elvis Presley, whom most think died on August 16, 1977. Over the years, however, *The Weekly World News*, *Globe*, and *Sun* have announced Elvis sightings. *OK*'s caption under the headshots declares that Beckham may be posh, but even with her pompadour and pout she'll never be the King. *OK*'s writer wonders if Beckham will wear blue suede shoes to complete the look. Probably unintentionally, she resembles Presley, who endures as a Prodigal Son hero in secular mythology as well as in rock and roll.

Grocery-Store Tabloids Grew from the Seeds of Sensationalism

Tabloids resemble their progenitors in the oral tradition even when they adopt the conventions of journalism. Early printing (ballads, broadsides, and newsbooks of the 17th century) celebrated universal themes: murders, natural disasters, unusual births, omens, accidents, and inscrutable occurrences. The Penny Press of the 1830s highlighted these same themes.

Intense focus on celebrities began in the mid-1920s with the birth of advertising and image-making careers in radio and movies that based fame on publicity, not heroism. During Prohibition, entertainers as well as gangsters like Al Capone fascinated media consumers.

The forerunner of American tabloids, the *Daily Graphic,* opened shop in 1872. To depict scenes at grisly murders that were not caught on film, it developed the precursor of "composography," the art of combining photos convincingly. The *Graphic* folded in 1889.

The British have always offered inspiration. In 1905, Alfred Harmsworth, who eventually became Lord Northcliffe, invented the "half-penny illustrated" (as the English called tabloids) with his *Daily Mirror*. The American weekly *National Police Gazette*, an illustrated macabre carnival of rape, murder, cannibalism, prostitution, kidnapping, train wrecks, fires, natural disasters, and sports, especially boxing, had thrived since its founding in 1845. Nevertheless, U.S. publishers ignored tabloids until Lord Northcliffe convinced the Chicago cousins, Joseph Patterson and R. R. McCormick, to start the *New York Daily News* (with Patterson at the helm) in June 1919.

The success of the *News* inspired publishers across the nation to develop tabloids. By 1925, tabloids had adopted the same formula for describing murders that ballads had invoked in the 17th century: "Discovery, Chase, Trial, Death Cell, Punishment," as Winifred Johnston summed it up. As did ballads, the tabloids developed stereotypes: baker, clubman, heiress, society leader, brownstone house, flapper, crooner, torch singer, sleuth, Red, love thief, love nest, love lure, love charm, love potion, and death car. Similar labels existed for celebrities: starlet, matinee idol, Latin lover, queen of the screen, box office hit, cowboy, and leading man or lady.

When Rudolph Valentino died, tabloids treated the silent-movie heartthrob like royalty. Although Valentino's talent in *The Sheik* made him immortal, it could not protect the Latin lover from a perforated ulcer and subsequent blood poisoning. His death on August 23, 1926, at age thirty-one fulfilled ancient plots about heroes, quests, and fate. Fans' passion transformed Valentino into an icon whose name has stayed in the tabloids long after his death. Ghost stories bring back public, secular heroes—like Elvis and Valentino.

Sometimes, exemplars emerge from athletics or exploration. For example, on May 27, 1927, "Lucky Lindy," aviator Charles Lindbergh, inspired a frenzy of tabloid conquering-hero tales about his transatlantic flight of the "Spirit of St. Louis" in 33.5 hours from Long Island, New York, to Paris. Sadly, in 1932, the "theft of the eaglet," as the press referred to the kidnapping of his son, Charles A. Lindbergh, Jr., once again put the famous flier in the spotlight.

In contrast, Mary Pickford, Douglas Fairbanks, Mae West, W. C. Fields, Clara Bow, Harold Lloyd, Janet Gaynor, Joan Crawford, John Barrymore, and Noah Beery needed publicity; even falsified love or vice narratives circulated their names.

Tabloids Move to Supermarkets

People escaped from the grim realities of the Great Depression of 1929 via radio programs and the cinema. In response to despair, many tabloids, including the *News*, changed from sensational rags to respectable publications offering serious coverage as well as gossip and advice. The *Graphic* folded, but the *News*'s series on syphilis won a Pulitzer Prize. Still, Clark Gable, Greta Garbo, Bob Hope, Bing Crosby, Fred Astair, Ginger Rogers, Bette Davis, and Spencer Tracy relied on tabloids and fan magazines to help them shine—as "stars" must do. Industry executives launched *Photoplay* and *Motion Picture Story* in 1911 to create celebrities whose glamour, wealth, and scandals would generate modern fairytales.

After World War II, tabloids were being published in many U.S. cities, covering thrilling murders minutely and continuing to run short news, rumors, gossip, and sports. In 1952, after Generoso Pope purchased the *New York Enquirer,* he changed the name to the *National Enquirer*. He transformed the failing mix of horseracing tips and scandals into a winning cocktail of gore, violence, and celebrity. Pope emphasized horrendous murders, gruesome accidents, unexplained mysteries, and grotesque ironies. Circulation zoomed from the initial 17,000 to 1 million by 1968.

In those days, blood often spiced with black humor, not sex, sold tabloids. Gossip columnists fabricated stories about Barbara Hutton drinking so much that her boy toy had to drag her out of a bar to stop her impromptu strip tease. They said Charles Laughton lay drunk on a pub floor for seven hours before a bartender found him. Headlines and graphic photos underscored detailed accounts of mayhem. The public enjoyed bizarre twists, such as an item about a woman fatally impaling two men with her stiletto pumps.

By 1970, Pope had toned down the *Enquirer* to distribute it in supermarkets rather than at declining newsstands. This new strategy launched the era of checkout-lane tabloids. He learned that regardless of accuracy, fans were not interested in negative news about major heroes like cowboy actor John Wayne and Elvis Presley. They expected tabloids to pay homage instead.

In the 21st century, American Media, Inc., publishes the best-known tabloids in the United States: the *National Enquirer*, the *Star*, the *Weekly World News* (an online venture since September of 2007), the *National Examiner*, the *Globe*, the *Sun,* and *Country Weekly*. Newcomers include glossy magazines *OK* (North and Shell Ltd.), *US* (US Weekly LLC), and *InTouch* and *Life & Style* (both Bauer Publishing Company). In addition, Time, Inc., publishes *People. See also*: **Criminals**; **Early Deaths**; **International Celebrity**; **Magazines' Role**; **Movies' Role**; **Newspapers' Role**; **Politics**; **Sex and Scandal**; **Supermodels**; **Tough Guys**.

Paulette D. Kilmer

For Further Reading

Beasley, Maurine H. "The Emergence of the Modern Media, 1900–1945." In *The Media in America: A History,* 7th ed., ed. William Sloan, 207–308. Northport, AL: Vision Press, 2008.

Bird, Elizabeth S. *For Enquiring Minds: A Cultural Study of Supermarket Tabloids.* Knoxville: University of Tennessee Press, 1992.

Bird, Elizabeth S. "Taking It Personally: Supermarket Tabloids after September 11." In *Journalism after September 11*, ed. Barbie Zelizer and Stuart Allan, 141–159. New York: Routledge, 2002.

Bird, Elizabeth S. "What a Story! Understanding the Audience for Scandal." In *Media Scandals: Morality and Desire in the Popular Culture Marketplace*, 99–121. New York: Columbia University Press, 1997.

Douglas, George H. "Tabloids." In *The Golden Age of the Newspaper*, 225–232. Westport, CT: Greenwood Press, 1999.

www.tvparty.com/tabloids.html.

www.tvparty.com/tabloids2.html.web loc.

TALK SHOW HOSTS

A talk show is a hosted television or radio program on which people discuss a variety of topics. Format is fairly predictable. It is host-centered and defined; a host controls much of the subject matter and tone, making it feel fresh and in the moment, whether the show is live or on tape, in front of an audience or not. The host creates a sense of intimate conversation with the guest and the audience. The host's give and take is structured around expected

King of late-night television Johnny Carson entertains at the 1981 Presidential Inaugural gala. Courtesy of the Department of Defense.

formulas and broadcast segments but appears to be spontaneous. While content can range from entertaining to thought-provoking, employing verbal mudslinging or highbrow conversations, it cannot alienate its advertisers or viewers. It may feature a single guest who discusses his or her work or embrace a panel of guests, usually a group of experts or people with experience in the show's daily focus. Talk show successes are tied to cultural issues and technological changes. These shows often use one of three distinctive formulas: morning magazine-format shows, late-night entertainment, and daytime audience participation.

Morning news talk magazines, featuring news and public affairs alongside entertainment, became familiar with the National Broadcasting Company's (NBC's) pioneering *The Today Show* (1952) with host Dave Garroway and the Columbia Broadcasting System's (CBS's) *Arthur Godfrey Time*. Hosts often come from the journalistic ranks and are expected to manage interviews on newsworthy issues, topics, and people, along with softer entertainment or lifestyle programming in the second or third programming hour. Extending the blurred distinction between morning news and entertainment, shows such as *Live with Regis and Kelly* and *The View* offer affable hosts who lead informal discussions with celebrities, politicians, and experts.

Late-night talk shows, like television's longest-running *Tonight Show* (NBC 1954), feature celebrity guests, **comedy** sketches, and a congenial host serving as social, political, and cultural barometer of public opinion, melding serious issues with entertainment. Late-night talk show hosts are often former stand-up comics, experienced as monologists, social commentators, and emcees. Most such talk shows have an in-house band playing musical interludes, along with an announcer or **sidekick**, and their humor is geared toward a male-dominated sensibility. Examples include *The Late Show with David Letterman*, *Late Night with Conan O'Brien*, and *Jimmy Kimmel Live*. On the syndicated late-night *Arsenio Hall Show* (1989–1994), presidential candidate Bill Clinton played "Heartbreak Hotel" on the saxophone (June 1992) with the house band, boosting Clinton's popularity among minority and young voters.

Daytime audience-participation shows (first attributed to Phil Donahue's 1967 Dayton, Ohio, show) pull the audience into full participation by engaging in direct dialogue with guest experts or celebrities. The host acts as a mediator who stirs live audience questions and represents the at-home audience in raising issues with the guest. Daytime audience hosts often boast public affairs or journalism training (Phil Donahue, Oprah Winfrey, Geraldo Rivera, Dr. Phil McGraw) and act as reporter, teacher, and counselor. Syndication, cable, and independent network competition accelerated an evolution in afternoon talk shows. In the early 1990s, some syndicated shows developed a new breed of confrontational, often sexually explicit tabloid talk shows. The *Jerry Springer Show,* the *Jenny Jones Show,* and *Geraldo* competed to be more edgy and provocative than each other, encouraging audience voyeurism. Guests discussed an emotional or provocative topic (Nazis, incest, fetishes, racism, the Ku Klux Klan), often egged on by the host to make public confessions and try to resolve their problems on camera. Featuring frequent obscenities and in-studio fighting, the shows appeared to be designed for controversy, confrontation, and theatricality. *The Morton Downey, Jr., Show* pioneered taboo talk television with foul language, violent in-studio fights, extremely dysfunctional guests, and an openly hostile host. In 1995, tabloid show outrageousness led to a talk summit attended by Secretary of Health and Human Services Donna Shalala to urge for moderation. The highest-rated talk show in American television history, *The Oprah Winfrey Show* (begun 1986), initially featured her personal confessions; like Donahue, Oprah explored provocative, taboo topics and sensationalistic social

issues. In 2001, Oprah shifted her content in a more spiritually uplifting direction framed by her self-improvement segments, book club, celebrity interviews, and philanthropic issues. By 2003, daytime talk shows (*The Ellen Show*, *The Tyra Banks Show*, *The Martha Stewart Show*) returned to a gentler focus on celebrities and lifestyle topics.

Other talk show formats are designed to cover **politics** and sports. Public affairs and political talk shows feature a host (or hosts) who interview national leaders in politics and public life, **military** leaders, ambassadors, religious leaders, and intellectuals. Most famous are the Sunday morning talk shows: NBC's *Meet the Press*, CBS's *Face the Nation*, American Broadcasting Company's (ABC's) *This Week*, Cable News Network's (CNN's) *Late Edition*, and *Fox News Sunday*. ABC's *Nightline* began during the Iranian hostage crisis and is pitted against the entertainment-focused late-night shows. The syndicated *McLaughlin Group* features five pundits who discuss current political issues in a round-table format. Comedy Central's *The Daily Show with Jon Stewart* and *The Colbert Report* parody political talk shows. Sports talk shows are also popular, ranging from *The Best Damn Sports Show Period* (Fox) to *Around the Horn* and *Pardon the Interruption* (ESPN), covering current sports issues, highlight packages, and statistics.

Parallel to talk television is talk radio, a discussion format about topical issues, individually hosted, featuring guest interviews. A major difference is that talk radio typically includes live conversations between the host and listeners who call in. Audience contributions are usually screened by a show's producer(s) to maximize audience interest, attract advertisers, and showcase the host. As with television, talk radio variations include politics, sports, health, and lifestyles, but shows also are dedicated to the paranormal, conspiracy theories, and fringe science. Closely identified with radio talk are its hosts. Shock jocks push the legal limits of obscenity and public taste with irreverent, often questionable comments. Howard Stern demeans politics and popular culture, joking about taboo subjects. Don Imus innovated by combining sexual banter with significant political discussions involving the media elite. While Stern glorified adolescent teen humor, Imus's show became a critical political must-listen. Conservative host Rush Limbaugh, using humor and antiestablishment talk, emerged as talk radio's number-one force in national politics in 1992. Limbaugh made fun of journalists (the drive-by media), Democrat politicians, and "feminazis," declaring that he had "talent on loan from God." Dwarfed by the more shock-oriented or politically leaning shows, programs such as *Talk of the Nation* (National Public Radio) present serious discourse that combine high journalistic standards and polite treatment of diverse topics and views. Satellite radio and Web Talk Radio have vastly expanded the talk show spectrum, and with podcasting, a talk show is now available for every taste and at any time.

Talk show topics range from tabloid to politics, entertainment to lifestyles. Syndication has allowed a diverse group of talent to establish themselves as celebrity hosts. Talk shows do not require elaborate sets or even an in-person audience. What they do offer is guest interviews and a clever host, entertainment or information, and a familiar, predictable format to meet the audience's needs. *See also*: **African American**; **Athletes**; **Internet's Role**; **Television's Role**.

Beth M. Waggenspack

For Further Reading

Jones, Jeffrey P. *Entertaining Politics: New Political Television and Civic Culture*. Lanham, MD: Rowman & Littlefield, 2004.

Timberg, Bernard. *Television Talk: A History of the TV Talk Show*. Austin: University of Texas Press, 2002.

"History of Talk Radio" (DVD). Kultur Films Inc., 1999.

The Museum of Broadcast Communications. "Talk Shows." www.museum.tv/archives/T/htmlT/talkshows.htm (accessed September 1, 2008).

TELEVISION'S ROLE

Movies feature glamorous, unattainable stars, radio provides intimate contact, but television delivers both celebrity and intimacy to a mass audience. With the advent of television, celebrities became more important than heroes. By the end of its first decade, more than eight of ten U.S. households had televisions, and viewership skyrocketed. Social psychologists noticed that television personalities such as Arthur Godfrey, Dave Garroway, and Art Linkletter—carryovers from radio—projected a familiarity that simulated friendship, a phenomenon termed

Television variety show host Ed Sullivan presents the Beatles in this 1964 show. Courtesy of Photofest.

"parasocial interaction." It was predicted that television would replace real friendships, particularly for lonely people and heavy viewers. Later, news and soap opera researchers found that the parasocial effect was caused by a television personality's reliable presence in the home more than by physical attractiveness or other personal qualities.

Entertainment

Most early television personalities came from radio and burlesque theater.

At first the Hollywood star system eschewed the new medium for fear of overexposure. However, some Hollywood crossovers, such as Lucille Ball, Jackie Gleason, and Raymond Burr achieved great popularity on the small screen. Elvis Presley's first appearance on *The Ed Sullivan Show* (1956) and the "Lucy Goes to the Hospital" episode of *I Love Lucy* (1953) claimed the largest television audiences of all time. Other top-rated shows were the final episodes of *The Fugitive* (1967), *Roots* (1977), *M*A*S*H* (1983), and several Super Bowl games.

The quiz show scandals of 1958–1959 gave the American television audience an early lesson in cynicism about celebrities' constructed personas. Hugely popular game shows such as *$64,000 Question, Dotto,* and *Twenty-One* were caught rigging what appeared to be fair contests. A celebrated champion of *Twenty-One*, Charles Van Doren, who had been featured on the cover of *Time* magazine and on National Broadcasting Company's (NBC's) *Today* as an outstanding American intellectual, admitted to a congressional committee that he had been fed answers by the show's producers and resigned his Columbia University professorship. Eventually, the disgraced producers and hosts continued their lucrative broadcasting careers.

Talk

Reminiscent of Edward R. Murrow's *Person to Person* (1953–1961) celebrity talk show for the Columbia Broadcasting System (CBS), *Lifestyles of the Rich and Famous* (1984–1995) starring Robin Leach capitalized on America's fascination with celebrities. Actors promoting their movie and television vehicles became staple guests of network morning news and late-night talk shows, as well as daytime syndicated shows such as *Regis Philbin, Rosie O'Donnell Show, Ellen DeGeneres Show,* and *The View.* Pioneered by the *Phil Donohue Show*'s (1970–1996) controversial public affairs segments, tabloid talk shows gravitated toward celebrities and reality guests. *Oprah!* became the highest-rated talk show in history, spawning a confessional style of public dialogue. Oprah Winfrey's media empire of worldwide television syndication, film production, and magazine publishing made her the richest and most philanthropic African American of all time. Other entries in confessional format included *Maury Povich, Jenny Jones, Ricki Lake,* and the *Jerry Springer Show,* which found its own "trash television" market niche. A new generation of news-oriented talk celebrities evolved for cable, including Larry King, Bill O'Reilly, and Chris Matthews. Comedy Central's "fake news" programs *The Daily Show* with Jon Stewart and the *Colbert Report* starring Stephen Colbert repudiated traditional news shows by becoming many U.S. viewers' preferred information sources—the ultimate victory of celebrity over substance.

Television transformed politics by emphasizing style and appearance over substance and statesmanship. The first live presidential debate, between Richard Nixon and John Kennedy in 1960, presaged television's determining role in elections. Kennedy appeared tanned, rested, and confident, whereas Nixon, suffering from a recent leg injury, was pallid and underweight. Radio listeners credited the college-trained debater

Nixon with having won the debate, but television viewers preferred the suave, handsome Kennedy. The debate helped Kennedy win a narrow election and taught Nixon to avoid televised debates when he ran for president again eight years later.

Sports

Television advertising transformed amateur college sports into big-time entertainment business and inflated professional salaries. Faster-paced, telegenic sports such as football and basketball, and even stock car racing, overtook the slow-moving, traditional American pastime of baseball in television audience ratings. Individual sports such as golf and tennis also televised well, with corresponding increases in player winnings. Sports leagues and major universities began to negotiate huge broadcasting deals with the networks, and the major sports championships (the Super Bowl, the World Series, and the Final Four) became the biggest broadcasting and advertising events of the year. The National Football League's (NFL's) Super Bowl became the biggest event of the broadcasting year by commanding the largest worldwide audience and advertising revenues. The NFL delayed the championship by an extra week to increase promotional opportunities. In 2009 NBC will earn $3 million per thirty-second Super Bowl advertising spot.

Athletes and coaches became role models for youth, and every sport touted its "hall of fame" as the ultimate recognition for its celebrity players. After sports leagues were desegregated, celebrity culture was blamed for tempting young African American men to disdain education for the promise of a professional sports career and as a shortcut to celebrity status. Athletes cultivate their celebrity images to attract **endorsement** contracts from advertisers, with endorsement earnings of the big stars eventually dwarfing their player salaries or tournament winnings. Team management hones players' on-screen presence by providing media training, and many athletes extend their sports careers by becoming broadcast announcers and commentators.

Global Celebrity Village

Celebrity culture in turn had a role in legitimizing television. Canadian English professor Marshall McLuhan himself became a celebrity in the 1960s when he described television as a prosocial force that would bring about a "Global Village." "Pop" **artists** of the New York gallery scene such as Andy Warhol and Roy Lichtenstein celebrated television's role in democratizing art. Warhol's famous prediction that, in a television society, everyone would enjoy "fifteen minutes of fame" acknowledged celebrity's fleeting nature and the media's short attention span. Because television was touted as the new panacea for learning, President Lyndon Johnson's Great Society social programs pumped millions of dollars into technologizing schools and universities.

Celebrity culture is driven by the profit motive. With the proliferation of cable television in the 1980s, the three major networks lost substantial audience share. Intense competition, combined with government deregulation, led to a flood of corporate mergers. Five global media conglomerates emerged: Disney,

AOL Time Warner, Viacom, General Electric, and News Corporation. To these are added the technology giants Microsoft, Google, and Yahoo! These megacorporations own television broadcast and cable networks, movie studios, amusement parks, newspapers, magazines, book publishing houses, music publishing, video rentals, computer software, and **Internet** properties. These conglomerates take advantage of media synergies and cross-marketing opportunities to promote celebrity-based entertainment worldwide, which has overtaken manufactured goods as the largest U.S. export. Some critics of the "mediagloms" point to collapsing ownership and control of the media as a threat to the free flow of information on which democracy depends.

News

News media performers became celebrities who literally embodied their stations and networks. The "eyewitness news" format, in which announcers who assumed the role of casual friends sharing "happy talk," came to dominate local news. Having more gravitas, network news celebrities became some of the most admired public figures in America. Suave, erudite NBC coanchors Chet Huntley and David Brinkley dominated ratings in the 1960s, while CBS's gravelly voiced, reassuring anchorman Walter Cronkite was named by polls as the most trusted man in America. Cronkite's special interests in the environment and the space program shaped his network's programming priorities and public awareness. His Vietnam War "quagmire" editorial on February 27, 1968, swayed public opinion against the war and convinced President Lyndon

Johnson not to seek reelection. After the Huntley-Brinkley-Cronkite era, the network anchors took editorial control of their newscasts and became powerful human marketing commodities.

Increased pressure to make news profitable happened at the same time the Federal Communications Commission tabled its *Fairness Doctrine* requirement that broadcasters address controversial issues. Traditional journalistic values of independence, reserve, and devotion to the public good gave way to popularity, sensation, and promotional self-interest. The line between news and entertainment became totally blurred. Starting in late 1980s, so-called tabloid news shows such as *Entertainment Tonight, A Current Affair, Hard Copy, Inside Edition, America's Most Wanted,* and *Unsolved Mysteries* featured celebrity gossip, flashy computer graphics, and recreations of events. Traditional newscasts condescended, but they soon adopted the same techniques. Tabloid shows were popular and much cheaper to produce than traditional news. Their popularity spawned a wave of **reality television** programs, such as *COPS, Survivor,* and *American Idol,* fulfilling Andy Warhol's prediction that anyone can become a celebrity for fifteen minutes. *See also*: **African American; Fan Clubs and Sites; Former Sports Stars as Media Celebrities; Halls of Fame; Television's Role; Temporary Celebrity**.

Russell J. Cook

For Further Reading

Fitzgerald, Terence J., ed. *Celebrity Culture in the United States*. Vol. 80, no. 1, *Reference Shelf Series*. New York: H. W. Wilson, 2008.

Giles, David. "Fame and the 'General Public.'" In *Illusions of Immortality: A Psychology of Fame and Celebrity*. New York: St. Martin's Press, 2000.

Halpern, Jake. *Fame Junkies: The Hidden Truth Behind America's Favorite Addiction*. Boston: Houghton Mifflin, 2007.

Marshall, P. David. "Television's Construction of the Celebrity." In *Celebrity and Power: Fame in Contemporary Culture*. Minneapolis: University of Minnesota Press, 1997.

Schickel, Richard. "Coherent Lives." In *Intimate Strangers: The Culture of Celebrity in America*. Chicago: Ivan R. Dee, 2000.

Museum of Broadcast Communications Archives. http://www.museum.tv/archives.

TEMPORARY CELEBRITY

The late celebrity **artist** Andy Warhol has been widely quoted as remarking, "In the future everybody will be world-famous for fifteen minutes." His use of hyperbole pointed out the hold that celebrity has on modern culture, a condition in which mass-mediated fame creates such a need for celebrity that a great many normally private people flash brightly onto the public screen, then—poof—are just as quickly returned to privacy. This is one area of celebrity about which relatively little has been written. In the late 1970s, author James Monaco gave brief mention to accidental celebrities, calling them "quasars." Twenty years later, writer David Brode published a book about individuals who had appeared in only one film, and a few years thereafter, author Chris Rojek gave mention to one-hit singers, lottery winners, **stalkers**, and other people who achieved temporary fame, calling them "celetoids." Rojek also wrote briefly about people who assumed fictitious and usually temporary show-business identities, such as the character Ali G, played on television by comedian Sacha Baron Cohen; Rojek called such people "celeactors." None of these new terms appears to have caught on, but the never-diminishing content needs of the media are such that a considerable number of these "shooting stars" come in a steady stream to media audiences from either the news or from various parts of the entertainment world. Some such individuals gained their temporary celebrity by something good they have done, others by villainy, and still others by having been victims of misfortune. A few temporary celebrities are hard to classify as to how they achieved their fleeting acclaim.

Only a few decades ago, many of our nation's biggest celebrities were people who became known for their work outside the entertainment field. Today, only a few political or **military** figures become widely recognized celebrities, especially among the young. It is shocking yet somehow understandable in 21st-century America that in a 2005 research study, the head shot of a successful contestant on the television show *Jeopardy*, Ken Jennings, was twice as well recognized by a large group of intelligent university students as was that of former President Gerald Ford. The adage *Sic transit Gloria mundi* seems to remain true: worldly glory does indeed pass fleetingly away, especially in **politics**.

In the 21st century, Americans tend to remember best those individuals who entertain them, especially those who look very, very good while doing so. Most U.S. megacelebrities look considerably better than the rest of us. Examples are easy to find: Julia Roberts, Keira Knightley, the late Princess Diana, Paris Hilton, Tom Cruise, or George Clooney, to name a few. Others who entertain well enough to achieve high-wattage celebrity are more powerful than most of their audience, witness sports stars such as Barry Bonds, Hulk Hogan, Lance Armstrong, Venus and Serena Williams, and Shaquille O'Neal. Other people—Oprah Winfrey, or Mick Jagger, or Woody Allen—manage to beat the odds, becoming major, durable celebrities by other means. All these public figures hold onto their celebrity for long periods of time, but what of those individuals who go from zero to hero (or miscreant) and back again to zero in terms of their familiarity to the general public? Just who are these people? From what sources do they come to our attention?

Some such people achieve their now-you-see-'em, now-you-don't celebrity in what might be thought of as our news culture. Surprisingly few of them can be called heroes, people such as Sally Ride, the first U.S. woman in space (1983); Oseola McCarthy, who in 1995 became known as the washerwoman philanthropist; Lenny Skutnik, who in January 1982 jumped into the icy Potomac River and saved a woman from drowning. For every temporary celebrity hero, there appear to be dozens of celebrity villains. Worst of them all are the mass or serial killers whose names and faces appear everywhere following their misdeeds and their

captures. David Berkowitz was arrested in 1977 as New York City's so-called Son of Sam serial killer; Ted Bundy was a handsome young man who stalked and killed young women in the 1970s; Jeffrey Dahmer, a cannibalistic serial killer, was at large from the late 1970s until 1991; John Allen Muhammad, the older of the two Beltway snipers, was captured in 2002. Other convicted murderers whose names have been well known to the public include white supremacist Byron De La Beckwith, who in 1963 killed civil rights figure Medgar Evers; Mark David Chapman, who in 1980 shot and killed singer John Lennon; Brynn Hartman, who in 1998 killed her husband, comedian Phil Hartman; Edgar Ray Killen, aptly named Baptist minister convicted of civil rights murders many years after his crimes in the 1960s; and Ronny Zamora, teenage killer of an elderly Miami woman and a lad who claimed to have been brainwashed by television crime shows.

Other recipients of celebrity infamy are spies and traitors, such as Robert Hanssen, Federal Bureau of Investigation (FBI) agent who spied for the Soviet Union, or John Walker Lindh, the so-called American Taliban caught in Afghanistan. Rapists and other sex-crime offenders are also temporary celebrities. Max Factor cosmetics heir Andrew Luster, caught in 2003, was a serial rapist, and Florida congress member Mark Foley disgraced himself in 2006 by writing suggestive e-mails to a congressional page. Similarly, Father John Geoghan was a notorious pedophile priest killed in his cell in 2003; Jim and Tammy Faye Bakker bilked the trusting through their Praise the Lord (PTL) Club; and homophobic preacher Fred Phelps of Kansas disgraced his Baptist faith, as did North Carolina minister Chan Chandler, who in 2004 kicked out church members out if they would not support George W. Bush for president. By like token, government, military, and business figures sometimes disgrace themselves and in the process become temporary celebrities. Congress member John Jenrette of South Carolina was caught in the ABSCAM FBI sting operation in 1980 for influence peddling; financier Billie Sol Estes was found guilty of a large-scale farm subsidy scam in the 1950s; Lt. William Calley led the infamous My Lai Massacre platoon in Vietnam; and David Vitter, pro-family values senator from Louisiana, was caught in 2007 with his pants down as a client of prostitutes. Disgraced media figures have included Edward Von Kloberg, flamboyant public relations representative for truly dreadful clients; Charles Van Doren, who confessed to fraudulent quiz show wins in the 1950s; and Jayson Blair, fast-track *New York Times* reporter fired in 2003 for plagiarism and other offenses.

Another kind of celebrity by way of notoriety is the hoaxer. Some of these figures do real harm, as did Elizabeth Chapman, who claimed her son Justin had an intelligence quotient of 298 and placed enormous pressure on the boy; Clifford Irving, who tricked publisher McGraw-Hill with his fake biography of reclusive tycoon Howard Hughes; and James Guckert, who was planted by the George W. Bush White House to ask fluff questions at presidential press conferences in the guise of "reporter" Jeff Gannon. Other hoaxers are benign, such as Atlanta radio host Ludlow Porch, who concocted a

spurious campaign ostensibly to stamp out animal nudity but actually to show up people's naïve and literal nature. Somewhere in between was Rosie Ruiz, who donned a track outfit and leaped in front of the actual runners just before the finish line, "winning" the 1980 Boston Marathon. Men and women who gain their fifteen minutes of fame through their sexual alliances with the wealthy or prominent include *femmes fatale* Tai Collins, a stunning blond who gave then-senator Chuck Robb a highly publicized "backrub"; Fanne Foxe, stripper playmate of influential congress member Wilbur Mills; and Donna Rice, cruise date of Sen. Gary Hart. Each of these liaisons contributed directly to the political demise of the politicians involved. Examples of *hommes fatale* are Clyde Tolson, long-time companion of FBI director and outspoken homophobe J. Edgar Hoover; Scott Thorson, who sued entertainer Liberace for palimony; and Marc Christian, who successfully sued Rock Hudson's estate for the same reason. A miscellany of infamous temporary celebrities includes Andrew Burnett, who in a 2001 fit of road rage, threw a small dog out into traffic; Wanda Holloway, who in 1991 conspired to murder her daughter's cheerleading rivals; Joey Buttafuoco, trouble-prone auto repairman who in 1992 figured in the Long Island Lolita case; and Valerie Solanas, who in 1968 shot and wounded Andy Warhol, thereby gaining her own fifteen minutes of fame.

Not exactly heroes, certainly not villains yet seldom liked for their contributions are whistle-blowers such as Herb Stempel, who exposed the quiz show scandals of the 1950s; Henry Hill, FBI mob informant from Brooklyn; and

Sherron Watkins, who brought the Enron scandal to light. Among the least-remembered temporary celebrities are inventors and other innovators, few of whom have curvy figures, bulging muscles, or electric guitars. Only a few celebrity watchers could likely identify Ray Tomlinson, who in 1971 originated e-mail; Alec Jeffries, who in 1983 developed DNA (Deoxyribonucleic acid) fingerprinting; Stephanie Kwolek, inventor of Kevlar in 1966; or Robert Ledley, who in 1990 invented the CAT (Computerized Axial Tomography) scan.

What governs the length of time a temporary celebrity remains fresh in the American audience's mind remains unproven. Some likely factors, however, are that persons having an unusual name might have a longer temporary celebrity "shelf life." A Herve Villechaize or a Fyvush Finkel might stick in one's mind longer than a Bob Smith or Ann Jones. Another factor might be the personal glamour or lack of same on the part of those who suddenly find themselves temporary household names, and a related factor might be how much entertainment value the person offers to the diversion-hungry public. One might also postulate that those temporary celebrities who are remembered best and longest are those from the world of entertainment. To be considered temporary celebrities, performers could not be a major star or a leading man or woman but instead, individuals who, no matter what else they did, had one iconic role, one song hit, or one sporting feat that allowed him or her to shine at least once. Of all these, one might hypothesize that since popular songs are played and heard for years, the one-hit recording wonders might be the best

remembered of the temporary celebrities of the entertainment culture. Or, one might instead postulate that the best recognized in the entertainment group might be the iconic television character actors, since their audiences both saw and heard them, and usually over time in a series of episodes. Already mentioned above were Fyvush Finkel, who played lawyer Douglas Wambaugh on *Picket Fences,* and the tiny actor Herve Villechaize, who as Tattoo on *Fantasy Island* each week shouted, "Da plane, boss, da plane!" Max Baer, Jethro on *The Beverly Hillbillies,* did such a fine job of playing a yokel that later he had great difficulty finding other roles. Similarly iconic roles were *Northern Exposure*'s native character Ed Chigliak, portrayed by actor Daren Burrows; *Frasier*'s ditsy Roz Doyle, played by Peri Gilpin; Jack McFarland, the gay pal of Will and Grace on the show of the same name, played by Sean Hayes; *M*A*S*H* heavy Major Frank Burns (actor Larry Linville) and from the same show, crazed Central Intelligence Agency officer Colonel Sam Flagg (Edward Winter); the lusty Peg Bundy of *Married With Children*, actress Katey Sagal; and perky *Love Boat* hostess Julie McCoy, actress Lauren Hewes. One of the best of all these show stealers was Polly Holliday, perfectly cast as the diner waitress Flo on the sitcom *Alice.* Other temporary celebrities appeared on variety shows; some examples are Bill Saluga, who, appearing on various programs in the character of Raymond Johnson, would wind up and let fly with, "Oh, you can call me Ray, or you can call me Jay," and Moreno Wenceslao, better known as Senor Wences, on *The Ed Sullivan Show.* Producing one instant celebrity after another have been television's reality shows. Some standouts in these programs have been Richard Hatch and Anh-Tuan "Cao Boi" Bui of *Survivor*, Omarosa Manigault-Stallworth of *The Apprentice,* and Evan Marriott, *Joe Millionaire*'s beefy construction-worker heartthrob. Similarly iconic have been supporting roles in some movies, such as the character Scout in *To Kill a Mockingbird*, played by child actress Mary Badham; the James Bond movies' intimidating strong-arm men Jaws, actor Richard Kiel, and Odd Job, actor Harold Sakata; and Bernice Lee, actress Sonya Wilde, who marries into a wealthy white family in *I Passed for White*.

Entertainment world temporary celebrities of another type are those singers who had only one big hit with which they remain closely identified. From the 1950s, there were Richard Berry's "Louie Louie," Rick Lewis's "Get a Job," Robin Luke's "Susie Darlin'," Sheb Wooley's "The Purple People Eater," and others. The 1960s produced Gene Chandler's "Duke of Earl," Mark Denning's "Teen Angel," Bobbie Gentry's "Ode to Billy Joe," and Boris Pickett's "Monster Mash." One-hit wonders of the 1970s included C. W. McCall's "Convoy," Billy Paul's "Me and Mrs. Jones," Mari Edgemon's "Telephone Man," and Billy Swan's "I Can Help." Recorded in the 1980s were Laurie London's "He's Got the Whole World in His Hands" and Toni Basil's "Mickey." In the 1990s, hits included Right Said Fred's (Richard and Fred Fairbrass) "I'm Too Sexy" and Billy Ray Cyrus's "Achy Breaky Heart."

Whereas sports celebrities tend to be more lasting, a few are remembered for a single remarkable accomplishment, such as the 1990 upset win by James "Buster" Douglas of the heavyweight boxing championship over the formidable Mike Tyson. (Douglas lost the title just as quickly later that year to Evander Holyfield.) Don Larsen is remembered as having pitched the only perfect World Series baseball game, in 1956. Despite her other accomplishments, tennis star Renee Richards is remembered mainly for her sex-change operation, just as former tennis champion Bobby Riggs is stuck with being remembered for his 1973 exhibition-match loss to a woman, Billie Jean King. And who could forget the endearing performance but last-place finish of Eddie "The Eagle" Edwards as he represented Britain in the 1988 Olympic ski-jump competition?

Finally, a modest number of temporary celebrities have come to us from advertising. Espera DeCorti was a Sicilian American who became at least temporarily famous as American Indian "Iron Eyes Cody." Clara Peller was the feisty little old lady known for the way she rasped her Wendy's commercial line, "Where's the beef?" For twenty-seven years, Jan Miner played "Madge the Manicurist" for Palmolive Detergent; Jesse White was the long-suffering "Maytag Repair Man"; and Dick Wilson was Charmin toilet tissue's "Mr. Whipple." Andy Lambros was the cute child actor known as the Oscar Mayer "Bologna Kid," and Benjamin Curtis was "Steven the Dell Dude." Gaining celebrity for appearing in their own companies' commercials and ads were popcorn king Orville Redenbacher, fried chicken king Harland Sanders, Wendy's chief executive Dave Thomas, and Perdue Chicken's chief executive Frank Perdue.

Temporary celebrities today come and go at such a rate that one might better speak of people's fifteen *seconds* of fame. This kind of celebrity can come in many different ways, sometimes when the people involved least expect it, and sometimes in an unwelcome way. But all these "celebrities with a lower-case c" are part of our lives—vivid splashes of color on America's wonderfully varied and ever-changing canvas. *See also*: **Athletes**; **Comedy**; **Criminals**; **Dream Girls**; **Hispanic/Latino**; **International Celebrity**; **Movies' Role**; **News Media Figures**; **Rock and Pop**; **Television's Role**.

Sam G. Riley

For Further Reading

Brode, David. *Once Was Enough: Celebrities (and Others) Who Appeared a Single Time on the Screen*. Secaucus, NJ: Carol Pub., 1997.

Monaco, James. *Celebrity: The Media as Image Makers*. New York: Dell, 1978.

Rojek, Chris. *Celebrity*. London: Reaktion Books, 2001.

www.celebrityblogsburg.blogspot.com.

TOUGH GUYS

From the start, entertainment executives have been convinced that women are from Venus, men are from Mars. Consequently, the leading men of many movies and television crime shows and Westerns have played characters who slugged or shot first and asked questions later, although many male stars, while manly enough, have fallen short of making completely convincing tough guys. To today's viewers, James Cagney, Edward G. Robinson, and Paul Muni seem too old. Jimmy Stewart, Henry Fonda, David Niven, and Cary Grant were much too gentlemanly to be remembered as tough guy actors. The same can be said of James Garner (*The Rockford Files*, 1974–1980), who was too droll; Pierce Brosnan (*Remington Steele*, 1982–1987, and James Bond movies), too elegant; Mike Connors (*Mannix*, 1967–1975), too sophisticated; Telly Savalas (*Kojak*, 1973–1978), too comedic; Dennis Weaver (*McCloud*, 1970–1977), too polite; Peter Falk (*Columbo*, 1971–1978), too bumbling; Craig Stevens (*Peter Gunn*, 1958–1961), too suave; James Drury (*The Virginian*, 1962–1971), too placid; and William Conrad (*Cannon*, 1971–1976), too heavy. In long-ago Westerns, Roy Rogers and Gene Autry could shoot straight but sang and were too mannerly, and except for the singing, the same could be said of The Lone Ranger (Clayton Moore) and Tom Mix. Plenty tough, but covered in the **martial arts** entry, are Chuck Norris, Steven Segal, Jean-Claude Van Damme, Bruce Lee, Jackie Chan, and other practitioners of Asian fighting styles.

The movie or television tough guy must look as though he could physically handle real-life bad guys and must be handy both in hand-to-hand combat and with weapons. To be an entertainment world tough guy, it helps to have a cold stare, firm jaw, and confident attitude. Clever remarks are permitted, but only after having dispatched the villain. Some entertainment-world tough guys are not only physically stronger and more agile than the

Sean Connery, greatest of the various James Bonds, appears in April 2001 with the U.S. Air Force Reserve Pipe Band from Georgia's Robbins Air Force Base. Courtesy of the Department of Defense.

average fellow but prior to their acting careers, held jobs that required real toughness. Some of these macho celebrities have served in the Marine Corps, others excelled in football or other sports, and still others have worked as bouncers or bodyguards.

For Americans who are in or past middle age, the gold standard for tough guy actors remains John Wayne, whose movies were usually Westerns or war films, even though Wayne never actually served in the military. During college, Wayne played football at the University of Southern California and began getting bit parts in movies. His first big role was in a 1930 Western, *The Big Trail*, and his breakthrough came in *Stagecoach* (1939). Movies such as *The Quiet Man* (1952), *The Man Who Shot Liberty Valance* (1962), and *True Grit* (1969) cemented his

reputation as an icon of American swagger and self reliance. In 1975, he played an aging tough guy in *Rooster Cogburn*; and decades before his death in 1979, virtually all Americans could recognize his nickname, The Duke, which was derived from a dog he owned in his youth.

Of the same generation as Wayne was Kirk Douglas (born Issur Danielovitch), son of Jewish immigrants from Russia. He was a college wrestler, even his voice sounded tough, and his cleft chin gave him a distinctive appearance in such films as *Gunfight at the OK Corral* (1957), *Spartacus* (1960), *The List of Adrian Messenger* (1963), and *Seven Days in May* (1964). Another tough guy in this age-group was Jack Palance (born Volodymyr Palahnyuk), son of Ukrainian immigrants. Palance mined coal and boxed professionally before serving in World War II. Reconstructive surgery to repair injuries incurred when a plane in which he was riding caught fire left his face with a diabolical look that served him well in *Shane* (1953), *Requiem for a Heavyweight* (1962), and other action movies. Many television viewers remember the one-armed pushups he did onstage at the 1992 Academy Awards—at age seventy-three. Just as tough was the late Charles Bronson, born Charles Buchinsky to parents who immigrated to America from Lithuania. The compact, muscular Bronson worked in the coal mines before breaking into acting in the 1950s. Among his best-known movies are *The Magnificent Seven* (1960), *The Great Escape* (1963), and, in 1974, *Mr. Majestyk* and *Death Wish*. He continued playing tough guy parts through the mid-1990s.

Rangy 6′2″ actor Lee Marvin introduced a new brand of attitude into his tough guy roles, having first served in combat as a Marine in World War II. He appeared in *The Dirty Dozen* (1967) and had other menacing roles before getting to show his comedic side in *Cat Ballou* (1965) and his singing ability in *Paint Your Wagon* (1969). Marvin studied martial arts for many years, some of that time with Bruce Lee.

A hugely popular tough guy actor is Clint Eastwood, whose big break was as role Rowdy Yates in the popular television Western *Rawhide* (1959–1966). He added to his reputation as a squinty-eyed shootist in such "spaghetti Westerns" as *A Fistful of Dollars* (1964) and *The Good, the Bad and the Ugly* (1960), in which his role was that of an **anti-hero**. Some of his fans remember him most as Harry Callahan (Dirty Harry), launched in 1971 in *Play Misty*

for Me, which prompted four sequels. *High Plains Drifter* (1973) and *The Outlaw Josey Wales* (1976) furthered his fame as an Old West good-bad guy.

Of comparable megapopularity is Scottish actor Sean Connery, who had been a bodybuilder before 1962, when he became the first of several actors to portray Commander James Bond, Agent 007 in Her Majesty's Secret Service. In seven of these films, Connery gave Bond a truly commanding presence and was never rivaled for sheer masculinity until the assumption of this role by English actor Daniel Craig. Other James Bonds have been George Lazenby, Roger Moore, and Pierce Brosnan.

Small for a tough guy, yet quick and wiry was Steve McQueen, who lent an air of devil-may-care "cool" to action roles. The former Marine first came to public attention in 1958 in the television series *Wanted Dead or Alive*. He moved to the big screen in 1960 in *The Magnificent Seven* and three years later appeared in *The Great Escape*. In *Bullitt* (1968), McQueen drove in one of Hollywood's best-ever car chases, and he was allowed greater acting latitude in *Papillon* (1973). The sleepy-eyed McQueen died at age fifty following surgery.

Lacking handsome good looks, yet having a rugged physical presence is another ex-Marine, Gene Hackman, who played Popeye Doyle in *The French Connection* (1971) and appeared in *The Poseidon Adventure* (1972) and *A Bridge Too Far* (1977). Soon thereafter, he played villain Lex Luthor in two *Superman* movies (1978 and 1980). A convincing although often comedic tough guy is Burt Reynolds, who played college football and was a bouncer and dockworker before landing the blacksmith role on *Gunsmoke* in 1962; his talent was fully recognized in the movie *Deliverance* (1972). In *Smokey and the Bandit* (1977) and *The Cannonball Run* (1981), Reynolds played action roles while giving viewers subtle indications that he knew those films were not of earthshaking quality yet he was having great fun making them. Born to play hard-nosed, sinister roles, former Marine Harvey Keitel appeared in *Mean Streets* (1973), *Thelma and Louise* (1991), *Reservoir Dogs* (1992), *The Piano* (1993), and *Pulp Fiction* (1994). In 2008, he continues to land such roles.

Movie tough guys come in many varieties. Bringing a distinctive persona to his roles, and one of the most financially successful of them all, Harrison Ford has been in many films but will be most remembered as sharp-tongued pilot Han Solo in the *Star Wars* series (1977, 1980, 1983, 1999, 2002, 2005) and as archaeologist *Indiana Jones* (1981, 1984, 1989, 2008) in that blockbuster series, just about the only movies in which the tough guy is a professor. Also having played recurring roles is Sylvester Stallone, who is South Philadelphia personified and who has played underdog boxer Rocky Balboa in the *Rocky* series, launched in 1976, and one-man army John Rambo in the *Rambo* movies, dating from 1982.

James Caan plays tough with teeth-gritting ferocity. He was a football player in both *The Rain People* (1969) and *Brian's Song* (1971), the impetuous Santino in *The Godfather* (1972), and a safecracker in *Thief* (1981). Caan took a suitably tough television role in 2003 in the series *Las Vegas*. A truly accomplished actor who makes a convincing

tough guy is Robert De Niro, the young Vito Corleone in *The Godfather, Part II* (1974) and two years later the tough-talking cabbie in *Taxi Driver*. He appeared in *The Deer Hunter* in 1978 and was at his semicrazed best as a boxer in *Raging Bull* (1980), and at his most menacing in *Cape Fear* (1991).

Compact and dependable-looking Tommy Lee Jones is a cum laude graduate of Harvard University, where he also played football. Some of the most popular of his many movie roles have been in *The Fugitive* (1993), *Batman Forever* (1995), *Rules of Engagement* (2000), and, in 2007, *No Country for Old Men* and *In the Valley of Elah*.

Now the governor of California, Austrian American Arnold Schwarzenegger became the world's most famous bodybuilder and won Mr. Olympia and Mr. Universe multiple times before getting into the movies. The 6'1.5" actor had no trouble looking tough in movies such as *Conan the Barbarian* (1982) and the *Terminator* series, which began in 1984. Schwarzenegger took a cue from Clint Eastwood by uttering snappy one-liners after having crushed his villainous opponents. A canny businessman, "The Gubanator" is now one of Hollywood's wealthiest celebrities. No account of durable tough-guy actors would be complete without Bruce Willis, closely identified with his portrayal of John McClane in the *Die Hard* series, dating from 1988. Although never having been in the armed forces, Willis is an outspoken supporter of the U.S. military, and before becoming an actor, briefly worked as a private investigator. Even more outspoken than Willis is Australian American Mel Gibson, a handsome, strongly built actor whose first big role was in the futuristic, immensely profitable Australian movie *Mad Max* (1979) and its three sequels. He costarred with Danny Glover in the *Lethal Weapon* movies, which began in 1987, and in 1995 was star and director of *Braveheart*. Gibson's reputation suffered a setback in 2006 when he made drunken, anti-Semitic comments while being **arrested** for driving under the influence.

A new generation of tough guy actors was ushered in by another Australian, Russell Crowe, who appeared in *L.A. Confidential* (1997) and in 2001 won many awards for *Gladiator*. After a successful non–tough guy part in *A Beautiful Mind* (2001), Crowe toughened back up for *Cinderella Man* (2005) and *American Gangster* (2007). His reputation as a tough guy has been underlined by his penchant for losing his temper and physically lashing out at people who irritate him in real life.

Except for a handful of tough guy celebrities whose birth names were extremely hard for U.S. audiences to pronounce or remember, most of the actors mentioned here worked under their original names. Not so for Vin Diesel, who was born Mark Vincent and who adopted his pseudonym while working as a bouncer. Diesel played the anti-hero role of Riddick in *Pitch Black* (2000), a hero in *The Fast and the Furious* (2001), and returned for a second Riddick movie in 2004. A new tough guy who has been well received by U.S. audiences is Daniel Craig, who played in *Lara Croft: Tomb Raider* (2001) and in *Layer Cake* (2004). His career shot skyward in 2006 when he stepped into the role of James Bond in *Casino Royale*. Among the macho actors who often play villain parts is Spaniard Javier Bardem, who gave a chilling performance in *No Country for Old Men* (2007); and one of the most convincingly intimidating new action heroes is Dwayne Johnson, better known by his ring name, The Rock. Johnson played college football, was a nine-time professional wrestling champion, and got his breakthrough movie role in 2001 in *The Scorpion King*. Half Samoan, half black, Johnson has muscles in places where most men do not even have places and brought in an enormous paycheck in *Walking Tall* (2004).

Television, too, has had its share of tough guys. Stacy Keach is closely identified with his private eye role in the three *Mike Hammer* series, which covered six years beginning in 1984, the year of his arrest in London for possession of cocaine. His two-fisted screen image seems at odds with his degrees from Berkeley and Yale and his experience in England as a Fulbright Scholar. Another imposing actor of similar age is Tom Selleck. Despite his 6'4" height and husky build, his preacting background included nothing rougher than basketball and modeling. After a supporting role with star James Garner on *The Rockford Files*, Selleck was cast in 1980 as Thomas Magnum on the Hawaii-set *Magnum, P.I.,* which lasted for eight seasons.

The title character of the detective show *Spenser: For Hire* (1983–1988) was Robert Urich, who was reasonably tough but was upstaged in steely toughness by Avery Brooks, who played the character Hawk. Brooks, who holds a master of fine arts from Rutgers, also sings and is a theater professor at his alma mater. A second tough guy who upstaged the lead character on an action show is mohawk-sporting Mr. T (born Lawrence Tureaud), who played B. A. Baracus on *The A-Team* (1983–1987), which starred George

Peppard. Rare is the long-time television viewer who does not recall Mr. T's famous line, "I pity the fool." Tureaud was an Army MP (military police officer), bouncer, and highly paid bodyguard to the likes of Steve McQueen, Bruce Lee, and boxers Leon Spinks and Joe Frazier.

Other television tough guys appeared in that medium's Westerns, especially popular in the late 1950s and the 1960s. One of the roughest, toughest such characters was Paladin, played with great menace by Richard Boone on the series *Have Gun—Will Travel* (1957–1963). The show had little plot and largely consisted of Paladin beating the daylights out of one hapless villain after another. Following this series, Boone himself turned to villain roles in a number of movies. Not remotely as mean, but with a looming 6'7" presence was James Arness, for twenty seasons Marshall Matt Dillon on *Gunsmoke* (1955–1975). Like Boone, Arness had fought in World War II. Almost as tall at 6'6" and more powerfully built is Clint Walker, who played Cheyenne Bodie on *Cheyenne* (1955–1962).

At roughly 300 pounds, 6'3" former bouncer Dan Blocker was the most massive of cowboy tough guys. From 1959 to 1973, he was Eric "Hoss" Cartright on *Bonanza*. When an ornery polecat would threaten a family of greenhorn settlers or his younger brother, Little Joe, played by Michael Landon, Hoss would lose his customarily sweet temperament and lower the boom.

In most Westerns, homesteaders were the people in need of the hero's protection, but in *The Rifleman* (1958–1963), Kevin "Chuck" Connors played fast-shooting homesteader Lucas McCain, also unusual in that he drilled the bad guys with a rifle rather than the customary six-gun. Connors is the only movie tough guy to have played both professional basketball and baseball. His most unusual fan was the Soviet Union's Leonid Brezhnev, who granted special permission for *The Rifleman* to be aired in the U.S.S.R. Smaller, but rattlesnake fast was Robert Conrad (born Conrad Robert Falk), Secret Service agent James West on *The Wild, Wild West* (1965–1969). *See also*: **Athletes; International Celebrity; Military Celebrity; Movies' Role; Pseudonyms; Television's Role.**

Sam G. Riley

For Further Reading

Bracken, Michael. *Fedora: Private Eyes and Tough Guys.* Doylestown, PA: Wildside Press, 2001.

Hossent, Harry. *Gangster Movies: Gangsters, Hoodlums and Tough Guys of the Screen.* London: Octopus Books, 1974.

Osgerby, Bill, and Anna Gough-Yates. *Action TV: Tough Guys, Smooth Operators and Foxy Chicks.* London and New York: Routledge, 2001.

Parish, James Robert. *The Tough Guys.* New Rochelle, NY: Arlington House, 1976.

Schlossheimer, Michael. *Gunmen and Gangsters: Profiles of Nine Actors Who Portrayed Memorable Screen Tough Guys.* Jefferson, NC: McFarland, 2002.

www.popculturist.net/movie-tough-guys.

www.suspense-movies.com/articles.

Selected Bibliography

Alger, Dean. *Megamedia: How Giant Corporations Dominate Mass Media, Distort Competition, and Endanger Democracy.* Lanham, MD: Rowman & Littlefield, 1998.

Altschuler, Glenn C. *All Shook Up: How Rock 'n' Roll Changed America.* Oxford; New York: Oxford University Press, 2003.

Amende, Coral. *Hollywood Confidential.* New York: Plume/Penguin, 1997.

Anderson, Iain. *This Is Our Music: Free Jazz, the Sixties, and American Culture.* Philadelphia: University of Pennsylvania Press, 2007.

Anderson, Robin. *Consumer Culture and TV Programming.* Boulder, CO: Westview, 1995.

Andrejevic, Mark. *Reality TV: The Art of Being Watched.* Lanham, MD: Rowman & Littlefield, 2004.

Andrews, David L., and Steven J. Jackson. *Sport Stars: The Cultural Politics of Sporting Celebrity.* London, New York: Routledge, 2001.

Anger, Kenneth. *Hollywood Babylon.* New York: Dell, 1975.

———. *Hollywood Babylon II.* New York: Dutton, 1984.

Austin, Thomas, and Martin Barker, eds. *Contemporary Hollywood Stardom.* London: Arnold, 2003.

Babington, Bruce, ed. *British Stars and Stardom: From Alma Taylor to Sean Connery.* Manchester, UK: Manchester University Press, 2001.

Banet-Weiser, Sarah. *Kids Rule! Nickelodeon and Consumer Citizenship.* Durham, NC: Duke University Press, 2007.

Barbas, Samantha. *Movie Crazy: Fans, Stars, and the Cult of Celebrity.* New York: Palgrave, 2001.

Barraclough, David. *Hollywood Heaven: From Valentino to John Belushi: The Film Stars Who Died Young.* London: Apple, 1991.

Barron, Lee. "'Elizabeth Hurley Is More Than a Model': Stars and Career Diversification in Contemporary Media." *Journal of Popular Culture* 39 (August 2006): 523–545.

Bauman, Zygmunt. "Consuming Life." *Journal of Consumer Culture* 1 (2001): 5–29.

Baumgartner, Jody C., and Jonathan S. Morris, eds. *Laughing Matters: Humor and American Politics in the Media Age.* New York: Routledge, 2008.

Bennett, W. Lance. *News: The Politics of Illusion,* 3rd ed. White Plains, NY: Longman, 1996.

Berlin, Joey. *Toxic Fame: Celebrities Speak on Stardom.* Detroit, MI: Visible Ink Press, 1996.

Bielby, Denise D. and C. Lee Harrington. *Global TV: Exporting Television and*

Culture in the World Market. New York: New York University Press, 2008.

Biressi, Anita, and Heather Nunn. *Reality TV: Realism and Revelation*, London: Wall-flower, 2005.

———. *The Tabloid Culture Reader*. Berkshire, UK: Open Universtiy Press, 2008.

Biskind, Peter. *Easy Riders, Raging Bulls: How the Sex-Drugs-and-Rock 'n' Roll Generation Saved Hollywood*. New York: Simon & Schuster, 1998.

Blake, David Haven. *Walt Whitman and the Culture of American Celebrity*. New Haven, CT: Yale University Press, 2006.

Blue, Anthony Dias. *Celebrity Chefs across America*. New York: RR Donnelly & Sons, 2000.

Blum, Virginia L. *Flesh Wounds: The Culture of Cosmetic Surgery*. Berkeley: University of California Press, 2003.

Bogle, Donald. *Bright Boulevards, Bold Dreams: the Story of Black Hollywood*. New York: One World Ballantine Books, 2005.

Bonds, Ray. *Movie Stars*. Edison, NJ: Chartwell, Books, 2006.

Bonner, Francis. *Ordinary Television: Analyzing Popular TV*. London: Sage, 2003.

Boorstin, Daniel. *The Image: A Guide to Pseudo-Events in America*. New York: Atheneum, 1987.

Boorstin, Daniel, and Ruth Frankel Boorstin. *Hidden History*. New York: Harper & Row, 1987.

Brasch, Walter M. *Sex and the Single Beer Can: Probing the Media and American Culture*. Spokane, WA: Marquette Books, 2007.

Braudy, Leo. *The Frenzy of Renown: Fame and Its History*. New York: Vintage Books, 1997.

Breitbart, Andrew, and Mark C. Ebner. *Hollywood Interrupted: Insanity Chic in Babylon—the Case against Celebrity*. New York: Wiley, 2004.

Brenton, Sam, and Reuben Cohen. *Shooting People: Adventures in Reality TV*. London: Sage, 2003.

Briggs, Asa, and Peter Burk. *A Social History of the Media: From Gutenberg to the Internet*. Cambridge, MA: Polity Press, 2002.

Brode, Douglas. *Once Was Enough: Celebrities (and Others) Who Appeared a Single Time on the Screen*. Secaucus, NJ: Carol Pub., 1997.

Brown, Tina. *The Diana Chronicles*. New York: Doubleday, 2007.

Cameron-Wilson, James. *Young Hollywood*. Lanham, MD: Madison Books, 1994.

Campbell, Beatrix. *Diana, Princess of Wales: How Sexual Politics Shook the Monarchy*. London: Women's Press, 1998.

Campbell, James T. "Print the Legend: John Wayne and Postwar American Culture." *Reviews in American History* 28 (2000): 465–477.

Carr, Graham. "Visualizing 'The Sound of Genius': Glenn Gould and the Culture of Celebrity in the 1950s." *Journal of Canadian Studies* 40 (Autumn 2006): 5–42.

Cashmore, Ernest. *Celebrity/Culture*. Abingdon, England and New York: Routledge, 2006.

Cashmore, Ernest, and A. Parker. "One David Beckham? Celebrity, Masculinity and the Soccerati." *Sociology of Sport Journal* 20 (2003): 214–231.

Chang, Jeff. *Can't Stop, Won't Stop: a History of the Hip-Hop Generation*. New York: St. Martin's Press, 2005.

Chung, Heejoon. "Sport Star vs. Rock Star in Globalizing Popular Culture: Similarities, Difference and Paradox in Discussion of Celebrities." *International Review for the Sociology of Sport* 38 (2003): 99–108.

Collins, Gail. *Scorpion Tongues: Gossip, Celebrity, and American Politics*. New York: William Morrow, 1998.

Corner, John, and Dick Pels, eds. *Media and the Restyling of Politics: Consumerism, Celebrity and Cynicism*. London: Thousand Oaks 2003.

Couldry, Nicki. *The Place of Media Power: Pilgrims and Witnesses of the Media Age*. London: Routledge, 2000.

Cowen, Tyler. *What Price Fame?* Cambridge, MA: Harvard University Press, 2000.

Crawford, Gary. *Consuming Sport: Fans, Sport and Culture.* London and New York: Routledge, 2004.

Cripps, Thomas. *Making Movies Black: The Hollywood Message Movie from World War II to the Civil Rights Era.* New York: Oxford University Press, 1993.

Cunneff, Tom. *Hollywood on the Links: A Collection of the Greatest Celebrity Golf Stories of All Time.* Lincolnwood, IL: Contemporary Books, 1998.

Currid, Elizabeth. *The Warhol Economy: How Fashion, Art and Music Drive New York City.* Princeton, NJ: Princeton University Press, 2007.

De Cordiva, Richard. *Picture Personalities: The Emergence of the Star System in America.* Champaign: University of Illinois Press, 1990.

De Zengotita, Thomas. "The Numbing of the American Mind." *Harper's Magazine* 304 (April 2002): 33–41.

———. *Mediated: How the Media Shapes Your World and the Way You Live in It.* New York: Bloomsbury, 2005.

Deery, June. "Reality TV as Advertainment." *Popular Communication* 2 (2004): 1–20.

Desser, David. "The Martial Arts Film in the 1990s." In *Film Genre 2000: New Critical Essays,* ed. by Wheeler Winston Dixon, 77–109. Albany: State University of New York Press, 2000.

Dixon, Wheeler W. *Disaster and Memory: Celebrity Culture and the Crisis of Hollywood Cinema.* New York: Columbia University Press, 1999.

Douglas, Susan J. *Where the Girls Are: Growing Up Female with the Mass Media.* New York: Times Books, 1994.

Drane, John William. *Celebrity Culture.* Edinburgh, Scotland: Rutherford House, 2005.

Drucker, Susan J., and Robert S. Cathcart. *American Heroes in a Media Age.* Cresskill, NJ: Hampton Press, 1994.

Dyer, Richard. *Heavenly Bodies: Film Stars and Society.* New York: St. Martin's Press, 1986.

———. *Only Entertainment.* New York: Routledge, 2002.

Edge, Alan. *Faith of Our Fathers: Football as a Religion.* London: Mainstream, 1997.

Edwards, Mona Shafer, and Jody Handley. *Captured!: Inside the World of Celebrity Trials.* Santa Monica, CA: Santa Monica Press, 2006.

Elliott, Anthony. *The Mourning of John Lennon.* Berkeley: University of California Press, 1999.

Ellis, Chris, and Julie Ellis. *The Mammoth Book of Celebrity Murders.* New York: Carroll & Graf, 2005.

Ellis, John. *Visible Fictions: Cinema, Television, Video.* London: Routledge, 1992.

Engelmann, Larry. *They Said That! The Wit and Wisdom of Modern Celebrity Culture.* Los Angeles: Renaissance Books, 2000.

Evans, Andrew, and Glenn Wilson. *Fame: The Psychology of Stardom.* London: Vision Paperbacks, 1999.

Evans, Christopher H., and William R. Herzog. *The Faith of 50 Million: Baseball, Religion, and American Culture.* Louisville, KY: Westminster John Knox Press, 2002.

Evans, Colin. *Super Lawyers: America's Courtroom Celebrities.* Detroit: Visible Ink Press, 1998.

Evans, Jessica, and David Hesmondhalgh. *Understanding Media: Inside Celebrity.* Maidenhead: Open University Press, 2005.

Evans, Peter William, and Celestino Deleyto, eds. *Terms of Endearment: Hollywood Romantic Comedy of the 1980s and 1990s.* Edinburgh: Edinburgh University Press, 1998.

Fallows, James. *Breaking the News: How the Media Undermine American Democracy.* New York: Vintage Books, 1996.

Fischer, Lucy, and Marcia Landy. *Stars: The Film Reader.* New York: Routledge, 2004.

Fiske, John. *Television Culture.* New York: Routledge, 1987.

Fitzgerald, Terence J. *Celebrity Culture in the United States.* New York: H. W. Wilson Co., 2008.

Forman, Murray. *The 'Hood Comes First: Race, Sports, and Place in Rap and Hip-Hop.* Middletown, CT: Wesleyan University Press, 2002.

Fowles, Jib. *Starstruck: Celebrity Performers and the American Public*. Washington, DC: Smithsonian Institution Press, 1992.

Friedlander, Paul, with Peter Miller. *Rock and Roll: a Social History*. Boulder, CO: Westview Press, 2006.

Funkhauser, G. Ray, and Eugene F. Shaw. "How Synthetic Experience Shapes Social Reality." *Journal of Communication* 40 (1990): 75–87.

Gabbard, Krin. *Black Magic: White Hollywood and African American Culture*. New Brunswick, NJ: Rutgers University Press, 2004.

Gabler, Neal. *Winchell: Gossip, Power, and the Culture of Celebrity*. New York: Knopf, 1994.

Gamson, Joshua. *Claims to Fame: Celebrity in Contemporary America*. Berkeley: University of California Press, 1994.

Garland, Robert. *Celebrity in Antiquity: From Media Tarts to Tabloid Queens*. London: Duckworth, 2006.

Garnham, Nicholas, and Fred Inglis. *Capitalism and Communication: Global Culture and the Economics of Information*. London: Sage, 1990.

Gever, Martha. *Entertaining Lesbians: Celebrity, Sexuality, and Self-Invention*. New York: Routledge, 2003.

Gianos, Phillip L. *Politics and Politicians in American Film*. Westport, CT: Praeger, 1998.

Giles, David. *Illusions of Immortality: a Psychology of Fame and Celebrity*. New York: St. Martin's Press, 1999.

Gitlin, Todd. *Media Unlimited: How the Torrent of Images and Sounds Overwhelms Our Lives*. New York: Metropolitan Books, 2001.

Giulianotti, Richard, and Norman Bonney. *Football, Violence, and Social Identity*. London and New York: Rouledge, 1994.

Glass, Loren Daniel. *Authors Inc.: Literary Celebrity in the Modern United States, 1880–1980*. New York: New York University Press, 2004.

Gledhill, Catharine, ed. *Stardom: Industry of Desire*. London: Routledge, 1991.

Gomery, Douglas. *The Hollywood Studio System: A History*. London: British Film Institute, 2005.

Goodwin, Andrew. *Dancing in the Distraction Factory: Music Television and Popular Culture*. Minneapolis: University of Minnesota Press, 1992.

Grace, Nancy, and Diane Clehane. *Objection! How High-Priced Defense Attorneys, Celebrity Defendants, and a 24/7 Media Have Hijacked Our Criminal Justice System*. New York: Hyperion, 2005.

Grainge, Paul. *Brand Hollywood: Selling Entertainment in a Global Media Age*. New York: Routledge, 2008.

Gritten, David. *Fame: Stripping Celebrity Bare*. London: Allen Lane, 2002.

Grossman, Lawrence K. *The Electronic Republic*. New York: Penguin, 1995.

Hadleigh, Boze. *Celebrity Feuds!* Dallas, TX: Taylor Pub., 1999.

———. *Celebrity Lies*. Fort Lee, NJ: Barricade Books, 2003.

———. *In or Out? Gay and Straight Celebrities Talk About Themselves and Each Other*. New York: Barricade Books, 2000.

Hall, Donald. "Death as a Career Move." *The Paris Review* 45 (Fall 2003): 255–258.

Hallin, Daniel C. "Sound Bite News: Television Coverage of Elections, 1968–1988." *Journal of Communication* 42 (Spring 1992): 5–24.

Halpern, Jake. "A School for the Starry-Eyed." *Psychology Today* 39 (November/December 2006): 84–88.

Harrington, C. Lee, and Denise D. Bielby, eds., *Popular Culture: Production and Consumption*. Oxford: Blackwell, 2001.

Harris, Cheryl, and Alison Alexander, eds. *Theorizing Fandom: Fans, Subculture and Identity*. Cresskill, NJ: Hampton Press, 1998.

Hart, Roderick P. *Seducing America: How Television Charms the Modern Voter*. Oxford: Oxford University Press, 1994.

Hartley, John. *Popular Reality: Journalism, Modernity, Popular Culture*. London: Edward Arnold, 1996.

Harvey, David. *Obsession: Stalking Celebrities*. Dublin, Ireland: Merlin, 2003.

Henderson, Amy. "Media and the Rise of Celebrity Culture." *Organization of American*

Historians Magazine of History 6 (Spring 1992): 1–6.

Holden, Anthony. *Behind the Oscar: The Secret History of the Academy Awards.* New York: Simon & Schuster, 1993.

Holmes, Su, and Sean Redmond. *Framing Celebrity: New Directions in Celebrity Culture.* London, New York: Routledge, 2006.

Holmes, Su, and Deborah Jermyn, eds. *Understanding Reality Television.* London: Routledge, 2004.

Hopkins, Susan. *Girl Heroes: The New Force in Popular Culture.* Sydney: Pluto Press, 2002.

Horfischer, Elsa, and David Hornfischer. *Mother Knew Best: Wit and Wisdom From the Moms of Celebrities.* Thorndike, ME: G.K. Hall, 1999.

Horne, John. *Sport in Consumer Culture.* Houndmills: Palgrave Macmillan, 2006.

Howe, Peter. *Paparazzi: And Our Obsession with Celebrity.* New York: Artisan, 2005.

Humphries, Jefferson. *The Red and the Black: Mimetic Desire and the Myth of Celebrity.* Boston: Twayne, 1991.

Illouz, Eva. *Oprah Winfrey and the Glamour of Misery: An Essay on Popular Culture.* New York: Columbia University Press, 2003.

Indiana, Gary. *Schwarzenegger Syndrome: Politics and Celebrity in the Age of Contempt.* New York: New Press, 2005.

Inglis, Ian, ed. *The Beatles, Popular Music, and Society.* London: Macmillan, 2000.

Iyengar, Shanto. *Is Anyone Responsible? How Television Frames Political Issues.* Chicago: University of Chicago Press, 1991.

Jacoby, Susan. *The Age of American Unreason.* New York: Pantheon Books, 2008.

Jaffe, Aaron. *Modernism and the Culture of Celebrity.* Cambridge: Cambridge University Press, 2005.

Jarman, Colin. *Barbed Quotes: Mudslinging, Backstabbing, and Celebrity Dirt Dishing.* Lincolnwood, IL: Contemporary Books, 1999.

Jeffords, Susan. *Hard Bodies: Hollywood Masculinity in the Reagan Era.* New York: Rutgers University Press, 1994.

Jenkins, Henry. *Textual Poachers: Television Fans and Participatory Culture.* New York: Routledge, 1992.

Jenkins, Philip. *Using Murder: The Social Construction of Serial Homicide.* New York: Aldine de Gruyter, 1994.

Karl, Michele. *What Celebrities Collect!* Gretna, LA: Pelican Pub., 2006.

Kaye, Andrew M. *The Pussycat of Prizefighting: Tiger Flowers and the Politics of Black Celebrity.* Athens, GA: University of Georgia Press, 2004.

Kear, Adrian, and Deborah Lynn Steinberg. *Mourning Diana: Nation, Culture, and the Performance of Grief.* London: Routledge, 1999.

Kellner, Douglas. *Media Culture.* London: Routledge, 1995.

Key, Donald R. *The Round-up: A Pictorial History of Western Movie and Television Stars Through the Years.* Madison, NC: Empire Pub., 1995.

Keyes, Cheryl Lynette. *Rap Music and Street Consciousness.* Urbana: University of Illinois Press, 2002.

Keyes, Dick. *True Heroism in a World of Celebrity Counterfeits.* Colorado Springs, CO: NavPress, 1995.

Kimball. Roger. *Art's Prospect: The Challenge of Tradition in an Age of Celebrity.* Chicago: Ivan R. Dee, 2003.

King, Geoff. *Film Comedy.* London: Wallflower Press, 2002.

Klapp, Orin E. *Heroes, Villains, and Fools: The Changing American Character.* Englewood Cliffs, NJ: Prentice-Hall, 1962.

Koestenbaum, Wayne. *Jackie under My Skin: Interpreting an Icon.* New York: Penguin, 1996.

Kozel, William, and Barrie Maguire. *What Were Their Names Before? Real Names of More Than 300 Celebrities and the Stories They Tell.* Chicago: Contemporary Books, 1993.

Kusinitz, Marc, and Solomon H. Snyder. *Celebrity Drug Use.* Bryn Mawr, PA: Chelsea House, 1988.

Lahusen, Christian. *The Rhetoric of Moral Protest: Public Campaigns, Celebrity Endorsement, and Political Mobilization.*

Berlin, Germany and New York: W. de Guyter, 1996.

Langham, Lauren. "Suppose They Gave a Culture War and No One Came: Zippergate and the Carnivalization of Politics." *The American Behavioral Scientist* 46 (December 2002): 501–537.

Lasch, Christopher. *The Culture of Narcissism: American Life in an Age of Diminishing Expectations*. London: Abacus, 1980.

Leff, Leonard. *Hemingway and His Conspirators: Hollywood, Scribners and the Making of American Celebrity Culture*. Lanham, MD: Rowman & Littlefield, 1997.

Lehman, Cheryl R., and Russell M. Moore. *Multinational Culture: Social Impacts of a Global Economy*. Westport, CT: Greenwood Press, 1992.

Leitch, Will, and Jim Cooke. *God Save the Fan: How Preening Sportscasters, Athletes Who Speak in the Third Person, and the Occasional Convicted Quarterback Have Taken the Fun Out of Sports*. New York: Harper, 2008.

Lerner, Barron H. *When Illness Goes Public: Celebrity Patients and How We Look at Medicine*. Baltimore, MD: Johns Hopkins University Press, 2006.

Levin, Martin. *Hollywood and the Great Fan Magazines*. New York: Arbor House, 1970.

Lewis, Lisa A., ed. *The Adoring Audience: Fan Culture and Popular Media*. London: Routledge, 1992.

Liguori, Ann. *A Passion for Golf: Celebrity Musings about the Game*. Dallas, TX: Taylor Pub., 1997.

Livingston, Sonia. *Making Sense of Television: The Psychology of Audience Interpretation*. London: Rutledge, 1990.

Loder, Kurt. *Bat Chain Puller: Rock and Roll in the Age of Celebrity*. New York: St. Martin's Press, 1990.

Lofman, Ron. *Goldmine's Celebrity Vocals: Attempts at Musical Fame from 1500 Major Stars and Supporting Players*. Iola, WI: Krause Publications, 1994.

Long, Kiane. *He's Just My Dad: Portraits of Celebrity Athletes and Their Children*. New York: HarperEntertainment, 2000.

Long, Rob. "Using Your Star Power." *Foreign Policy* (May/June 2006): 74–78.

Lopate, Phillip, ed. *American Movie Critics: An Anthology from the Silents until Now*. New York: Library of America, 2006.

Lowenthal, Leo. *Literature, Popular Culture and Society*. Palo Alto, CA: Pacific Books, 1961.

Lucaire, Ed. *The Celebrity Almanac*. New York: Prentice Hall, 1991.

———. *Celebrity Setbacks: 800 Stars Who Overcame the Odds*. New York: Prentice Hall, 1993.

Lule, Jack. *Daily News, Eternal Stories: The Mythological Role of Journalism*. New York: Guilford Press, 2001.

Lumby, Catherine. *Bad Girls: The Media, Sex and Feminism in the 90s*. Sydney, AU: Allen and Unwin, 1997.

———. *Gotcha! Life in a Tabloid World*. Sydney, AU: Allen and Unwin, 1999.

Lury, Celia. *Consumer Culture*. Cambridge, UK: Polity, 1996.

Madsen, Axel. *The Sewing Circle: Female Stars Who Loved Other Women*. New York: Birch Lane Press, 1995.

Marshall, P. David. *Celebrity and Power: Fame in Contemporary Culture*. Minneapolis: University of Minnesota Press, 1997.

———. *New Media Cultures*. London: Arnold, 2004.

———, ed. *The Celebrity Culture Reader*. New York and London: Routledge, 2006.

McChesney, Robert. *Corporate Media and the Threat to Democracy*. New York: Seven Stories, 1997.

———, Robert Waterman, and Ellen Meiksins. *Capitalism and the Information Age: The Political Economy of the Global Communication Revolution*. New York: Monthly Review Press, 1998.

McCutcheon, Lynn E., Rense Lange, and James Houran. "Conceptualization and Measurement of Celebrity Worship." *British Journal of Psychology* 93 (2002): 67–87.

McDonald, Archie P. *Shooting Stars: Heroes and Heroines of Western Film*. Bloomington: Indiana University Press, 1987.

McLean, Adrienne L., and David A. Cook. *Headline Hollywood: A Century of Film Scandal*. New Brunswick, NJ: Rutgers University Press, 2001.

McLuhan, Marshall. *The Medium Is the Message*. New York: Bantam Books, 1967.

McManus, John H. *Market-Driven Journalism: Let the Citizen Beware?* Thousand Oaks, CA: Sage, 1994.

Melcher, Charles, and Valerie Virga. *National Enquirer: Thirty Years of Unforgettable Images*. New York: Talk Miramax Books, 2001.

Miler, Patrick B., and David Kenneth Wiggins, eds. *Sport and the Color Line: Black Athletes and Race Relations in Twentieth-Century America*. New York: Routledge, 2004.

Miller, Jim. *Flowers in the Dustbin: The Rise of Rock and Roll, 1947–1977*. New York: Simon & Schuster, 1999.

Mills, Robert Lockwood. *The Lindbergh Syndrome: Heroes and Celebrities in a New Gilded Age*. Tucson, AZ: Fenestra Books, 2005.

Monaco, James. *Celebrity: The Media as Image Makers*. New York: Dell Pub. Co., 1978.

Moran, Joe. *Star Authors: Literary Celebrity in America*. Sterling, VA: Pluto Press, 2000.

Moser, Margaret, Michael Bertin, and Bill Crawford. *Movie Stars Do the Dumbest Things*. Los Angeles, CA: Renaissance Books, 1999.

Murray, Susan, and Laurie Ouellette, eds. *Reality TV: Remaking Television Culture*. New York: New York University Press, 2004.

Nash, Jay Robert. *Murder among the Rich and Famous: Celebrity Slayings That Shocked America*. New York: Arlington House, 1987.

Nataraajan, Rajan, and Sudhir K. Chawla. "'Fitness Marketing: Celebrity or Non-Celebrity Endorsement?" *Journal of Professional Services Marketing* 15 (1997): 119–130.

Negra, Diane. *Off-White Hollywood: American Culture and Ethnic Female Stardom*. London: Routledge, 2001.

Neimark, Jill. "The Culture of Celebrity." *Psychology Today* (May/June 1995): 54–57, 87–90.

Neuman, W. Russell. *The Future of the Mass Audience*. Cambridge: Cambridge University Press, 2002.

Newbury, Michael. "Celebrity Watching." *American Literary History* 12 (2000): 272–283.

Nolan, Maggie. *Champagne—and Real Pain: Celebrities in Paris in the Fifties*. Buffalo, NY: Mosaic Press, 1998.

Null, Gary. *Black Hollywood: From 1970 to Today*. Secaucus, NJ: Carol Pub. Group, 1993.

O'Donnell, Rosie. *Celebrity Detox*. New York: Warner Books, 2004.

O'Neal, Bill. *Reel Cowboys: Western Movie Stars Who Thrilled Young Fans and Helped Them Grow Up Decent and Strong*. Austin, TX: Eakin Press, 2000.

O'Neill, Terry. *Celebrity*. London: Little, Brown, 2003.

Ogbar, Jeffrey Ogbanna Green. *Hip-Hop Revolution: The Culture and Politics of Rap*. Lawrence: University Press of Kansas, 2007.

Ogg, Alex, and David Upshal. *The Hip Hop Years: A History of Rap*. New York: Fromm International, 2001.

Olsen, Marilyn. *Arrested! Celebrities Caught in the Act*. New York: Hatherleigh Press, 2002.

Orth, Maureen. *The Importance of Being Famous: Behind the Scenes of the Celebrity-Industrial Complex*. New York: Henry Holt, 2004.

Ouellette, Laurie, and James Hay. *Better Living through Reality TV: Television and Post-Welfare Citizenship*. Malden, MA: Blackwell, 2008.

Parenti, Michael. *Make-Believe Media: The Politics of Entertainment*. New York: St. Martin's Press, 1991.

Parish, James Robert. *Today's Black Hollywood*. New York: Pinnacle Books, 1995.

Peary, Danny. *Cult Movie Stars*. New York: Simon & Schuster, 1991.

Petras, Kathryn, and Ross Petras. *Unusually Stupid Celebrities: A Compendium of All-Star Stupidity*. New York: Villard, 2007.

Phillips, Robert H. *Rising to the Challenge: Celebrities and Their Very Personal Health Stories*. Garden City Park, NY: Avery Pub. Group, 1990.

Ponce de Leon, Charles L. *Self-Exposure: Human Interest Journalism and the Emergence of Celebrity in America, 1890–1940*. Chapel Hill: University of North Carolina Press, 2002.

Postman, Neil. *Amusing Ourselves to Death*. New York: Penguin, 1985.

Poutain, Dick, and David Robins. *Cool Rules: Anatomy of an Attitude*. London: Reaktion, 2000.

Prindle, David F. *Risky Business: The Political Economy of Hollywood*. Boulder, CO: Westview Press, 1993.

Quinlan, David. *Quinlan's Illustrated Registry of Film Stars*. New York: H. Holt, 1991.

———. *The Film Lover's Companion: An A to Z Guide to 2,000 Stars and the Movies They Made*. Secaucus, NJ: Carol Pub. Group, 1997.

Ramsey, Guthrie P. *Race Music: Black Cultures from Bebop to Hip-Hop*. Berkeley: University of California Press, 2003.

Redfern, Nicholas. *Celebrity Secrets: Government Files on the Rich and Famous*. New York: Paraview Pocket Books, 2007.

Rein, Irving J., Philip Kotler, and Martin R. Stoller. *High Visibility: The Making and Marketing of Professionals into Celebrities*. Lincolnwood, IL: NTC Pub. Group, 1997.

Reynolds, Joshua, Martin Posle, Mark Hallett, Tim Clayton, and S. K. Tillyard. *Joshua Reynolds: The Creation of Celebrity*. London: Tate, 2005.

Riesman, David. *The Lonely Crowd: A Study of the Changing American Character*. New York: Yale University Press, 1950.

Ritzer, George. *The McDonaldization of Society*. Thousand Oaks, CA: Pine Forge Press, 1993.

Robinson, John P., and Mark R. Levy. "News Media and the Informed Public." *Journal of Communication* 46 (1996): 129–135.

Roche, George Charles. *A World without Heroes: The Modern Tragedy*. Hillsdale, MI: Hillsdale College Press, 1987.

Rojek, Chris. *Celebrity*. London: Reaktion Books, 2001.

Rose, Tricia. *Black Noise: Rap Music and Black Culture in Contemporary America*. Hanover, NH: University Press of New England, 1994.

Ross, Andrew. *No Respect: Intellectuals and Popular Culture*. New York: Routledge, 1989.

Ryan, Bill. *Making Capital from Culture: The Corporate Form of Capitalist Cultural Production*. Berlin and New York: Walter de Gruyter, 1992.

Sabato, Larry. *Feeding Frenzy: How Attack Journalism Has Transformed American Politics*. New York: The Free Press, 1991.

Salmon, R. "Signs of Intimacy: The Literary Celebrity in an Age of Interviewing." *Victorian Literature and Culture* 25 (1997): 159–177.

Samuels, Allison. *Off the Record: A Reporter Unveils the Celebrity Worlds of Hollywood, Hip Hop and Sports*. New York: Amistad/HarperCollins, 2007.

Sanders, John. *Celebrity Slayings That Shocked the World*. London: True Crime Library, 2001.

Sayre, Shay. *Entertainment Marketing and Communication: Selling Branded Performance, People, and Places*. Saddle River, NJ: Pearson Education, Inc., 2008.

Scheurer, Timothy E. *The Age of Rock*. Bowling Green, OH: Bowling Green University Popular Press, 1989.

Schickel, Richard. *Intimate Strangers: The Culture of Celebrity*. Garden City, NY: Doubleday, 1985.

Schiller, Herbert. *Mass Communication and American Empire*. 2nd ed. Boulder, CO: Westview Press, 1992.

Schmid, David. *Natural Born Celebrities: Serial Killers in American Culture*. Chicago: University of Chicago Press, 2005.

Schor, Juliet B. *Born to Buy: The Commercialized Child and the New Consumer Culture*. New York: Scribner, 2004.

Schultz, David A. *It's Show Time! Media, Politics, and Popular Culture.* New York: P. Lang, 2000.

Sebba, Anne. *Mother Teresa: Beyond the Image.* London: Weidenfeld and Nicolson, 1997.

Seminara, George. *Mug Shots: Celebrities under Arrest.* London: Plexus, 2003.

Sentilles, Renee M. *Performing Mencken: Adah Isaacs Menken and the Birth of American Celebrity.* Cambridge: Cambridge University Press, 2003.

Sharkey, Jacqueline. "The Diana Aftermath." *American Journalism Review* 19 (1997): 18–25.

Shields, David. *Remote: Reflections on Life in the Shadow of Celebrity.* Madison: University of Wisconsin Press, 2004.

Shindler, Colin. *Garbo and Gilbert in Love: Hollywood's First Great Celebrity Couple.* London: Orion, 2005.

Shipman, David. *The Great Movie Stars.* Boston: Little, Brown and Co., 1995.

Shropshire, Kenneth L. *Being Sugar Ray: The Life of Sugar Ray Robinson, America's Greatest Boxer and First Celebrity Athlete.* New York: BasicCicitas, 2007.

Smart, Barry. *The Sport Star: Modern Sport and the Culture Economy of Sporting Celebrity.* London and Thousand Oaks, CA: SAGE, 2005.

Smith, Robert, and John Wiebusch. *The Rest of the Iceberg: An Insider's View on the World of Sport and Celebrity.* Minneapolis, MN: Inkwater Press, 2004.

Smith, Robert Ellis. *Celebrities and Privacy.* Washington, DC: Privacy Journal, 1985.

Smulyan, Susan. *Popular Ideologies: Mass Culture at Mid-Century.* Philadelphia: University of Pennsylvania Press, 2007.

Snead, James A., Colin MacCabe, and Cornel West. *White Screens, Black Images: Hollywood from the Dark Side.* New York: Routledge, 1994.

Snyder, Robert W. "American Journalism and the Culture of Celebrity." *Reviews in American History* 31 (2003): 440–448.

Sochen, June. *From Mae to Madonna: Women Entertainers in Twentieth-Century America.* Lexington: University Press of Kentucky, 1999.

Spohrer, Erika. "Becoming Extra-Textual: Celebrity Discourse and Paul Robeson's Political Transformation." *Critical Studies in Mass Communication* 24 (June 2007): 151–168.

Stephens, Autumn. *Drama Queen: Wild Women of the Silver Screen.* Berkeley, CA: Conari Press, 1998.

Stewart, Joseph. *Famous Movie Stars and Directors.* Santa Monica, CA: Santa Monica Press, 1993.

Straka, Mike. *Grrr! Celebrities Are Ruining Our Country—and Other Reasons We're All in Trouble.* New York: St. Martin's Press, 2007.

Street, John. *Politics and Popular Culture.* Cambridge, MA: Polity Press, 1997.

———. "Celebrity Politicians: Popular Culture and Political Representation." *British Journal of Politics and International Relations* 6 (November 2004): 435–452.

Stromberg, Gary, and Jane Merrill. *Feeding the Fame: Celebrities Tell Their Real-Life Stories of Eating Disorders and Recovery.* Center City, MN: Hazelden, 2006.

Sullivan, Steve. *Va-Va-Voom: Bombshells, Pinups, Sexpots, and Glamour Girls.* Los Angeles: GPC/Rhino Books, 1995.

Thomas, Gareth. *Movie Stars: Unseen Archives.* Bath, UK: Paragon Pub., 2005.

Thompson, Thomas. *Celebrity.* Garden City, NY: Doubleday, 1982.

Turner, Graeme. *Understanding Celebrity.* London: Thousand Oaks, 2004.

Turner, Graeme, Frances Bonner, and P. David Marshall. *Fame Game: The Production of Celebrity in Australia.* Cambridge: Cambridge University Press, 2000.

Waak, Erika. "Celebrities Counter the War." *The Humanist* (August 2003): 20–23.

Walker, John Albert. *Art and Celebrity.* Sterling, VA: Pluto Press, 2003.

Wann, Daniel L. *Sport Fans: The Psychology and Social Impact of Spectators.* New York: Routledge, 2001.

Warhol, Andy, and Laura L. Morris. *Andy Warhol Celebrities: More Than Fifteen*

Minutes. Las Vegas: PaperBall Las Vegas, 2003.

Wark, McKenzie. *Celebrities, Culture and Cyberspace*. Sydney, AU: Pluto Press Australia, 1999.

Watkins, S. Craig. *Hip Hop Matters: Politics, Pop Culture, and the Struggle for the Soul of a Movement*. Boston: Beacon Press, 2005.

Wernick, Andrew. *Promotional Culture: Advertising, Ideology and Symbolic Expression*. London: Sage, 1991.

West, Darrell M., and John M. Orman. *Celebrity Politics*. Upper Saddle River, NJ: Prentice Hall, 2003.

Whannel, Gary. *Media Sport Stars: Masculinities and Moralities*. London: Routledge, 2002.

Wicke, Jennifer. "Celebrity Material: Materialist Feminism and the Culture of Celebrity." *South Atlantic Quarterly* 93 (1994): 751–778.

Wiggins, David Kenneth. *Out of the Shadows: a Biographical History of African American Athletes*. Fayetteville: University of Arkansas Press, 2006.

Willis, Andrew. *Film Stars: Hollywood and Beyond*. Manchester: Manchester University Press, 2004.

Wills, Gary. *John Wayne's America: The Politics of Celebrity*. New York: Simon & Schuster, 1997.

Wilson, Cintra. *A Massive Swelling: Celebrity Re-examined as a Grotesque, Crippling Disease, and Other Cultural Revelations*. New York: Penguin Books, 2001.

Wilson, Colin, and Donald Seaman. *The Serial Killers*. London: W. H. Allen, 1990.

Wilson, Pamela and Michelle Stewart, eds. *Global Indigenous Media: Cullture,*

Poetics, and Politics. Durham, NC: Duke University Press, 2008.

Wilson, Scott. *Encyclopedia of Celebrity Burial Places*. Jefferson, NC: McFarland, 2001.

Winfield, Betty Houchin, and Janice Hume. "The American Hero and the Evolution of the Human Interest Story." *American Journalism* 15 (1998): 79–99.

Wise, James E., and Paul W. Wilderson. *Stars in Khaki: Movie Actors in the Army and the Air Services*. Annapolis, MD: Naval Institute Press, 2000.

Wise, James E., and Anne Collier Rehill. *Stars in the Corps: Movie Actors in the United States Marines*. Annapolis, MD: Naval Institute Press, 1999.

Wolf, Michael J. *The Entertainment Economy: How Mega-Media Forces Are Transforming Our Lives*. New York: Times Books, 1999.

Zaslow, Jeffrey. *Take It from Us: Advice from 262 Celebrities on Everything That Matters—to Them and to You*. Chicago: Bonus Books, 1994.

Zeitz, Joshua. *Flapper: A Madcap Story of Sex, Style, Celebrity, and the Women Who Made America Modern*. New York: Crown, 2006.

Ziegler, Ronald M. *Celebrity Sources: A Guide to Biographical Information about Famous People in Showbusiness and Sports Today*. New York: Garland, 1990.

Zizek, Slavoj. *For They Know Not What They Do: Enjoyment as a Political Factor*. London: Verso, 1991.

Zollo, Paul. *Hollywood Remembered: An Oral History of the Golden Age*. New York: Cooper Square Press, 2002.

Index

Avalon, Frankie (Francis Thomas Avallone), 79, 257
Avery, James, 4
Aviation Hall of Fame, 129
Aykroyd, Dan, 55, 57, 106, 137, 155, 222

Bacall, Lauren (Betty Joan Perske), 92, 114, 118, 187, 264
Bacharach, Burt, 101
Bachman, Richard (Stephen King), 244
Bacon, Kevin, 103, 137
Badham, Mary, 298
Baer, Max, 297
Baer, Parley, 270
Baez, Joan, 17, 167
Bahner, Adam Nyerere ("Tay Zonday"), 148, 149
Bailey, F. Lee, 159, 160
Bailey, Mark, 274
Bailey, Pearl, 2
Baio, Scott, 40
Baker, Chet, 96–97, 277
Baker, Josephine, 2, 81
Baker, Ray Stannard, 199
Bakker, Jim, 68, 159, 265, 295
Bakker, Tammy Faye, 68, 295
Baldwin, Alec, 137
Baldwin, James, 6
Baldwin, Tammy, 168
Ball, Lucille, 28, 39, 56, 132, 155, 205, 261, 271, 291
Ballentine, Carl, 177
Bambaataa, Afrika, 3, 130
Banachek (Seven Shaw), 212
Bancroft, Anne (Anna Maria Italiano), 245
Bandaras, Antonio, 137
Bankhead, Tallulah, 88
Banks, Tyra, 4, 283, 288
Banner, John, 106
Bara, Theda (Theodosia Goodman), 245
Barber, Ronde, 28
Barber, Tiki, 28, 120

Bardem, Javier, 10, 303
Bardo, Robert, 273
Bardot, Brigette, 93
Barkley, Charles, 5, 101, 120, 136
Barnard, A. M. (Louisa May Alcott), 243
Barnett, Marilyn, 167
Barnum, P. T., 58, 171
Barr, Roseanne, 54
Barry, Don "Red," 277
Barrymore, Drew, 97, 110, 262
Barrymore, Ethel, 110
Barrymore, John, 110, 285
Barrymore, John Drew, 110
Barrymore, Lionel, 110
Bartley, Dick, 84
Baryshnikov, Mikhail, 81
Basie, William "Count," 1, 151, 208
Basil, Toni, 298
Basinger, Kim, 94
Basquiat, Jean Michele, 95
Bateman, James (Henry Gibson), 55
Beach Boys, The, 41, 115, 258
Bean, Billy, 168
Beard, James, 74, 75
Beastie Boys, The, 131
Beatles, The, 2, 17, 41, 62, 85, 124, 142, 143, 178, 206, 257, 258, 290
Beatty, Clyde, 46, 47
Beatty, Warren (Henry Warren Beaty), 190
Beckham, David, 102, 124, 138
Beckham, Victoria, 28, 109, 117, 241, 284
Bee Gees, The, 259
Beery, Noah, 285
Behar, Joy (Josephine Occhiuto), 88
Belafonte, Harry, 2, 53, 103
Bell, Acton (Anne Bronte), 243
Bell, Currier (Charlotte Bronte), 243
Bell, Ellis (Emily Bronte), 243
Bell, James "Cool Pap," 204
Belmonts, The, 213
Belushi, John, 55, 97, 155, 222
Benatar, Pat, 114

U2, 17, 126, 137, 145, 213
Udall, Morris "Mo," 227
Uggams, Leslie, 4
UGK, 131
Underwood, Blair, 4
Unitas, Johnny, 26
Unser, Al, 111
Unser, Al, Jr., 111
Unser, Al, III, 111
Upton, Lauren Caitlin, 148–149
Urban, Keith, 283
Ure, Midge, 138
Urich, Robert, 303
Uris, Leon, 29
Usher (Usher Raymond), 42, 103, 213

Vadim, Roger, 89
Vai, Steve, 137
Valens, Richie (Richard Steven
    Valenzuela), 41, 184
Valentino, Rudolph (Rudolfo Guglielmi),
    187, 239, 244–245, 285
Valvano, Jimmy, 121
Vance, Vivian (Vivian Roberta Jones),
    271
Van Damme, Jean-Claude, 181, 299
Vanderbilt, Cornelius, 57
Van Doren, Charles, 291, 296
Van Doren, Mamie (Joan Lucille
    Olander), 93
Van Dyke, Richard Wayne "Dick," 56
Vanilla Ice (Robert Van Winkle), 12,
    131
Vanity Fair Hall of Fame, 163
Van Zandt, Townes, 63
Vanzetti, Bartolomeo, 157
Vareen, Ben, 4
Vasquez, Miguel, 48
Vaughan, Sarah, 2
Veblen, Thorstein, 25, 229
Veeck, Bill, 22
Veloso, Caetano, 126
Vendela (Thomessen), 211
Ventura, Jesse (James George Janos),
    227

Venturi, Ken, 120
Versace, Donatella, 116, 224
Versace, Gianni, 115, 116, 192, 274
Veruschka (Vera von Lehndorff-
    Steinort), 213, 278
Vicious, Sid (John Simon Ritchie), 11,
    12, 97, 193–194, 276, 277
Vick, Michael, 14, 102, 115
Victoria (Lisa Marie Varon), 88
Vidal, Eugene Luther "Gore," 29
Villa, Pancho, 200
Villechaize, Herve, 268, 277, 297
Virgil, Mike, 237
Virgil v. Time Inc., 237
Vitter, David, 266, 296
Vives, Carlos, 134
Voight, John, 110
Von Bulow, Claus, 159, 161
Von Kloberg, Edward, 296
Vonnegut, Kurt, 29, 262
Vuitton, Louis, 117, 118

Waddell, Tom, 167
Waggoner, Lyle, 222
Wagner, Lindsay, 101
Wagner, Raymond "Gorgeous
    George," 209
Wahlberg, Mark, 136
Waitkus, Eddie, 272
Waits, Tom, 96, 239
Walken, Christopher, 77
Walker, Alice, 6, 29
Walker, Clint (Norman Walker), 245,
    304
Walker, James Carter "Jimmy," 106
Wallace, Ben, 243
Wallace, Chrissy, 111
Wallace, George, 160
Wallace, Kenny, 111
Wallace, Mike, 111, 163, 201
Wallace, Rusty, 111
Wallenda, Karl, 46
Wallendas, The, 46
Waller, Robert, 29
Waller, Thomas "Fats," 208

About the Editor and Contributors

SAM G. RILEY, editor of this encyclopedia, is professor of communication at Virginia Tech, where he has taught a variety of journalism courses since 1981. His earlier books include ten on the history of magazine publishing, three about newspaper columnists and their work, two about prominent African Americans working in the news media, and one trade paperback. He has written for a variety of academic journals, has been a newspaper columnist, and writes occasional commentary pieces for the Roanoke and Richmond newspapers in Virginia. His blog on temporary celebrity is at www.celebrityblogsburg.blogspot.com.

TAMARA BALDWIN is professor of communication at Southeast Missouri State University in Cape Girardeau, Missouri. She is president of the American Journalism Historians Association and has published extensively in the areas of mass communication history and women in mass media education.

RANDLE B. CARPENTER, JR. is an attorney and negotiation consultant practicing in the New York metropolitan area. He is a Duke University Law School graduate, an arbitrator, and a former adjunct professor of law at the Pace University School of Law in White Plains, New York.

GINGER CARTER-MILLER is a professor of mass communication at Georgia College and State University in Milledgeville, Georgia. She has written extensively about media coverage of Project Mercury, America's first manned space mission, and she is currently working on a project about controversial journalist and First Amendment advocate Ralph Ginzburg.

JAMES COMBS is the author or coauthor of many books on popular culture and related subjects. His most recent book is *Movie Time*; others include *Polpop: Politics and Popular Culture in America, The Reagan Range: The Nostalgic Myth in American Politics, Phony Culture*, and *Play World: The Emergence of the New Ludenic Age*. He resides in a cabin in the Virginia woods near the Appalachian Trail.

RUSSELL J. COOK is professor and chair of the Department of Communication at Loyola College in Maryland, where he teaches broadcasting and media aesthetics. His research on journalism history includes *The Vietnam War* (2005), a volume in the Greenwood Library of American War Reporting, as well as book sections on press coverage of the Vietnam War, Watergate, and the Persian Gulf War. In 2004, his documentary video production, "3625," which documents a Pacific-to-Atlantic bicycle trip, won the grand prize from the National Broadcasting Society.

DOUGLAS CUMMING teaches journalism at Washington and Lee University. During his twenty-six years of reporting and editing, he worked at newspapers and magazines in Raleigh, Providence, and Atlanta. He was a Nieman Fellow at Harvard University and in 1982 won a George Polk Award.

KATHLEEN L. ENDRES is distinguished professor of communication at the University of Akron. Her scholarly work appears in books, journals, and documentaries, as well as on Web sites.

JACK ESTES completed his graduate work in popular culture at Bowling Green State University. He spent most of his career teaching in the state of Washington and has been at Borough of Manhattan Community College in New York City since 2002. In addition to his work in popular culture, he is the publisher of Pleasure Boat Studio: A Literary Press.

BRUCE J. EVENSEN is professor of journalism at DePaul University. A former broadcast journalist, he has published five books and numerous articles on journalistic practice, ethics, and history.

VICTORIA GOFF was a newspaper and magazine writer, columnist, book publisher, and author of two books before becoming an academic. She is associate professor of communication and history at the University of Wisconsin–Green Bay and has written journal articles and chapters in scholarly books. She is completing a book about the history of Spanish-language journalism in the United States; is editor of *Voyageur*, a regional history magazine; and is president of Stirling Communication, a media-consulting firm.

ELIZABETH HENDRICKSON is an Assistant Professor at the University of Tennessee, Knoxville. She has researched the relationship between magazine editors and celebrity publicists during booking negotiations, how media framing can recast politicians as celebrities, and the use of computer-mediated communication as an organizational tool. Also, she has worked as an entertainment editor at *Ladies' Home Journal, Glamour,* and *First for Women.*

JANICE HUME is associate professor in the Grady College of Journalism and Mass Communications at the University of Georgia, where she teaches magazine writing and historical research methods. She is author of *Obituaries in American Culture* (2000) and coauthor of *Journalism in a Culture of Grief* (2008). She formerly was lifestyle and arts editor at the Mobile, Alabama, *Register.*

JAMES D. IVORY is assistant professor in the Department of Communication at Virginia Tech. He earned his doctorate in mass communication from the University of North Carolina at Chapel Hill in 2005. His primary research and teaching areas are media effects and communication technologies.

NANCY JUREK was an instructor of communication at Virginia Tech. Her bachelor's degree and master's degree are in English literature, and her focus was film theory and criticism.

PAULETTE D. KILMER is associate professor of communication at the University of Toledo in Ohio. She writes about archetypes, folklore, memory, and narrative elements in the media, particularly the press. She has published two books, most recently *We Are One Organism: The Adventures of IBEW Local 8 in Keeping Current*. She has won teaching awards and has been nominated by her students three times for inclusion in *Who's Who among America's Teachers*.

CRAIG A. LOCKARD is the Rosenberg Professor of History in the Social Change and Development Department at the University of Wisconsin–Green Bay. His most recent books include *Societies, Networks and Transitions: A Global History*; *Dance of Life: Popular Music and Politics in Southeast Asia*; and *Southeast Asia in World History*.

THERESE L. LUECK is a professor of communication at the University of Akron. Her research publications and presentations focus primarily on women and media. She has served as a Fulbright Fellow, teaching journalism in China.

ROBERT MAGEE is an assistant professor of communication at Virginia Tech. Before entering academe, he was an editor at the English-language service of Agencia EFE, Spain's official news agency, and was a contributing editor for *HISPANIC Magazine*. His teaching and research focus on new technology, persuasion, and international communication.

JAMES BRIAN McPHERSON is an associate professor of communication studies at Whitworth University in Spokane, Washington. He is author of *The Conservative Resurgence and the Press: The Media's Role in the Rise of the Right* (2008) and *Journalism at the End of the American Century, 1965–Present* (2006). He also contributes to blogs about the media and politics at http://jmcpherson.wordpress.com.

RANDY MILLER is an associate professor of mass communications at the University of South Florida. He has worked as a sportswriter and copy editor and has written about sports journalism. He has also coauthored a textbook on media writing.

KEN MUIR is a professor of sociology at Appalachian State University. A Fulbright Senior Specialist, he has done research on women's rugby in the United States, New Zealand, and Australia and has written extensively on issues dealing with the sociology of sport.

VANESSA MURPHREE is associate professor of communication at the University of South Alabama and is author of *The Selling of Civil Rights: The Student Nonviolent*

Coordinating Committee and the Use of Public Relations (2006). She has written about the birth control movement, crisis communication, and historical perspectives of public relations. The American Journalism Historians Association presented her the 2005 award for best article in its journal, *American Journalism.*

STEPHEN PRINCE is professor of theater and cinema at Virginia Tech. He is author of numerous books on the film industry. His latest book is *Firestorm: American Film in the Age of Terrorism.*

HENRY SESSOMS is Professor Emeritus of English at Southeast Missouri State University in Cape Girardeau, Missouri. He served as chair of English for twenty-five years and was instrumental in creating his university's Department of Mass Communication in 1983.

EDWARD H. SEWELL, JR., is Associate Professor Emeritus in the Virginia Tech Department of Communication. He is a Multicultural Fellow, past chair of the university's Commission on Equal Opportunity and Diversity, and past cochair of the university's Lesbian, Gay, Bisexual, and Transgendered (LGBT) Caucus.

ROBERT SUGARMAN is chair of the Circus and Circus Culture area of the Popular Culture Association and edited a collection of this subject area's papers, *The Many Worlds of Circus* (2007). He is a contributing editor of *Spectacle, the Circus Arts Quarterly,* and is president of the Vermont Tent chapter of the Circus Fans Association of America. He wrote *Circus for Everyone: Circus Learning around the World* (2001) and has taught at the State University of New York–Albany, Bennington College, Southern Vermont College, and Cazenovia College.

JOHN C. TEDESCO is an associate professor and was director of graduate studies in the Virginia Tech Department of Communication. He is widely published in the areas of political and public relations campaigns. His work has appeared in such journals as *Harvard International Journal of Press/Politics, Journal of Advertising, Journalism Studies,* and *Journal of Broadcasting and Electronic Media.*

BETH M. WAGGENSPACK is an associate professor of communication at Virginia Tech, where she teaches rhetorical history, theory, and criticism, and director of graduate studies. She is a member of the university's Academy of Teaching Excellence and a recipient of the Alumni Teaching Award. Her research focuses on women's roles in political communication and on media and adoption. She is coauthor of *Communication: Principles of Tradition and Change* (2009).

DANNA L. WALKER is the James B. Simpson Fellow at American University in Washington, D.C. She has done extensive research and authored papers on women and media for various journals.

AMY WIDMAYER is preparing to enter a doctoral program and is living in Philadelphia. At the time her entries were written, she was working for Condé Nast in New York City and was completing a Master's degree.